Mastering Hadoop 3

Big data processing at scale to unlock unique
business insights

Chanchal Singh
Manish Kumar

BIRMINGHAM - MUMBAI

Mastering Hadoop 3

Commissioning Editor: Amey Varangaonkar
Acquisition Editor: Porous Godhaa
Content Development Editor: Ronnel Mathew
Technical Editor: Sushmeeta Jena
Copy Editor: Safis Editing
Project Coordinator: Namrata Swetta
Proofreader: Safis Editing
Indexer: Priyanka Dhadke
Graphics: Jisha Chirayil
Production Coordinator: Shraddha Falebhai

First published: February 2019

Production reference: 1280219

Published by Packt Publishing Ltd.
Livery Place
35 Livery Street
Birmingham
B3 2PB, UK.

ISBN 978-1-78862-044-4

www.packtpub.com

To my mother, Usha Singh, and my father, Parasnath Singh, for their sacrifices and for exemplifying the power of determination.

To my wife Jyoti for being my loving partner throughout our joint life journey

– Chanchal Singh

`mapt.io`

Mapt is an online digital library that gives you full access to over 5,000 books and videos, as well as industry leading tools to help you plan your personal development and advance your career. For more information, please visit our website.

Why subscribe?

- Spend less time learning and more time coding with practical eBooks and Videos from over 4,000 industry professionals

- Improve your learning with Skill Plans built especially for you

- Get a free eBook or video every month

- Mapt is fully searchable

- Copy and paste, print, and bookmark content

Packt.com

Did you know that Packt offers eBook versions of every book published, with PDF and ePub files available? You can upgrade to the eBook version at `www.packt.com` and as a print book customer, you are entitled to a discount on the eBook copy. Get in touch with us at `customercare@packtpub.com` for more details.

At `www.packt.com`, you can also read a collection of free technical articles, sign up for a range of free newsletters, and receive exclusive discounts and offers on Packt books and eBooks.

Foreword

In today's fast-moving world, many people have moved their learning from reading a book to looking at a computer screen (maybe even a mobile phone screen). As a college professor, I can see there are pros and cons to this way of learning. Learners learning in this way typically look for different topics and sub topics by searching the web for pages that provide snippets of information for video clips. This type of learning lacks the proper steps and tends to be incomplete because learners often skip the fundamentals, go straight to the core based on the search keywords they chose, and therefore do not get the whole picture.

During the course of writing this book, Chanchal Singh and myself taught a big data course together in college. We wanted to learn for ourselves the best way to pass on knowledge to a group of eager learners. During this process, we gained valuable insight into how we should structure the book to provide step-by-step, uncluttered learning. Therefore, we are confident that this book is suitable for use as a college textbook on Hadoop. It can also be used as a reference text for experienced big data developers.

Mastering Hadoop 3 starts with what's new in Hadoop, and then it dives into the Hadoop Distributed File System, the core of big data in Hadoop. The book moves on to YARN, MapReduce, and SQL in Hadoop. With that foundation laid, it covers real-time processing, widely used Hadoop ecosystem components, and how to design applications. Machine learning is one of today's hot topics, and this book illustrates how it can work in a Hadoop environment. The book wraps up with security for Hadoop systems and how to monitor it.

In my long career in the IT industry, constantly keeping myself up to date has become a habit. I still read a lot of books because books structure learning for me. They also ensure I get the whole picture of the subject. Being able to recall knowledge is a demonstration of successful learning. To achieve that, I often re-read the same book several times to make sure I can recall the knowledge gained from it effectively and apply it in real life. I am confident *Mastering Hadoop 3* is well-structured when it comes to presenting the subject.

To close, I recall that I built my first database for a customer back in 1982, 37 years ago. There was no big data because storage was expensive, CPU power was limited, and data could not move quickly because networking at the time could not move that fast. All these factors are no longer valid today. That's why anyone can build a database using a big data architecture such as Hadoop. Not only is the required technology now very accessible, the ecosystem around it is also mature. I encourage the new generation of data and application architects to consider leveraging big data in every project they conceive. This book, *Mastering Hadoop 3*, will be a good reference to have.

Timothy Wong

PhD, Founder and President, Codehesive Solutions

Professor, Humber College

Contributors

About the authors

Chanchal Singh has over five years of experience in product development and architect design. He has been working very closely with the leadership teams of various companies including directors CTOs, and founding members, to define technical roadmaps. He is the founder of and speaker at the meetup group big bata and AI Pune Meetup-Experience Speaks. He is the co-author of *Book Building Data Streaming Application with Apache Kafka*.

He has a bachelor's degree in Information Technology from the University of Mumbai and a master's degree in computer applications from Amity University. He was also part of the entrepreneur cell in IIT Mumbai. His Linkedin Profile can be found by searching for Chanchal Singh.

Manish Kumar is a technical architect at DataMetica Solutions Pvt. Ltd. He has approximately 11 years' experience in data management, working as a data architect and product architect. He has extensive experience of building effective ETL pipelines, implementing security over Hadoop, and providing the best possible solutions to data science problems. Before joining the world of big data, he worked as a tech lead for Sears Holding, India. Manish has a bachelor's degree in information technology, and he is a co-author of *Building Data Streaming Applications with Apache Kafka*.

About the reviewer

Ravishankar Nair's prowess with big data platforms and his passion in applying technology to solve complex data challenges has earned him the tag of Hadoopean. Based in the U.S., Ravi has 22 years of technology experience. He was responsible as SVP for Business Intelligence for a global consumer group of a fortune 500 Financial organization. He is an active big data and Spark blogger, and speaks at international data conferences (he has presented to over 8,000 data enthusiasts) and webinar presentations. Ravi is an ACM member and is the CEO of PassionBytes, a US-based distributed computing solution company. Ravi runs many big data-focused user groups, is an Amazon-certified solution architect associate and Hadoop/Spark certified professional.

Packt is searching for authors like you

If you're interested in becoming an author for Packt, please visit `authors.packtpub.com` and apply today. We have worked with thousands of developers and tech professionals, just like you, to help them share their insight with the global tech community. You can make a general application, apply for a specific hot topic that we are recruiting an author for, or submit your own idea.

Table of Contents

Section 3: Hadoop in the Real World

Preface

In this book, we will examine advanced concepts of the Hadoop ecosystem and build high-performance Hadoop data pipelines with security, monitoring, and data governance.

We will also promote enterprise-grade applications using Apache Spark and Flink. This book teaches the internal workings of Hadoop, which includes building solutions to some real-world use cases. We will master the best practices for enterprises using Hadoop 3 as a data platform, including authorization and authentication. We will also learn how to model data in Hadoop, gain an in-depth understanding of distributed computing using Hadoop 3, and explore the different batch data-processing patterns.

Lastly, we will understand how components in the Hadoop ecosystem can be integrated effectively to implement a fast and reliable big data pipeline.

Who this book is for

If you want to become a big data professional by mastering the advanced concepts of Hadoop, this book is for you. You'll also find this book useful if you're a Hadoop professional looking to strengthen your knowledge of the Hadoop ecosystem. Fundamental knowledge of the Java programming language and of the basics of Hadoop is necessary to get started with this book.

What this book covers

Chapter 1, *Journey to Hadoop 3*, introduces the main concepts of Hadoop and outlines its origin. It further focuses on the features of Hadoop 3. This chapter also provides a logical overview of the Hadoop ecosystem and different Hadoop distributions.

Chapter 2, *Deep Dive into the Hadoop Distributed File System*, focuses on the Hadoop Distributed File System and its internal concepts. It also covers HDFS operations in depth, and introduces you to the new functionality added to the HDFS in Hadoop 3, along with covering HDFS caching and HDFS Federation in detail.

Chapter 3, *YARN Resource Management in Hadoop*, introduces you to the resource management framework of YARN. It focuses on efficient scheduling of jobs submitted to YARN and provides a brief overview of the pros and cons of the scheduler available in YARN. It also focuses on the YARN features introduced in Hadoop 3, especially the YARN REST API. It also covers the architecture and internals of Apache Slider. It then focuses on Apache Tez, a distributed processing engine, which helps us to optimize applications running on YARN.

Chapter 4, *Internals of MapReduce*, introduces a distributed batch processing engine known as Map Reduce. It covers some of the internal concepts of Map Reduce and walks you through each step in detail. It then focuses on a few important parameters and some common patterns in Map Reduce.

Chapter 5, *SQL on Hadoop*, covers a few important SQL-like engines present in the Hadoop ecosystem. It starts with the details of the architecture of Presto and then covers some examples with a few popular connectors. It then covers the popular query engine, Hive, and focuses on its architecture and a number of advanced-level concepts. Finally, it covers Impala, a fast processing engine, and its internal architectural concepts in detail.

Chapter 6, *Real-Time Processing Engines*, focuses on different engines available for processing, discussing each processing engine individually. It includes details on the internal workings of Spark Framework and the concept of **Resilient Distributed Datasets (RDDs)**. An introduction to the internals of Apache Flink and Apache Storm/Heron are also focal points of this chapter.

Chapter 7, *Widely Used Hadoop Ecosystem Components*, introduces you to a few important tools used on the Hadoop platform. It covers Apache Pig, used for ETL operations, and introduces you to a few of the internal concepts of its architecture and operations. It takes you through the details of Apache Kafka and Apache Flume. Apache HBase is also a primary focus of this chapter.

Chapter 8, *Designing Applications in Hadoop*, starts with a few advanced-level concepts related to file formats. It then focuses on data compression and serialization concepts in depth, before covering concepts of data processing and data access and moving to use case examples.

Chapter 9, *Real-Time Stream Processing in Hadoop*, is focused on designing and implementing real-time and microbatch-oriented applications in Hadoop. This chapter covers how to perform stream data ingestion, along with the role of message queues. It further penetrates some of common stream data-processing patterns, along with low latency design considerations. It elaborates on these concepts with real-time and microbatch case studies.

`Chapter 10`, *Machine Learning in Hadoop*, covers how to design and architect machine learning applications on the Hadoop platform. It addresses some of the common machine learning challenges that you can face in Hadoop, and how to solve those. It walks through different machine learning libraries and processing engines. It covers some of the common steps involved in machine learning and further elaborates on this with a case study.

`Chapter 11`, *Hadoop in the Cloud*, provides an overview of Hadoop operations in the cloud. It covers detailed information on how the Hadoop ecosystem looks in the cloud, how we should manage resources in the cloud, how we create a data pipeline in the cloud, and how we can ensure high availability across the cloud.

`Chapter 12`, *Hadoop Cluster Profiling*, covers tools and techniques for benchmarking and profiling the Hadoop cluster. It also examines aspects of profiling different Hadoop workloads.

`Chapter 13`, *Who Can Do What in Hadoop*, is about securing a Hadoop cluster. It covers the basics of Hadoop security. It further focuses on implementing and designing Hadoop authentication and authorization.

`Chapter 14`, *Network and Data Security*, is an extension to the previous chapter, covering some advanced concepts in Hadoop network and data security. It covers advanced concepts, such as network segmentation, perimeter security, and row/column level security. It also covers encrypting data in motion and data at rest in Hadoop.

`Chapter 15`, *Monitoring Hadoop*, covers the fundamentals of monitoring Hadoop. The chapter is divided into two major sections. One section concerns general Hadoop monitoring, and the remainder of the chapter discusses specialized monitoring for identifying security breaches.

To get the most out of this book

You won't need too much hardware to set up Hadoop. The minimum setup is a single machine / virtual machine, and the recommended setup is three machines.

It is better to have some hands-on experience of writing and running basic programs in Java, as well as some experience of using developer tools such as Eclipse.

Download the example code files

You can download the example code files for this book from your account at `www.packt.com`. If you purchased this book elsewhere, you can visit `www.packt.com/support` and register to have the files emailed directly to you.

You can download the code files by following these steps:

1. Log in or register at `www.packt.com`.
2. Select the **SUPPORT** tab.
3. Click on **Code Downloads & Errata**.
4. Enter the name of the book in the **Search** box and follow the on screen instructions.

Once the file is downloaded, please make sure that you unzip or extract the folder using the latest version of:

- WinRAR/7-Zip for Windows
- Zipeg/iZip/UnRarX for Mac
- 7-Zip/PeaZip for Linux

The code bundle for the book is also hosted on GitHub at `https://github.com/PacktPublishing/Mastering-Hadoop-3`. In case there's an update to the code, it will be updated on the existing GitHub repository.

We also have other code bundles from our rich catalog of books and videos available at `https://github.com/PacktPublishing/`. Check them out!

Download the color images

We also provide a PDF file that has color images of the screenshots/diagrams used in this book. You can download it here: `https://www.packtpub.com/sites/default/files/downloads/9781788620444_ColorImages.pdf`.

Code in action

Visit the following link to check out videos of the code being run:
`http://bit.ly/2XvW2SD`

Conventions used

There are a number of text conventions used throughout this book.

`CodeInText`: Indicates code words in text, database table names, folder names, filenames, file extensions, pathnames, dummy URLs, user input, and Twitter handles. Here is an example: "Mount the downloaded `WebStorm-10*.dmg` disk image file as another disk in your system."

A block of code is set as follows:

```
<property>
        <name>dfs.ha.namenodes.mycluster</name>
        <value>nn1,nn2,nn3</value>
    </property>
```

When we wish to draw your attention to a particular part of a code block, the relevant lines or items are set in bold:

```
<property>
        <name>dfs.ha.namenodes.mycluster</name>
        <value>nn1,nn2,nn3</value>
    </property>
```

Any command-line input or output is written as follows:

```
hdfs dfsadmin -fetchImage /home/packt
```

Bold: Indicates a new term, an important word, or words that you see onscreen. For example, words in menus or dialog boxes appear in the text like this. Here is an example: "Select **System info** from the **Administration** panel."

Warnings or important notes appear like this.

Tips and tricks appear like this.

Get in touch

Feedback from our readers is always welcome.

General feedback: If you have questions about any aspect of this book, mention the book title in the subject of your message and email us at customercare@packtpub.com.

Errata: Although we have taken every care to ensure the accuracy of our content, mistakes do happen. If you have found a mistake in this book, we would be grateful if you would report this to us. Please visit www.packt.com/submit-errata, selecting your book, clicking on the Errata Submission Form link, and entering the details.

Piracy: If you come across any illegal copies of our works in any form on the internet, we would be grateful if you would provide us with the location address or website name. Please contact us at copyright@packt.com with a link to the material.

If you are interested in becoming an author: If there is a topic that you have expertise in, and you are interested in either writing or contributing to a book, please visit authors.packtpub.com.

Reviews

Please leave a review. Once you have read and used this book, why not leave a review on the site that you purchased it from? Potential readers can then see and use your unbiased opinion to make purchase decisions, we at Packt can understand what you think about our products, and our authors can see your feedback on their book. Thank you!

For more information about Packt, please visit packt.com.

Section 1: Introduction to Hadoop 3

This section will help you to understand Hadoop 3's features and provides a detailed explanation of the **Hadoop Distributed File System** (**HDFS**), YARN, and MapReduce jobs.

This section consists of the following chapters:

- Chapter 1, *Journey to Hadoop 3*

- Chapter 2, *Deep Dive into the Hadoop Distributed File System*

- Chapter 3, *YARN Resource Management in Hadoop*

- Chapter 4, *Internals of MapReduce*

Journey to Hadoop 3

Hadoop has come a long way since its inception. Powered by a community of open source enthusiasts, it has seen three major version releases. The version 1 release saw the light of day six years after the first release of Hadoop. With this release, the Hadoop platform had full capabilities that can run MapReduce-distributed computing on **Hadoop Distributed File System** (**HDFS**) distributed storage. It had some of the most major performance improvements ever done, along with full support for security. This release also enjoyed a lot of improvements with respect to HBASE.

The version 2 release made significant leaps compared to version 1 of Hadoop. It introduced YARN, a sophisticated general-purpose resource manager and job scheduling component. HDFS high availability, HDFS federations, and HDFS snapshots were some other prominent features introduced in version 2 releases.

The latest major release of Hadoop is version 3. This version has seen some significant features such as HDFS erasure encoding, a new YARN Timeline service (with new architecture), YARN opportunistic containers and distributed scheduling, support for three name nodes, and intra-data-node load balancers. Apart from major feature additions, version 3 has performance improvements and bug fixes. As this book is about mastering Hadoop 3, we'll mostly talk about this version.

In this chapter, we will take a look at Hadoop's history and how the Hadoop evolution timeline looks. We will look at the features of Hadoop 3 and get a logical view of the Hadoop ecosystem along with different Hadoop distributions.

In particular, we will cover the following topics:

- Hadoop origins
- Hadoop Timelines
- Hadoop logical view
- Moving towards Hadoop 3
- Hadoop distributions

Hadoop origins and Timelines

Hadoop is changing the way people think about data. We need to know what led to the origin of this magical innovation. Who developed Hadoop and why? What problems existed before Hadoop? How has it solved these problems? What challenges were encountered during development? How has Hadoop transformed from version 1 to version 3? Let's walk through the origins of Hadoop and its journey to version 3.

Origins

In 1997, Doug Cutting, a co-founder of Hadoop, started working on project Lucene, which is a full-text search library. It was completely written in Java and is a full-text search engine. It analyzes text and builds an index on it. An index is just a mapping of text to locations, so it quickly gives all locations matching particular search patterns. After a few years, Doug made the Lucene project open source; it got a tremendous response from the community and it later became the Apache foundation project.

Once Doug realized that he had enough people who can look into Lucene, he started focusing on indexing web pages. Mike Cafarella joined him for this project to develop a product that can index web pages, and they named this project Apache Nutch. Apache Nutch was also known to be a subproject of Apache Lucene, as Nutch uses the Lucene library to index the content of web pages. Fortunately, with hard work, they made good progress and deployed Nutch on a single machine that was able to index around 100 pages per second.

Scalability is something that people often don't consider while developing initial versions of applications. This was also true of Doug and Mike and the number of web pages that could be indexed was limited to 100 million. In order to index more pages, they increased the number of machines. However, increasing nodes resulted in operational problems because they did not have any underlying cluster manager to perform operational tasks. They wanted to focus more on optimizing and developing robust Nutch applications without worrying about scalability issues.

Doug and Mike wanted a system that had the following features:

- **Fault tolerant**: The system should be able to handle any failure of the machines automatically, in an isolated manner. This means the failure of one machine should not affect the entire application.
- **Load balancing**: If one machine fails, then its work should be distributed automatically to the working machines in a fair manner.

- **Data loss**: They also wanted to make sure that, once data is written to disk, it should never be lost even if one or two machines fail.

They started working on developing a system that can fulfill the aforementioned requirements and spent a few months doing so. However, at the same time, Google published its Google File System. When they read about it, they found it had solutions to similar problems they were trying to solve. They decided to make an implementation based on this research paper and started the development of **Nutch Distributed File System (NDFS)**, which they completed in 2004.

With the help of the Google File System, they solved the scalability and fault tolerance problem that we discussed previously. They used the concept of blocks and replication to do so. Blocks are created by splitting each file into 64 MB chunks (the size is configurable) and replicating each block three times by default so that, if a machine holding one block fails, then data can be served from another machine. The implementation helped them solve all the operational problems they were trying to solve for Apache Nutch. The next section explains the origin of MapReduce.

MapReduce origin

Doug and Mike started working on an algorithm that can process data stored on NDFS. They wanted a system whose performance can be doubled by just doubling the number of machines running the program. At the same time, Google published *MapReduce: Simplified Data Processing on Large Clusters* (`https://research.google.com/archive/mapreduce.html`).

The core idea behind the MapReduce model was to provide parallelism, fault tolerance, and data locality features. Data locality means a program is executed where data is stored instead of bringing the data to the program. MapReduce was integrated into Nutch in 2005. In 2006, Doug created a new incubating project that consisted of **HDFS (Hadoop Distributed File System)**, named after NDFS, MapReduce, and Hadoop Common.

At that time, Yahoo! was struggling with its backend search performance. Engineers at Yahoo! already knew the benefits of Google File System and MapReduce implemented at Google. Yahoo! decided to adopt the capability of Hadoop and they employed Doug to help their engineering team to do so. In 2007, a few more companies who started contributing to Hadoop and Yahoo! reported that they were running 1,000 node Hadoop clusters at the same time.

NameNodes and DataNodes have a specific role in managing overall clusters. NameNodes are responsible for maintaining metadata information. MapReduce engines have a job tracker and task tracker whose scalability is limited to 40,000 nodes because the overall work of scheduling and tracking is handled by only the job tracker. YARN was introduced in Hadoop version 2 to overcome scalability issues and resource management jobs. It gave Hadoop a new lease of life and Hadoop became a more robust, faster, and more scalable system.

Timelines

We will talk about MapReduce and HDFS in detail later. Let's go through the evolution of Hadoop, which looks as follows:

Year	Event
2003	• Research paper for Google File System released
2004	• Research paper for MapReduce released
2006	• JIRA, mailing list, and other documents created for Hadoop • Hadoop Nutch created • Hadoop created by moving out NDFS and MapReduce from Nutch • Doug Cutting names the project Hadoop, which was the name of his son's yellow elephant toy • Release of Hadoop 0.1.0 • 1.8 TB of data sorts on 188 nodes, which took 47.9 hours • Three hundred machines deployed at Yahoo! for the Hadoop cluster • Cluster size at Yahoo! increases to 600
2007	• Two clusters of 1,000 machines run by Yahoo! • Hadoop released with HBase • Apache pig created at Yahoo!
2008	• JIRA for YARN opened • Twenty companies listed on the Powered by Hadoop page • Web index at Yahoo! moved to Hadoop • 10,000-core Hadoop cluster used to generate Yahoo!'s production search index • First ever Hadoop summit • World record created for the fastest sorting (one terabyte of data in 209 seconds) by using 910 node Hadoop clusters • Hadoop bags record for terabyte sort • Hadoop bags record for terabyte sort benchmark • The Yahoo! cluster now has 10 TB loaded to Hadoop every day • Cloudera founded as a Hadoop distribution company • Google claims to sort 1 terabyte in 68 seconds with its MapReduce implementation

2009	• 24,000 machines with seven clusters run at Yahoo! • Hadoop records sorting petabyte storage • Yahoo! claims to sort 1 terabyte in 62 seconds • Second Hadoop summit • Hadoop core renamed Hadoop Common • MapR distribution founded • HDFS becomes a separate subproject • MapReduce becomes a separate subproject
2010	• Authentication using Kerberos added to Hadoop • Stable version of Apache HBase • Yahoo runs 4,000 nodes to process 70 PB • Facebook runs 2,300 clusters to process 40 petabytes • Apache Hive released • Apache Pig released
2011	• Apache Zookeeper released • Contribution of 200,000 lines of code from Facebook, LinkedIn, eBay, and IBM • Media Guardian Innovation Awards Top Prize for Hadoop • Hortonworks started by Rob Beardon and Eric Badleschieler, who were core members of Hadoop at Yahoo • 42,000 nodes of Hadoop cluster at Yahoo, processing petabytes data
2012	• Hadoop community moves to integrate YARN • Hadoop Summit at San Jose • Hadoop version 1.0 released
2013	• Yahoo! deploys YARN in production • Hadoop Version 2.2 released
2014	• Apache Spark becomes an Apache top-level project • Hadoop Version 2.6 released
2015	• Hadoop 2.7 released
2017	• Hadoop 2.8 released

Hadoop 3 has introduced a few more important changes, which we will discuss in upcoming sections in this chapter.

Overview of Hadoop 3 and its features

The first alpha release of Hadoop version 3.0.0 was on 30 August 2016. It was called version **3.0.0-alpha1**. This was the first alpha release in a series of planned alphas and betas that ultimately led to **3.0.0 GA**. The intention behind this alpha release was to quickly gather and act on feedback from downstream users.

With any such releases, there are some key drivers that lead to its birth. These key drivers create benefits that will ultimately help in the better functioning of Hadoop-augmented enterprise applications. Before we discuss the features of Hadoop 3, you should understand these driving factors. Some driving factors behind the release of Hadoop 3 are as follows:

- **A lot of bug fixes and performance improvements**: Hadoop has a growing open source community of developers regularly adding major/minor changes or improvements to the Hadoop trunk repository. These changes were growing day by day and they couldn't be accommodated in minor version releases of 2.x. They had to be accommodated with a major version release. Hence, it was decided to release the majority of these changes committed to the trunk repository with Hadoop 3.

- **Overhead due to data replication factor**: As you may be aware, HDFS has a default replication factor of 3. This helps make things more fault-tolerant with better data locality and better load balancing of jobs among DataNodes. However, it comes with an overhead cost of around 200%. For non-frequently accessed datasets that have low I/O activities, these replicated blocks are never accessed in the course of normal operations. On the other hand, they consume the same number of resources as other main resources. To mitigate this overhead with non-frequently accessed data, Hadoop 3 introduced a major feature, called **erasure coding**. This stores data durably while saving space significantly.

- **Improving existing YARN Timeline services**: YARN Timeline service version 1 has limitations that impact reliability, performance, and scalability. For example, it uses local-disk-based LevelDB storage that cannot scale to a high number of requests. Moreover, the Timeline server is a single point of failure. To mitigate such drawbacks, YARN Timeline server has been re-architected with the Hadoop 3 release.

- **Optimizing map output collector**: It is a well-known fact that native code (written correctly) is faster to execute. In lieu of that, some optimization is done in Hadoop 3 that will speed up mapper tasks by approximately two to three times. The native implementation of map output collector has been added, which will be used in the Java-based MapReduce framework using the **Java Native Interface (JNI)**. This is particularly useful for shuffle-intensive operations.

- **The need for a higher availability factor of NameNode**: Hadoop is a fault-tolerant platform with support for handling multiple data node failures. In the case of NameNodes versions, prior to Hadoop version 3 support two NameNodes, Active and Standby. While it is a highly available solution, in the case of the failure of an active (or standby) NameNode, it will go back to a non-HA mode. This is not very accommodative of a high number of failures. In Hadoop 3, support for more than one standby NameNode has been introduced.
- **Dependency on Linux ephemeral port range**: Linux ephemeral ports are short-lived ports created by the **OS (operating system)** when a process requests any available port. The OS assigns the port number from a predefined range. It then releases the port after the related connection terminates. With version 2 and earlier, many Hadoop services' default ports were in the Linux ephemeral port range. This means starting these services sometimes failed to bind to the port due to conflicts with other processes. In Hadoop 3, these default ports are moved out of the ephemeral port range.
- **Disk-level data skew**: There are multiple disks (or drives) managed by DataNodes. Sometimes, adding or replacing disks leads to significant data skew within a DataNode. To rebalance data among disks within a DataNode, Hadoop 3 has introduced a CLI utility called **hdfs diskbalancer**.

Well! Hopefully, by now, you have a clear understanding of why certain features were introduced in Hadoop 3 and what kinds of benefits are derived from them. Throughout this book, we will look into these features in detail. However, our intent in this section was to ensure that you get a high-level overview of the major features introduced in Hadoop 3 and why they were introduced. In the next section, we will look into Hadoop Logical view.

Hadoop logical view

The Hadoop Logical view can be divided into multiple sections. These sections can be viewed as a logical sequence, with steps starting from **Ingress/Egress** and ending at **Data Storage Medium**.

The following diagram shows the Hadoop platform logical view:

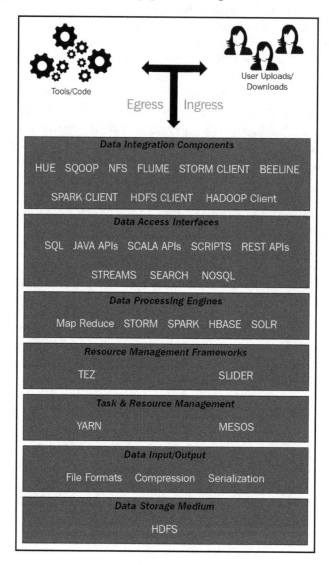

We will touch upon these sections as shown in the preceding diagram one by one, to understand them. However, when designing any Hadoop application, you should think in terms of those sections and make technological choices according to the use case problems you are trying to solve. Without wasting time, let's look at these sections one by one:

- **Ingress/egress/processing**: Any interaction with the Hadoop platform should be viewed in terms of the following:
    - Ingesting (ingress) data
    - Reading (Egress) data
    - Processing already ingested data

These actions can be automated via the use of tools or automated code. This can be achieved by user actions, by either uploading data to Hadoop or downloading data from Hadoop. Sometimes, users trigger actions that may result in Ingress/egress or the processing of data.

- **Data integration components**: For ingress/egress or data processing in Hadoop, you need data integration components. These components are tools, software, or custom code that help integrate the underlying Hadoop data with user views or actions. If we talk about the user perspective alone, then these components give end users a unified view of data in Hadoop across different distributed Hadoop folders, in different files and data formats. These components provide end users and applications with an entry point for using or manipulating Hadoop data using different data access interfaces and data processing engines. We will exlpore the definition of data access interfaces and processing engines in the next section. In a nutshell, tools such as Hue and software (libraries) such as `Sqoop`, `Java Hadoop Clients`, and `Hive Beeline Clients` are some examples of data integration components.

- **Data access interfaces**: Data access interfaces allow you to access underlying Hadoop data using different languages such as SQL, NoSQL, or APIs such as Rest and JAVA APIs, or using different data formats such as search data formats and streams. Sometimes, the interface that you use to access data from Hadoop is tightly coupled with underlying data processing engines. For example, if you're using SPARK SQL then it is bound to use the SPARK processing engine. Something similar is true in the case of the SEARCH interface, which is bound to use search engines such as **SOLR** or **elastic search**.

- **Data Processing Engines**: Hadoop as a platform provides different processing engines to manipulate underlying data. These processing engines have different mechanisms to use system resources and have completely different SLA guarantees. For example, the MapReduce processing engine is more disk I/O-bound (keeping RAM memory usage under control) and it is suitable for batch-oriented data processing. Similarly, SPARK in a memory processing engine is less disk I/O-bound and more dependent on RAM memory. It is more suitable for stream or micro-batch processing. You should choose processing engines for your application based on the type of data sources you are dealing with along with SLAs you need to satisfy.

- **Resource management frameworks**: Resource management frameworks expose abstract APIs to interact with underlying resource managers for task and job scheduling in Hadoop. These frameworks ensure there is a set of steps to follow for submitting jobs in Hadoop using designated resource managers such as YARN or MESOS. These frameworks help establish optimal performance by utilizing underlying resources systematically. Examples of such frameworks are Tez or Slider. Sometimes, data processing engines use these frameworks to interact with underlying resource managers or they have their own set of custom libraries to do so.

- **Task and resource management**: Task and resource managment has one primary goal: sharing a large cluster of machines across different, simultaneously running applications in a cluster. There are two major resource managers in Hadoop: YARN and MESOS. Both are built with the same goal, but they use different scheduling or resource allocation mechanisms for jobs in Hadoop. For example, YARN is a Unix process while MESOS is Linux-container-based.

- **Data input/output**: The data input/output layer is primarily responsible for different file formats, compression techniques, and data serialization for Hadoop storage.

- **Data Storage Medium**: HDFS is the primary data storage medium used in Hadoop. It is a Java-based, high-performant distributed filesystem that is based on the underlying UNIX File System. In the next section, we will study Hadoop distributions along with their benefits.

Hadoop distributions

Hadoop is an open-source project under the Apache Software Foundation, and most components in the Hadoop ecosystem are also open-sourced. Many companies have taken important components and bundled them together to form a complete distribution package that is easier to use and manage. A Hadoop distribution offers the following benefits:

- **Installation**: The distribution package provides an easy way to install any component or rpm-like package on clusters. It provides an easy interface too.

- **Packaging**: It comes with multiple open-source tools that are well configured to work together. Assume that you want to install and configure each component separately on a multi-node cluster and then test whether it's working properly or not. What if we forget some testing scenarios and the cluster behaves unexpectedly? The Hadoop distribution assures us that we won't face such problems and also provides upgrades or installations of new components by using their package library.

- **Maintenance**: The maintenance of a cluster and its components is also a very challenging task, but it is made very simple in of all these distribution packages. They provide us with a nice GUI interface to monitor the health and status of a component. We can also change the configuration to tune or maintain a component to perform well.

- **Support**: Most distributions come with 24/7 support. That means that, if you are stuck with any cluster-or distribution-related issue, you don't need to worry much about finding resources to solve the problem. Hadoop Distribution comes with a support package that assures you of technical support and help as and when needed.

On-premise distribution

There are many distributions available in the market; we will look at the most widely used distributions:

- **Cloudera**: Cloudera is an open source Hadoop distribution that was founded in 2008, just when Hadoop started gaining popularity. Cloudera is the oldest distribution available. People at Cloudera are committed to contributing to the open source community and they have contributed to the building of Hive, Impala, Hadoop, Pig, and other popular open-source projects. Cloudera comes with good tools packaged together to provide a good Hadoop experience. They also provide a nice GUI interface to manage and monitor clusters, known as Cloudera manager.

- **Hortonworks**: Hortonworks was founded in 2011 and it comes with the **Hortonworks Data Platform** (**HDP**), which is an open-source Hadoop distribution. Hortonworks Distribution is widely used in organizations and it provides an Apache Ambari GUI-based interface to manage and monitor clusters. Hortonworks contributes to many open-source projects such as Apache tez, Hadoop, YARN, and Hive. Hortonworks has recently launched a **Hortonworks Data Flow** (**HDF**) platform for the purpose of data ingestion and storage. Hortonworks distribution also focuses on the security aspect of Hadoop and has integrated Ranger, Kerberos, and SSL-like security with the HDP and HDF platforms.

- **MapR**: MapR was founded in 2009 and it has its own filesystem called MapR-FS, which is quite similar to HDFS but with some new features built by MapR. It boasts higher performance; it also consists of a few nice sets of tools to manage and administer a cluster, and it does not suffer from a single point of failure. It offers some useful features, such as mirroring and snapshots.

Cloud distributions

Cloud services offer cost-effective solutions in terms of infrastructure setup, monitoring, and maintenance. A large number of organizations do prefer moving their Hadoop infrastructure to the cloud. There are a few popular distributions available for the cloud:

- **Amazon's Elastic MapReduce**: Before moving to Hadoop, Amazon had already acquired a large space on the cloud in their infrastructure setup. Amazon provides Elastic MapReduce and many other Hadoop ecosystem tools in their distribution. They have the s3 File System, which is another alternative to HDFS. They offer a cost-effective setup for Hadoop on cloud and it is currently the most actively used cloud on Hadoop distributions.
- **Microsoft Azure**: Microsoft offers HDInsight as a Hadoop distribution. It also offers a cost-effective solution for Hadoop infrastructure setup, monitoring and managing cluster resources. Azure claims to provide a fully cloud-based cluster with 99.9% **Service Level Agreements (SLA)**.

Other big companies have also started providing Hadoop on cloud such as Google Cloud Platform, IBM BigInsight, and Cloudera Cloud. You may choose any distribution based on the feasibility and stability of Hadoop tools and components. Most companies offer a free trial for 1 year with lots of free credits for organizational use.

Points to remember

We provided a basic introduction to Hadoop and the following are a few points to remember:

- Doug Cutting, the founder of Hadoop, started the development of Hadoop at Nutch based on a Google research paper on Google File System and MapReduce.
- Apache Lucene is a full-text open-source search library initially written by Doug Cutting in Java.
- Hadoop consists of two important parts, one called the Hadoop Distributed File System and the other called MapReduce.
- YARN is a resource management framework used to schedule and run applications such as MapReduce and Spark.
- Hadoop distributions are a complete package of all open source big data tools integrated together to work with each other in an efficient way.

Summary

In this chapter, we covered Hadoop's origins and how Hadoop evolved over time with more performance-optimized features and tools. We also covered a logical view of the Hadoop platform in detail and understood its different layers. Hadoop distribution was also covered, to help you understand which distribution you should choose. We described the new features available in Hadoop version 3 and will discuss these in more detail in upcoming chapters.

In the next chapter, we will cover HDFS and will walk you through the HDFS architecture and its component in detail. We will go much deeper into the internals of HDFS and HDFS high availability features. We will then look into HDFS read-write operations and how the HDFS caching and federation service works.

2
Deep Dive into the Hadoop Distributed File System

Today, data is being used to generate new opportunities, and companies can generate more business using data analytics. A single machine is not enough to handle growing volumes of data. Hence, it is necessary to distribute data between multiple machines. The Distributed File System consists of a number of machines, with data distributed between them. Hadoop offers a distributed storage File System, which is known as the **Hadoop Distributed File System (HDFS)**. HDFS is capable of handling high volumes of data and is easily scalable. It also handles machine failure without any data loss.

In this chapter, we will look at the following topics:

- The details of the HDFS architecture
- Read/write operations
- The internals of HDFS components
- HDFS commands and understanding their internal working

Technical requirements

You will be required to have basic knowledge of Linux and Apache Hadoop 3.0.

The code files of this chapter can be found on GitHub:
`https://github.com/PacktPublishing/Mastering-Hadoop-3/tree/master/Chapter02`

Check out the following video to see the code in action:
`http://bit.ly/2SxtIvJ`

Defining HDFS

HDFS is designed to run on a cluster of commodity hardware. It is a fault-tolerant, scalable File System that handles the failure of nodes without data and can scale up horizontally to any number of nodes. The initial goal of HDFS was to serve large data files with high read and write performance.

The following are a few essential features of HDFS:

- **Fault tolerance**: Downtime due to machine failure or data loss could result in a huge loss to a company; therefore, the companies want a highly available fault-tolerant system. HDFS is designed to handle failures and ensures data availability with corrective and preventive actions.
  Files stored in HDFS are split into small chunks and each chunk is referred to as a **block**. Each block is either 64 MB or 128 MB, depending on the configuration. Blocks are replicated across clusters based on the replication factor. This means that if the replication factor is three, then the block will be replicated to three machines. This assures that, if a machine holding one block fails, the data can be served from another machine.
- **Streaming data access**: HDFS works on a **write once read many** principle. Data within a file can be accessed by an HDFS client. Data is served in the form of streams, which means HDFS enables streaming access to large data files where data is transferred as a continuous stream. HDFS does not wait for the entire file to be read before sending data to the client; instead, it sends data as soon as it reads it. The client can immediately process the received stream, which makes data processing efficient.

- **Scalability**: HDFS is a highly scalable File System that is designed to store a large number of big files and allows you to add any number of machines to increase its storage capability. Storing a huge number of small files is generally not recommended; the size of the file should be equal to or greater than the block size. Small files consume more RAM space on master nodes, which may decrease the performance of HDFS operations.
- **Simplicity**: HDFS is easy to set up and manage. It is written in Java. It provides easy command-line interface tools that are very much similar to Linux commands. Later in this chapter, we will see how easy it is to operate HDFS via a command-line utility.
- **High availability**: HDFS is a highly available distributed File System. Every read and write request goes to a master node, and a master node can be a single point of failure. Hadoop offers the high availability feature, which means a read and write request will not be affected by the failure of the active master node. When the active master node fails, the standby master node takes over. In Hadoop version 3, we can have more than two master nodes running at once to make high availability more robust and efficient.

You will be able to relate to the features we have mentioned in this section as we dive deeper into the HDFS architecture and its internal workings.

Deep dive into the HDFS architecture

As a big data practitioner or enthusiast, you must have read or heard about the HDFS architecture. The goal of this section is to explore the architecture in depth, including the main and essential supporting components. By the end of this section, you will have a deep knowledge of the HDFS architecture, along with the intra-process communication of architecture components. But first, let's start by establishing definition of **HDFS** (**Hadoop Distributed File System**). HDFS is the storage system of the Hadoop platform, which is distributed, fault-tolerant, and immutable in nature. HDFS is specifically developed for large datasets (too large to fit in cheaper commodity machines). Since HDFS is designed for large datasets on commodity hardware, it purposely mitigates some of the bottlenecks associated with large datasets.

We will understand some of these bottlenecks and how HDFS mitigates them here:

- With large datasets comes the problem of slow processing they are run on only one computer. The Hadoop platform consists of two logical components, distributed storage and distributed processing. HDFS provides distributed storage. MapReduce and other YARN-compatible frameworks provide distributed processing capabilities. To mitigate this, Hadoop offers distributed data processing, which has several systems processing a chunk of data simultaneously.

- With distributed processing of large datasets, one of the challenges is to mitigate large data movements over the network. HDFS makes provisions for applications or code to move the computation closer to where the data is located. This ensures less utilization of cluster bandwidth. Moreover, data in HDFS is replicated by default and each replica is hosted by a different node. This replication helps in moving computation closer to the data. For example, if the node hosting one of the replicas of the HDFS block is busy and does not have any open slots for running jobs, then the computation would be moved to another node hosting some other HDFS block replica.

- With large datasets, the cost of failure is greater. So, if a complex process on large datasets (running over a longer duration) fails, then rerunning that complex data processing job is significant in terms of resource costs and time consumption. Moreover, one of the side effects of distributed processing is that the chances of failure are high due to high network communication and coordination across a large number of machines. Lastly, it runs on commodity hardware, where failure is unavoidable. To mitigate such risks, HDFS is built with an automated mechanism to detect and recover from faults.

- HDFS is designed to be a File System that is used for multiple access by end users and processes in a distributed cluster. In the case of multiple random access, having provisions for modifying files at arbitrary positions is error-prone and difficult to manage. To mitigate this risk, HDFS is designed to support a simple coherency model where the file is not allowed to be modified at arbitrary points once it has been written, created, and closed for the first time. You can only add content at the end of a file or truncate it completely. This simple coherency model keeps the HDFS design simple, scalable, and less buggy.

HDFS logical architecture

We'll now gain an understanding of some of the design decisions of HDFS and how they mitigate some of the bottlenecks associated with a large dataset's storage and processing in a distributed manner. It's time to take a deep dive into the HDFS architecture. The following diagram represents the logical components of HDFS:

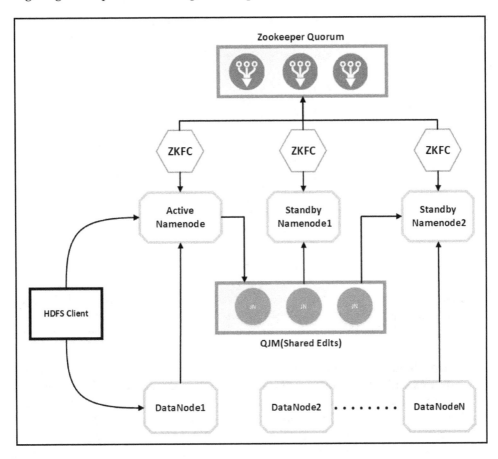

For simplicity's sake, you can divide the architecture into two groups. One group can be called the **data group**. It consists of processes/components that are related to file storage. The other group can be called the **management group**. It consists of processes/components that are used to manage data operations such as read, write, truncate, and delete.

So, the data group is about data blocks, replication, checkpoints, and file metadata. The management group is about NameNodes, DataNodes, JournalNodes, and Zookeepers. We will first take at the management group's components and then we will talk about the data group's components:

- **NameNode**: HDFS is a master-slave architecture. The NameNode plays the role of a master in the HDFS architecture. It is the regulator that controls all operations on the data and stores all relevant metadata about data that's stored in HDFS. All data operations will first go through a NameNode and then to other relevant Hadoop components. The NameNode manages the File System namespace. It stores the File System tree and metadata of files and directories. All of this information is stored on the local disk in three types of files, namely File System namespace, image (fsimage) files, and edit logs files.

    The fsimage file stores the state of the File System at a point in time. The edit logs files contains a list of all changes (creation, modification, truncation, or deletion) that are made to each HDFS file after the last fsimage file was created. A new fsimage file is created after collaborating the content of the most recent fsimage files with the latest edit logs. This process of merging fsimage files with edit logs is called checkpointing. It is system-triggered and is managed by system policies. NameNode also maintains a mapping of all data blocks to DataNode.

- **DataNode**: DataNodes plays the role of slaves in the HDFS architecture. They perform data block operations (creation, modification, or deletion) based on instructions that are received from NameNodes or HDFS clients. They host data processing jobs such as MapReduce. They report back block information to NameNodes. DataNodes also communicate between each other in the case of data replication.

- **JournalNode**: With NameNode high availability, there was a need to manage edit logs and HDFS metadata between a active and standby NameNodes. JournalNodes were introduced to efficiently share edit logs and metadata between two NameNodes. JournalNodes exercise concurrency write locks to ensure that edit logs are written by one active NameNode at a time. This level of concurrency control is required to avoid the state of a NameNode from being managed by two different services that act as failovers of one another at the same time. This type of scenario, where edit logs are managed by two services at the same time, is called **HDFS split brain scenario**, and it can result in data loss or inconsistent state. JournalNodes avoid such scenarios by allowing only one NameNode to be writing to edit logs at a time.

- **Zookeeper failover controllers**: With the introduction of **high availability** (**HA**) in NameNodes, automatic failover was introduced as well. HA without automatic failover would have manual intervention to bring NameNode services back up in the event of failure. This is not ideal. Hence, the Hadoop community has introduced two components: **Zookeeper Quorum** and Zookeeper Failover controller, also known as **ZKFailoverController** (**ZKFC**). Zookeeper maintains data about NameNode health and connectivity. It monitors clients and notifies other clients in the event of failure. Zookeeper maintains an active persistent session with each of the NameNodes, and this session is renewed by each of them upon expiry. In the event of a failure or crash, the expired session is not renewed by the failed NameNode. This is when Zookeeper informs other standby NameNodes to initiate the failover process. Every NameNode server has a Zookeeper client installed on it. This Zookeeper client is called ZKFC. Its prime responsibilities are monitoring the health of the NameNode processes, managing sessions with Zookeeper servers, and acquiring write lock concurrency in the case of its local NameNode being active. ZKFC monitors NameNode health with periodic health check pings. If a NameNode responds to those pings in a timely manner, then ZKFC considers that NameNode to be healthy. If not, then ZKFC considers it to be unhealthy and accordingly notifies the Zookeeper servers about it. In the case of the local NameNode being healthy and active, ZKFC opens a session in Zookeeper and creates a *lock* znode on the Zookeeper servers. This znode is ephemeral in nature and will be deleted automatically when the session expires.

Concepts of the data group

There are two concepts that belong to the data group: blocks and replication. We will look at each of them in detail.

Blocks

Blocks define the minimum amount of data that HDFS can read and write at a time. HDFS, when storing large files, divides them into sets of individual blocks and stores each of these blocks on different data nodes in a Hadoop cluster. All files are divided into data blocks and then stored in HDFS. The default value of a HDFS block size is either 64 MB or 128 MB. This is large compared to Unix-level File System blocks. Having a large HDFS data block size is beneficial in the case of storing and processing large volumes of data in Hadoop. One of the reasons for this is to efficiently manage the metadata associated with each data block. If the size of the data blocks are too small, then more metadata will be stored in NameNodes, causing its RAM to be filled up quickly. This will also result in more **remote procedural calls** (**RPCs**) to NameNode ports, which may result in resource contention.

The other reason is that large data blocks would result in higher Hadoop throughput. With an appropriate data block size, you can strike a balance between how many data nodes would be running parallel processes to perform operations on a given dataset and how much data can be processed by an individual process given the amount of resources allocated to it. Larger data blocks also result in less time being spent in disk-seeking operations or finding out the start of the data block. In addition to the advantages of having a large HDFS block size, the concept of HDFS block abstraction have other advantages in Hadoop operations. One such benefit is that you can store files larger than the size of a disk of an individual machine. The other benefit is that it provides better replication strategy and failover. Corrupted disk blocks can be easily replaced by replicated blocks from some other DataNode.

Replication

HDFS replication is critical for reliability, scalability, and performance. By default, HDFS has a replication factor of three. Therefore, Hadoop creators have given careful thought on where each data block replica should be placed. It is all policy-driven. The current implementation follows the rack-aware replica management policy. Before we look at that in detail, we should first go through some of the facts about server racks. Any communication between two racks goes through switches, and the available network bandwidth between two racks is generally less than the bandwidth between machines on the same rack. Large Hadoop clusters spread across multiple racks. Hadoop tries to place replicas onto different racks. This prevents data loss in the case of an entire rack unit failing and utilizes multiple available rack bandwidth for reading data.

However, this increases write latency as data needs to be transferred to multiple racks. If the replication factor is three, then HDFS would put one replica on the local machine where the writer is present, otherwise it would put on a random DataNode. Another replica would be placed on the DataNode on a different remote rack, and the last replica would be placed on another DataNode in the same remote rack. The HDFS replication policy makes an assumption that rack failures are less probable than node failures. A block is only placed in two different racks, not three, which reduces the probability of network bandwidth being used. The current replication policy does not equally distribute files across racks—if the replication factor is three, then two replicas will be on the same rack and the third one will be on another rack. In bigger clusters, we may have more replication factors. In such cases, two thirds of the replicas will be placed on one rack, one thirds of the replicas will be placed on another block, and the rest of the replicas will be equally distributed between the remaining racks.

The maximum number of replicas that we can have on HDFS is equal to the number of DataNodes because a DataNode cannot keep multiple copies of the same block. HDFS always tries for direct read requests to the replica that's closest to the client. If the reader node is under the same rack where the replica is, then it is assigned for reading the block. If the replication factor is more than the default replication factor, which is three, then the fourth and following replicas are placed randomly by sticking to the per rack replica limit. This can be calculated using the following formula:

(number_of_replicas-1)/number_of_racks+2

HDFS communication architecture

One of the important aspects of understanding HDFS is taking a look at how different components interact with each other programmatically and which type of network protocols or method invocations they use. All communication between HDFS components happens over the TCP/IP protocol. Different protocol wrappers are defined for different types of communication. The following diagram represents such protocol wrappers, which we will look into in this section:

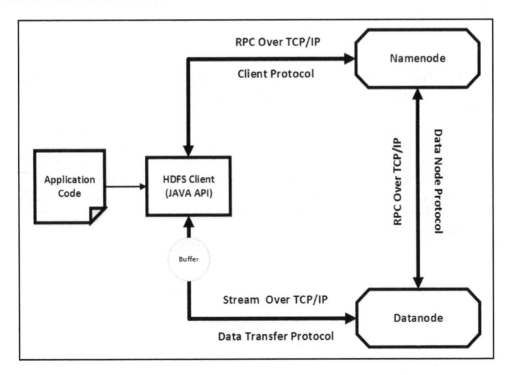

The preceding diagram can be explained as follows:

- **Client Protocol**: This is a communication protocol that's defined for communication between the **HDFS Client** and the **Namenode** server. It is a **remote procedure call** (RPC) that communicates with **NameNode** on a defined port using a TCP protocol. All user code and client-side libraries that need to interact with **Namenode** use this protocol. Some of the important methods in this protocol are as follows:

    - create: Creates a new empty file in the HDFS namespace
    - append: Appends to the end of file
    - setReplication: Sets replication of the file
    - addBlock: Writes additional data blocks to a file and assigns DataNodes for replication

    There are multiple methods that are supported by the client protocol. All of these are with respect to client interaction with NameNode. We suggest you go over the Hadoop source code on GitHub to understand client and NameNode communication in more detail. This is the location of ClientProtocol.java in the Hadoop source code: hadoop-hdfs-project/hadoop-hdfs-client/src/main/java/org/apache/hadoop/hdfs/protocol/ClientProtocol.java.

- **Data Transfer Protocol**: The **HDFS Client**, after receiving metadata information from **Namenode**, establishes communication with **Datanode** to read and write data. This communication between the client and the **Datanode** is defined by the **Data Transfer Protocol**. Since this type of communication does most of the data heavy lifting in terms of high volume read and writes, it is defined as a streaming protocol and is unlike the RPC protocol we defined earlier. Moreover, for efficiency purposes, the client buffers data up to a certain size of HDFS data blocks (64 MB by default) and then writes one complete block to the respective DataNodes. This protocol is mostly defined around data blocks. Some of the important methods that are included in this protocol are as follows:

    - readBlock: Reads a data block from a DataNode.
    - writeBlock: Writes a data block to a DataNode.
    - transferBlock: Transfers a data block from one DataNode to another.
    - blockChecksum: Gets the checksum value of a data block. This can be an MD5 or a CRC32 value.

The data transfer protocol is an important protocol that defines communication (read/write) between client and data nodes. Additional details about the methods it supports can be found in the Hadoop source code on GitHub. The following is the link for the same is: `https://github.com/lpcclown/hadoop_enhancement/tree/master/hadoop-hdfs-project/hadoop-hdfs-client/src/main/java/org/apache/hadoop/hdfs/protocol/datatransfer`.

- **Data Node Protocol**: This is another important protocol that you should understand in detail. This protocol defines communication between **Namenode** and **DataNode**. The **Data Node Protocol** (**DNP**) is mostly used by **Datanode** to provide its operation, health, and storage information to **Namenode**. One of the important aspects of this protocol is that it is a one-way protocol. This means that all requests are always initiated by DataNode. NameNodes only respond to requests that are initiated by DataNodes. Unlike the previous protocol, this is a RPC protocol that's defined over TCP. The following are some of the important methods that are included in this protocol:
    - `registerDatanode`: This registers new or rebooted data nodes to NameNode.
    - `sendHeartbeat`: This tells NameNode that the DataNode is alive and working properly. This method is not only important from the point of view of knowing which DataNode is alive, but it also gives NameNode a chance to respond back to DataNodes with a set of commands that it wants them to execute. For example, at times, NameNode wants to invalidate some of the blocks stored in data nodes. In that case, in response to the `sendHeartbeat()` method, NameNode sends an invalidate block request to the DataNode.
    - `blockReport`: This method is used by DataNode to send all of its locally stored block-related information to NameNode. In response to this, NameNode sends DataNodes blocks that are obsolete and should be deleted.

Additional details about methods supported by the Data Node Protocol can be found in the Hadoop source code on GitHub. This the link for that: `hadoop/hadoop-hdfs-project/hadoop-hdfs/src/main/java/org/apache/hadoop/hdfs/server/protocol/DatanodeProtocol.java`.

NameNode internals

HDFS is a distributed File System for storing and managing large datasets. It divides large datasets into small data chunks where each data chunk is stored on different nodes that are part of the Hadoop cluster. However, HDFS hides these underlying complexities of dividing data into smaller chunks and copying that data to different nodes behind abstract file operation APIs. For HDFS users, these file operation APIs are just read/write/create/delete operations. All a HDFS user needs to know about is the Hadoop namespace and file URIs. But in reality, lots of steps are performed before those operations are completed. One of the key HDFS components in achieving all of these activities is NameNode. NameNode in Hadoop is a central component that regulates any operations on HDFS using file metadata that's stored in it. In other words, it manages HDFS file namespaces. NameNode performs the following functions:

- It maintains the metadata of files and directories stored in HDFS. Metadata mostly consists of file creation/modification timestamps, access control lists, block or replica storage information, and files' current state.
- It regulates any file operations in terms of access control lists stored in files or directories, and which blocks and replicas will be handled by which DataNode. It also denies an operation if a user is not allowed to perform that operation.
- It gives the client information about data blocks and which data node will serve the read/write request.
- It also issues commands to DataNodes such as delete corrupted data blocks and also maintains a list of healthy DataNodes.

NameNodes maintains a data structure called INodes in memory. INodes have all the information regarding files and directories. All of these INodes constitute a tree-like structure that is maintained by the Namenodes. INodes contain information such as file or directory name, username, group name, permissions, authorization ACLs, modification time, access time, and disk space quotas. The following diagram shows the high-level classes and interfaces that are used in implementing INodes:

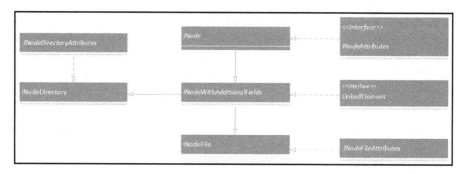

Data locality and rack awareness

One of the design goals of Hadoop is to move computation to data rather than moving data to computation. This goal was set because Hadoop was created for processing high-volume datasets. Moving large datasets can decrease performance. For example, if Hadoop is running MapReduce on a large volume of data, it would first try to run mapper tasks on the DataNodes that have the relevant input data (**Data Local**). This is generally referred to as data locality optimization in Hadoop. One of the key points to remember here is that reduce tasks do not use data locality, because a single reduce task can use output from multiple mappers. To achieve data locality, Hadoop uses all three replications (**Data Local**, **Rack Local**, and **Off rack**). But sometimes, in a very busy cluster, if there are no task slots available on the nodes hosting input data replicas, job schedulers would first try to run jobs on the node that have free slots on the same rack (**Rack Local**). If Hadoop does not find any free slots on the same rack, then tasks are run on different racks. However, this will result in data transfer (**Off rack**). The following diagram shows different types of data locality in Hadoop:

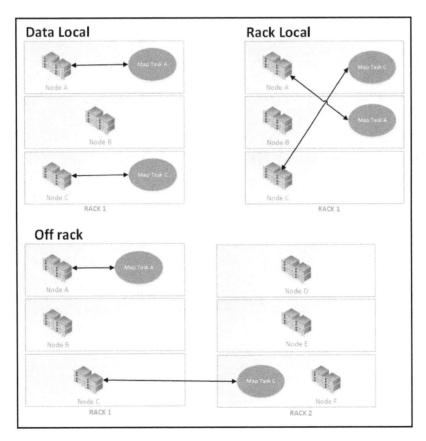

Hadoop understands that any communication between nodes within a rack would be of a lower latency as more network bandwidth is available within a rack than going outside the rack. Therefore, all components in Hadoop are rack-aware. Rack awareness basically means that Hadoop and its components have complete knowledge of the Cluster topology. By cluster topology, we mean how data nodes are placed onto different racks that are part of the Hadoop cluster. Hadoop uses this information to ensure data availability in the case of failures and for better the performance of Hadoop jobs.

DataNode internals

HDFS is built based on a master/worker architecture where NameNode is the master and DataNodes are the workers. DataNode follows NameNode's instructions, such as block creation, replication, and deletion. Read and write requests from clients are served by DataNodes. All the files in HDFS are split into blocks and actual data is then stored in the DataNodes. Each DataNode periodically sends its heartbeat to the NameNode to acknowledge that it is still alive and functioning properly. DataNodes also send block reports to the NameNodes.

When the DataNodes receives a new block request, it sends a block received acknowledgement to the NameNode. The `Datanode.Java` class contains the majority of the implementation of Datanode's functionality. This class has the implementation code for communicating with the following:

- Client code for read and write operations
- DataNode for replication operations
- NameNode for block report and heartbeats

The DataNode follows instructions from the NameNode and may delete block replicas or copy replicas to some other DataNodes as per instruction. The NameNode does not connect to a DataNode directly for instruction; instead, a client takes metadata information from the NameNode and then instructs the DataNode to read/write or copy block replica. An open server socket connection is maintained by the DataNode for client or other DataNodes to read and write data. Server information such as host and port number are sent to the NameNode, and the latter sends this information to the client when it receives a request for read and write operations.

The NameNode must know which DataNode is functioning properly and thus each DataNode sends a heartbeat to the NameNode at regular intervals. The interval is 3 seconds by default. Similarly, block information is also sent to a NameNode by DataNodes at a regular configured interval. In short, DataNodes are involved in the following operations:

- **Heartbeat**: All the DataNodes send a regular heartbeat to the NameNode so that the NameNode knows that the DataNodes are working properly and can satisfy read/write/delete requests from clients. If the DataNode does not send a heartbeat for a configured period of time, NameNode marks the DataNode as dead and does not use that DataNode for any read and write requests.
- **Read/write**: A DataNode opens a socket connection for clients to read and write data blocks to its storage. The client sends a request to the NameNode and NameNode replies with a list of DataNodes that can be used for read and write operations. The client then directly uses DataNodes to read or write data.
- **Replication and block report**: During write or replica balance operations, one DataNode may receive a write request for data block write from another DataNode. DataNodes also send block reports to the NameNode at regular intervals. This keeps the NameNode up to date regarding the location and other details of each block.

Quorum Journal Manager (QJM)

NameNode used to be a single point of failure before the release of Hadoop version 2. In Hadoop 1, each cluster consisted of a single NameNode. If this NameNode failed, then the entire cluster would be unavailable. So, until and unless the NameNode service restarted, no one could use the Hadoop cluster. In Hadoop 2, the high availability feature was introduced. It has two NameNodes, one of the NameNodes is in active state while the other NameNode is in standby state. The active NameNode serves the client requests while the standby NameNode maintains synchronization of its state to take over as the active NameNode if the current active NameNode fails.

There is a **Quorum Journal Manager** (QJM) runs in each NameNode. The QJM is responsible for communicating with JournalNodes using RPC; for example, sending namespace modifications, that is, edits to JournalNodes, and so on. A JournalNode daemon can run on *N* machines where *N* is configurable. A QJM writes edits to the local disk of a JournalNode running on N machines in the cluster. These JournalNodes are shared with NameNode machines and any modifications performed by the active NameNode is logged into edit files on these shared nodes. These files are then read by the standby NameNode, which applies these modification onto its own `fsimage` to keep its state in sync with the active NameNode. In case the active NameNode fails, the standby NameNode will apply all the changes from the edit logs before changing its state to active and thus making sure that the current namespace is fully synchronized. The QJM performs the following operations when it writes to the JournalNode:

- The writer makes sure that no other writers are writing to the edit logs. This is to guarantee that even if the two NameNodes are active at a same time, only one will be allowed to make namespace changes to the edit logs.
- It is possible that the writer has not logged namespace modifications to all the JournalNodes or that some JournalNodes have not completed the logging. The QJM makes sure that all the JournalNodes are in sync based on file length.
- When one of the preceding two things are verified, the OJM can start a new log segment to write to edit logs.
- The writer sends current batch edits to all the JournalNodes in the cluster and waits for an acknowledgement based on the quorum of all the JournalNodes before considering the write a success. Those JournalNodes who failed to respond to the write request will be marked as `OutOfSync` and will not be used for the current batch of the edit segment.
- A QJM sends a RPC request to JournalNodes to finalize log segmentation. After receiving confirmation from quorum of JournalNodes, QJM can begin the next log segment.

The DataNode sends block information and a heartbeat to both the DataNodes to make sure that both have up to date information about the block. In Hadoop 3, we can have more than two NameNodes, and the DataNode will send information to all of those NameNodes. In this way, QJM helps in achieving high availability.

HDFS high availability in Hadoop 3.x

With Hadoop 2.0, active and standby NameNodes were introduced. At any point, out of two NameNodes, one will always be in active state and other will be in standby state. The active NameNode is the one that's responsible for any client requests in the cluster. Standby NameNodes are slave nodes whose responsibility is to keep its state in sync with the active NameNode so that it can provide fast failover in the event of failover. However, what if one of the NameNodes fails? In that case, the NameNode would become non-HA. This means that NameNodes can only tolerate up to one failure. This behavior is the opposite of the core fault -tolerant behavior of Hadoop, which certainly can accommodate more than one failure of DataNodes in a cluster. Keeping that in mind, provisions of more than one standby NameNode was introduced in Hadoop 3. The behavior of additional standby NameNodes will still be the same as any other standby NameNode. They will have their own IDs, RPC, and HTTP addresses. They will use QJM to get the latest edit logs and update their `fsimage`.

The following are the core configurations that are required for HA in NameNode:

- First, you need to define the `nameservice` for the cluster:

```
<property>
   <name>dfs.nameservices</name>
   <value>mycluster</value>
</property>
```

- Then, you have to give the IDs of all the NameNodes in the named service, `mycluster` , which we defined previously:

```
<property>
   <name>dfs.ha.namenodes.mycluster</name>
   <value>nn1,nn2,nn3</value>
</property>
```

- After giving the identifiers to the NameNodes, you need to add RPC and HTTP addresses for those NameNodes. Here, we will define RPC and HTTP addresses for `nn1`, `nn2`, and `nn3`:

```
<property>
   <name>dfs.namenode.rpc-address.mycluster.nn1</name>
   <value>masternode1.example.com:9820</value>
</property>
<property>
   <name>dfs.namenode.rpc-address.mycluster.nn2</name>
   <value>masternode2.example.com:9820</value>
</property>
```

```
<property>
  <name>dfs.namenode.rpc-address.mycluster.nn3</name>
  <value>masternode3.example.com:9820</value>
</property>

<property>
  <name>dfs.namenode.http-address.mycluster.nn1</name>
  <value>masternode1.example.com:9870</value>
</property>
<property>
  <name>dfs.namenode.http-address.mycluster.nn2</name>
  <value>masternode2.example.com:9870</value>
</property>
<property>
  <name>dfs.namenode.http-address.mycluster.nn3</name>
  <value>masternode3.example.com:9870</value>
</property>
```

 The preceding configurations are just a small snippet of what more than NameNodes HA configuration would look like in Hadoop 3. If you are looking for comprehensive configuration steps for HA, then you should refer to this link:
https://hadoop.apache.org/docs/current/hadoop-project-dist/
hadoop-hdfs/HDFSHighAvailabilityWithNFS.html.

Data management

We discussed HDFS blocks and replication in the previous sections. NameNode stores all metadata information and is a single point of failure, which means that no one can use HDFS if NameNode is down. This metadata information is important and can be used to restart NameNode on other machines. Thus, it is important to take multiple backup copies of a metadata file so that, even if metadata is lost from the primary NameNode, the backup copy can be used to restart the NameNode on the same machine or another machine. In this section, we will discuss NameNode metadata files such as `fsimage` and edit log. We will discuss data integrity further by using checksum and taking snapshots of the directory to avoid data loss and modification.

Metadata management

HDFS stores a large amount of structured and unstructured data in various formats. While the data is continuously growing to terabytes and petabytes, and your data is being used by Hadoop, you are likely to come across questions, such as what data is available on HDFS, how it is being used, and what type of users are using the data, the data creation timeline, and so on. Well-maintained metadata information can effectively answer these questions and thus improve the usability of the data store over HDFS.

NameNode keeps the complete fsimage in memory so that all the metadata information requests can be served in the smallest amount of time possible and persist fsimage and edit logs on the disk. fsimage contains HDFS directory information, file information, permissions, quotas, last access times and last modification times, and block IDs for files.

HDFS metadata information includes various attributes of directories and files, such as ownership, permissions, quotas, replication factors, and much more. This information is in two files:

- fsimage: An fsimage file contains the complete state of the File System to which every File System modification is assigned a unique and an unmodulated increasing transaction ID. An fsimage file represents the File System state up to a specific transaction ID.
  Let's see how we can analyze the content of fsimage by taking various usage patterns that can help us check the health of the File System. The following command can be used to fetch the latest fsimage from NameNode:

```
hdfs dfsadmin -fetchImage /home/packt
```

The fsimage file is not in a human-readable format. The Offline Image Viewer tool is used to convert fsimage file content into a human-readable format. It also provides the WebHDFS API, which helps with offline fsimage analysis. Let's see how we can use it and what options are available with the Offline Image Viewer tool:

```
hdfs oiv --help
```

The preceding command will return the following output, which contains details about its usage and options:

```
chanchal@chanchal-Lenovo-ideapad-510-15IKB:~$ hdfs oiv --help
Error parsing command-line options:
Usage: bin/hdfs oiv [OPTIONS] -i INPUTFILE -o OUTPUTFILE
Offline Image Viewer
View a Hadoop fsimage INPUTFILE using the specified PROCESSOR,
saving the results in OUTPUTFILE.

The oiv utility will attempt to parse correctly formed image files
and will abort fail with mal-formed image files.

The tool works offline and does not require a running cluster in
order to process an image file.

The following image processors are available:
  * XML: This processor creates an XML document with all elements of
    the fsimage enumerated, suitable for further analysis by XML
    tools.
  * FileDistribution: This processor analyzes the file size
    distribution in the image.
    -maxSize specifies the range [0, maxSize] of file sizes to be
     analyzed (128GB by default).
    -step defines the granularity of the distribution. (2MB by default)
  * Web: Run a viewer to expose read-only WebHDFS API.
    -addr specifies the address to listen. (localhost:5978 by default)
  * Delimited (experimental): Generate a text file with all of the elements common
    to both inodes and inodes-under-construction, separated by a
    delimiter. The default delimiter is \t, though this may be
    changed via the -delimiter argument.

Required command line arguments:
-i,--inputFile <arg>   FSImage file to process.

Optional command line arguments:
-o,--outputFile <arg>  Name of output file. If the specified
                       file exists, it will be overwritten.
                       (output to stdout by default)
-p,--processor <arg>   Select which type of processor to apply
                       against image file. (XML|FileDistribution|Web|Delimited)
                       (Web by default)
-delimiter <arg>       Delimiting string to use with Delimited processor.
-t,--temp <arg>        Use temporary dir to cache intermediate result to generate
                       Delimited outputs. If not set, Delimited processor constructs
                       the namespace in memory before outputting text.
```

We will convert `fsimage` content into a tab delimited file:

```
hdfs oiv -i /home/packt/fsimage_00000000007685439 -o
/home/packt/fsimage_output.csv -p Delimited
```

Now, we have the available information stored in `fsimage` in the form of a tab delimited file and we can expose a hive table on top of it after removing the header from the file. The header can be removed using the linux utility or any file editor. You can use the following command to do this:

```
sed -i -e "1d" /home/packt/fsimage_output.csv
```

Once the header has been removed, we can expose the hive table on top of this `fsimage` file:

- `edits`: An `edits` log file contains a list of changes that are applied on the File System after the most recent `fsimage`. The edit log contains an entry for each operation and the checkpoint operation periodically merges `fsimage` and the edit log by applying all of the changes that are available in the edit logs in `fsimage` before saving the new `fsimage`.
  The edit log file is available in binary format and we can convert it into human-readable XML format using the following command:

```
sudo hdfs oev -i /hadoop/hdfs/namenode/current/
edits_0000000000000488053-0000000000000488074 -o editlog.xml
```

After using the preceding command, we will see the content of the edit log file, which consists of different attributes:

```xml
<?xml version="1.0" encoding="UTF-8"?>
<EDITS>
  <EDITS_VERSION>-63</EDITS_VERSION>
  <RECORD>
    <OPCODE>OP_START_LOG_SEGMENT</OPCODE>
    <DATA>
      <TXID>488053</TXID>
    </DATA>
  </RECORD>
  <RECORD>
    <OPCODE>OP_MKDIR</OPCODE>
    <DATA>
      <TXID>488054</TXID>
      <LENGTH>0</LENGTH>
      <INODEID>190335</INODEID>
      <PATH>/tmp/hive/hive/124dd7e2-d4d3-413e-838e-3dbbbd185a69</PATH>
      <TIMESTAMP>1509663411129</TIMESTAMP>
      <PERMISSION_STATUS>
        <USERNAME>hive</USERNAME>
        <GROUPNAME>hdfs</GROUPNAME>
        <MODE>448</MODE>
      </PERMISSION_STATUS>
    </DATA>
  </RECORD>
  <RECORD>
    <OPCODE>OP_ADD</OPCODE>
    <DATA>
      <TXID>488055</TXID>
      <LENGTH>0</LENGTH>
      <INODEID>190336</INODEID>
      <PATH>/tmp/hive/hive/124dd7e2-d4d3-413e-838e-3dbbbd185a69/inuse.info</PATH>
      <REPLICATION>3</REPLICATION>
      <MTIME>1509663411169</MTIME>
      <ATIME>1509663411169</ATIME>
      <BLOCKSIZE>134217728</BLOCKSIZE>
      <CLIENT_NAME>DFSClient_NONMAPREDUCE_1006023362_1</CLIENT_NAME>
      <CLIENT_MACHINE>10.1.2.26</CLIENT_MACHINE>
      <OVERWRITE>true</OVERWRITE>
      <PERMISSION_STATUS>
        <USERNAME>hive</USERNAME>
        <GROUPNAME>hdfs</GROUPNAME>
        <MODE>420</MODE>
```

A new record entry is made for every new operation. The structure of the record entry is as follows:

```
<RECORD>
    <OPCODE>OP_ADD</OPCODE>
    <DATA>
      <TXID>488055</TXID>
      <LENGTH>0</LENGTH>
      <INODEID>190336</INODEID>
      <PATH>/tmp/hive/hive/124dd7e2-
d4d3-413e-838e-3dbbbd185a69/inuse.info</PATH>
      <REPLICATION>3</REPLICATION>
      <MTIME>1509663411169</MTIME>
      <ATIME>1509663411169</ATIME>
      <BLOCKSIZE>134217728</BLOCKSIZE>
      <CLIENT_NAME>DFSClient_NONMAPREDUCE_1006023362_1</CLIENT_NAME>
      <CLIENT_MACHINE>10.1.2.26</CLIENT_MACHINE>
      <OVERWRITE>true</OVERWRITE>
      <PERMISSION_STATUS>
        <USERNAME>hive</USERNAME>
        <GROUPNAME>hdfs</GROUPNAME>
        <MODE>420</MODE>
      </PERMISSION_STATUS>
      <RPC_CLIENTID>ad7a6982-fde8-4b8a-8e62-f9a04c3c228e</RPC_CLIENTID>
      <RPC_CALLID>298220</RPC_CALLID>
    </DATA>
  </RECORD>
```

Here, `OPCODE` represents the type of operation that's performed on the file that's available at the `PATH` location.

Now, we will see how the checkpoint operation works and what steps are involved in the operation.

Checkpoint using a secondary NameNode

Checkpoint is the process of merging an fsimage with edit logs by applying all the actions of the edit log on the fsimage. This process is necessary to make sure that the edit log does not grow too large. Let's go into further details of how the checkpoint process works in Hadoop.

In the previous section, we discussed the fsimage and the edit log file. NameNode loads the fsimage into memory when it starts and then applies edits from the edit log file to the fsimage. Once this process is complete, it then writes a new fsimage file to the system. At the end of this operation, the edit log file does not have anything in it. This process starts only during NameNode startup—it does not perform merging operations while the NameNode is live and is busy serving a request. If the NameNode is up for a long period of time, then the edit log file could get too big. Therefore, we may need to have a service that periodically merges edit logs and the fsimage file. The Secondary NameNode does the job of merging the fsimage and the edit log file. The interval for the checkpoint operation and the number of transactions in the edit log is controlled by two configuration parameters: `dfs.namenode.checkpoint.period` for intervals and `dfs.namenode.checkpoint.txns` for the number of transactions. This means that if the limit is reached, then the checkpoint process will be forcefully started, even if the interval period has not been reached. The secondary NameNode also stores the latest fsimage file so that it can be used if anything is required.

Data integrity

Data integrity ensures that no data is lost or corrupted during storage or processing of data. HDFS stores huge volumes of data that consists of a large number of HDFS blocks. Typically, in a big cluster that consist of thousands of nodes, there are more chances of machine failures. Imagine that your replication factor is three and two of the machines storing replication for a particular block failed and that the last replica block is corrupted. You may lose your data in such cases, and so it is necessary to configure a good replication factor and do regular block scanning to verify that the block is not corrupted. HDFS maintains data integrity using the checksum mechanism.

Checksum: Checksum is calculated for each block that is written to HDFS. HDFS maintains checksum for each block and verifies checksum when it reads data. The DataNode is responsible for storing data and checksum is responsible for all of the data stored on it. In this way, when the client reads data from the DataNode, they also read the checksum of data. The DataNode regularly runs a block scanner to verify the data blocks stored on them. If a corrupt block is found, HDFS reads a replica of the corrupted block and replaces the block with a new replica. Let's see how checksum verification happens in read and write operations:

- **HDFS write**: The DataNode is responsible for verifying the checksum of the block. During the write operation, the checksum is created for a file that has to be written to HDFS. Previously, we discussed the HDFS write operation, where a file is split into blocks and HDFS creates a block pipeline. The DataNode, which is responsible for storing the last block in the pipeline, compares the checksum, and if the checksum does not match, it sends `ChecksumException` to the client and the client can then take necessary action, such as retrying the operation and so on.
- **HDFS read**: When the clients starts reading data from the DataNode, it also compares the checksum of the block and if the checksum is not equal, then it sends information to the NameNode so that the NameNode marks the block as corrupted and takes necessary action to replace the corrupted block with another replica. The NameNode does not use these DataNodes for any other client request until it is replaced or removed from the corrupted entry list.

HDFS Snapshots

Today, data is the backbone of businesses, and users do not want to lose data due to any machine failure or disaster. In the event of failures or disasters, a File System user may want to have a plan to take a backup and restore their important data. Because of this, HDFS introduced the Snapshots. Snapshots are point-in-time images that are a part of a File System or are the entire File System. In other words, HDFS Snapshots are snapshots of a subtree of the HDFS, such as directories, sub-directories, or the entire HDFS. Let's look into a few of the common use cases of HDFS Snapshots:

- **Backup:** The admin may want to do a backup of the entire File System, a subtree in the File System, or just a file. Depending on the requirements, the admin can take a read-only snapshot. This snapshot could be used to recover data or could be used to send data to remote storage.

- **Protection**: The user may accidentally delete files on HDFS or delete the entire directory. However, these files go into the trash and can be recovered, but once the files have been deleted using the File System, the operation does not go into the trash and is recoverable. The admin can set up a job that can take a HDFS snapshot on a regular basis so that if any file is deleted, it can be restored using a HDFS Snapshot.

- **Application Testing**: Testing the application with the original dataset is a common requirement of an application developer or application users. The application may not perform as per expectations, which may lead to data loss or may corrupt the production data. In such cases, the admin can create a read/write HDFS Snapshot of the original data and assign that snapshot to a user for testing. Any changes done to this dataset will not reflect the original dataset.

- **Distributed Copy (distcp)**: distcp is used to copy data from one cluster to another cluster. But think about scenarios where you are copying data and someone has deleted the source file or moved data to some other location—this will put distcp in an inconsistent state. HDFS Snapshot can be used to address this problem where the snapshot can be used with distcp to copy data from one cluster to another cluster.

- **Legal and Auditing**: Organizations may want to store data for a certain period of time for legal or internal processes to see what data has changed over a period of time or to take an aggregated report from data. They may want to do auditing of the File System. Snapshots are taken regularly and contain information for data that can be used for auditing or legal purposes.

Let's see how we can take a snapshot of HDFS tree, sub-tree, or sub-directories. Before you can take a snapshot, you have to allow snapshot for the tree, sub-tree, or directory. This can be done by using the following command:

```
hdfs dfsadmin -allowSnapshot <path>
```

Once the directory is snapshottable, then you can take a snapshot of the directory using the following command:

```
hdfs dfs -createSnapshot <path> [<snapshotName>]
```

Here, `path` is the path of the tree, sub-tree, directory, or file that you want to take a snapshot of. Remember that, until and unless you allow the directory to be snapshottable, you cannot execute the preceding command successfully. SnapshotName is a name that you can assign to a snapshot. It is good practice to attach the date to the snapshot's name for identification.

Data rebalancing

HDFS is a scalable distributed storage File System, and data stored on it increases over time. As data volume increases, a few DataNodes may hold more blocks than other DataNodes, and this may cause more read and write requests to DataNodes with more blocks. Thus, these DataNodes will be very busy serving requests compared to other DataNodes.

HDFS is a scalable system and consists of commodity hardware. On large clusters where data volumes are high, the chances of DataNodes failing is higher. Also, adding new DataNodes to manage data volume is common. The removal or addition of DataNodes can cause data to be skewed where a few DataNodes hold more blocks than others. To avoid such problems, HDFS has a tool known as a **balancer**. Let's see how HDFS stores blocks and what scenario it takes into consideration.

When a new request comes to store a block, HDFS considers the following approaches:

- Distributing data uniformly across the DataNode in a cluster.
- Storing one replica on the same rack where the first block was written. This helps optimize cross-rack I/O.
- Storing another replica on a different rack to support fault-tolerance in the case of rack failure.
- When a new node is added, HDFS does not distribute previously stored blocks to it. Instead, it uses this DataNode to store new blocks.
- If a failed DataNode is removed, then a few of the blocks will be under-replicated. Therefore, HDFS will balance the replicas by storing them in different DataNodes.

 The balancer is used to balance the HDFS cluster, and by doing so it evenly distributes blocks across all the DataNodes in a cluster. Now, the obvious question is, *when do we call a cluster a balance cluster?* We can call a cluster a balanced cluster when the percentage of free space or utilized space of all DataNodes is above or below the specified threshold size. The balancer maintains the threshold by moving data from over-utilized DataNodes to under-utilized DataNodes, which ensures that all DataNodes have an equal amount of free space.

Let's check how we can run `balancer` using the command-line interface and what options are available with it:

```
hdfs balancer --help
```

The preceding command will give the following output:

```
sshuser@hn0-apdc-s:~$ hdfs balancer --help
Usage: hdfs balancer
        [-policy <policy>]       the balancing policy: datanode or blockpool
        [-threshold <threshold>]     Percentage of disk capacity
        [-exclude [-f <hosts-file> | <comma-separated list of hosts>]] Excludes the specified datanodes.
        [-include [-f <hosts-file> | <comma-separated list of hosts>]] Includes only the specified datanodes.
        [-source [-f <hosts-file> | <comma-separated list of hosts>]]  Pick only the specified datanodes as source nodes.
        [-idleiterations <idleiterations>]     Number of consecutive idle iterations (-1 for Infinite) before exit.
        [-runDuringUpgrade]     Whether to run the balancer during an ongoing HDFS upgrade.This is usually not desired since it will not
    used space on over-utilized machines.

Generic options supported are
-conf <configuration file>     specify an application configuration file
-D <property=value>            use value for given property
-fs <local|namenode:port>      specify a namenode
-jt <local|resourcemanager:port>     specify a ResourceManager
-files <comma separated list of files>     specify comma separated files to be copied to the map reduce cluster
-libjars <comma separated list of jars>    specify comma separated jar files to include in the classpath.
-archives <comma separated list of archives>    specify comma separated archives to be unarchived on the compute machines.

The general command line syntax is
bin/hadoop command [genericOptions] [commandOptions]
```

Let's look at two important properties that are used with the balancer:

- **Threshold**: The threshold is used to ensure that the overall usage of all DataNodes does not exceed or drop lower than the configured threshold percentage for the overall cluster usage. Simply, if the overall cluster usage is 60% and the threshold that's been configured is 5%, then each DataNode usage capacity should be between 55% to 65%. The default threshold is 10%, but you can change it by using the following command when you are running the balancer:

```
$ hdfs balancer –threshold 15
```

In the preceding case, if the overall disk usage is 60% and we run the balancer using the preceding command, then the balancer will make sure that the cluster usage at each DataNode is between 45% and 75%. This means that the balancer will only balance those DataNodes whose usage percentage is less than 45% and more then 75%.

- **Policy**: Policy is of two types: one is DataNode and the other is Blockpool. By default, the value is used to balance storage at the DataNode level, but for clusters where we are using the HDFS Federation service, we should change it to a Blockpool so that balancer ensures that blocks from one Blockpool do not move to another.

 The primary objective of balancer is to move data from the DataNode whose threshold is higher than DFS usage to a DataNode whose threshold is lower than the DFS usage. The balancer also takes care of the rack policy, where it minimizes the data transfer between two different racks.

Best practices for using balancer

In this section, we will talk about how we can optimize a balancer job, when to use balancer, and some best practices regarding it.

We should always run balancer when a new node is added to a cluster because the newly added node will have no block initially and it will be under-utilized. Normally, in a big cluster that consists of a large number of DataNode servers, it is good practice to run balancer at regular intervals. The idea is to a schedule one job, which will take care of running the balancer at regular intervals. Don't worry if the balancer is already running and the cron job has scheduled another balancing job—the new balancer will not start until the previous ends its execution.

Balancer is also a task and it must finish as early as possible. Each DataNode allocates 10 MBPS bandwidth for the balancer job. We may want to take care of two things: allocating more bandwidth to the DataNode should not affect other jobs, and getting the maximum performance from the balancer by increasing the bandwidth. Generally, if you have 200 MBPS bandwidth, you can allocate 10% of it, that is, 20 MBPS for the balancer without impacting on other jobs. You can use the following command to increase the bandwidth to 15 MBPS:

```
$ su hdfs -c 'hdfs dfsadmin -setBalancerBandwidth 15728640'
```

It is good practice to invoke the balancer when the cluster is not using its resources extensively. In such a case, it is easy to ask for more bandwidth for the balancer and the balancer will finish earlier than expected.

HDFS reads and writes

HDFS is a Distributed File Storage system in which we write data and then read that same data. NameNode is a master node that contains metadata information about all the files and DataNode space. The DataNode is a worker node that stores real files. Every read and write request will go through NameNode. HDFS is known for the write once read many pattern, meaning that the file is written in HDFS only once and can be read many times. Files stored in HDFS are not editable but appending new data to a file is allowed.

In this section, we will cover the internals of HDFS read and write operations, and will see how clients communicate with NameNode and DataNode for read/write operations.

Write workflows

HDFS provides us with the capability to write, read, and delete files from its storage system. You can write data using the command-line utility or by using the programming API interface. However, the write workflow remains the same in both cases. We will go through the internals of HDFS write in this section. The following diagram gives a high-level overview of HDFS write:

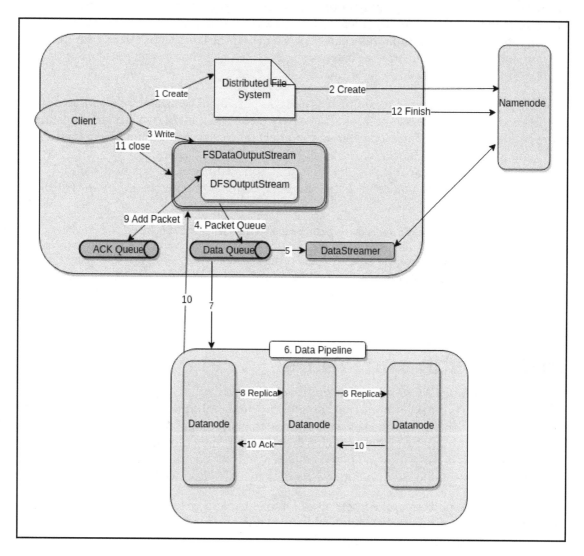

To write a file to HDFS, the HDFS client uses the `DistributedFileSystem` API and calls its `create()` method. The signature of the create method is given as follows, which is a part of the `FileSystem` class. The File System is the parent class of `DistributedFileSystem`:

```
public FSDataOutputStream create(Path f) throws IOException {
  return create(f, true);
}

public FSDataOutputStream create(Path f, boolean overwrite)
    throws IOException {
  return create(f, overwrite,
            getConf().getInt(IO_FILE_BUFFER_SIZE_KEY,
                IO_FILE_BUFFER_SIZE_DEFAULT),
            getDefaultReplication(f),
            getDefaultBlockSize(f));
}
```

The methods that are mentioned in the preceding code are abstract methods whose implementation is in `DistsibutedFileSystem`:

```
public abstract FSDataOutputStream create(Path f,
    FsPermission permission,
    boolean overwrite,
    int bufferSize,
    short replication,
    long blockSize,
    Progressable progress) throws IOException;
```

`DistributedFileSystem` makes an RPC call to NameNode by creating a new file. NameNode checks whether the file exists or not. If it already exists, it will throw `IOException` with a message stating that the file already exists. If the file does not exist, NameNode then uses `FSPermission` to check whether the user has permission to write the file to the mentioned location. Once the permission check is successful, the NameNode makes a record of the new file. If it isn't successful, it will return `IOException` with a message stating that permission was denied.

The return type of `create()` is `FSDataOutputStream`, which is written to that client after the successful execution of `create()`. The client uses `FsDataOutputStream` and we call the write method to write data.

DFSOutputStream is responsible for splitting data into packets of block size. Data is written to an internal data queue called DFSPacket , which contains data, its checksum, sequence number, and other information.

DataStreamer contains a Linked List of DFSPacket, and for each packet it asks NameNode for new DataNodes to store packets and their replicas. DataNodes returned by NameNode form a pipeline, and DataStreamer writes a packet to the first DataNode in the pipeline. The first DataNode stores the packet and forwards it to the second DataNode in the pipeline. This process is repeated until the last DataNode in the pipeline stores the packet. The number of DataNodes in the pipeline depends on the replication factor that's been configured. All of the data blocks are stored in parallel.

DFSOutputStream also maintains an acknowledgement queue (Linked List) of packets for which acknowledgement is not received from the DataNode. Once the packet is copied by the DataNode in the pipeline, the DataNode sends an acknowledgement. This acknowledgement queue is used to restart the operation if the data node in the pipeline fails.

Once the HDFS client finishes writing data, it closes the stream by calling close() on the stream. The close operation flushes the remaining data to the pipeline and then waits for an acknowledgement.

Finally, the client sends a completion signal to the NameNode after its final acknowledgement is received. Thus, NameNode has information about all of the packets and their block location, which can be accessed while reading the file.

Read workflows

We have seen how a file can be written to HDFS and how HDFS works internally to make sure that the file is written in a distributed fashion. Now, we will see how a file is read using the HDFS client and how it works internally. Similar to HDFS write, NameNode is also a primary contact for the read operation. The following diagram shows the detailed steps of the file read operation of HDFS:

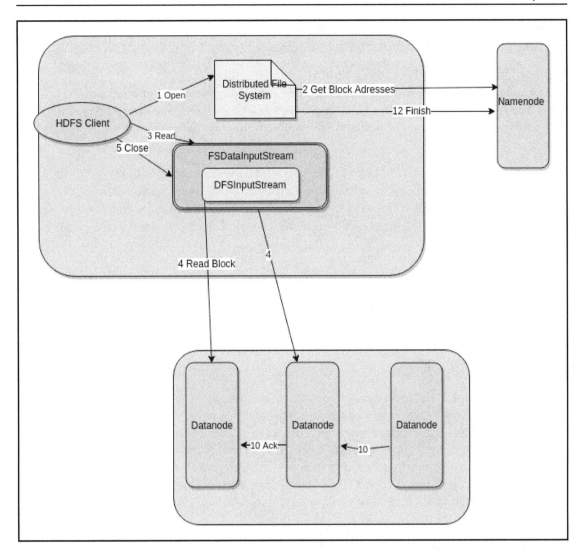

HDFS calls open() on a particular file that it wants to use by using the FileSystem object, which internally calls open() of DistributedFileSystem:

```
public FSDataInputStream open(Path f) throws IOException {
   return open(f, getConf().getInt(IO_FILE_BUFFER_SIZE_KEY,
      IO_FILE_BUFFER_SIZE_DEFAULT));
}

public abstract FSDataInputStream open(Path f, int bufferSize)
   throws IOException;
```

NameNode returns IOException with the appropriate message the client does not have permission to read the file or the file does not exist.

NameNode contains all the metadata information about the files. DistributedFileSystem makes an RPC call to the NameNode to get blocks of files. NameNode returns a list of DataNodes for each block, which are sorted based on the proximity of the HDFS client, that is, the NameNode nearest to the client will be first in the list.

The open() method returns FSDataInputStream to the client to read data. DFSInputStream is wrapped within FSDataInputStream and is responsible for managing the DataNodes. DFSInputStream connects to the DataNode using the DataNode addresses, which it received in the first block. Data is returned to the client in the form of a stream.

When data from the block is read successfully, DFSInputStream will close the connection with the DataNode and then take the nearest DataNode for the next block of the file. Data is then streamed from the DataNode back to the client to which the client calls the read() method repeatedly on the stream. When the block ends, DFSInputStream closes the connection to the DataNode to which the DFSInputStream then finds the suitable DataNode for the next block.

It's obvious that the DataNode may fail or return an error to DFSInputStream. In the case of an error or failure, DFSInpurStream makes an entry of failed DataNodes so that it does not connect to these DataNodes for the next blocks and then connects to the next closest DataNode that contains a replica for the block. Then, it reads the data from there. DFSInputStream also verifies the checksum of the block and if it does not match and finds that the block is corrupted, it reports it to NameNode and then selects the next closest DataNode that contains a replica of the block to read data.

Once the client has finished reading data from all the blocks, it closes the connection using close() on the stream.

Every operation request will go through the NameNode, and the NameNode helps the client by providing metadata information about the request.

Short circuit reads

We walked through the HDFS read steps in the previous sections and have seen how DataNode is involved in the read operation. In short, the HDFS client receives block details from the NameNode and asks the DataNode to read a file. The DataNode reads the file and sends the data to the client using TCP sockets. In a short circuit read, the DataNode is not involved and the HDFS client reads the file directly. However, this is only possible when the client is on the same machine where the data is being kept.

Earlier, even if the client was on the same machine where the data was, DataNode was used to read data and serve packets using TCP sockets. This involved having an overhead of threads and other processing resources. Short circuit read optimizes this by reducing this overhead. The following configuration enables short circuit read:

```
<configuration>
  <property>
    <name>dfs.client.read.shortcircuit</name>
    <value>true</value>
  </property>
  <property>
    <name>dfs.domain.socket.path</name>
    <value>socketPath</value>
  </property>
</configuration>
```

Managing disk-skewed data in Hadoop 3.x

Over any period of time, when you're producing a Hadoop cluster, there is always a need to manage disks on DataNodes. It could be the case that you must replace corrupted disks or you must add more disks for more data volumes. Another possibility is that your disks volumes vary in same data nodes. All such cases would result in uneven data distribution across all of the disks in a DataNode. Another reason that can result in uneven data distribution is round robin-based disk writes and random deletes.

To prevent such problems from occurring prior to the release of Hadoop 3, Hadoop administrators were applying methods that were far from ideal. One solution was to shut down your data node and use the UNIX mv command to move block replicas along with supported metadata files from one directory to another directory. Each of those directories should be using different disks. You need to ensure that subdirectory names are not changed, otherwise, upon rebooting, the DataNode would not be able to identify that block replica. This is cumbersome and not ideal if you have a very large Hadoop cluster. What you actually need is a diskbalancer tool that will do these operations for you automatically. That tool should also give you a complete picture of disk usage and how much of the disk is occupied on each DataNode. With those concerns in mind, the Hadoop community introduced a DataNode diskbalancer tool that has the following abilities:

- **Disk data distribution report**: The HDFS diskbalancer tool generates reports to identify DataNodes that suffer from asymmetric data distribution. There are two types of reports that can be generated. One report is about top nodes that have possible data skew and that can benefit from running this tool, while the other report is about detailed information about data nodes that you want information about. A node's IPs/DNS can be passed into a file as an argument.
- **Performing disk balancing on live DataNodes**: This is the core functionality of this tool. It can move data block folders from one volume to another. This works in three phases: discover, plan and execute. The discover phase is more about cluster discovery, where information such as the physical layout of cluster computes and storage types is stored. The plan phase is about steps that should be performed for each user-specified data node, and how data should be moved and in what sequence. This phase takes input from the discover phase. The execute phase is about executing plans that are received from the planning phase by each DataNode. This runs in the background without affecting user activity.

The HDFS diskbalancer tool, after executing the balancing activity, generates two types of reports per DataNode for debugging and verification purposes. One is called `<datanode>.before.json` and the other is called `<datanode>.after.json`. These reports include disk storage state information about each DataNode before running the tool and after running the tool. You can always compare the two reports and see whether you want to re-run the balancer or whether it is sufficient at any given point in time. The following table presents some of the commands that can be used to run `hdfs diskbalancer`:

Command	Description
`hdfs diskbalancer -plan datanode1.haoopcluster.com -out <file_folder_location>`	The plan command is used to run against `datanode1` on your Hadoop cluster. `<file_folder_location>` is the place where you want to save the plan's output JSON. This command outputs two files: `<datanode1>.before.json`, which captures the state of the cluster before the diskbalancer is run, and `<datanode1>.plan.json`. `<datanode1>.plan.json` will be used in the execute phase.
`hdfs diskbalancer -execute <file_folder_location>/<datanode1>.plan.json`	The execute command runs the plan that was generated from the plan phase.
`hdfs diskbalancer -query datanode1.hadoopcluster.com`	The query command gets the current status of the diskbalancer from a DataNode.

The preceding table covers some of the `diskbalancer` commands at a high level. If you need more details about `hdfs diskbalancer` commands, then check out this link: `https://hadoop.apache.org/docs/current/hadoop-project-dist/hadoop-hdfs/HDFSDiskbalancer.html`.

Lazy persist writes in HDFS

Enterprise adoption of Hadoop is growing day by day. With increased adoption, there are a variety of application types that are using Hadoop for their enterprise goals. One such adoption is for applications that need to deal with data that amounts to only a few GBs. Keeping performance goals in mind with such small records would incur more latency costs when DISK I/O writes are involved during its execution—especially when such volumes of data can easily fit into memory without any DISK I/O. With the release of Hadoop 2.6, provisions for writes have been introduced that will use the off-heap memory of DataNodes. Eventually, data from memory will be flushed out to disk asynchronously. This will remove any expensive Disk I/O and computations for checksum while write operations are initiated from the HDFS client. Such asynchronous writes are called lazy persist writes, where persistence to disk does not happen immediately but asynchronously after some time. HDFS provides a best effort guarantee against data loss. However, there are some rare chances of data loss. In case a data node restarts before replicas are persisted to disk, there are some chances of data loss. We can minimize this risk by avoiding any such writes for an amount of time before restarting. However, there is never an absolute guarantee against data loss due to restarts. For precisely this reason, we should always use this feature for data that is temporary in nature and can be regenerated by rerunning the operation. Another important aspect of lazy writes is that you should use a file with one replica configured for it. If you enable multiple replicas for a file, then write operations cannot be completed unless all replicas are written to different DataNodes. This would defeat the low-latency purpose of memory writes as replication would involve multiple data transfers over a network. If you want, you can enable this off the hot write path by enabling replication of files later (probably asynchronously) when writes are complete. However, there is a chance of data loss in the event of disk failure before you have completed data replication.

Generally, to set up lazy persists optimization in Hadoop, you need to set up RAM disks. RAM disks are virtual hard drives on your RAM memory. At first glance, it looks like a regular drive on your PC, but it segregates a fixed amount of RAM memory and it will not be available for any other processes. For Hadoop memory storage support, RAM disks were chosen as they have better persistence support in the event that the DataNode restarts. RAM disks have provisions for automatically saving content to the hard drive before it restarts.

Additional details about HDFS Memory Storage and its configuration can be found at the following link:
`https://hadoop.apache.org/docs/r3.0.0-beta1/hadoop-project-dist/`
`hadoop-hdfs/MemoryStorage.html#Use_the_LAZY_PERSIST_Storage_`
`Policy.`

Erasure encoding in Hadoop 3.x

HDFS achieves fault-tolerance by replicating each block three times by default. However, in big clusters, the replication factor can be more. The purpose of replication is to handle data loss against machine failure, providing data locality for the MapReduce job, and so on. The replication takes more storage space, which means that if our replication factor is three, HDFS will take an extra 200% space to store file. In short, storing 1 GB of data will require 3 GB of memory. This also causes metadata memory on NameNode.

HDFS introduced **erasure coding** (**EC**) for storing data by taking less storage space. Now, data is labelled based on their usage access pattern, and after the conditions for erasure coding have been satisfied, data will be applicable for erasure coding. The term Data Temperature is used to identify the data usage pattern. The different types of data are as follows:

- **Hot data**: By default, all data is considered HOT. Data that is accessed more than 20 times a day and whose age is less than seven days is considered HOT data. Data in this storage layer will have all of its replicas in the disk tier and will still utilize 200% extra storage if the replication factor is three.
- **Warm data**: Data whose access frequency is only a few times over the course of the week comes under the warm data layer. Warm data will have one replica available in the disk tier and the rest will go into the archive tier.
- **Cold data**: Data that is accessed only a few times a month and has an age more than a month goes into the COLD layer. This data can be used for erasure coding.

As we have already discussed, initially, all blocks will be replicated as configured per the replication factor. When the erasure code condition is met, then the blocks will be changed into an erasure coding form. The following flowchart shows erasure encoding in Hadoop 3.x:

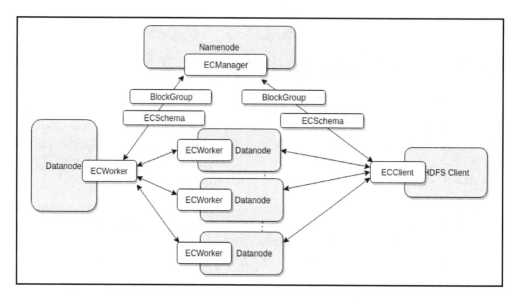

Erasure encoding is the process of encoding a message with additional parity data so that even if a portion of data is lost, then it can be recoverable using an encoded value. An architecture improvement has been done for HDFS so that it can support erasure coding. The following components were added as extensions:

- **ECManager**: The ECManager is added as a Namenode extension and resides on Namenode. It manages the EC block group and does group allocation, placement of blocks, health monitoring, and coordinates for the recovery of blocks. Erasure coding stripes HDFS file data and these stripes may contain a large number of internal blocks. NameNode may require more space to store metadata for these blocks. ECManager reduces the space consumption on the NameNode by managing these internal blocks efficiently.

- **ECClient**: ECClient is an extention to HDFS client that stripes data to and from multiple DataNodes in parallel. The block group consists of multiple internal blocks and ECClient helps the client perform read and write operations on multiple internal blocks of the block group.

- **ECWorker**: ECWorkers are available on Datanodes and can be used to recover a failed erasure coded block. ECManager tracks the failed erasure coded block and gives instructions to the ECWorker to recover these blocks. DataNodes doesn't know about EC or striping during normal I/O operations. ECWorkers listen for any instructions from the ECManager. The ECWorker then pulls data from peer DataNodes, does codec calculation, builds converted blocks, and then pushes this to additional ECWorkers.

Advantages of erasure coding

- **Saving storage**: Data which terms as cold data still takes 200 percent extra space on HDFS. Erasure coding reduces the storage overhead for data by more than 50%.
- **Configurable policy**: Admin can mark data as hot or cold by just running simple command. Data marked as hot will be replicated according to replication factor configured.
- **Easily recoverable**: Even if some percentage of data is lost, with the help of erasure code one can easily recover it.

Disadvantages of erasure coding

Erasure coding can help us save lot of storage space but still has some limitations, as follows:

- **Data locality**: Erasure coding only keeps one replica for data blocks, and so programs like MapReduce that work on data locality need to be run on a machine where this block resides. If not, then the data block needs to be transferred across the network.
- Encoding and decoding operations are computationally expensive.
- **Expansive copy operation**: Erasure coding keeps only one replica and encodes data. Encoded data can't be read without moving most of the data over the network. The computation time for decoding, network transfer, and parallel reading with only one replica for a block makes copy operations expansive.

HDFS common interfaces

In this section, we will dig into the HDFS Java interfaces and APIs that can be used to interact with the HDFS File System. We will also to focus on the method implementation of `FileSystem` classes so that you can understand how to write your own implementation if needed. This will also help you when you test your program against certain test cases.

HDFS read

We will talk about two approaches to reading a file and will discuss when to use what. In the first approach, we can use the URL class, which is part of the `java.net` package and can be used to read files stored on HDFS. The URL calls `setURLStreamHandlerFactory()`, which requires an instance of `FsUrlStreamHandlerFactory()`. This initialization is a part of a static block that is executed before any instance creation. This method is in a static block because it can only be called once per JVM and hence, if any third-party program sets `URLStreamHandlerFactory`, we won't be able to use it for reading files from HDFS:

```
static {
 URL.setURLStreamHandlerFactory(new FsUrlStreamHandlerFactory());
 }
```

Once the URL has been initialized, it opens a stream on the file that returns `InputStream`. Then, the `IOUtils` class can be used to copy stream data to the output stream, as shown in the following code:

```
import java.io.InputStream;
import java.net.URL;
import org.apache.hadoop.fs.FsUrlStreamHandlerFactory;
import org.apache.hadoop.io.IOUtils;

public class HDFSReadUsingURL {
    static {
        URL.setURLStreamHandlerFactory(new FsUrlStreamHandlerFactory());
    }

    public static void   main(String[]  args)  throws Exception  {
        InputStream fileInputStream   =  null;
        try    {
            fileInputStream   =  new    URL(args[0]).openStream();
            IOUtils.copyBytes(fileInputStream, System.out,   4096,
false);
        }  finally   {
            IOUtils.closeStream(fileInputStream);
```

```
        }
    }
}
```

Once the program is ready, you can package it into a `.jar` and deploy it to the Hadoop classpath:

```
export HADOOP_CLASSPATH=HdfS_read.jar
```

Now, you can use classname as a command to read the file from HDFS, as shown in the following code:

```
hadoop HDFSReadUsingURL hdfs://localhost/user/chanchals/test.txt
```

We have already mentioned that this approach will not work in every scenario. Due to this, we have another approach, where the `FileSystem` class API can be used to read a HDFS file. There are basically two steps involved when we use the `FileSystem` class to read a file from HDFS:

- **Creating a File System Instance**: The first step is to create a `FileSystem` instance. HDFS provides different static factory methods to create a `FileSystem` instance, and each method can be used in different scenarios:

```
public static FileSystem get(Configuration conf) throws IOException
public static FileSystem get(URI uri, Configuration conf) throws
IOException
public static FileSystem get(URI uri, Configuration conf, String user)
throws IOException
```

  The configuration object is common in all of these methods, which contains client and server configuration parameters. These parameters are set by reading a property from the `core-site.xml` and `core-default.xml` files. In the second method, the URI object tells the `FileSystem` about what URI scheme to use.

- **Calling an open method to read a file**: Once the `FileSystem` instance has been created, we can call `open()` to get the input stream from a file. `FileSystem` has two method signatures for the open method, as follows:

  - ```
public FSDataInputStream open(Path f) throws IOException

    public abstract FSDataInputStream open(Path f, int bufferSize)
    throws IOException
```
```

In the first method, the buffer size is not specified and it uses the default buffer size of 4 KB, while in the second method you can specify the default buffer size. The return type of the method is FSDataInputStream, which extends DataInputStream and allows you to read any part of a file. The class is as follows:

```
package org.apache.hadoop.fs;
public class FSDataInputStream  extends    DataInputStream
        implements Seekable,  PositionedReadable {
}
```

The Seekable and PositionedReadable interfaces allow you to read a file from any seekable position. When we say seekable position, we mean that a position value should not be greater than the file length, otherwise it will result in IOException. The interface definition is given as follows:

```
public  interface  Seekable   {
    void    seek(long  pos)    throws IOException;
    long    getPos()   throws IOException;
}
```

Now, let's write a program to read the HDFS file by using the FileSystem API:

```
import org.apache.hadoop.conf.Configuration;
import org.apache.hadoop.fs.FileSystem;
import org.apache.hadoop.fs.Path;
import org.apache.hadoop.io.IOUtils;

import java.io.InputStream;
import java.net.URI;

public class HDFSReadUsingFileSystem {
    public static void main(String[] args) throws Exception {
        String uri = args[0];
        Configuration conf = new Configuration();
        FileSystem fileSystem = FileSystem.get(URI.create(uri),
conf);
        InputStream fileInputStream = null;
        try {
            fileInputStream = fileSystem.open(new Path(uri));
            IOUtils.copyBytes(fileInputStream, System.out, 4096,
false);
        } finally {
            IOUtils.closeStream(fileInputStream);
        }
    }
}
```

To execute and test this program, we need to package it into a `.jar`, as we did previously, copy it to the `hadoop` classpath, and use it as follows:

```
hadoop HDFSReadUsingFileSystem filepath
```

HDFS write

The `FileSystem` class also provides a number of methods for creating a file. `FileSystem` has different overloaded versions of the `create()` method, and a few of them are given as follows:

```java
public FSDataOutputStream create(Path f) throws IOException {
}

public FSDataOutputStream create(Path f, boolean overwrite) throws
IOException {
}

public FSDataOutputStream create(Path f, Progressable progress) throws
IOException {
}

public FSDataOutputStream create(Path f, short replication) throws
IOException {
}
```

The first method is the simplest version to use, which uses a `Path` object so that a file is created and returns `FSDataOutputStream`. There are some other versions of this method as well, which allow us to overwrite an existing file, change the replication factor for a file, and change the block size and file permissions. The `create()` method with `Progressable` allows you to track the progress of data writes operations to a DataNode.

HDFSFileSystemWrite.java

The following is the code for HDFS write:

```java
import org.apache.hadoop.conf.Configuration;
import org.apache.hadoop.fs.FSDataOutputStream;
import org.apache.hadoop.fs.FileSystem;
import org.apache.hadoop.fs.Path;
import org.apache.hadoop.io.IOUtils;

import java.io.BufferedInputStream;
import java.io.FileInputStream;
```

```
import java.io.IOException;
import java.io.InputStream;
import java.net.URI;

public class HDFSFileSystemWrite {
    public static void main(String[] args) throws IOException {
        String sourceURI = args[0];
        String targetURI = args[1];
        Configuration conf = new Configuration();
        FileSystem fs = FileSystem.get(URI.create(targetURI), conf);

        FSDataOutputStream out = null;
        InputStream in = new BufferedInputStream(new
FileInputStream(sourceURI));
        try {
            out = fs.create(new Path(targetURI));
            IOUtils.copyBytes(in, out, 4096, false);

        } finally {
            in.close();
            out.close();
        }
    }
}
```

FSDataOutputStream has a method for returning the current position of a file but, unlike the read operation, writing to a file in HDFS cannot start from any position other than the end of the file. FileSystem also provides a method for creating directories. mkdirs() is used to create directories, and there are a number of overloaded versions available inside the FileSystem class:

```
public boolean mkdirs(Path f) throws IOException
```

This method will create all the parent directories if they do not exist. Remember that, while creating a file using create(), you don't need to explicitly call mkdirs() because create() automatically creates directories in the path if they don't exist.

HDFS delete

A user may want to delete files or directories that are already available on HDFS. The `FileSystem` class provides the `delete()` method, which can be used to permanently delete files or directories:

```
public boolean delete(Path filePath, boolean recursive) throws IOException
```

If the `filePath` is an empty directory or file, then the value or recursive is ignored and the file or directory is removed. The true value of recursive will delete all the files and directories inside the HDFS path.

HDFS command reference

HDFS offers a command-line utility where we can execute HDFS shell commands. These commands are very much similar to Linux-based commands.

File System commands

File System commands can be used to directly interact with HDFS. These commands can also be executed on an HDFS supported File System such as WebHDFS, S3, and so on. Let's walk through a few basic, important commands:

- **-ls**: The `ls` command lists all the directories and files within a specified path:

```
hadoop fs -ls /user/packt/
```

  The `ls` command returns the following information:

```
File_Permission numberOfReplicas userid groupid filesize
last_modification_date last_modification_time
filename/directory_name
```

  A few options are also available that you can use with the `ls` command, such as sorting output based on size and showing only limited information:

```
hadoop fs -ls -h /user/packt
```

The -h option is used to display file sizes in a readable format. For example, it would use 230.8 MB or 1.24 GB instead of putting the file size in bytes. You can check out other options for this by using --help options:

- -copyFromLocal and -put: Users may want to copy data from a local File System to HDFS, which is possible if you use the -copyFromLocal and -put commands:

```
hadoop fs -copyFromLocal /home/packt/abc.txt /user/packt
hadoop fs -put /home/packt/abc.txt /user/packt
```

You can also use these options to copy the data from a local File System to an HDFS supported File System. For example, the -f option can be used to forcefully copy a file to an HDFS supported File System, even if the file already exists at that destination.

- -copyToLocal and -get: These commands are used to copy data from an HDFS supported File System to a local File System:

```
hadoop fs -copyToLocal /user/packt/abc.txt /home/packt
hadoop fs -get /user/packt/abc.txt /home/packt
```

- -cp: You can copy data from one HDFS location to another HDFS location by using the -cp command:

```
hadoop fs -cp /user/packt/path1/file1 /user/packt/path2/
```

- -du: The du command is used to display the size of files and directories contained in the given path. It is a good option to include the -h option so that you can view the size in a readable format:

```
hadoop fs -du -h /user/packt
```

- -getmerge; The getmerge command takes all the files from a specified source directory and concatenates them into a single file before storing it in a local File System:

```
hadoop fs -getmerge /user/packt/dir1 /home/sshuser
```

- -skip-empty-file: This option can be used to skip empty files.

- −mkdir: Users often create directories on HDFS, and the mkdir command is used to serve this purpose. You can use the −p option to create all the directories along this path. For example, if you create a directory called /user/packt/dir1/dir2/dir3, dir1 and dir2 do not exist, but if you use the −p option, it will create dir1 and dir2 before creating dir3:

```
hadoop fs -mkdir -p /user/packt/dir1/dir2/dir3
```

If you don't use the −p option, then the preceding command has to be written like this:

```
hadoop fs -mkdir /user/packt/dir1   /user/packt/dir2
/user/packt/dir3
```

- −rm: The rm command is used to remove a file or directory from an HDFS supported File System. By default, all the deleted files go into the trash, but if you use the −skipTrash option with it, the file will be immediately deleted from the File System and will not go into the trash. −r can be used to recursively delete all the files within a specified path:

```
hadoop fs -rm -r -skipTrash /user/packt/dir1
```

- −chown: Sometimes, you may want to change the owner of a file or directory. −chown is used for this purpose. Users must have valid permission to change permissions, otherwise a super user must do this. The −R option can be used to change the ownership of all the files within a specified path:

```
hadoop fs -chown -R /user/packt/dir1
```

- −cat: The use of this command is similar to what it does in Linux; it is used to copy file data to a standard output:

```
hadoop fs -cat /user/packt/dir1/file1
```

Distributed copy

You may want to copy data from one cluster to another cluster. This may be due to the decommission of an old cluster or because of a requirement for similar data for some reporting or processing purpose. The −distcp command is used to copy data from one HDFS supported system to another HDFS supported system.

`distcp` uses the MapReduce job to perform data distribution, error handling, recovery, and reporting. It generates certain map tasks, where each task is responsible for copying a few files to another cluster:

```
hadoop distcp hdfs://198.20.87.78:8020/user/packt/dir1 \
hdfs://198.89.76.34:8020/user/packt/dir2
```

You can also specify multiple sources for data copy:

```
hadoop distcp hdfs://198.20.87.78:8020/user/packt/dir1 \
              hdfs://198.20.87.78:8020/user/packt/dir2 \
              hdfs://198.89.76.34:8020/user/packt/dir3
```

When multiple sources are specified, `distcp` will abort the operation if a source has a collision. By default, if a file already exists at the destination, the new file will not be skipped, but we can use the different available options to overwrite the destination file.

Admin commands

The admin is responsible for maintaining clusters and continuously checking the reports of DataNode. There are a few commands that the admin uses frequently for a File System. Admin commands start with `hadoop dfsadmin command`.

`-report`: This command is used to generate a report of DataNodes, such as basic File System information, statistics about used space and free space, and so on. You can also use options to filter live or dead DataNodes by using the `-live` and `-dead` options:

```
hdfs dfsadmin -report -live
hdfs dfsadmin -report -dead
```

The admin uses this command to check which DataNode has higher or lower uses than average cluster uses to ascertain whether any node needs to be excluded or included in a balancer operation or to check whether a new node needs to be added.

`- safemode`: This is a maintenance state of NameNode, during which NameNode doesn't allow any changes to the `FileSystem`.

In the `safemode` state, the HDFS cluster is read-only and it doesn't replicate or delete blocks. Generally, when nameNode starts, it automatically goes into `safemode` and does the following:

- Loads `fsimage` and edits the log into memory
- Applies edit log changes to `fsimage`, which gives a new `FileSystem` namespace
- Finally, it receives a block report from the DataNode, which contains information about the block's location

The admin can also enter the `safemode` state manually or check the `safemode` status. Manually entering NameNode into `safemode` does not allow NameNode to leave `safemode` automatically—you must explicitly leave it, as shown in the following command:

```
hdfs dfsadmin -safemode enter/get/leave
```

There are hundreds of commands available that can be used with HDFS, but covering all of these commands is outside the scope of this book. You can refer to the HDFS documentation to understand the uses of all the commands.

Points to remember

We have covered the HDFS in detail and the following are a few points to remember:

- HDFS consists of two main components: NameNode and DataNode. NameNode is a master node that stores metadata information, whereas DataNodes are slave nodes that store file blocks.
- Secondary NameNode is responsible for performing checkpoint operations in which edit log changes are applied to fsimage. This is also known as a checkpoint node.
- Files in HDFS are split into blocks and blocks are replicated across a number of DataNodes to ensure fault tolerance. The replication factor and block size are configurable.

- HDFS Balancer is used to distribute data in an equal fashion between all DataNodes. It is a good practice to run balancer whenever a new DataNode is added and schedule a job to run balancer at regular intervals.
- In Hadoop 3, high availability can now have more than two NameNodes running at a time. If an active NameNode fails, a new NameNode will be elected from an other NameNode and will become an active NameNode.
- Quorum Journal Manager writes namespace modifications into multiple JournalNodes. These changes are then read by the Standby NameNode and they apply these changes to their fsimage file.
- Erasure coding is a new feature that was introduced in Hadoop 3, which reduces storage overhead by up to 50%. The replication factor in HDFS costs us 200% more space. Erasure coding provides the same durability guarantee using less disk storage.

Summary

In this chapter, our focus was to cover the architecture of HDFS and its components. We covered the internals of NameNode and DataNode internals. We explained the work of the Quorum Journal Manager and HDFS high availability in Hadoop 3. Data management was also a focus of this chapter, and we covered edit logs and fsimage in detail. We looked at a brief overview of the checkpoint process. We also covered the internals of the HDFS write and read operations. The interface and HDFS commands were explained with examples.

In the next chapter, we will cover **Yet Another Resource Manager** (**YARN**) in detail. We will dive deep into the YARN architecture and will cover its components in detail. We will gain an understanding of the different types of schedulers that are available in YARN and their detailed uses. A few new features were added to YARN in the Hadoop 3 release, such as the YARN timeline server and the opportunist container, and so on. We will also cover these features in detail.

3
YARN Resource Management in Hadoop

From the very beginning of Hadoop's existence, it has consisted of two major parts, the storage part, which is known as the **Hadoop Distributed File System (HDFS)**, and the processing part, which is known as MapReduce. In the previous chapter, we discussed the Hadoop Distributed File System, its architecture, and its internals. In Hadoop version 1, the only job that can be submitted and executed to Hadoop is MapReduce. In the present era of data processing, real-time and near real-time processing are favored over batch processing. Thus, there is a need for a generic application executor and Resource Manager that can schedule and execute all types of applications, including MapReduce, in real time or near real time. In this chapter, we will learn about YARN and will cover the following topics:

- YARN architecture
- YARN job scheduling and different types of scheduling
- Resource Manager high availability
- What node labels are and their advantages
- Improvements in the YARN Timeline server
- Opportunistic containers to improve performance
- Running YARN containers as Docker containers
- Using YARN REST API
- Commonly used YARN commands and their uses

Architecture

YARN stands for **Yet Another Resource Negotiator**, and was introduced with Apache Hadoop 2.0 to address the scalability and manageability issues that existed with the previous versions. In Hadoop 1.0, we have two major components for job execution: JobTracker and task tracker. JobTracker is responsible for managing resources and scheduling jobs. It is also responsible for tracking the status of each job and restarting them if there is any failure. The task trackers are responsible for running tasks and sending progress report to JobTracker. The JobTracker also reschedules failed tasks on different task trackers. As JobTracker could be overloaded with multiple tasks, Hadoop 1.0 made several changes in its architecture to eliminate the following limitations:

- **Scalability**: In Hadoop 1.0, the JobTracker is responsible for scheduling the jobs, monitoring each job, and restarting them on failure. It means JobTracker spends the majority of its time managing the application's life cycle. In a larger cluster with more nodes and more tasks, the burden of scheduling and monitoring increases. The work overhead limits the scalability of Hadoop version 1 to 4,000 nodes and 40,000 tasks.

- **High availability**: High availability ensures that even if one node serving the request goes down, the other standby active node can assume the responsibility for the failed node. In this case, the state of the failed node should be in sync with the state of the standby active node. The JobTracker is a single point of failure. Every few seconds, task trackers send the information about tasks to the JobTracker, which makes it difficult to implement high availability for the JobTracker because of the large number of changes in a very short span of time.

- **Memory utilization**: Hadoop version 1 required preconfigured task tracker slots for map and reduce tasks. The slot reserved for the map task cannot be used for the reduce task or the other way around. The efficient utilization of task trackers' memory was not possible on account of to this setup.

- **Non MapReduce jobs**: Every job in Hadoop version 1 required MapReduce for its completion because scheduling was only possible through the JobTracker. The JobTracker and the task tracker were tightly coupled with the MapReduce framework. Since the adoption of Hadoop has been growing fast, there were a lot of new requirements, such as graph processing and real-time analytics that needed processing over the same HDFS storage to reduce complexity, infrastructure, maintenance cost, and so on.

Let us discuss the YARN architecture and see how it helps to resolve the limitations discussed before. The initial idea of YARN was to split the resource management and job scheduling responsibilities of the JobTracker. YARN consists of two major components: **Resource Manager** and the **Node Manager**. The **Resource Manager** is a master node that is responsible for managing resources in the cluster. Per-application Application Master running on the **Node Manager** is responsible for launching and monitoring containers of jobs. The cluster consists of one **Resource Manager** and multiple **Resource Manager**,as seen in the following diagram:

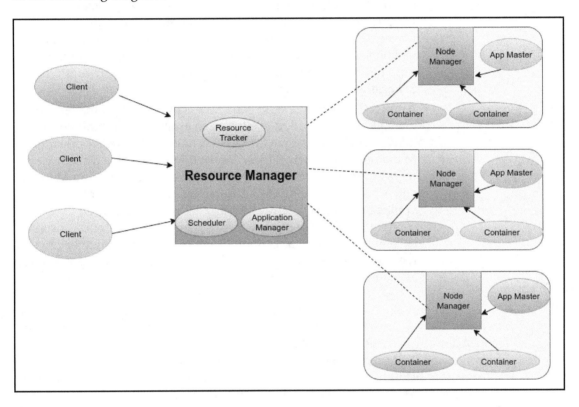

The preceding diagram can be explained as follows:

- **Resource Manager**: The **Resource Manager** is a master daemon that is responsible for managing the resources of submitted applications. It has two primary components:

  - **Scheduler**: The job of **Resource Manager Scheduler** is to allocate the required resources requested by the per application application master. The job of **Scheduler** is to only schedule the job, which means it does not monitor any task and is not responsible for relaunching any failed application container. The application makes a request of job scheduling to the YARN and YARN sends detailed scheduling information, including the amount of memory required for the job. Upon receiving the scheduling request, the **Scheduler** simply schedules the job.

  - **Application Manager**: The job of the **Application Manager** is to manage per application master. Each application submitted to the YARN will have its own application master and the **Application Manager** keeps track of each application master. Each client request for job submission is received by the **Application Manager** and it provides resources to launch application master for the application. It also destroys the application master upon completion of the application execution. When cluster resources become limited and already in use, the **Resource Manager** can request back the resources from a running application so that it can allocate it to the application.

- **Node manager**: The **Node Manager** is a slave that runs on every worker node of a cluster and has responsibility for launching and executing containers based on instructions from the **Resource Manager**. The **Node Manager** sends heartbeat signals to the **Resource Manager**, and which also contain some other information,including **Node Manager** machine details, and available memory. The **Resource Manager** regularly updates the information of each **Node Manager** upon receiving the request, which helps in planning and scheduling upcoming tasks. The containers are launched on the **Node Manager** and the application master is also launched on the **Node Manager** container.

- **Application master**: The first step of the application is to submit the job to YARN, and upon receiving the request of a job submission, YARN's **Resource Manager** launches the application master for that particular job on one of the **Node Manager Container**. The application master is then responsible for managing application execution in the cluster. For each application, there will be a dedicated application master running on some **Node Manager Container** that is responsible for coordinating between **Resource Manager** and **Node Manager** in order to complete the execution of the application. The application master requests the required resources for application execution from the **Resource Manager** and the **Resource Manager** sends the detailed information about the **Resource Container** to the application master, which then coordinates with the respective **Node Manager** to launch the container to execute the application task. The application master sends heartbeats at regular intervals to the **Resource Manager** and updates its resource usage. The application master changes the plan of execution depending upon the response received from the **Resource Manager**.

Resource Manager component

The Resource Manager is a primary core component of YARN. Each client interaction will always involve the Resource Manager for some reason. YARN provides a few major components for the Resource Manager, as shown here:

- **Client component**: The Resource Manager has exposed methods to clients for initiating RPC communication with itself. The YARN Resource Manager provides the `ClientRMService` class, exposes the API for application requests, such as submitting a new job, or a new application request, and killing the application. It also contains the API to get the cluster metrics. It also provides the `AdminService` class, which is used by the cluster administrator for managing the Resource Manager services. Admin can check cluster health, access information, and refresh cluster nodes. Admin uses the `rmadmin` command to execute any operation that internally uses the service provided by the `AdminService` class.
- **Core component:** The scheduler and the application manager are the major part of the Resource Manager core interface. The following are a few interfaces provided by the Resource Manager:
  - `YarnScheduler` provides APIs for resource allocation and cleanup operation. `YarnScheduler` works on the pluggable policy and based on the configuration, it distributes cluster resources to the applications.

- RMStateStore is another core interface that provides implementation for the Resource Manager state store so that in case of failure, the Resource Manager can recover its state using the implementation provided. A few implementation of this class are FileSystemRMStateStore, MemoryRMStateStore, ZKRMStateStore, NullRMStateStore. The state of the Resource Manager plays an important role in the Resource Manager high availability implementation. The ZKRMStateStore is a very reliable implementation for this purpose as it uses the ZooKeeper to maintain state.

- SchedulingMonitor provides an interface to define the scheduling policy and a way to edit schedules at regular intervals. It also interfaces to monitor containers and the tuning of resources.

- RMAppManager is responsible for managing the list of applications running on the YARN cluster. It collects and stores runtime information of the application and provides information to YARN on request.

- **Node Manager component**: The Resource Manager is a master node and Node Manager is slave node. Node Manager sends heartbeats, resource information, status information, and so on to the Resource Manager at regular intervals. The Resource Manager keeps an updated status of each Node Manager, which helps it in allocating resource to the application master. ResourceTrackerService is responsible for responding to the Node Managers' RPC requests. It contains APIs for the registration of new nodes to the cluster and receiving heartbeats from the Node Managers. It also contains the NMLivelinessMonitor object, which helps in monitoring all the live and dead nodes. In general, if the node does not send a heartbeat for 10 minutes, it is considered as dead and will not be used to launch any new containers. You can increase or decrease the interval by setting YARN.am.liveness-monitor.expiry-interval-ms in the YARN configuration (time in milliseconds). The constructor of ResourceTrackerService looks like the following code:

```
public ResourceTrackerService(RMContext rmContext,
NodesListManager nodesListManager, NMLivelinessMonitor
nmLivelinessMonitor, RMContainerTokenSecretManager
containerTokenSecretManager, NMTokenSecretManagerInRM
nmTokenSecretManager
```

- `NMLivelinessMonitor` is responsible for tracking all the dead and live nodes. As discussed earlier, any Node Manager that does not send a heartbeat to the Resource Manager for 10 minutes is considered dead and will not be used for running any container on it.

- **Application master component**: YARN launches a new application master for every new application request it receives from a client. The application master acts as a mediator between the Resource Manager and the Node Manager for resource requirements of its application. The Resource Manager provides an API to manage the application master. The following are some classes and internals of how it works:
  - `AMLivelinessMonitor` works very similarly to `NMLivelinessMonitor` and sends heartbeats to the Resource Manager. The Resource Manager keeps track of all the live and dead application masters and if it does not receive heartbeats from any application master for 10 minutes, then it marks the application master as dead. The containers used by these dead application masters are then destroyed and the Resource Manager launches a new application master for the application on a new container. If still the application master fails, the Resource Manager repeats the process for four attempts and then sends a failure message to the client. The number of attempts for relaunching the application master is configurable.
  - `ApplicationMasterService` is responsible for responding to the application master's RPC request and provides an API for the new application master registration, container requests from all application masters, and so on. It then forwards the request to the YARN scheduler for further processing.

Node manager core

The Node Managers are worker nodes and thus each worker node has one Node Manager. This means if we have five worker nodes in a cluster, we will have five Node Managers running on the node. The job of the Node Manager is to run and manage containers on worker nodes, send heartbeats and node information at regular intervals to the Resource Manager, manage already running containers, manage utilization of containers, and so on.

Let us talk about a few important components of the Node Manager:

- **Resource manager component**: Node Managers are worker nodes and work closely with resource managers. The `NodeStatusUpdater` is responsible for sending updated information about node resources to the Resource Manager at regular intervals and at the first time when the machine starts. `NodeHealthCheckerService` works closely with `NodeStatusUpdater` and any change in node health will be reported to `NodeStatusUpdater` from `NodeHealthCheckerService`.

- **Container component**: The primary work the Node Manager is to manage the life cycle of containers and `ContainerManager` is responsible for starting, stopping, or getting status of the already running containers. The `ContainerManagerImpl` contains the implementation part of starting or stopping containers and checking the status of containers. The following are the components of containers:

  - **Application master request**: The application master request requires resource from Resource Manager and then sends a request to the Node Manager to launch a new container. It can also send a request to stop an already running container. The RPC server running on Node Manager is responsible for receiving requests from application masters to launch the new container or stop already running containers.

  - `ContainerLauncher`: The requests received from application masters or Resource Managers go to the `ContainerLauncher`. Once the request is received, the `ContainerLauncher` launches the containers. It can also clean up the container resources based on demand.

  - `ContainerMonitor`: The Resource Manager provides a resource to the application masters to launch containers, and containers are launched with the provided configuration. The `ContainersMonitor` is responsible for monitoring container health, resources utilization, and sending signals for cleaning up the container when it exceeds the resource utilization assigned to it. This information can be very helpful in debugging application performance and memory utilization, which can further help in performance tuning.

  - `LogHandler`: Each container generates a log of its life cycle and the `LogHandler` allows us to specify the log location either on the same disk or some other external storage location. These logs can be used to debug the applications.

Introduction to YARN job scheduling

In the previous sections, we talked about the YARN architecture and its components. The Resource Manager has two major components; namely, the application manager and the scheduler. The Resource Manager scheduler is responsible for allocating the required resources to an application based on schedule policies. Before YARN, Hadoop used to allocate slots for map and reduce tasks from available memory, which restricts reduce tasks to run on slots allocated for map tasks and the other way around. YARN does not define map and reduce slots initially. Based on a request, it launches containers for tasks. This means that if any free container is available, it will be used for map or reduce tasks. As previously discussed in this chapter, the scheduler will not perform monitoring or status tracking for the any application. The scheduler receives requests from per application application masters with the resources requirement detail and executes its scheduling function.

Hadoop provides us with the opportunity to run many applications at a time and it is important to effectively utilize the cluster's memory. Selecting the correct scheduling strategy is not easy and YARN provides a configurable scheduling policy that allows us to choose the right strategy based on an application's need. There are by default three schedulers available in YARN, which are as follows:

- FIFO scheduler
- Capacity scheduler
- Fair scheduler

We will study each of them in the following sections.

FIFO scheduler

The FIFO scheduler uses the simple strategy of first come first serve. Memory will be allocated to applications based on the sequence of request time, which means the first application in the queue will be allocated the required memory, then the second, and so on. In case memory is not available, applications have to wait for sufficient memory to be available for them to launch their jobs. When the FIFO scheduler is configured, YARN will make a queue of requests and add applications to the queue, then launch applications one by one.

Capacity scheduler

The capacity scheduler makes sure that users get the guaranteed minimum amount of configured resources in the YARN cluster. The use of the Hadoop cluster increases with the use cases in the organization and it is very unlikely that organization creates separate Hadoop clusters for each use case because this will increase maintenance. One use case may be that different users in the same organization want to have a certain amount of resources reserved when they want to execute their tasks. The capacity scheduler helps in sharing the cluster resources in a cost-effective manner across different users in the same organization to meet the SLA by ensuring no other user uses resources configured for some other user in the cluster. In short, the cluster resources are shared across multiple user groups.

The capacity scheduler works on the concept of queues. A cluster is divided into partitions known as queues and each queue is assigned with a certain percentage of resources. The capacity scheduler is responsible for making sure that each queue gets its resource share from the cluster resource pool when a job is submitted to that queue.

Let us try to explain this with an example. Suppose we created two queues; A and B. Queue A has been allocated with 60% and queue B has been allocated 40% of resource share. When we submit first job to queue A, the capacity scheduler will allocate all 100% of the available resources to queue A because there are no other tasks or jobs running in the cluster at that moment. Now suppose while the first job is running another user submits a second job to queue B, than the capacity scheduler will kill a few tasks of first job and assign it to the second job to ensure that queue B gets its guaranteed minimum share from the cluster resources.

Configuring capacity scheduler

The capacity scheduler allows sharing of resources across an organization, which enables multi tenancy and helps in increasing the utilization of a Hadoop cluster. Different departments in the organization have different cluster requirements and thus they require specific amounts of resources reserved for them when they submit their jobs. The reserved memory will be used by the users belonging to the department. If there are no other applications submitted to the queue, then resources will be available for other applications.

The first step to configure the capacity scheduler to set the scheduler class of the Resource Manager scheduler to capacity scheduler in `YARN-site.xml` is shown as follows:

```
<property>
     <name>YARN.resourcemanager.scheduler.class</name>
     <value>org.apache.hadoop.YARN.server.resourcemanager.scheduler.
capacity.CapacityScheduler
     </value>
</property>
```

The queues properties are set in the capacity value in the `scheduler.xml` file. The queue allocation is defined as follows:

```
<?xml version="1.0"?>
<configuration>
     <property>
          <name>YARN.scheduler.capacity.root.queues</name>
          <value>A,B</value>
     </property>
     <property>
          <name>YARN.scheduler.capacity.root.B.queues</name>
          <value>C,D</value>
     </property>
     <property>
          <name>YARN.scheduler.capacity.root.A.capacity</name>
          <value>60</value>
     </property>
     <property>
          <name>YARN.scheduler.capacity.root.B.capacity</name>
          <value>40</value>
     </property>
     <property>
          <name>YARN.scheduler.capacity.root.B.maximum-capacity</name>
          <value>75</value>
     </property>
     <property>
          <name>YARN.scheduler.capacity.root.B.C.capacity</name>
          <value>50</value>
     </property>
     <property>
          <name>YARN.scheduler.capacity.root.B.D.capacity</name>
          <value>50</value>
     </property>
</configuration>
```

The capacity scheduler also provides a way to configure ACLs for queues and some advance configurations.

Fair scheduler

In fair scheduling, all applications get almost an equal amount of the available resources. In fair scheduler, when the first application is submitted to YARN, it will assign all the available resources to the application. Now in any scenario, if the new application is submitted to the scheduler, the scheduler will start allocating resources to the new application until both the applications have almost an equal amount of resources for their execution. Unlike the two schedulers discussed before, the fair scheduler prevents applications from resource starvation and assures that the applications in the queue get the required memory for execution. The distribution of the minimum and maximum share resources are calculated by the scheduling queue by using the configuration provided in the fair scheduler. The application will get the amount of resources configured for the queue where the application is submitted and if a new application is submitted to the same queue, the total configured resources will be shared between both applications.

Scheduling queues

The scheduler assigns the application into a queue by using the identity of the job submitter. We can also configure the queue in the configuration of the application at the time of application submission. The application first falls into the default queue that is shared by all the users and then applications are further divided into different queues. Queues are organized hierarchically and are assigned with weights. These weights indicate the proposition of cluster resources. The following diagram gives a better explanation of the queue hierarchy:

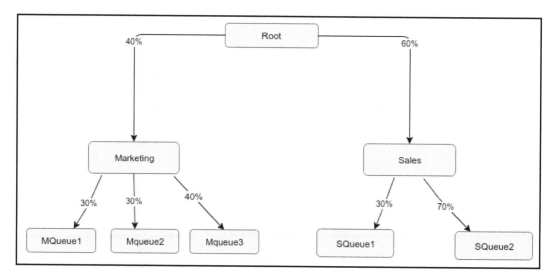

The fair scheduler guarantees the configured minimum amount of resources share to the queue. Remember the guaranteed minimum share of resources is applicable for any application submitted to the queue. If the application is not submitted to any particular queue, then the resources belonging to that queue will be allocated to the queues running the application. These processes make sure that resources are not under utilized and that applications are not suffering resource starvation.

Configuring fair scheduler

YARN provides a plugin policy for scheduler. By default, the capacity scheduler is configured to be used. In this section, we will see how to configure and set up queues for the fair scheduler. By default, a fair scheduler lets you run all the applications but if configured properly, the number of applications that can be run per user and per queue can be limited. Sometimes, it is important to restrict the number of applications per user so that other applications do not wait longer in the queue submitted by other users.

The first configuration change would go in `YARN-site.xml` to enable YARN to use a fair scheduler. To use the fair scheduler we need to first configure the appropriate scheduler class in `YARN-site.xml` as follows:

```
<property>
    <name>YARN.resourcemanager.scheduler.class</name>
    <value>org.apache.hadoop.YARN.server.resourcemanager.scheduler.
fair.FairScheduler
    </value>
</property>
```

The next step is to specify the scheduler configuration file location into `YARN-site.xml` by adding the following:

```
<property>
    <name>YARN.scheduler.fair.allocation.file</name>
    <value>/opt/packt/Hadoop/etc/Hadoop/fair-scheduler.xml</value>
</property>
```

Once it is done, the next step is to configure the scheduler properties and the next changes will go to the `fair-scheduler.xml` file. The first change in `fair-scheduling.xml` is to make queue allocation policy which will look as follows:

```
<?xml version="1.0"?>
<allocations>
    <defaultQueueSchedulingPolicy>fair</defaultQueueSchedulingPolicy>
<queue name="root">
    <queue name="dev">
```

```
        <weight>40</weight>
    </queue>

    <queue name="prod">
        <weight>60</weight>
        <queue name="marketing"/>
        <queue name="finance" />
        <queue name ="sales" >
    </queue>
</queue>
    <queuePlacementPolicy>
        <rule name="specified" create="false" />
        <rule name="primaryGroup" create="false" />
    </queuePlacementPolicy>
</allocations>
```

The preceding allocation configuration has a `root` queue, which means all jobs submitted to YARN will go into the `root` queue first. The `prod` and `dev` are two sub queues of the `root` queue. They share `60` and `40` percentage of resources.

Resource Manager high availability

Resource Manager (**RM**) is the single point of failure in a YARN cluster as every request from a client goes through it. The Resource Manager also acts as a central system to allocate resources for various tasks. The failure of the resource manager will lead to failure of YARN and thus a client cannot obtain any information about the YARN cluster or a client cannot submit any application for execution. Therefore, it is important to implement high availability of Resource Manager to prevent any cluster failure. The following are a few important considerations for high availability:

- **Resource Manager state**: It is very important to persist a resource manager state, which if stored in memory may be lost upon resource manager failure. If the state of the Resource Manager is available even after failure, we can restart the Resource Manager from the last failure point based on the last state.
- **Running application state**: The Resource Manager persistent state store allows YARN to continue to function in the RM restart in a user transparent manner. Once the last state is loaded by the Resource Manager, it will restart all the application masters, kill all the running containers, and start them from a clean state. In this process, the work already done by containers will be lost and it will lead to an increase in the application completion time. There is a need to preserve the state of containers, which upon failure will not require restarting the application masters and killing existing containers.

- **Automatic failover**: Automatic failover refers to the control transfer from a failed resource manager to a standby resource manager. The failover fencing mechanism is a popular method to implement failover as one of the controllers will trigger the failover if the specified condition is met. Remember, transferring control will always require the transfer of the old state to the new resource manager.

Architecture of RM high availability

The Resouces Manager high availability also works on the Active/Standby architecture where the standby resource manager will take over control upon receiving the signal from the ZooKeeper. The following diagram shows the high level design of Resouces Manager high availability:

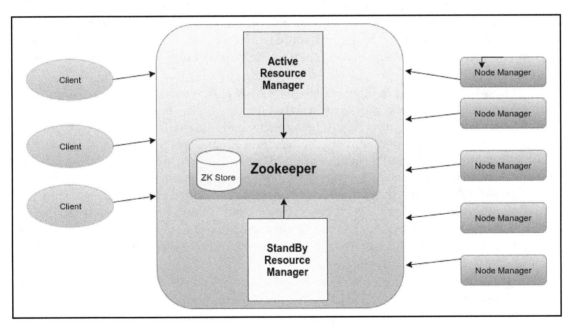

Components of Resouces Manager HA:

- **Resource Manager state store**: As discussed previously, it is important to store the state of the Resource Manager. So in case of failure, the standby resource manager will reload the state from the store during startup and will start from the last execution point. The Resource Manager state store provides the ability to store the internal state of the Resource Manager such as application and its attempts, version, tokens, and so on. There is no need to store the cluster information as it will be reconstructed when the **Node Manager** sends a heartbeat to the new Resource Manager. It provides file-based and **ZooKeeper** based state store implementation.

- **Resource Manager restart and failover**: The Resource Manager loads the internal application state from the Resource Manager state store. The scheduler of the Resource Manager reconstructs its state of cluster information when the **Node Manager** sends heartbeats. The Resource Manager makes a re-attempt for an application submitted to the failed resource manager. The checkpoint process allows the Resource Manager to only work on failed, running, or pending tasks and avoids restarting already completed task that helps to save significant time cost.

- **Failover fencing**: In high availability YARN clusters, there can be two or more than two Resource Managers in active/standby mode. It is possible at times that two managers assume themselves as active and that will lead to a split brain situation. When that happens, both resource managers will control cluster resources and handle client requests. The failover fencing mechanism enables the active Resource Manager to restrict other resource managers' operation. The state store that we discussed previously provides the **ZooKeeper** based state store `ZKResourceManagerStateStore`, which only allows a single Resource Manager to write to it at a time. It does so by maintaining an ACL where only the active Resource Manager will have create-delete access and the other will only have read-admin access.

- **Leader elector**: The ZooKeeper-based leader elector `ActiveStandbyElector` is used to elect a new active Resource Manager and implements fencing internally. When the current active Resource Manager goes down, a new resource manager will be elected by `ActiveStandbyElector` and take over the control. If automatic failover is not enabled, then admin has to manually make the transition of the active RM to standby and the other way around.

Configuring Resource Manager high availability

Let's look into how we configure Resource Manager high availability and what are the configuration changes required in the YARN cluster. The YARN configuration changes are available in `YARN-site.xml` and the following changes are required in order to enable HA:

- **Enabling high availability**: The first step is to enable the YARN cluster for resource manager high availability and change the `YARN.resourcemanager.ha.enabled` property to true as shown in the code:

```
<property>
  <name>YARN.resourcemanager.ha.enabled</name>
   <value>true</value>
</property>
```

- **Assign IDs to Resource Manager**: Each Resource Manager in the YARN cluster must be configured with unique IDs for its identification. That means if we have three Resource Managers, we must have three IDs, for example:

```
<property>
  <name>YARN.resourcemanager.ha.rm-ids</name>
  <value>rm1,rm2,rm3</value>
</property>
```

- **Attaching Resource Manager hostname to IDs**: The IDs configured will be linked with the Resource Manager hostname, which will be uniquely assigned. The hostname mentioned in the following configuration must be replaced by your resource manager hostname or IP address, for example:

```
<property> <name>YARN.resourcemanager.hostname.rm1</name>
<value>resourcemanager1</value> </property> <property>
<name>YARN.resourcemanager.hostname.rm2</name>
<value>resourcemanager2</value> </property><property>
<name>YARN.resourcemanager.hostname.rm3</name>
<value>resourcemanager3</value> </property>
```

- **Configuring Resource Manager web application**: The following properties set the port for the RM web application:

```
<property>
  <name>YARN.resourcemanager.webapp.address.rm1</name>
  <value>resourcemanager2:8088</value>
</property>
<property>
  <name>YARN.resourcemanager.webapp.address.rm2</name>
  <value>resourcemanager2:8088</value>
```

```
    </property>
    <property>
      <name>YARN.resourcemanager.webapp.address.rm3</name>
      <value>resourcemanager3:8088</value>
    </property>
```

- **ZooKeeper address**: The ZooKeeper plays a very important role in the state store and leader election. It also provides the fencing mechanism for failover. The following property must be set with all zooKeeper node address:

```
    <property>
      <name>YARN.resourcemanager.zk-address</name>
      <value>Zkhost1:2181,Zkhost2:2181,Zkhost3:2181</value>
    </property>
```

You can then check the Resource Manager state using the ID assigned to each resource manager and YARN admin commands. For example, the following command will give the state of `resourcemanager1`:

```
YARN rmadmin -getServiceState rm1
```

Node labels

The use of Hadoop in the organization increases over time and they board more use cases to the Hadoop platform. The data pipeline in an organization consists of multiple jobs. A Spark job may need machines with more RAM and powerful processing capabilities but, on the other hand, MapReduce can run on less powerful machines. Therefore, it is obvious that a cluster may consist of different types of machines to save infrastructure costs. A Spark job may need machines with high processing capability.

YARN label is nothing but a marker for each machine so that machines with the same label name can be used for specific jobs. The nodes with more powerful processing capabilities can be labelled with the same name and then jobs that require more powerful machines can use the same node label during submission. Each node can only have one label assigned to it, which means the cluster will have a disjointed set of nodes or we can say a cluster is partitioned based on node labels. The YARN also provides capabilities to set queue level configuration, which defines how much of a partition a queue can use. There are two types of node labels available for now, which are as follows:

- **Exclusive**: The exclusive node label ensures that it is the only queue permitted or allowed to access node label. The application submitted by queue having an exclusive label will have exclusive access to the partition so that no other queue can get resources.

- **Non-exclusive**: The non-exclusive label allows or permits idle resources sharing with other applications. The queues are assigned the node labels and applications submitted to these queues will get first priority over the respective node labels. If there is no application or job submitted by a queue to these node labels, then resources will be shared between other non-exclusive node labels. If the queue with the node label submits an application or job in between processing, the resources will be preempted from the running task and assigned to associated queues on priority basis.

Configuring node labels

In this section we will talk about configuring node labels in a Hadoop cluster. Every request to YARN goes through the Resource Manager therefore the first step is to enable node label configuration to resource manager:

- **Enabling node label and setting node label path**: The YARN-site.xml file contains the configuration related to YARN, as follows:

```
<property>
    <name>YARN.node-labels.enabled</name>
    <value>true</value>
    <description>Enabling node label feature</description>
</property>

<property>
 <name>YARN.node-labels.fs-store.root-dir</name>
 <value>http://namemoderpc:port/YARN/packt/node.labels</value>
 <description>The path to the node labels file.</description>
</property>
```

- **Creating directory structure on HDFS**: The next step is to create a node label directory where node label information will be stored. The permission should be set so that YARN will be able to access this directories, for example:

```
sudo su hdfs
Hadoop fs -mkdir -p /YARN/packt/node-labels
Hadoop fs -chown -R YARN:YARN /YARN
Hadoop fs -chmod -R 700 /YARN
```

- **Granting permission to YARN**: The YARN user directory must be present on HDFS. If not, create the directory and assign the permission to the directory to the YARN user, as follows:

```
sudo su hdfs
Hadoop fs -mkdir -p /user/YARN
Hadoop fs -chown -R YARN:YARN /user/YARN
Hadoop fs -chmod -R 700 /user/YARN
```

- **Creating node label**: Once the preceding steps are done, we can create node labels using the following command:

```
sudo -u YARN YARN rmadmin -addToClusterNodeLabels "<node-label1>
(exclusive=<true|false>),<node-label2>(exclusive=<true|false>)"
```

By default, the exclusive property is `true`. It is good to check whether the node labels are created or not. We can list the node labels to verify it as shown in the following code:

```
sudo -u YARN YARN rmadmin -addToClusterNodeLabels
"spark(exclusive=true),Hadoop(exclusive=false)"

YARN cluster --list-node-labels
```

- **Assigning node with node label**: Once node label is created, we can now assign node labels to nodes. Each node will have only one node label assigned to it. Use the following command to assign a node with a node label:

```
YARN rmadmin -replaceLabelsOnNode "<nodeaddress1>:<port>=<node-label1> <nodeaddress2>:<port>=<node-label2>"
```

The following shows an example:

```
sudo su YARN
YARN rmadmin -replaceLabelsOnNode "packt.com=spark
packt2.com=spark,packt3.com=Hadoop,packt4.com=Hadoop"
```

- **Queue-node label association**: The last step is to assign each queue with a node label so that the job submitted by the queue goes to the node label assigned to it, for example:

```
<property>
 <name>YARN.scheduler.capacity.root.queues</name>
 <value>marketing,sales</value>
</property>

<property>
```

```
<name>YARN.scheduler.capacity.root.accessible-node-
      labels.spark.capacity</name>
<value>100</value>
</property>

<property>
<name>YARN.scheduler.capacity.root.accessible-node-
      labels.Hadoop.capacity</name>
<value>100</value>
</property>

<!-- configuration of queue-a -->
<property>
<name>YARN.scheduler.capacity.root.marketing.accessible-node
      -labels</name>
<value>x,y</value>
</property>

<property>
<name>YARN.scheduler.capacity.root.marketing.capacity</name>
<value>40</value>
</property>

<property>
<name>YARN.scheduler.capacity.root.sales.accessible-node
      -labels.spark.capacity</name>
<value>100</value>
</property>

<property>
<name>YARN.scheduler.capacity.root.sales.accessible-node-
      labels.Hadoop.capacity</name>
<value>50</value>
</property>

<property>
<name>YARN.scheduler.capacity.root.marketing.queues</name>
<value>product,service</value>
</property>

<!-- configuration of queue-b -->
<property>
<name>YARN.scheduler.capacity.root.sales.accessible-node-
      labels</name>
<value>Hadoop</value>
</property>

<property>
```

```
    <name>YARN.scheduler.capacity.root.sales.capacity</name>
    <value>60</value>
    </property>

    <property>
    <name>YARN.scheduler.capacity.root.sales.accessible-node-
        labels.Hadoop.capacity</name>
    <value>50</value>
    </property>

    <property>
    <name>YARN.scheduler.capacity.root.sales.queues</name>
    <value>product_sales</value>
    </property>

    <!-- configuration of queue-a.a1 -->
    <property>
   <name>YARN.scheduler.capacity.root.marketing.product.
        ccessible-node-labels</name>
    <value>spark,Hadoop</value>
    </property>

    <property>
    <name>YARN.scheduler.capacity.root.marketing.
        product.capacity</name>
    <value>40</value>
    </property>

    <property>
    <name>YARN.scheduler.capacity.root.marketing.product.
        accessible-node-labels.spark.capacity</name>
    <value>30</value>
    </property>

    <property>
  <name>YARN.scheduler.capacity.root.marketing.product.accessible-
        node-labels.Hadoop.capacity</name>
    <value>50</value>
    </property>

    <!-- configuration of queue-a.a2 -->
    <property>
<name>YARN.scheduler.capacity.root.marketing.service.
    accessible-node-labels</name>
    <value>spark,Hadoop</value>
    </property>

    <property>
```

```
        <name>YARN.scheduler.capacity.root.marketing.service.
            capacity</name>
        <value>60</value>
        </property>

        <property>
      <name>YARN.scheduler.capacity.root.marketing.service.
            accessible-node-labels.spark.capacity</name>
        <value>70</value>
        </property>

        <property>
        <name>YARN.scheduler.capacity.root.marketing.service.
 accessible-node-labels.Hadoop.capacity</name>
        <value>50</value>
        </property>

        <!-- configuration of queue-b.b1 -->
        <property>
        <name>YARN.scheduler.capacity.root.sales.product_sales.accessible-
node-
            labels</name>
        <value>y</value>
        </property>

        <property>
<name>YARN.scheduler.capacity.root.sales.product_sales.capacity</name>
        <value>100</value>
        </property>

        <property>
        <name>YARN.scheduler.capacity.root.sales.product_sales.accessible-
node-
            labels.Hadoop.capacity</name>
        <value>100</value>
        </property>
```

- **Refreshing the queue**: Once the configuration and queue assignment with the node label is done, we can proceed with refreshing the queues. Use following command to refresh the queue:

```
sudo su YARN
YARN rmadmin -refreshQueues
```

- **Submitting job**: The basic idea of a node label is to create the partition of nodes so that each partition can be used for a specific use case. The user can submit jobs to the queue and specify the node label application that should be used for execution of tasks. We can do it using the following command:

```
Hadoop jar wordcount.jar –num_containers 4 –queue product –
node_label_expression Hadoop
```

A node can be removed and reassigned to another node label. Any node label configured with exclusive set to false will be treated as non-exclusive node labels and resources available with those non-exclusive nodes that will be shared with other node labels.

YARN Timeline server in Hadoop 3.x

The job history server in MapReduce provides the information about all the current and historical MapReduce. jobs details. The job history server was only able to capture the information about MapReduce jobs and it was not able to capture YARN level events and metrics. As we know, YARN has a capability to run applications other than MapReduce and thus, there was a need to have a YARN-specific application that can capture information about all the applications. The YARN Timeline server is responsible for retrieving current as well as historic information about applications. The metrics and information collected through a YARN Timeline server are generic in nature and hence have a common structure that helps in debugging the logs and capturing other metrics for any specific use. The Timeline server captures two types of information, which are as follows:

- **Application information**: The application is submitted to the queue by the user and each application can have multiple application attempts. Each application attempt can launch multiple containers to complete the job. The Timeline server captures and provides detailed information and logs for each step involved in the application life cycle. It also provides a web interface to view the information.
- **Framework information**: YARN is capable of launching different types of applications such as map-reduce, spark, Tez, and so on. A MapReduce job may contain information such as the number of map and reduce tasks. A Spark job may contain information such as the number of executors and cores. This information changes based on the framework from which the YARN job is submitted. The Timeline server provides a web interface and a REST API to access this information.

In Hadoop version 3, there are major changes in the YARN Timeline server architecture. It addresses two major challenges that were in previous versions. They are solved in the current version, and are as follows:

- **Scalability and reliability**: The writer and reader in previous versions are limited to a single instance and thus it was difficult to handle a big cluster as the processing capabilities were limited. The current version of YARN in Hadoop version 3 uses a distributed writer and scalable storage. The reader and writer are loosely coupled and the readers instances are responsible to serve read requests received via the REST API. The primary storage for the current version of the Timeline server is HBase because of its ability to deliver a fast response for read and write requests.
- **Flows and aggregation**: The application life cycle in YARN consists of various steps. YARN may launch a set of applications to complete a logical application life cycle. A single application can consist of many sub applications, and we need to have aggregated metrics of the application. YARN aggregates the metrics from all sub applications and their attempts and make it available as an aggregated report of a application.

Configuring YARN Timeline server

The Timeline server requires a few basic configurations to start but it also provides various configuration options for specific purposes. Let's look at a few configurations of a Timeline server:

- **Basic configuration**: The basic configuration is good enough to start a Timeline server, which generally allows the client and resource manager to publish their metrics, as follows:

```
<property>
  <description>
  If enabled, the end user can post entities using TimelineClient
library.
  </description>
  <name>YARN.timeline-service.enabled</name>
  <value>true</value>
</property>

<property>
  <description>if enabled the  system metrics send by Resource
Manager will be
            published on the timeline server..</description>
  <name>YARN.resourcemanager.system-metrics-
```

```
publisher.enabled</name>
        <value>true</value>
    </property>

    <property>
        <description> if enabled Client can query application data
directly from                          Timeline server.</description>
        <name>YARN.timeline-service.generic-application-
history.enabled</name>
        <value>true</value>
    </property>
```

- **Host configuration**: The host for a Timeline server is set via the following configuration. It indicates the web address of the Timeline server, for example:

```
    <property>
        <name>YARN.timeline-service.hostname</name>
        <value>0.0.0.0</value>
    </property>
    <property>
        <description>Address for the Timeline server to start the RPC
server.
        </description>
        <name>YARN.timeline-service.address</name>
        <value>${YARN.timeline-service.hostname}:10200</value>
    </property>

    <property>
        <description>The http address of the Timeline service web
application.
        </description>
        <name>YARN.timeline-service.webapp.address</name>
        <value>${YARN.timeline-service.hostname}:8188</value>
    </property>

    <property>
        <description>The https address of the Timeline service web
application.
        </description>
        <name>YARN.timeline-service.webapp.https.address</name>
        <value>${YARN.timeline-service.hostname}:8190</value>
    </property>

    <property>
        <description>Handler thread count to serve the client RPC
requests.
        </description>
```

```
<name>YARN.timeline-service.handler-thread-count</name>
<value>10</value>
</property>
```

- **Starting the Timeline server**: Finally we can start the Timeline server using following command:

```
YARN timelineserver
```

Opportunistic containers in Hadoop 3.x

Containers are allocated to nodes by the scheduler only when there is sufficient unallocated resources at a node. YARN guarantees that once the application master dispatches a container to a node, the execution will immediately start. The execution of a container will only be completed if there is no violation of fairness or capacity, which means until some other containers ask for preemption of resources from the node, the container is guaranteed to run to completion.

The current container execution design allows an efficient task execution but it has two primary limitations, which are as follows:

- **Heartbeat delay**: The Node Manager at regular intervals sends heartbeats to its resource manager and the heartbeat request also contains the resource metrics of a Node Manager. If any container running on a Node Manager finishes its execution then the information is sent as part of request in the next heartbeat, which means that the Resource Manager knows that there are available resources on a Node Manager to launch a new container. It will schedule a new container at that node and the application master of the application who requested the resource gets notified by the Resource Manager and the application master then launches the container at the node. The delay between the steps discussed previously can be longer and until then, the resources will be idle.
- **Resource allocation and utilization**: The resources allocated to a container by the Resource Manager can be significantly higher than what is actually being utilized by the container. For example, 6 GB of a container is only using 3 GB, but this doesn't mean that the container will not use more memory than 3 GB. These problems should be addressed in such a way that a container should only use the utilized memory and get more memory whenever it requires it in the future.

To address the preceding limitation, YARN has introduced a new type of container called an opportunist container. Opportunist containers can be sent to a Node Manager even if there are no sufficient resources available on the Node Manager for processing the request. The opportunist container will be queued until there are resources available for its execution. The opportunist container priority is lower than the guaranteed container and because of this an opportunist container can be killed when there is resources requested for guaranteed containers. The applications can be configured to use both opportunist and guaranteed containers for execution of its tasks.

There are two ways in which opportunist containers are allocated to an application, which are as follows:

- **Centralized**: The containers are allocated through a YARN resource manager. The application master requests a container from the Resource Manager. The request for a guaranteed container goes to the `ApplicatonMasterService` and gets handled by the scheduler. The request for an opportunist container is handled by the `OpportunisticContainerAllocator`, which schedules a container to a node.

- **Distributed**: The resources are allocated through the local scheduler, which is available at each Node Manager. The current version of YARN has `AMRMProxyService` at every node. The `AMRMProxyService` works as a proxy between the Resource Manager and the application master. An application master does not directly interact with a resource manager. Instead, it interacts with a `AMRMProxyService` of the same node where it is running. In the event of an application master, a new application master is launched and YARN allocates a `AMRMToken` to a new application master.

The number of currently running guaranteed containers, opportunist containers, and queued opportunist containers at every node are updated to the Resource Manager by the Node Manager during the heartbeat. The Resource Manager collects the information about each node and determines the least busy node. The default allocation is centralized, hence in such cases, allocation happens centrally.

Configuring opportunist container

The opportunist container configuration goes into `YARN-site.xml`. The first step is to enable opportunist container allocation, as follows:

```
<properties>
    <name>YARN.resourcemanager.opportunistic-container-
allocation.enabled</name>
      <value>true</value>
</properties>
```

The minimum number of opportunist containers that can be queued at a Node Manager is determined by the following property:

```
<properties>
 <name>YARN.nodemanager.opportunistic-containers-max-queue-length</name>
 <value>15</value>
</properties>
```

An efficient value is determined by job characteristics, the cluster configuration, and the target utilization. The allocation can happen using either a centralized or distributed node. By default, YARN uses the centralized way to allocate resources. But if we want to enable the distributed allocation method, we can enable the following property:

```
<properties>
    <name>YARN.nodemanager.distributed-scheduling.enabled</name>
    <value>true</value>
</properties>
```

The following parameter tells us the amount of memory that can be used while submitting the job to indicate the percentage of mappers that can run using an opportunist container:

```
-Dmapreduce.job.num-opportunistic-maps-percent="30"
```

Docker containers in YARN

Docker has been widely used as a light weighted container for various applications. YARN is now widely used as a resource manager for diverse applications and it uses Linux to launch containers. YARN has added support for Docker containerization. The Docker image can be specified to run the YARN container and the Docker container has custom libraries to run the application.

The Docker environment is completely different from those of a Node Manager. The user does not need to worry about additional software or modules required to run the application and can focus on running and fine tuning the application. Different versions of the same application can be run in parallel and they will be completely isolated from one another.

The `ContainerExecutor` abstraction provides four implementations that are responsible for providing the resources required for running the application, setting up the environment, and managing the life cycle of containers, which are as follows:

- `DefaultContainerExecutor`
- `LinuxContainerExecutor`
- `WindowsSecureContainerExecutor`
- `DocketContainerExecutor`

The `DockerContainerExecutor` allows the Node Manager to launch YARN containers into Docker containers. YARN has added support for Docker commands to allow the Node Manager to launch, monitor, and clean up Docker containers, the same as it does for any YARN container. Using the `DockerContainerExecutor` is not recommended because we can only specify one `ContainerExecutor` per Node Manager and, hence, we will not be able to launch any other job such as Spark, tez, or MapReduce. `DockerContainerExecutor` will be removed in the future Hadoop release.

Configuring Docker containers

The first step is to specify the Docker configuration in `YARN-site.xml`. The Docker image that will be used for the YARN container must satisfy requirements such as Java home variable, and Hadoop home environment variables, including `HDFS`, `YARN`, and `MAPRED`, must be set. The variable names are `JAVA_HOME`, `HADOOP_COMMON_PATH`, `HADOOP_HDFS_HOME`, `HADOOP_MAPRED_HOME`, `HADOOP_YARN_HOME`, and `HADOOP_CONF_DIR`, as follows:

```
<property>
    <name>YARN.nodemanager.docker-container-executor.exec-    name</name>
      <value>docker -H=tcp://0.0.0.0:4243</value>
      <description> path to docker client </description>
</property>
<property>
    <name>YARN.nodemanager.container-executor.class</name>
<value>org.apache.Hadoop.YARN.server.nodemanager.DockerContainerExecutor</v
alue>
```

```
    <description> all job will be started as DockerCntainerExecutor.
</description>
</property>
```

Running the Docker image

Apache Hadoop 2.7.1 Docker image can be downloaded from `https://github.com/sequenceiq/Hadoop-docker`. The Hadoop Docker image has preconfigured variables that are required to run YARN container as Docker container, as follows:

```
docker pull sequenceiq/Hadoop-docker:2.7.1
docker run -it sequenceiq/Hadoop-docker:2.7.1 /etc/bootstrap.sh -bash
```

Running the container

The following command will run YARN container as a Docker container:

```
bin/Hadoop jar /share/Hadoop/mapreduce/Hadoop-mapreduce-examples-3.0.0.jar \
  teragen \
     -Dmapreduce.map.env="YARN.nodemanager.docker-container-executor.image-name=sequenceiq/Hadoop-docker:2.7.1" \
   -Dyarn.app.mapreduce.am.env="YARN.nodemanager.docker-container-executor.image-name=sequenceiq/Hadoop-docker:2.7.1" \
  1000 \
  output
```

YARN REST APIs

YARN also introduced REST API to access the information of the cluster, nodes of the cluster, applications, and so on. You can also build your own application to interact with YARN services by using these REST APIs. The important REST APIs provided by the YARN service are explained in the following sections.

Resource Manager API

The Resource Manager is the primary contact for any application and therefore it contains around 80% of the information that can be accessed via YARN's REST API. The YARN REST API has many retrieval applications, which will be explained as follows:

- **Retrieving cluster information**: The basic API is used to access cluster information that contains information such as clusterID, when did the cluster start, what is the state of the cluster, versions of Hadoop, the Resource Manager, and so on. The CURL request on the REST API will look as follows:

```
curl -X GET http://localhost:8088/ws/v1/cluster/info
```

  The default response would be in JSON, but you can also specify an XML response in the request header.

- **Retrieving cluster metrics**: The cluster metrics contains detailed information about the total number of applications submitted, total number of failed, running, killed, and completed applications counts, information about memory and containers, number of active and non active nodes, and so on. You can use following HTTP request to get the information:

```
curl -X GET http://localhost:8088/ws/v1/cluster/metrics
```

- **Retrieving application information**: YARN keeps information about all the applications whether they finished successfully, killed by any error, killed forcefully, pending for execution, and so on. We can easily get information about all the applications using the following REST API, which will return the information about each application and get details such as ID, username, start and finish time, resource allocation, container log location, and so on. We can extract the information of the applications using the following command:

```
curl -X GET http://localhost:8088/ws/v1/cluster/apps
```

  We can also easily extract the information of a specific application using its application ID in the preceding request as follows:

```
curl -X GET http://localhost:8088/ws/v1/cluster/apps/{APP_ID}
```

The APP_ID should be replaced by the real application ID; for example, here is a request URL: `http://localhost:8088/ws/v1/cluster/apps/application_1415159230 5_01`.

YARN can make multiple attempts to run an application because of a number of reasons. We can also see the detailed information about the number of attempts and location of logs for those attempts in order to debug and correctly identify the root cause of failure. The REST API looks like the following:

```
curl -X GET http://localhost:8088/ws/v1/cluster/apps/{APP_ID}/
appattempts
```

The APP_ID should be replaced by a valid application ID.

- **Retrieving node information**: A YARN cluster consists of multiple nodes and each node may have different configurations and types. YARN also provides an API to extract information about all the nodes configured with cluster. The response includes information such as Node ID, rack information, status, memory and container information, and so on. We can use the following curl request to retrieve information:

  ```
  curl -X GET http://localhost:8088/ws/v1/cluster/nodes
  ```

We can also get the specific node information by providing a node ID to the REST request. To retrieve information of a node with ID node1, a request would look like the following:

```
curl -X GET http://localhost:8088/ws/v1/cluster/nodes/node1
```

- **Application API**: YARN has a REST API to create new application requests and then it uses the response to submit new applications to a YARN resource manager. There are two steps to submit jobs, which are as follows:
  - **Creating new application request**: The first step is to create an application request to YARN. YARN will then respond with a new application ID, which will be used for the new application. The creation REST API will be as follows:

    ```
    curl -X POST http://localhost:8088/ws/v1/
    cluster/apps/new-application
    ```

The response for the preceding HTTP request will be as follows:

```
{
    "application-id":"application_1412438797841_0001",
    "maximum-resource-capability":
        {
            "memory":10456,
            "vCores":40
        }
}
```

- **Submitting new application**: Once we have a new application ID available, we can use it to submit a new application using the job submit API. The POST request for the job submit API will contain a request body that has the detailed information about the application, as follows:

```
curl -v -X POST -d new_application.json -H "Content-type:
application/json"'http://localhost:8088/ws/v1/cluster/apps'
```

The following is the code for the application API new_application.json:

```
{
    "application-id":"application_1412438797841_0001",
    "application-name":"new_application",
    "am-container-spec":
    {
        "local-resources":
        {
            "entry":
            [
                {
                    "key":"AppMaster.jar",
                    "value":
                    {
                        "resource":"hdfs://hdfs-
                        namenode:9000/user/packt/DistributedShell/demo-
app/AppMaster.jar",
                        "type":"FILE",
                        "visibility":"APPLICATION",
                        "size": "43004",
                        "timestamp": "1405452071209"
                    }
                }
            ]
        },
```

```
        "commands":
        {
            "command":"{{JAVA_HOME}}/bin/java -Xmx10m
org.apache.Hadoop.YARN.applications.distributedshell.ApplicationMaster --
            container_memory 10 --container_vcores 1 --num_containers 1 --
priority 0 1>
            <LOG_DIR>/AppMaster.stdout 2><LOG_DIR>/AppMaster.stderr"
        },
        "environment":
        {
            "entry":
            [
                {
                    "key": "DISTRIBUTEDSHELLSCRIPTTIMESTAMP",
                    "value": "1405459400754"
                },
                {
                    "key": "CLASSPATH",
                    "value":
"{{CLASSPATH}}<CPS>./*<CPS>{{HADOOP_CONF_DIR}}<CPS>{{HADOOP_COMMON_HOME}}/s
hare/Hadoop/common/*<CPS>{{HADOOP_COMMON_HOME}}/share/Hadoop/common/lib/*<C
PS>{{HADOOP_HDFS_HOME}}/share/Hadoop/hdfs/*<CPS>{{HADOOP_HDFS_HOME}}/share/
Hadoop/hdfs/lib/*<CPS>{{HADOOP_YARN_HOME}}/share/Hadoop/YARN/*<CPS>{{HADOOP
_YARN_HOME}}/share/Hadoop/YARN/lib/*<CPS>./log4j.properties"
                },
                {
                    "key": "DISTRIBUTEDSHELLSCRIPTLEN",
                    "value": "6"
                },
                {
                    "key": "DISTRIBUTEDSHELLSCRIPTLOCATION",
                    "value": "hdfs://hdfs-
namenode:9000/user/packt/example/shellCommands"
                }
            ]
        }
    },
    "unmanaged-AM":"false",
    "max-app-attempts":"2",
    "resource":
    {
        "memory":"1024",
        "vCores":"1"
    },
    "application-type":"YARN",
    "keep-containers-across-application-attempts":"false"
}
```

- **Retrieving application status**: We can retrieve the current status of an application using the REST API, which provides the status by using an application ID, as follows:

```
curl -X GET 'http://localhost:8088/ws/v1/cluster/apps/
application_1412438797841_0001/state'
```

- **Killing application**: Sometime we may want to kill an application because of reasons such as application taking too long for execution, some mistakes in the application code, or undesired output. Any application that is in a running or pending state can be killed and YARN provides a REST API to kill the application. The preceding submitted application can be killed using following request:

```
curl -v -X PUT -d '{"state":
"KILLED"}''http://localhost:8088/ws/v1/cluster/apps/
application_1412438797841_0001'
```

Node Manager REST API

The Node Manager is responsible for running containers and executing tasks inside containers. The Node Manager API provides information about particular nodes, applications running on that node, and their containers. Let's look at each API and their uses:

- **Retrieve Node Manager information**: YARN exposes the REST API to get information about any particular node. The response contains information such as node ID, node hostname, health report, container memory, and core information, for example:

```
curl -X GET http://nodemanagerIP:port/ws/v1/node/info
```

An example would look like the following:

```
curl -X GET http://10.20.28.19:8042/ws/v1/node/info
```

- **Application information on Node Manager**: We can also get the information about what applications are running on a Node Manager and their containers. Remember, the same application may be running on other Node Managers as well with different containers and tasks. To get the application information, we can use following REST API:

```
curl -X GET http://nodemanagerIP:port/ws/v1/node/apps
```

An example would look like the following:

```
curl -X GET http://10.20.28.19:8042/ws/v1/node/apps
```

We can also get the information about specific applications running on a Node Manager by providing an application ID to the API. The REST call would look as follows:

```
      curl -X GET
  http://nodemanagerIP:port/ws/v1/node/apps/{APP_ID}
```

An example would look like the following:

```
      curl -X GET
  http://10.20.28.19:8042/ws/v1/node/apps/application_1412438797813_0
  01
```

- **Retrieving container information**: The Node Manager launches containers to execute various tasks such as running the application master, map task or reduce task, and so on. The container REST APIs for YARN provide information about all the containers running on a Node Manager. The response contains information about all the containers such as container ID, container log location, memory required by container, container status, user, and so on. The REST call would look like the following:

```
curl -X GET http://nodemanagerIP:port/ws/v1/node/containers
```

An example would look like the following:

```
curl -X GET http://10.20.28.19:8042/ws/v1/node/apps/containers
```

We can also retrieve information about a specific container by passing a container ID to the REST call mentioned previously, as follows:

```
      curl -X GET
  http://nodemanagerIP:port/ws/v1/node/containers/{containerID}
```

An example would look like the following:

```
  curl -X GET http://10.20.28.19:8042/ws/v1/node/apps/containers/
  container_1423657897651_0002_01_000020
```

The REST APIs are currently configured to return responses in either JSON or XML. The default return type is JSON. If you would like to receive response in XML format, you need to mention the content type of XML in the request header, as follows:

```
curl-X GET -H "Content-Type: application/xml" RESTURL
```

YARN command reference

Similar to HDFS, YARN also has its own commands to manage the overall YARN cluster. YARN provides two command-line interfaces, one is for users who want to run any service on a YARN cluster and the other is for administrators who will manage the overall YARN cluster.

User command

The user command in a Hadoop cluster is the one who submits applications to the Hadoop cluster. The application may fail or sometimes they do not perform well. In such scenarios, logs are the first step to debug your application and YARN stores logs for applications and containers that can be accessed via a command-line interface.

Application commands

The application command is used to perform operations with applications submitted to the YARN cluster. The operation can include listing all the applications with a specific state, killing the application, debugging application logs, and so on. Let's look into a few commands and how to use them:

- -appStates: This command is used along with -list command to list all the application with a particular state. The following command will list all the applications that are in a killed state. The possible states are ALL, NEW, NEW_SAVING, SUBMITTED, ACCEPTED, RUNNING, FINISHED, FAILED, KILLED:

```
YARN application -list -appStates killed
```

The output of the preceding command is as follows:

```
[root@ip-10-254-0-45 hadoop]# yarn application -list -appStates failed
18/01/18 08:08:03 INFO impl.TimelineClientImpl: Timeline service address: http://ip-10-254-0-45.ap-south-1.compute.internal:8188/ws/v1/timelin
18/01/18 08:08:03 INFO client.RMProxy: Connecting to ResourceManager at ip-10-254-0-45.ap-south-1.compute.internal/10.254.0.45:8032
Total number of applications (application-types: [] and states: [FAILED]):5
                Application-Id      Application-Name        Application-Type          User        Queue              State
inal-State              Progress                    Tracking-URL
application_1513582536692_0011  HIVE-dcbc8001-3339-470e-a303-b367d17fa83c                   TEZ        hadoop          default
        FAILED              FAILED          0% http://ip-10-254-0-45.ap-south-1.compute.internal:8088/cluster/app/application_1513582
6692_0011
application_1513582536692_0009  select count(*) from tests3...service_region(Stage-1)        MAPREDUCE        hadoop          default
        FAILED              FAILED          0% http://ip-10-254-0-45.ap-south-1.compute.internal:8088/cluster/app/application
513582536692_0009
application_1513582536692_0010  HIVE-9a9368ef-6e76-4ddb-8d72-e8b0dccaa534                   TEZ        hadoop          default
        FAILED              FAILED          0% http://ip-10-254-0-45.ap-south-1.compute.internal:8088/cluster/app/application_1513582
6692_0010
application_1513582536692_0007  select sum(transaction_amou...service_region(Stage-1)       MAPREDUCE        hadoop          default
        FAILED              FAILED          0% http://ip-10-254-0-45.ap-south-1.compute.internal:8088/cluster/app/application
513582536692_0007
application_1513582536692_0008  select sum(transaction_amount) from tests3(Stage-1)         MAPREDUCE        hadoop          default
        FAILED              FAILED          0% http://ip-10-254-0-45.ap-south-1.compute.internal:8088/cluster/app/application
513582536692_0008
[root@ip-10-254-0-45 hadoop]#
```

- -kill: The user may want to kill the running applications due to certain reasons such as visualized a bug in the execution process, application taking too long to execute, and so on. The -kill command will kill the submitted or running application, as follows:

  YARN application -kill applicationId

- -status: The status of an application can be tracked using the -status command. It gives detailed information about an application like user, start time, end time, queue name, and so on, for example:

  YARN application -status applicationID

The output of the preceding command is as follows:

```
[root@ip-10-254-0-45 hadoop]# yarn application -status application_1513582536692_0119
18/01/18 08:20:26 INFO impl.TimelineClientImpl: Timeline service address: http://ip-10-254-0-45.ap-south-1.compute.internal:8188/ws/v1/timeline/
18/01/18 08:20:26 INFO client.RMProxy: Connecting to ResourceManager at ip-10-254-0-45.ap-south-1.compute.internal/10.254.0.45:8032
Application Report :
        Application-Id : application_1513582536692_0119
        Application-Name : HIVE-a34d1844-cdb8-4691-a289-8a53a55f9dec
        Application-Type : TEZ
        User : root
        Queue : default
        Start-Time : 1515995486809
        Finish-Time : 1515995488561
        Progress : 100%
        State : KILLED
        Final-State : KILLED
        Tracking-URL : http://ip-10-254-0-45.ap-south-1.compute.internal:8088/cluster/app/application_1513582536692_0119
        RPC Port : -1
        AM Host : N/A
        Aggregate Resource Allocation : 1337 MB-seconds, 1 vcore-seconds
        Diagnostics : Application killed by user.
[root@ip-10-254-0-45 hadoop]#
```

- -movetoqueue: The application submitted to YARN by a queue can be moved to a different queue by the user using the -movetoqueue command, as follows:

```
YARN application -movetoqueue applicationID -queue queuename
```

Logs command

The application logs are important for debugging and tuning the performance of an application. The logs can be seen via the command-line interface using following command:

```
YARN logs -applictationId applicationID
```

We can also view a specific log file for an application. For example, to view only the error log, we can use following command:

```
YARN logs -applicationId application_15145363773_001_00 -log_files stderr
```

The Node Manager can launch multiple containers for a single application and sometimes, due to an error in the data format or application code, a few containers may fail. We have to debug an application at the container level to identify the problems and correct them. The following command can be used to list all the containers for an application ID:

```
YARN logs -applicationId application_154356768798_0001_001 -
show_application_log_info
```

Once we have the container information available, we can view container logs using the following command:

```
YARN logs -applicationId application_151345678971_0001_001 -containerId
container_151345678652_001_001
```

Administration commands

Hadoop admin is responsible for managing the YARN cluster and configuring the scheduler, queue, and other properties. YARN provides a command-line interface to admin to manage the cluster. The following are a few important commands that are used frequently:

- nodemanager: The nodemanager is available on every worker node in the YARN cluster. The following command is used to start the nodemanager service:

```
YARN nodemanager
```

- `rmadmin`: The Resource Manager is a master node in the YARN cluster and the `rmadmin` command is used to manage services at the Resource Manager level. The following is the syntax for `rmadmin`:

    YARN -rmadmin option

The options that can be used with the `rmadmin` command are as follows:

- `-refreshQueues`: Sometimes, queue configurations such as ACLs, and queue info, may require changing. Once the changes are made, admin needs to refresh the queue so that the Resource Manager will reload the configuration file and the queue configuration, such as ACLs, state, and scheduler properties, as follows:

    YARN rmadmin -refreshQueues

- `-refreshNodes`: Decommissioning and commissioning a node are the basic commands in any YARN cluster. These commands will refresh the host information of the node at the Resource Manager, as follows:

    YARN rmadmin -refreshNodes

- `-refreshNodesResources`: The Node Manager contains the resource information about the node they manage. At regular intervals, the information is sent to the Resource Manager. The admin can manually refresh the node information, as follows:

    `YARN rmadmin refreshNodesResources`

- `-refreshAdminAcls`: The cluster can have more than one admin and each one of them can have different ACLs. The ACL for admins can be changed or new ACLs can be added for admins. The `refreshAdminAcls` will reload the ACLs to the Resource Manager.
- `-refreshServiceAcl`: The services that YARN manages may not be accessible to all users. This command will trigger the Resource Manager to reload the service ACL policy.
- `-getGroups username`: This returns the group name to which the user belongs.

- **service commands**: There are a list of service commands that admin can execute to get the state of the service, check service health, or change the state of the service from active to standby, and the other way around, which are as follows:

```
YARN rmadmin -transitionToActive serviceId
YARN rmadmin -transitionToActive serviceId
YARN rmadmin -getServiceState serviceId
YARN rmadmin -checkHealth serviceId
```

- `schedulerconf`: The scheduler configuration of a YARN cluster can be changed by this command. The queue can be modified, added, and removed using the `schedulerconf` command, as follows:

```
YARN schedulerconf -add
<"queuePath1:key1=val1,key2=val2;queuePath2:key3=val3">
```

- **Removing queue**: The queues can be removed using the following command:

```
YARN schedulerconf -remove
<"queuePath1;queuePath2;queuepath3">
```

Summary

This chapter focused on YARN and its components. We covered various concepts, such as YARN architecture and resource manager HA in detail. We then went through YARN schedulers and how they work. We also covered some basic configurations for the scheduler and explained when to use what. The primary focus was to introduce the new features that have been added to Hadoop version 3. Thus, we covered the opportunist container and the Timeline server. In the last part, we went through the Docker container executor and a few commonly used Hadoop commands.

In the next chapter, we will cover MapReduce processing in detail, we will deep dive into MapReduce flow, and will look into each step in detail. We will go through different examples and look into a few techniques to improve the performance of applications.

4
Internals of MapReduce

The last chapter was all about managing resources on a Hadoop cluster and we went through details of the YARN architecture, execution, and a few examples. In this chapter, we will talk more about the MapReduce processing framework and how it has evolved over time. We will try to simplify how the overall MapReduce processing works and learn about what the major steps involved in the process are. The topics that will be covered in this chapter are as follows:

- Deep dive into the Hadoop MapReduce framework
- YARN and MapReduce
- MapReduce workflow in a Hadoop framework
- Important MapReduce parameters
- Common MapReduce patterns
- MapReduce examples in our use case
- Optimizing MapReduce
- MapReduce command reference

Technical requirements

You will be required to have Hadoop 3.0.

The code files of this chapter can be found on GitHub:
https://github.com/PacktPublishing/Mastering-Hadoop-3/tree/master/Chapter04

Check out the following video to see the code in action:
http://bit.ly/2PY4oP

Deep dive into the Hadoop MapReduce framework

The story of Hadoop started with HDFS and MapReduce. Hadoop version 1 has the basic features for storing and processing data over a distributed platform and since then it has evolved a lot. Hadoop version 2 added major changes, such as NameNode, high availability, and a new resource management framework called **YARN**. However, the high-level flow for MapReduce processing did not change despite various changes in its API.

MapReduce consists of two major steps: map and reduce, and multiple minor steps that are part of the process flow from map to reduce tasks. The mappers are responsible for performing map tasks while reducers are responsible for the reduce tasks. The job of the mapper is to process the blocks stored on HDFS, like the distributed storage system. Let's us look at the following MapReduce flow diagram:

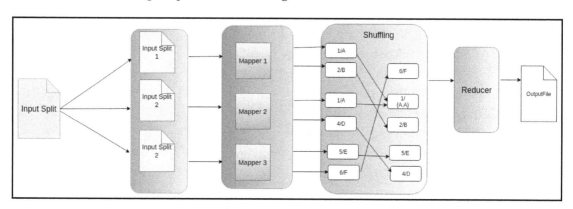

We will understand the processing flow as follows:

- **InputFileFormat**: The MapReduce process starts with reading the file stored on HDFS. These files can be of any specific type, such as Text, Avro, and so on. The processing of the file is controlled by `InputFormat`. There are multiple implementations for `InputFormat`. One such implementation is `TextInputFormat`. The abstract `InputFormat` class looks as follows:

  ```
  public abstract class InputFormat<K, V>

  {

      public abstract List<InputSplit> getSplits(JobContext
      context) throws IOException, InterruptedException;
      public abstract RecordReader<K, V>
  ```

```
createRecordReader(InputSplit split,
TaskAttemptContext context) throws IOException,
InterruptedException;

}
```

- **RecordReader and input split**: The input file is divided into chunks and these chunks are known as **input split**. The input split is nothing but the individual chunks of the file and the size is controlled by the `mapred.max.split.size` and `mapred.min.split.size` parameters. By default, the input split size is the same as block size and you must not change this unless required for a specific case. For non-splittable file formats such as `.gzip`, the input split will be equal to the size of a single `.gzip` file, which means that if there are 12 `.gzip` files then there will be 12 input splits and for each input split there will be one mapper launched to process it.

  The `RecordReader` function is responsible for reading data from the input splits stored on HDFS. The default input file format is `TextInputFileFormat` and the `RecordReader` delimiter is `/n`, which means the one line will be treated as one record by the `RecordReader`. Remember you can always customize the behavior of the `RecordReader` by passing the implementation of your own `RecordReader`.

  The `RecordReader` knows how to read records from the input split. By default, the `RecordReader` reads a record with a new line record delimiter for `TextInputFileFormat`. However, you can modify the behavior of `RecordReader` by passing your own implementation. The `RecordReader` reads the record and passes it to mapper.

- **Mapper**: The `Mapper` class is responsible for processing the input split. The `RecordReader` function reads the record from input split and passes each record to the `map` function of the mapper. The mapper contains the `map` method, which takes input from `RecordReader` and processes the record. The `map` function gets executed for each record, which means if one input split has 100 records, then the `map` function will be executed 100 times.

  The mapper also contains the `setup` and `cleanup` methods. The `setup` method gets executed before the mapper starts processing the records for input split, thus any initialization operation, such as reading from distributed cache and initializing connection, should be done inside the `setup` method. The `cleanup` method gets executed once all records in the input split have been processed and thus any `cleanup` operation should be performed inside this method.

- The `Mapper` processes the record and emits the output using the `context` object. The `context` object enables `Mapper` and `Reducer` to interact with other Hadoop systems, such as availing configuration to mappers and reducers, writing mappers and reducers emitted records to file, and so on. It also enables communication between `Mapper`, `Combiner`, and `Reducer`. The `Mapper` class looks as follows:

```
import org.apache.Hadoop.io.IntWritable;
import org.apache.Hadoop.io.LongWritable;
import org.apache.Hadoop.io.Text;
import org.apache.Hadoop.mapreduce.Mapper;

import java.io.IOException;

public class DemoMapper extends Mapper<LongWritable,
   Text, Text, IntWritable> {

   @Override
   protected void setup(Context context) throws IOException,
     InterruptedException {
    super.setup(context);
   }

   @Override
   protected void map(LongWritable key, Text value, Context
   context) throws IOException, InterruptedException {
       //Record Processing Logic Here
   }

   @Override
   protected void cleanup(Context context) throws IOException,
InterruptedException {
       super.cleanup(context);
   }

}
```

- **Partitioner**: The job of a `Partitioner` is to assign a partition number to the record emitted by mapper so that records with the same key always get the same partition number, which ensures the records with the same key will always go to the same reducer. For each record, there is a specific partition index associated and the value of the partition index is calculated inside.
  mapper `Context.write()`. The general formula of partition index is
  `partitionIndex = (key.hashCode() & Integer.MAX_VALUE) %
  numReducers`

- **Shuffling and sorting**: The process of transferring data from mapper to reducer is known as **shuffling**. The reducer launches threads to read data from the mapper machine and reads all the partitions that belong to them for processing using the HTTP protocol. The different mappers may have the record for the same and thus the reducer merge sorts the records by key. The shuffling and sorting phases occur in parallel, which means while outputs are being fetched, they are merged so that the reducer receives multiple records for the same key in a list as a value.

- **Reducer**: The number of reducers that the Hadoop framework can launch depends on the number of map outputs and various other parameters, but we can also control the number of reducers that can be launched. The formula for calculating the number of reducers is as follows:

  1.75 * no. of nodes * mapred.tasktracker.reduce.tasks.maximum.
  The Reducer contains reduce(), which gets executed for each unique key emitted by mappers, as follows:

```
import org.apache.Hadoop.io.IntWritable;
import org.apache.Hadoop.io.Text;
import org.apache.Hadoop.mapreduce.Reducer;

import java.io.IOException;

public class DemoReducer extends Reducer<Text, IntWritable, Text,
IntWritable> {
    @Override
    protected void setup(Context context) throws IOException,
InterruptedException {
        super.setup(context);
    }

    @Override
    protected void reduce(Text key, Iterable<IntWritable> values,
Context context) throws IOException, InterruptedException {
        super.reduce(key, values, context);
    }

    @Override
    protected void cleanup(Context context) throws IOException,
InterruptedException {
        super.cleanup(context);
    }
}
```

- **Combiner**: The combiner, also known as **mini reducer** or localized reducer, runs on the mappers machine. It takes the intermediate key emitted by the mapper and applies the user-defined `reduce` function of the combiner on the same machine. For each mapper, there will be one combiner available on the mappers machine. The combiner significantly reduces the amount of data shuffling from mapper to reducer and thus helps in performance improvement. The combiners are not guaranteed to be executed.

- **Output format**: The output format translates the `reduce` functions key/value pair output and record writer writes it to the file on HDFS. By default, the key values of the output are separated by tab and records are separated by a newline character. The output format translates the final key/value pair from the `reduce` function and writes it out to a file by a record writer. By default, it will separate the key and value with a tab and separate records with a newline character. The default behavior can be changed by implementing your own output format.

We have covered the important components of the MapReduce framework. We will examine how execution flow works in the upcoming sections. The idea is to give you enough understanding of the framework. To make any significant changes, you must know where the impact of changes will be.

YARN and MapReduce

We have covered enough information about YARN in previous chapters. In this section, we will talk about the execution of MapReduce over YARN. The JobTracker in Hadoop version 1 has a bottleneck due to a scalability limit of 4,000 nodes. Yahoo realizes that their current requirement needs a scaling of up to 20,000 nodes. The latter was certainly not possible due to the legacy architecture of the job tracker. Yahoo then introduced YARN, which broke the function of the job tracker for efficient management. We covered the detail architecture in `Chapter 3`, *YARN Resource Management in Hadoop*.

The **node manager** in YARN has enough memory to launch multiple containers. The **application master** can request any number of containers from the **resource manager**, which keeps track of the available resources in the YARN cluster. The job type is not limited to MapReduce; instead, YARN can launch any type of application. Let's take a look at the life cycle of a MapReduce application on YARN in the following diagram:

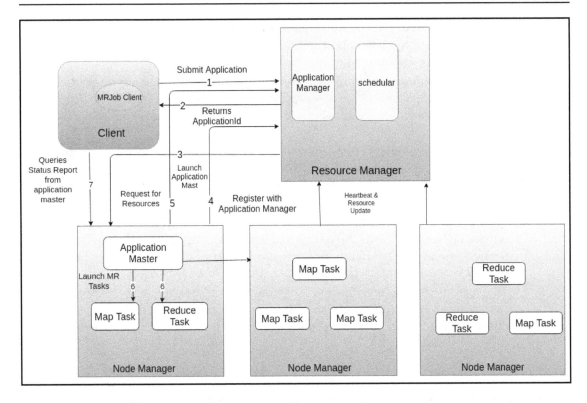

The preceding diagram can be explained as follows:

- The MapReduce job **client** requests a new application ID from the **application manager**. The **resource manager** sends the unique application ID to the **client** after validating the authentication and authorization of client. The **MR job client** encloses the metadata information about the application into `ApplicationSubmissionContext`, which also contains information to start the **application master**.
- The **resource manager** starts the **application master** on one of the **node managers**, which fulfils that container requirement for the **application master**. The **resource manager scheduler** selects the **node manager** where the **application master** will be launched.
- The **application master** creates a **client** object to make communication with the **resource manager** and **node manager**. The **application master** registers itself with the **resource manager** and the latter responds back with information such as access tokens, ACL list, and so on.

- The **MR job client** queries the **application manager** to obtain the information about a**pplication master** and can then talk directly to the **application master** for status, counter, and any other information.
- The **application master** computes the number of splits and sends a resource request for mappers and reducers to the **resource manager scheduler**. The request contains information about memory and CPU information that's required for the container.
- The **application master** receives the container for **map task** and **reduce task** and then it communicates with specific **node managers** to launch containers. The **node manager** in YARN can launch multiple containers on the same **node manager**.
- The **application master** also manages and monitors the individual **nap task** and **reduce task** and requests the additional container from **resource manager** if needed. It also ensures that if any task has failed or not responding, it can restart with new resources until the maximum attempt of retry is reached.
- The **application master** runs a task cleanup operation after all the **map tasks** and **reduce tasks** are completed. Finally the **application master** sends the unregistered request to **resource manager**, exits the execution, and frees up the container occupied.

MapReduce workflow in the Hadoop framework

The MapReduce execution goes through various steps and each step has scope for a little optimization. In the previous sections, we have covered the components of the MapReduce framework and now we will briefly look into the MapReduce execution flow, which will help us understand how each component interacts with each other. The following diagram gives a brief overview about the MapReduce execution flow. We have divided the diagram into smaller parts so that each step looks easier to understand. The step numbers are mentioned over arrow connectors and the last arrow in the diagram connects to the following diagram in the section:

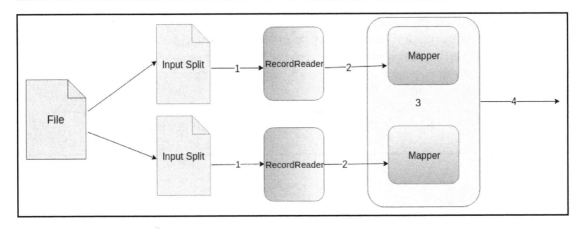

We will explain the different steps of the MapReduce internal flow here as follows:

1. The InputFormat is the starting point of any MapReduce application. It is defined in the job configuration in the `Driver` class of the application, for example, `job.setInputFormatClass(TextInputFormat.class)`. The `InputFormat` helps in understanding the type of input and how to read it. It returns the input split and record reader, which helps in reading records from the file. The size of the input split again depends on `InputFormat`, for example, the `TextInputFormat` split size will be equal to the `hdfs` block size that is defined with the property `dfs.blocksize`. For a non-splittable file format such as `.gzip`, the input split size will be equal to the single file size, which means that if there are 10 gzip files, then there will be a 10 input split.

2. For every input split, one mapper will be launched. That means that if `getsplit()` returns five splits, then five map tasks will be launched to process the splits. The `map` function defined in the `Mapper` class will be executed for each key-value pair of input splits returned by `RecordReader`. The RecordReader implementation depends on InputFileFormat and for TextInputFormat, every new line is considered as a new record.

3. The mapper processes the record. For every record, we may choose to emit one or more output and write it to the context object provided in the map function. The class that is responsible for collecting the map output is defined using the property `mapreduce.job.map.output.collector.class` and the default implementation is the `org.apache.Hadoop.mapred.MapTask.MapOutputBuffer` class. The following diagram is the continuation of the preceding diagram:

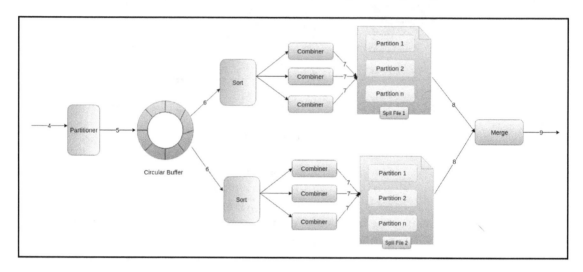

4. The output emitted by the map function goes to the `partition` class, which has the `getPartition()` method. The method calculates the partition number based on a specific algorithm and by default it uses `HashPartitioner`. The code for it looks as follows:

```
package org.apache.Hadoop.mapreduce.lib.partition;

import org.apache.Hadoop.mapreduce.Partitioner;

/** Partition keys by their {@link Object#hashCode()}. */
public class HashPartitioner<K, V> extends Partitioner<K, V> {

    /** Use {@link Object#hashCode()} to partition. */
    public int getPartition(K key, V value,
                            int numReduceTasks) {
        return (key.hashCode() & Integer.MAX_VALUE) %
numReduceTasks;
    }

}
```

5. The emitted output with a partition is now written to the circular buffer in memory. By default, the size of the circular buffer is 100 MB. It can be changed by assigning a new value to the property `mapreduce.task.io.sort.mb`. If the size of the output data exceeds, the data stored in the circular buffer will spill to the disk.

> **Spilling**: The data is spilled to the disk if the size of the data exceeds the limit specified in `mapreduce.map.sort.spill.percentage`, which means
>
> if `mapreduce.map.sort.spill.percent` is `0.8` and `mapreduce.task.io.sort.mb` is 100 MB, then the buffer size reaches 80 MB, which is 80% of 100 MB and it will be spilled to the disk. The spilling process runs in parallel and does not affect the `Mapper` function. Remember that the mapper process will only get blocked if the mapper processes the data much faster than spilling, because the buffer will get full and mapper have to wait until there is some space in the buffer to accept new records.

6. Before the data gets spilled to the disk, it is sorted by partition key and inside each partition, it is sorted with record keys. After the sorting, the combiner processes the records to reduce the amount of data that is written to the disk. The combiner is not guaranteed to be executed and if the size of the record emitted by mapper is larger than the buffer size, then both the sorting and combiner phases will be skipped and data will directly spill to disk.

7. For every spilling operation there will be a new file created on the local disk of the mapper. The location of the directory can be configured using the `mapreduce.job.local.dir` property.

8. After all the records are processed and spilled tasks are completed, the spill files are merged together to form a single map output file. This phase is called the **merge phase**. The merge process can process up to 100 files by default. This setting can be changed by changing the value of `mapreduce.task.io.sort.factor`.

If the number of files is greater than the value specified, the merge step will recursively merge files until all files are merged to a single file. If the total number of spill files is greater than `min.num.spills.for.combine`, the **Combiner** will be executed on the final merge result. The MapOutput File along with the index file are written to the mapper's local disk. The index file contains information such as number of partitions, start, end points of partition, and so on. The following diagram is the continuation of the preceding diagram:

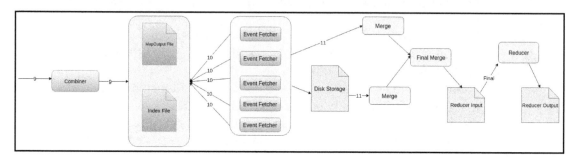

9. The next step is the shuffling of data from mapper to reducer. The reducer runs an event fetcher thread whose task is to poll the application master for the status of the mappers. After receiving the execution finish status of the mapper, it passes the mapper's information to another thread, which starts copying the data from the mapper using the HTTP protocol. By default, the number of fetcher threads is five and it can be changed by assigning a new value to `mapred.reduce.parallel.copies`. The data copied by fetcher threads is stored in the memory, and the size of the memory is 1 GB by default. The memory can be increased or decreased by changing `mapreduce.reduce.memory.totalbytes`. When the size of map output exceeds the specified percentage of memory that is defined using `mapreduce.reduce.shuffle.input.buffer.percent` (default 0.7) 70%, then the fetcher saves the output into the local disk of the reducer.

10. The merger is the next step after fetcher. The merger thread can run in parallel with the fetcher jobs and it merges all the records fetched by the fetcher. The final step in the overall process is running the reducer task. The reducer reads the record from the merged file and processes it inside the `reduce` method. For each key, the reduce task will be executed once, which means if there are 55 keys in the output merged file, the reducer will run the reduce function 55 times.

Common MapReduce patterns

The design patterns are the solution templates for solving specific problems. Developers can reuse templates for similar problems across domains so that they save time in solving problems. If you are a programmer, you would have used the abstract factory pattern, builder pattern, observer pattern, and so on before. These patterns are discovered by people who have been solving similar problems for many years. The MapReduce framework has existed for almost a decade now. Let's look into a few of the commonly used MapReduce design patterns across industries.

Summarization patterns

Summarization problems use the pattern widely across domains. It's all about grouping similar data together and then performing an operation such as calculating a minimum, maximum, count, average, median-standard deviation, building an index, or just simply counting based on key. For example, we might want to calculate the total amount of money our website has made by country. As another example, let's say you want to get the average number of times the users login to our website. One more example can be finding the minimum and maximum number of users by state. The MapReduce works with key-value pair. Thus, operations on keys are commonly used operations. The mapper emits the key-value pairs and the values of these keys are aggregated on the reducer. The following are a few commonly used examples of the summarization pattern.

Word count example

Many people who start to learn MapReduce development would have written Word count as their first program. Thus, it is sometimes known as the **Hello World** program of MapReduce. The basic idea of this program is to show how the MapReduce framework works. The pattern of Word count can be applied to use cases such as counting population by state, counting the total number of crime by state, finding total spending per person, and so on. Let's briefly discuss the word count program with a Mapper, Reducer, and combiner example.

Mapper

The job of a `Mapper` is to split the record, get each word from record, and emit a value of one with a word. The output key and the output value is of type `Text` and `IntWritable`, as shown in the following code:

```
import org.apache.Hadoop.io.IntWritable;
import org.apache.Hadoop.io.LongWritable;
import org.apache.Hadoop.io.Text;
import org.apache.Hadoop.mapreduce.Mapper;

import java.io.IOException;

public class WordcountMapper extends Mapper<LongWritable, Text, Text,
IntWritable> {

    public static final IntWritable ONE = new IntWritable(1);

    @Override
    protected void map(LongWritable offset, Text line, Context context)
            throws IOException, InterruptedException {
        String[] result = line.toString().split("    ");

        for (String word : result) {
            context.write(new Text(word), ONE);
        }
    }
}
```

Reducer

The MapReduce framework uses partitions to make sure that all the records with the same key always go to the same reducer. The reducer receives the list of values for the key and thus can easily perform aggregated operations such as `count` and `sum`, as follows:

```
import org.apache.Hadoop.io.IntWritable;
import org.apache.Hadoop.io.Text;
import org.apache.Hadoop.mapreduce.Reducer;

import java.io.IOException;

public class WordcountReducer extends Reducer<Text, IntWritable, Text,
IntWritable> {

    @Override
    protected void reduce(Text key, Iterable<IntWritable> values, Context
context)
```

```
        throws IOException, InterruptedException {

    int count = 0;
    for (IntWritable current : values) {
        count += current.get();

    }
    context.write(key, new IntWritable(count));
    }

}
```

Combiner

The combiner would be same as the Reducer in most of the cases and it can be added to the Driver class with the same class as that of the reducer. The advantage of the combiner is that it works as a mini reducer and runs on the same machine as the mapper, thus reducing the amount of data shuffling. The Driver class of the word count application as follows:

```
import org.apache.Hadoop.conf.Configuration;
import org.apache.Hadoop.conf.Configured;
import org.apache.Hadoop.fs.Path;
import org.apache.Hadoop.io.IntWritable;
import org.apache.Hadoop.io.Text;
import org.apache.Hadoop.mapreduce.Job;
import org.apache.Hadoop.mapreduce.lib.input.FileInputFormat;
import org.apache.Hadoop.mapreduce.lib.input.TextInputFormat;
import org.apache.Hadoop.mapreduce.lib.output.FileOutputFormat;
import org.apache.Hadoop.mapreduce.lib.output.TextOutputFormat;
import org.apache.Hadoop.util.Tool;
import org.apache.Hadoop.util.ToolRunner;

public class Driver extends Configured implements Tool {


    public static void main(String[] args) throws Exception {
        int res = ToolRunner.run(new Configuration(), (Tool) new Driver(),
args);
        System.exit(res);
    }

    public int run(String[] args) throws Exception {

        Configuration conf = new Configuration();
        Job job = Job.getInstance(conf, "WordCount");
```

```
    job.setJarByClass(Driver.class);


    if (args.length < 2) {
        System.out.println("Jar requires 2 paramaters :  \""
                + job.getJar()
                + " input_path output_path");
        return 1;
    }

    job.setMapperClass(WordcountMapper.class);

    job.setReducerClass(WordcountReducer.class);

    job.setCombinerClass(WordcountReducer.class);

    job.setOutputKeyClass(Text.class);
    job.setOutputValueClass(IntWritable.class);
    job.setInputFormatClass(TextInputFormat.class);

    job.setOutputFormatClass(TextOutputFormat.class);

    Path filePath = new Path(args[0]);
    FileInputFormat.setInputPaths(job, filePath);

    Path outputPath = new Path(args[1]);
    FileOutputFormat.setOutputPath(job, outputPath);

    job.waitForCompletion(true);
    return 0;
    }
}
```

Minimum and maximum

The minimum and maximum calculation for a specific field is a commonly used use case in MapReduce. Once the mapper completes its operation, the reducer simply iterates through all the key values and finds out the minimum and maximum in the key grouping:

- **Writables**: The idea behind writing custom writables was to save extra effort in splitting data at the reducer side and avoiding unnecessary problems that can occur from the delimiter. Most of the time, we choose the delimiter that is already present in the record and then it leads to the incorrect mapping of records with the field.

We will use the following `import` packages:

```
import org.apache.Hadoop.io.IntWritable;
import org.apache.Hadoop.io.LongWritable;
import org.apache.Hadoop.io.Text;
import org.apache.Hadoop.io.Writable;
import java.io.DataInput;
import java.io.DataOutput;
import java.io.IOException;
```

The custom `Writable` class encapsulates the details inside the `Writable` object, which can be used at the reducer side to fetch values for the records:

```
public class PlayerDetail implements Writable {
    private Text playerName;
    private IntWritable score;
    private Text opposition;
    private LongWritable timestamps;
    private IntWritable ballsTaken;
    private IntWritable fours;
    private IntWritable six;


    public void readFields(DataInput dataInput) throws IOException
{

        playerName.readFields(dataInput);
        score.readFields(dataInput);
        opposition.readFields(dataInput);
        timestamps.readFields(dataInput);
        ballsTaken.readFields(dataInput);
        fours.readFields(dataInput);
        six.readFields(dataInput);

    }

    public void write(DataOutput dataOutput) throws IOException {
        playerName.write(dataOutput);
        score.write(dataOutput);
        opposition.write(dataOutput);
        timestamps.write(dataOutput);
        ballsTaken.write(dataOutput);
        fours.write(dataOutput);
        playerName.write(dataOutput);

    }

    public Text getPlayerName() {
        return playerName;
```

```
    }

    public void setPlayerName(Text playerName) {
        this.playerName = playerName;
    }

    public IntWritable getScore() {
        return score;
    }

    public void setScore(IntWritable score) {
        this.score = score;
    }

    public Text getOpposition() {
        return opposition;
    }

    public void setOpposition(Text opposition) {
        this.opposition = opposition;
    }

    public LongWritable getTimestamps() {
        return timestamps;
    }

    public void setTimestamps(LongWritable timestamps) {
        this.timestamps = timestamps;
    }

    public IntWritable getBallsTaken() {
        return ballsTaken;
    }

    public void setBallsTaken(IntWritable ballsTaken) {
        this.ballsTaken = ballsTaken;
    }

    public IntWritable getFours() {
        return fours;
    }

    public void setFours(IntWritable fours) {
        this.fours = fours;
    }

    public IntWritable getSix() {
        return six;
```

```
        }

        public void setSix(IntWritable six) {
            this.six = six;
        }

        @Override
        public String toString() {
            return playerName +
                    "\t" + score +
                    "\t" + opposition +
                    "\t" + timestamps +
                    "\t" + ballsTaken +
                    "\t" + fours +
                    "\t" + six;
        }

    }
```

We will import the following packages and implement the custom `Writable` class:

```
import org.apache.Hadoop.io.IntWritable;
import org.apache.Hadoop.io.Text;
import org.apache.Hadoop.io.Writable;

import java.io.DataInput;
import java.io.DataOutput;
import java.io.IOException;

public class PlayerReport implements Writable {

    private Text playerName;
    private IntWritable maxScore;
    private Text maxScoreopposition;
    private IntWritable minScore;
    private Text minScoreopposition;


    public void write(DataOutput dataOutput) throws IOException {
        playerName.write(dataOutput);
        maxScore.write(dataOutput);
        maxScoreopposition.write(dataOutput);
        minScore.write(dataOutput);
        minScoreopposition.write(dataOutput);

    }

    public void readFields(DataInput dataInput) throws IOException {
```

```
        playerName.readFields(dataInput);
        maxScore.readFields(dataInput);
        maxScoreopposition.readFields(dataInput);
        minScore.readFields(dataInput);
        minScoreopposition.readFields(dataInput);

    }

    public Text getPlayerName() {
        return playerName;
    }

    public void setPlayerName(Text playerName) {
        this.playerName = playerName;
    }

    public IntWritable getMaxScore() {
        return maxScore;
    }

    public void setMaxScore(IntWritable maxScore) {
        this.maxScore = maxScore;
    }

    public Text getMaxScoreopposition() {
        return maxScoreopposition;
    }

    public void setMaxScoreopposition(Text maxScoreopposition) {
        this.maxScoreopposition = maxScoreopposition;
    }

    public IntWritable getMinScore() {
        return minScore;
    }

    public void setMinScore(IntWritable minScore) {
        this.minScore = minScore;
    }

    public Text getMinScoreopposition() {
        return minScoreopposition;
    }

    public void setMinScoreopposition(Text minScoreopposition) {
        this.minScoreopposition = minScoreopposition;
    }
```

```
@Override
public String toString() {
    return playerName +
            "\t" + maxScore +
            "\t" + maxScoreopposition +
            "\t" + minScore +
            "\t" + minScoreopposition;
    }
}
```

- **Mapper class**: The `Mapper` class in the MinMax algorithm maps the record with the custom writable object and emits the record for each player using the player name as key and `PlayerDetail` as value, as follows:

```
import org.apache.Hadoop.io.IntWritable;
import org.apache.Hadoop.io.LongWritable;
import org.apache.Hadoop.io.Text;
import org.apache.Hadoop.mapreduce.Mapper;
import java.io.IOException;

public class MinMaxMapper extends
        Mapper<LongWritable, Text, Text, PlayerDetail> {

    private PlayerDetail playerDetail = new PlayerDetail();

    @Override
    protected void map(LongWritable key, Text value, Context
context) throws IOException, InterruptedException {

        String[] player = value.toString().split(",");

        playerDetail.setPlayerName(new Text(player[0]));
        playerDetail.setScore(new
IntWritable(Integer.parseInt(player[1])));
        playerDetail.setOpposition(new Text(player[2]));
        playerDetail.setTimestamps(new
LongWritable(Long.parseLong(player[3])));
        playerDetail.setBallsTaken(new
IntWritable(Integer.parseInt(player[4])));
        playerDetail.setFours(new
IntWritable(Integer.parseInt(player[5])));
        playerDetail.setSix(new
IntWritable(Integer.parseInt(player[6])));

        context.write(playerDetail.getPlayerName(), playerDetail);

    }
}
```

- **Reducer class**: The `Reducer` is responsible for calculating the minimum and maximum scores of each individual by iterating through the list of records of players and emit the record using the `PlayerReport` writable object, as follows:

```
import org.apache.Hadoop.io.IntWritable;
import org.apache.Hadoop.io.Text;
import org.apache.Hadoop.mapreduce.Reducer;
import java.io.IOException;

public class MinMaxReducer extends Reducer<Text, PlayerDetail,
Text, PlayerReport> {

    PlayerReport playerReport = new PlayerReport();

    @Override
    protected void reduce(Text key, Iterable<PlayerDetail> values,
Context context) throws IOException, InterruptedException {
        playerReport.setPlayerName(key);
        playerReport.setMaxScore(new IntWritable(0));
        playerReport.setMinScore(new IntWritable(0));
        for (PlayerDetail playerDetail : values) {
            int score = playerDetail.getScore().get();
            if (score > playerReport.getMaxScore().get()) {
                playerReport.setMaxScore(new IntWritable(score));
playerReport.setMaxScoreopposition(playerDetail.getOpposition());
            }
            if (score < playerReport.getMaxScore().get()) {
                playerReport.setMinScore(new IntWritable(score));
playerReport.setMinScoreopposition(playerDetail.getOpposition());
            }
            context.write(key, playerReport);
        }
    }
}
```

- **Driver class**: The `Driver` class provides the basic configuration to run MapReduce applications and defines the protocol that cannot be violated by the MapReduce framework. For example, the `Driver` class mentions the output key class as `IntWritable` and the value as text, but the reducer tries to emit the key as text and the value as `IntWritable`. Due to this, the job will fail and an error will be thrown, as follows:

```
import org.apache.Hadoop.conf.Configuration;
import org.apache.Hadoop.fs.Path;
import org.apache.Hadoop.io.Text;
import org.apache.Hadoop.mapreduce.Job;
import org.apache.Hadoop.mapreduce.lib.input.FileInputFormat;
```

```
import org.apache.Hadoop.mapreduce.lib.input.TextInputFormat;
import org.apache.Hadoop.mapreduce.lib.output.FileOutputFormat;
import org.apache.Hadoop.mapreduce.lib.output.TextOutputFormat;
import org.apache.Hadoop.util.Tool;
import org.apache.Hadoop.util.ToolRunner;

public class MinMaxDriver {


    public static void main(String[] args) throws Exception {
        int res = ToolRunner.run(new Configuration(), (Tool) new
MinMaxDriver(), args);
        System.exit(res);
    }

    public int run(String[] args) throws Exception {

        Configuration conf = new Configuration();
        Job job = Job.getInstance(conf, "MinMax");

        job.setJarByClass(MinMaxDriver.class);


        if (args.length < 2) {
            System.out.println("Jar requires 2 paramaters :  \""
                    + job.getJar()
                    + " input_path output_path");
            return 1;
        }

        job.setMapperClass(MinMaxMapper.class);

        job.setReducerClass(MinMaxReducer.class);

        job.setCombinerClass(MinMaxReducer.class);

        job.setOutputKeyClass(Text.class);
        job.setOutputValueClass(PlayerReport.class);
        job.setInputFormatClass(TextInputFormat.class);

        job.setOutputFormatClass(TextOutputFormat.class);

        Path filePath = new Path(args[0]);
        FileInputFormat.setInputPaths(job, filePath);

        Path outputPath = new Path(args[1]);
        FileOutputFormat.setOutputPath(job, outputPath);
```

```
            job.waitForCompletion(true);
            return 0;
        }
    }
```

Filtering patterns

The filtering pattern is simply filtering out records based on a particular condition. Data cleansing is one of the commonly used examples of a filtering pattern. The raw data may have records in which a few fields are not present or it's just junk that we cannot use in further analysis. Filtering logic can be used to validate each record and remove any junk records. The other example could be web article filtering based on particular word/regex matches. These web articles can be further used in classification, tagging, or machine learning use cases. The other use case could be filtering out all the customers who do not buy anything that is more than 500 dollars in value and then process it further for any other analysis. Let's look at the following regex filtering example:

```java
import org.apache.Hadoop.io.NullWritable;
import org.apache.Hadoop.io.Text;
import org.apache.Hadoop.mapreduce.Mapper;

import java.io.IOException;

public class RegexFilteringMapper extends Mapper<Object, Text,
NullWritable, Text> {

    private String regexPattern = "/* REGEX PATTERN HERE */";

    @Override
    protected void map(Object key, Text value, Context context) throws
IOException, InterruptedException {

        if (value.toString().matches(regexPattern)) {
            context.write(NullWritable.get(), value);
        }
    }
}
```

The other example could be random sampling of data, which is required in many use cases such as data for testing applications, training machine learning models, and so on. The other common use case is to find out top-k records based on a specific condition. In most organizations, it is important to find out the outliers/customers who are genuinely loyal to the merchant and offer them good rewards or to find out about customers who have not used the application for a long time and offer them a good discount to get them to re-engage. Let's look into how we can find out about the top-k records using MapReduce based on a particular condition.

Top-k MapReduce implementation

The top-k reduce algorithm is a popular algorithm in MapReduce. The mappers are responsible for emitting top-k records at its level and then reducer filters out top-k records from all the records it received from the mapper. We will be using an example of player score that we used previously. The objective is to find out top-k players with the lowest score. Let's look onto the mapper implementation. We are assuming that each player has a unique score, otherwise the logic will require a little change, and we need to keep a list of players' details in values and emit only 10 records from the `cleanup` method.

The code for `TopKMapper` can be seen as follows:

```
import org.apache.Hadoop.io.IntWritable;
import org.apache.Hadoop.io.LongWritable;
import org.apache.Hadoop.io.Text;
import org.apache.Hadoop.mapreduce.Mapper;
import java.io.IOException;
import java.util.Map;
import java.util.TreeMap;

public class TopKMapper extends
        Mapper<LongWritable, Text, IntWritable, PlayerDetail> {
    private int K = 10;
    private TreeMap<Integer, PlayerDetail> topKPlayerWithLessScore = new
TreeMap<Integer, PlayerDetail>();
    private PlayerDetail playerDetail = new PlayerDetail();

    @Override
    protected void map(LongWritable key, Text value, Context context)
throws IOException, InterruptedException {

        String[] player = value.toString().split(",");

        playerDetail.setPlayerName(new Text(player[0]));
        playerDetail.setScore(new
```

```
IntWritable(Integer.parseInt(player[1])));
        playerDetail.setOpposition(new Text(player[2]));
        playerDetail.setTimestamps(new
LongWritable(Long.parseLong(player[3])));
        playerDetail.setBallsTaken(new
IntWritable(Integer.parseInt(player[4])));
        playerDetail.setFours(new
IntWritable(Integer.parseInt(player[5])));
        playerDetail.setSix(new IntWritable(Integer.parseInt(player[6])));

        topKPlayerWithLessScore.put(playerDetail.getScore().get(),
playerDetail);
        if (topKPlayerWithLessScore.size() > K) {
topKPlayerWithLessScore.remove(topKPlayerWithLessScore.lastKey());
        }

    }

    @Override
    protected void cleanup(Context context) throws IOException,
InterruptedException {
        for (Map.Entry<Integer, PlayerDetail> playerDetailEntry :
topKPlayerWithLessScore.entrySet()) {
            context.write(new IntWritable(playerDetailEntry.getKey()),
playerDetail);
        }
    }
}
```

The `TopKReducer` has the same logic as that of the reducer and we are assuming that scores are unique for players. We can also have logic for duplicate player scores and emit records for the same. The code for `TopKReducer` can be seen as follows:

```
import org.apache.Hadoop.io.IntWritable;
import org.apache.Hadoop.mapreduce.Reducer;
import java.io.IOException;
import java.util.Map;
import java.util.TreeMap;

public class TopKReducer extends Reducer<IntWritable, PlayerDetail,
IntWritable, PlayerDetail> {
    private int K = 10;
    private TreeMap<Integer, PlayerDetail> topKPlayerWithLessScore = new
TreeMap<Integer, PlayerDetail>();
    private PlayerDetail playerDetail = new PlayerDetail();

    @Override
    protected void reduce(IntWritable key, Iterable<PlayerDetail> values,
```

```
Context context) throws IOException, InterruptedException {

        for (PlayerDetail playerDetail : values) {
            topKPlayerWithLessScore.put(key.get(), playerDetail);

            if (topKPlayerWithLessScore.size() > K) {
topKPlayerWithLessScore.remove(topKPlayerWithLessScore.lastKey());
            }
        }
    }

    @Override
    protected void cleanup(Context context) throws IOException,
InterruptedException {
        for (Map.Entry<Integer, PlayerDetail> playerDetailEntry :
topKPlayerWithLessScore.entrySet()) {
            context.write(new IntWritable(playerDetailEntry.getKey()),
playerDetail);
        }
    }
}
```

The `Driver` class has a configuration of `job.setNumReduceTasks(1)`, which means that only one reducer will be running to find out the top-k records, otherwise, in case of multiple reducers, we will have multiple top-k files. The code for `TopKDriver` can be seen as follows:

```
import org.apache.Hadoop.conf.Configuration;
import org.apache.Hadoop.fs.Path;
import org.apache.Hadoop.io.Text;
import org.apache.Hadoop.mapreduce.Job;
import org.apache.Hadoop.mapreduce.lib.input.FileInputFormat;
import org.apache.Hadoop.mapreduce.lib.input.TextInputFormat;
import org.apache.Hadoop.mapreduce.lib.output.FileOutputFormat;
import org.apache.Hadoop.mapreduce.lib.output.TextOutputFormat;
import org.apache.Hadoop.util.Tool;
import org.apache.Hadoop.util.ToolRunner;

public class TopKDriver {


    public static void main(String[] args) throws Exception {
        int res = ToolRunner.run(new Configuration(), (Tool) new
TopKDriver(), args);
        System.exit(res);
    }

    public int run(String[] args) throws Exception {
```

```
Configuration conf = new Configuration();
Job job = Job.getInstance(conf, "TopK");
job.setNumReduceTasks(1);

job.setJarByClass(TopKDriver.class);


if (args.length < 2) {
    System.out.println("Jar requires 2 paramaters :  \""
            + job.getJar()
            + " input_path output_path");
    return 1;
}

job.setMapperClass(TopKMapper.class);

job.setReducerClass(TopKReducer.class);


job.setOutputKeyClass(Text.class);
job.setOutputValueClass(PlayerDetail.class);
job.setInputFormatClass(TextInputFormat.class);

job.setOutputFormatClass(TextOutputFormat.class);

Path filePath = new Path(args[0]);
FileInputFormat.setInputPaths(job, filePath);

Path outputPath = new Path(args[1]);
FileOutputFormat.setOutputPath(job, outputPath);

job.waitForCompletion(true);
return 0;
        }

    }
```

Join pattern

The join is commonly used across companies where reports are being created. The two datasets are joined together to extract meaningful analysis, which can be helpful for decision makers. The join queries are simple in SQL but achieving this in MapReduce is a bit complex. Both mappers and reducers operate on a single key at a time. Joining two datasets of equal size will require two times the network bandwidth as all data from both datasets will have to be sent to the reducer for joining.

The join operation is very costly in Hadoop as it requires data traversal from one machine to another over the network and thus it is important to make sure that enough effort is made to save network bandwidth. Let's look into a few join patterns.

Reduce side join

The simplest form of join available in the MapReduce framework and nearly any type of SQL join such as inner, left outer, full outer, and so on can be done using reduce side join. The only difficulty is that nearly all the data will be shuffled across the network to go to the reducer. Two or more datasets will be joined together using a common key. Multiple large datasets can be joined by a foreign key. Remember that you should go with map side join if one of the datasets can fit into the memory. Reduce side join should be used when both datasets cannot fit into memory.

MapReduce has the capability of reading data from multiple inputs and different formats in the same MapReduce program and it also allows different mappers to be used for a specific `InputFormat`. The following configuration needs to be added to the `Driver` class so that the MapReduce program reads the input from multiple paths and redirects to the specific mapper for processing, for example:

```
MultipleInputs.addInputPath(job, new Path(args[0]), TextInputFormat.class,
UserMapper.class);

MultipleInputs.addInputPath(job, new Path(args[1]), TextInputFormat.class,
PurchaseReportMapper.class);
```

Let's look into some sample code of the reduce side join and see how it works. The mappers emit the records with a key as `userId` and a value as an identifier appended to the whole record. The X is appended to the record so that on the reducer we can easily identify that the record is coming from which `Mapper`. The `UserMapper` class will look as follows:

```
import org.apache.Hadoop.io.Text;
import org.apache.Hadoop.mapreduce.Mapper;

import java.io.IOException;

public class UserMapper extends Mapper<Object, Text, Text, Text> {
    private Text outputkey = new Text();
    private Text outputvalue = new Text();

    public void map(Object key, Text value, Context context)
            throws IOException, InterruptedException {

        String[] userRecord = value.toString().split(",");
```

```
        String userId = userRecord[0];
        outputkey.set(userId);
        outputvalue.set("X" + value.toString());
        context.write(outputkey, outputvalue);
    }
}
```

Similarly, the second `Mapper` processes the purchase history of the users and emits the IDs of the users who purchase the goods, and appends `Y` to the value as the identifier, as follows:

```
import org.apache.Hadoop.io.Text;
import org.apache.Hadoop.mapreduce.Mapper;

import java.io.IOException;

public class PurchaseReportMapper {
    private Text outputkey = new Text();
    private Text outputvalue = new Text();

    public void map(Object key, Text value, Mapper.Context context)
            throws IOException, InterruptedException {

        String[] purchaseRecord = value.toString().split(",");
        String userId = purchaseRecord[1];
        outputkey.set(userId);
        outputvalue.set("Y" + value.toString());
        context.write(outputkey, outputvalue);
    }
}
```

On the `Reducer` side, the idea is to simply keep two lists and add user records to one list and purchase records to the other list, then perform a join based on the condition. The sample `Reducer` code will look as follows:

```
import org.apache.Hadoop.io.Text;
import org.apache.Hadoop.mapreduce.Reducer;

import java.io.IOException;
import java.util.ArrayList;

public class UserPurchaseJoinReducer extends Reducer<Text, Text, Text,
Text> {
    private Text tmp = new Text();
    private ArrayList<Text> userList = new ArrayList<Text>();
    private ArrayList<Text> purchaseList = new ArrayList<Text>();
```

```
        public void reduce(Text key, Iterable<Text> values, Context context)
throws IOException, InterruptedException {
            userList.clear();
            purchaseList.clear();

            while (values.iterator().hasNext()) {
                tmp = values.iterator().next();
                if (tmp.charAt(0) == 'X') {
                    userList.add(new Text(tmp.toString().substring(1)));
                } else if (tmp.charAt('0') == 'Y') {
                    purchaseList.add(new Text(tmp.toString().substring(1)));
                }
            }

            /* Joining both dataset */

            if (!userList.isEmpty() && !purchaseList.isEmpty()) {
                for (Text user : userList) {
                    for (Text purchase : purchaseList) {
                        context.write(user, purchase);
                    }
                }
            }
        }
    }
```

The joining operation is a more costly operation that requires shuffling of data over the network. If there is scope, the data should be filtered at the mapper side to avoid unnecessary data movement.

Map side join (replicated join)

If any of the data is small enough to fit into the main memory, then a map side join can be a good choice. In a map side join, the small dataset is loaded into the memory map during the setup phase of mapper. Large datasets will be read as input to the mapper so that each record gets joined with a small dataset and output is then emitted to a file. There is no reduce phase and therefore there will be no shuffling and sorting phases.
Map side join is widely used for left outer join and inner join use cases. Let's look into examples of how we can create a Mapper class for map side join and Driver class:

- **Mapper class**: The following Mapper class is a template for using map side join and you can use it and modify the logic according to your input dataset. The data that's read from a distributed cache is stored in RAM and therefore it can throw an out of memory exception if the file size does not fit into memory. The only option to solve this problem is to increase the memory space.

- The `setup` method is executed only once during the mapper life cycle and the `map` function is called for each record. Inside the `map` function, each record is processed and checked for any matching record available in memory to perform any join operation.

Let's look into the `Mapper` class template. The following is the code for the `Mapper` class:

```
import org.apache.Hadoop.conf.Configuration;
import org.apache.Hadoop.fs.Path;
import org.apache.Hadoop.io.LongWritable;
import org.apache.Hadoop.io.Text;
import org.apache.Hadoop.mapreduce.Job;
import org.apache.Hadoop.mapreduce.Mapper;

import java.io.*;
import java.net.URI;
import java.util.HashMap;

public class UserPurchaseMapSideJoinMapper extends
        Mapper<LongWritable, Text, Text, Text> {
    private HashMap<String, String> userDetails = new
HashMap<String, String>();

    private Configuration conf;

    public void setup(Context context) throws IOException {

        conf = context.getConfiguration();
        URI[] URIs = Job.getInstance(conf).getCacheFiles();
        for (URI patternsURI : URIs) {
            Path filePath = new Path(patternsURI.getPath());
            String userDetailFile = filePath.getName();
            readFile(userDetailFile);
        }


    }


    private void readFile(String filePath) {
        try {

            BufferedReader bufferedReader = new BufferedReader(new
FileReader(filePath));

            String userInfo = null;
```

```
            while ((userInfo = bufferedReader.readLine()) != null)
{
                /* Add Record to map here. You can modify value and
key accordingly.*/
                userDetails.put(userInfo.split(",")[0],
userInfo.toLowerCase());
            }

        } catch (IOException ex) {
            System.err.println("Exception while reading stop words
file: " + ex.getMessage());
        }

    }

    @Override
    protected void map(LongWritable key, Text value, Context
context) throws IOException, InterruptedException {
        String purchaseDetailUserId =
value.toString().split(",")[0];
        String userDetail = userDetails.get(purchaseDetailUserId);

        /*Perform the join operation here*/
    }
}
```

- **Driver class**: In the `Driver` class, we add the path of the input file that will be shipped to each mapper during their execution. Let's look into the `Driver` class template, as follows:

```
import org.apache.Hadoop.conf.Configuration;
import org.apache.Hadoop.fs.Path;
import org.apache.Hadoop.io.Text;
import org.apache.Hadoop.mapreduce.Job;
import org.apache.Hadoop.mapreduce.lib.input.FileInputFormat;
import org.apache.Hadoop.mapreduce.lib.input.TextInputFormat;
import org.apache.Hadoop.mapreduce.lib.output.FileOutputFormat;
import org.apache.Hadoop.mapreduce.lib.output.TextOutputFormat;
import org.apache.Hadoop.util.Tool;
import org.apache.Hadoop.util.ToolRunner;

import java.util.Map;

public class MapSideJoinDriver {


    public static void main(String[] args) throws Exception {
        int res = ToolRunner.run(new Configuration(), (Tool) new
```

```
MapSideJoinDriver(), args);
        System.exit(res);
    }

    public int run(String[] args) throws Exception {

        Configuration conf = new Configuration();
        Job job = Job.getInstance(conf, "map join");

        job.setJarByClass(MapSideJoinDriver.class);


        if (args.length < 3) {
            System.out.println("Jar requires 3 paramaters :  \""
                    + job.getJar()
                    + " input_path output_path
distributedcachefile");
            return 1;
        }

        job.addCacheFile(new Path(args[2]).toUri());

        job.setMapperClass(UserPurchaseMapSideJoinMapper.class);
        job.setOutputKeyClass(Text.class);
        job.setOutputValueClass(Text.class);
        job.setInputFormatClass(TextInputFormat.class);

        job.setOutputFormatClass(TextOutputFormat.class);

        Path filePath = new Path(args[0]);
        FileInputFormat.setInputPaths(job, filePath);

        Path outputPath = new Path(args[1]);
        FileOutputFormat.setOutputPath(job, outputPath);

        job.waitForCompletion(true);
        return 0;
    }
}
```

Composite join

The map side join on a very large dataset is known as a **composite join**. The advantage will be the same as we discussed in map side join previously in that the shuffling and sorting phase will be skipped as there will be no reducer. The only condition for composite join is that data needs to be prepared with a specific condition before it gets processed.

One of the conditions is that the dataset must be sorted with the key that was used for the join. It must also partition by the key and both datasets must have the same number of partitions. Hadoop provides a special InputFormat to read such datasets with `CompositeInputFormat`.

Before using the following template, you must process your input data to sort and partition to make the data be in the format that's required for composite join. The first step should be to prepare the input data and we must preprocess input data to sort and partition it using a join key. Let's look into mapper and reducer to sort and partition the input data.

Sorting and partitioning

The following `Mapper` swaps the first key with the index key. In our case, the index is already at the first position, so we may not require `getRecordInCompositeJoinFormat()` here:

```
import com.google.common.base.Joiner;
import com.google.common.base.Splitter;
import com.google.common.collect.Iterables;
import com.google.common.collect.Lists;
import org.apache.Hadoop.io.LongWritable;
import org.apache.Hadoop.io.Text;
import org.apache.Hadoop.mapreduce.Mapper;

import java.io.IOException;
import java.util.List;

public class PrepareCompositeJoinRecordMapper extends Mapper<LongWritable,
Text, Text, Text> {

    private int indexOfKey=0;
    private Splitter splitter;
    private Joiner joiner;
    private Text joinKey = new Text();
    String separator=",";

    @Override
    protected void setup(Context context) throws IOException,
InterruptedException {
        splitter = Splitter.on(separator);
        joiner = Joiner.on(separator);
    }

    @Override
    protected void map(LongWritable key, Text value, Context context)
```

```
throws IOException, InterruptedException {
        Iterable<String> recordColumns = splitter.split(value.toString());
        joinKey.set(Iterables.get(recordColumns, indexOfKey));
        if(indexOfKey != 0){
            value.set(getRecordInCompositeJoinFormat(recordColumns,
indexOfKey));
        }
        context.write(joinKey,value);
    }


    private String getRecordInCompositeJoinFormat(Iterable<String> value,
int index){
        List<String> temp = Lists.newArrayList(value);
        String originalFirst = temp.get(0);
        String newFirst = temp.get(index);
        temp.set(0,newFirst);
        temp.set(index,originalFirst);
        return joiner.join(temp);
    }
}
```

Reducer: The reducer emits the record with the key as the join key and the value as the entire record. The value is kept as key because in the composite join `Driver` class, we are going to use the `KeyValueTextInputFormat` class as the input format class for `CompositeInputFormat`, as shown in the following code:

```
import org.apache.Hadoop.io.Text;
import org.apache.Hadoop.mapreduce.Reducer;

import java.io.IOException;

public class PrepareCompositeJoinRecordReducer extends
Reducer<Text,Text,Text,Text> {
    @Override
    protected void reduce(Text key, Iterable<Text> values, Context context)
throws IOException, InterruptedException {
        for (Text value : values) {
            context.write(key,value);
        }
    }
}
```

Composite join template: The following template can be used to create and run your composite join example. You can modify the logic with respect to your use case. Let's look into its implementation.

`Driver` class: The `Driver` class takes four input arguments. The first two are input data files, the third one is the output file path, and the fourth one is the join type. The composite join supports only inner and outer join type, as follows:

```
import org.apache.Hadoop.fs.Path;
import org.apache.Hadoop.io.Text;
import org.apache.Hadoop.mapred.*;
import org.apache.Hadoop.mapred.join.CompositeInputFormat;

public class CompositeJoinExampleDriver {

    public static void main(String[] args) throws Exception {

        JobConf conf = new JobConf("CompositeJoin");
        conf.setJarByClass(CompositeJoinExampleDriver.class);

        if (args.length < 2) {
            System.out.println("Jar requires 4 paramaters :  \""
                    + conf.getJar()
                    + " input_path1 input_path2 output_path jointype[outer
or inner] ");
            System.exit(1);
        }


        conf.setMapperClass(CompositeJoinMapper.class);
        conf.setNumReduceTasks(0);
        conf.setInputFormat(CompositeInputFormat.class);

        conf.set("mapred.join.expr", CompositeInputFormat.compose(args[3],
                KeyValueTextInputFormat.class, new Path(args[0]), new
Path(args[1])));
        TextOutputFormat.setOutputPath(conf,new Path(args[2]));
        conf.setOutputKeyClass(Text.class);
        conf.setOutputValueClass(Text.class);
        RunningJob job = JobClient.runJob(conf);
        System.exit(job.isSuccessful() ? 0 : 1);
    }
}
```

Mapper class: The `Mapper` class takes join keys as the mapper's input key and `TupleWritable` as the value. Remember the join key will be fetched from the input files and that is why we said the input data should be in specific format, for example:

```
import org.apache.Hadoop.io.Text;
import org.apache.Hadoop.mapred.MapReduceBase;
import org.apache.Hadoop.mapred.Mapper;
import org.apache.Hadoop.mapred.OutputCollector;
import org.apache.Hadoop.mapred.Reporter;
import org.apache.Hadoop.mapred.join.TupleWritable;

import java.io.IOException;

public class CompositeJoinMapper extends MapReduceBase implements
        Mapper<Text, TupleWritable, Text, Text> {
    public void map(Text text, TupleWritable value, OutputCollector<Text,
Text> outputCollector, Reporter reporter) throws IOException {
        outputCollector.collect((Text) value.get(0), (Text) value.get(1));
    }
}
```

There are many more design patterns available in MapReduce, but covering all of the patterns is outside the scope of for this book.

MapReduce use case

We will cover a use case to find out the top 20 highly rated movies and will consider the condition that movies should have been rated by more than 100 people. The filter pattern we discussed earlier is a good fit for the use case. The format of the data is as follows:

title	averageRating	numVotes
tt0000001	5.8	1374

The title code refers to the specific movie. The rating is based on a 10 point scale. Let's look into the mapper, reduce code, and driver code. The template can also be used for similar use cases.

MovieRatingMapper

The job of the mapper is to process the record and emit the top 20 records it has processed for input split. We are also filtering out movies that have not been rated by at least 100 people. The code is as follows:

```java
import org.apache.Hadoop.io.LongWritable;
import org.apache.Hadoop.io.Text;
import org.apache.Hadoop.mapreduce.Mapper;

import java.io.IOException;
import java.util.Map;
import java.util.TreeMap;

public class MovieRatingMapper extends
        Mapper<LongWritable, Text, Text, Text> {
    private int K = 10;
    private TreeMap<String, String> movieMap = new TreeMap<>();

    @Override
    protected void map(LongWritable key, Text value, Context context)
throws IOException, InterruptedException {

            String[] line_values = value.toString().split("\t");
            String movie_title = line_values[0];
            String movie_rating = line_values[1];
            int noOfPeople=Integer.parseInt(line_values[2]);
            if(noOfPeople>100) {
                movieMap.put(movie_title, movie_rating);
                if (movieMap.size() > K) {
                    movieMap.remove(movieMap.firstKey());
                }
            }

    }


    @Override
    protected void cleanup(Context context) throws IOException,
InterruptedException {
            for (Map.Entry<String, String> movieDetail : movieMap.entrySet()) {
                context.write(new Text(movieDetail.getKey()), new
Text(movieDetail.getValue()));
            }
    }
}
```

MovieRatingReducer

The job of the `Reducer` is to filter out the top 20 movies by rating from all the output of multiple mappers. The `Reducer` simply iterates through values and maintains the top 20 movies by rating in memory. The records are flushed to the file once reducer completed its processing, as follows:

```java
import org.apache.Hadoop.io.Text;
import org.apache.Hadoop.mapreduce.Reducer;

import java.io.IOException;
import java.util.Map;
import java.util.TreeMap;

public class MovieRatingReducer extends Reducer<Text, Text, Text, Text> {
    private int K = 20;
    private TreeMap<String, String> topMiviesByRating = new TreeMap<>();

    @Override
    protected void reduce(Text key, Iterable<Text> values, Context context)
throws IOException, InterruptedException {

        for (Text movie : values) {
            topMiviesByRating.put(key.toString(), movie.toString());
            if (topMiviesByRating.size() > K) {
                topMiviesByRating.remove(topMiviesByRating.firstKey());
            }
        }
    }

    @Override
    protected void cleanup(Context context) throws IOException,
InterruptedException {
        for (Map.Entry<String, String> movieDetail :
topMiviesByRating.entrySet()) {
            context.write(new Text(movieDetail.getKey()), new
Text(movieDetail.getValue()));
        }
    }
}
```

MovieRatingDriver

The configuration is set in the `Driver` class and the total number of reducers is set to 1 because if we have multiple reducers, it will result in multiple top 20 movies and the final result may not meet the expectation, for example:

```
import org.apache.Hadoop.conf.Configuration;
import org.apache.Hadoop.conf.Configured;
import org.apache.Hadoop.fs.Path;
import org.apache.Hadoop.io.Text;
import org.apache.Hadoop.mapreduce.Job;
import org.apache.Hadoop.mapreduce.lib.input.FileInputFormat;
import org.apache.Hadoop.mapreduce.lib.input.TextInputFormat;
import org.apache.Hadoop.mapreduce.lib.output.FileOutputFormat;
import org.apache.Hadoop.mapreduce.lib.output.TextOutputFormat;
import org.apache.Hadoop.util.Tool;
import org.apache.Hadoop.util.ToolRunner;

public class MovieRatingDriver extends Configured implements Tool {


    public static void main(String[] args) throws Exception {
        int res = ToolRunner.run(new Configuration(), (Tool) new
MovieRatingDriver(), args);
        System.exit(res);
    }

    public int run(String[] args) throws Exception {

        Configuration conf = new Configuration();
        Job job = Job.getInstance(conf, "TopMoviwByRating");
        job.setNumReduceTasks(1);

        job.setJarByClass(MovieRatingDriver.class);


        if (args.length < 2) {
            System.out.println("Jar requires 2 paramaters :  \""
                    + job.getJar()
                    + " input_path output_path");
            return 1;
        }

        job.setMapperClass(MovieRatingMapper.class);

        job.setReducerClass(MovieRatingReducer.class);
```

```
        job.setOutputKeyClass(Text.class);
        job.setOutputValueClass(Text.class);
        job.setInputFormatClass(TextInputFormat.class);

        job.setOutputFormatClass(TextOutputFormat.class);

        Path filePath = new Path(args[0]);
        FileInputFormat.setInputPaths(job, filePath);

        Path outputPath = new Path(args[1]);
        FileOutputFormat.setOutputPath(job, outputPath);

        job.waitForCompletion(true);
        return 0;
    }
}
```

We have not used the combiner as we are only flushing out 20 records from the mapper at the end and therefore there is no need for the combiner here. Now let's look into how we can optimize MapReduce applications.

Optimizing MapReduce

The MapReduce framework provides a massive advantage for improving performance for large datasets as we can add more nodes to get more performance. The resources such as node, memory, and disk require significant investment, thus only adding the node should not be a parameter for performance optimization. Sometimes, adding more nodes does not help in getting more performance as the application performance could be something else, such as code optimization, unwanted data transfer, and so on. In this section, we will discuss some of the best practices to optimize the MapReduce application.

The performance of the application is measured by the overall processing time taken by the application. MapReduce processes data in parallel and thus it already provides a performance advantage over your MapReduce application. The following factors play important roles in optimizing MapReduce performance.

Hardware configuration

Hardware setup is the first step in the Hadoop installation. The performance is always dependent on the hardware configuration that's used for the application. The system with higher processing power will always give better performance than the system with lower processing power. The system with more memory will always give higher performance than the system with less memory. In Hadoop, the network bandwidth also plays a critical role as MapReduce jobs may require shuffling of data from one machine to another. Thus, we will need more network bandwidth to finish the process as fast as possible.

Operating system tuning

The operating system is responsible for most of the system level tasks, such as the following:

- **Transparent Huge Pages (THP)**: The machines that are used in Hadoop must have THP disabled. Let's understand what a THP is. In most Linux systems, the default block size is 4 KB and thus large files will have more physical blocks. The processing of files will require more blocks to be loaded to memory and thus require more iteration, which can cause slower performance. The THP allocates single memory addresses for all the blocks that are referred to as Huge Pages and thus require less iteration to read and process file.
  Hadoop already has a larger block size of 128 MB and blocks are not stored in contiguous memory. The blocks allow Hadoop to process data in parallel.

  The THP does not perform well in a Hadoop cluster and causes high CPU usage. The recommendation is to disable THP on each worker node. This sometimes results in higher performance improvement. The following code can be added to the `/etc/rc.local` file to disable THP:

  ```
      if test -f /sys/kernel/mm/redhat_transparent_hugepage/defrag; then
  echo never >
          /sys/kernel/mm/redhat_transparent_hugepage/defrag ;fi
  ```

- **Avoid unnecessary memory swapping**: In Hadoop, swapping may affect job performance and thus we should avoid unnecessary data swapping from memory to swap space and it should only be done whenever required. The swappiness setting can be made to 0 (zero) to avoid swapping unless absolutely required. The value 100 means it will immediately swap data to swap space. The swap space is backed by disk space and it is always slower than in memory. We need to add `vm.swappiness=0` to the `/etc/sysctl.conf` file to enable this.

- **CPU configuration**: In most operating systems, the CPU is configured to save power and thus not optimized for systems like Hadoop where the CPU is busy executing tasks most of the time. By default, the scaling governor is set to power save mode and we need to change it to performance mode by running the following command:

```
cpufreq-set -r -g performance
```

- **Network tuning**: The shuffling of data takes significant time in Hadoop and thus optimal use of network bandwidth can help us achieve higher performance. The master and worker interact with each other but the number of connections the master can make with the worker at a time is limited with net.core.somaxconn. In Hadoop, the connection between master and worker happens very frequently, so net.core.somaxconn should be set to a higher value. It can be done by adding or editing /etc/sysctl.conf in the following file:

```
net.core.somaxconn=1024
```

- **Choosing file system**: The Linux distribution comes with a default filesystem and it can have significant impact on Hadoop performance as it is designed to handle highly IO intensive workloads. The latest Linux distribution comes with EXT4 as the default file system, which performs better than the EXT3 file system. The file system logs a last access time for every read operation to file and thus causes a disk write operation for every read operation. The logging setting can be disabled by adding a noatime attribute to the file system mount option. Some use cases have noticed more than 20% performance improvement by adding noatime.

Optimization techniques

Good hardware selection does 30% of the job, but it is always good to have optimized and balanced cluster configuration based on the application requirement. Let's look into a few techniques that can help us increase the performance of MapReduce applications:

- **Using combiner**: The shuffling of data over the network is costly and thus the transfer of more data will always result in high processing time. The combiner acts as a mini reducer and it runs on the mappers machine. The reducer cannot be used in all the use cases but in most of the use cases we can use the combiner. It reduces the size of data that will be transferred over the network during the shuffling phase.

- **Map output compression**: The mapper processes the output and stores it in the local disk. This intermediate result can be compressed using LZO compression so that it reduces the disk I/O during shuffling. The results are more visible in cases where the mapper generates a large amount of output. To enable the LZO compression, we need to set `mapred.compress.map.output` to true.

- **Filter records**: It's always a good idea to filter out records at the mapper side so that the mapper always writes less data to the local disk. All the subsequent steps will run faster as they have to operate on comparatively less data than it had before. The majority of time will be saved during the shuffling phase as data has to move over the network to the reducer.

- **Avoid too many small files**: Too many small files may cause your application to take more time to execute. HDFS will store these files as a separate block and there will be an overhead of starting too many mappers to process these files. It is a good idea to compact the small files into a single large file and then run the MapReduce application over it. In some cases, I have seen around 100% performance improvement.

- **Avoid non-splittable file format**: The non-splittable file format such as `.gzip` will be processed at once instead of in chunks. If these files are too small in size, it's going to take more time to process because for each file, one mapper will be launched. If there are 200 files, then 200 mappers will be launched. The time to start and stop the mapper will take more time than processing the files. The best idea is to use a splittable file format such as Text, AVRO, ORC, and so on.

Runtime configuration

Hadoop comes with a set of options to tune memory, disk, and optimize the network performance of Hadoop jobs. Let's look into a few of them:

- **Java memory for tasks**: The map and reduce tasks are JVM processes and they take JVM memory for execution. More memory will eventually lead to better performance. The memory size can be set using the `mapred.child.java.opts` property.

- **Map spill memory**: The output records emitted by the mapper are stored in a circular buffer and the default buffer size is 100 MB. Remember that once the output size exceeds 70% of 100 MB, which means 70 MB, then data will spill to disk in the file. So if there are 7 spill operations then there will be 7 spill files. These files then merge together to form the single file. Our goal is to have a low number of spill files and to reduce I/O time for writing spill files to disk. This can be done by increasing buffer memory in case the mapper creates more spills. The size can be set using the `io.sort.mb` property.

- **Tuning map task**: The number of mappers are decided implicitly by the Hadoop framework and it is controlled by `mapred.min.split.size`. The idea is to control the number of mappers launched by the application so that there is a balance between the size of input data and the number of mappers. If there are too many small tasks running after each other, then it is good to set `mapred.job.reuse.jvm.num.tasks` to `-1`. Please do not use this property if you have long running tasks as launching a new JVM overhead will not add any boost to performance Instead, it may decrease the performance. In most cases, if the input data size is too big, then it is a good practice to increase the input split to a higher number.

File System optimization

The HDFS disk comes with specific file systems such as Ext4, Ext3, or XFS, and tuning the file system for better performance will significantly improve the processing performance. Let's look into a few commonly known options for HDFS tuning:

- **Mount option**: There are a few mount options that are efficient for Hadoop clusters. A right mount option provides good performance benefits. Remember to reboot the system after applying the setting as just changing the configuration will not work. You need to remount the system and then reboot it. Ext4 and XFS should have `noatime` configured.

- **HDFS block size**: The block size plays an important role in boosting the performance of NameNode as well as job execution performance. The NameNode keeps metadata for each block that it stores on `datanode` and thus takes more memory in case of a block size that is much less than the recommended block size. A processing engine such as MapReduce will also launch the number of mappers equal to the split size, which is generally equal to the block size. The recommended value for `dfs.blocksize` should be in a range of 134,217,728 to 1,073,741,824.

  Having an optimal HDFS block size boosts NameNode performance as well as job execution performance.

- **Short circuit read**: The `read` operation in HDFS goes through DataNode, which means that the client requests DataNode to read a file and DataNode sends the file data over TCP socket to the client. In short circuit read, the client directly reads the file and thus bypasses DataNode in the process, but remember it can only happen when the client is co-located with the data. In most cases, short circuit read provides significant improvement in performance. The following property can be added to `hdfs-site.xml` to enable short circuit read:

```
dfs.client.read.shortcircuit=true
dfs.domain.socket.path=/var/lib/Hadoop-hdfs/dn_socket
```

- **Small file problem**: Hadoop is optimized for storing large files and it is recommended to have a file size at list equal to the block size of HDFS. If there are too many small files, it will increase the NameNode memory overhead and will have a negative impact on performance during processing, as for each block, a new mapper will be launched.
  Therefore, it is recommended to perform compaction on such small files to make them a single large file.

- **Stale DataNode**: The DataNode sends a heartbeat to the NameNode at regular intervals so that the NameNode knows that its DataNode is still alive. The DataNodes that have not sent a heartbeat to the NameNode for a defined interval are assumed to have become `stale`. We should avoid sending any read or write requests to such DataNodes. This can be done by adding the following property to `hdfs-site.xml`:

```
dfs.namenode.avoid.read.stale.datanode=true
dfs.namenode.avoid.write.stale.datanode=true
```

Summary

In this chapter, we learned about MapReduce processing and overall processing works internally. We also looked into how MapReduce jobs are submitted to YARN and how YARN works to make sure your MapReduce job runs with efficiency and delivers status to you on successful completion. In the latter half of the chapter, we covered different design patterns that are commonly used in the industry and also covered basic templates to use these patterns.

In the next chapter, we will look into various Hadoop components added for efficient processing over HDFS. We will also look into some of the SQL engines used for data analytics and report generation.

Section 2: Hadoop Ecosystem

2

This section will introduce popular tools such as Kafka, Flume, Spark, Hive, and Flink. It covers information about these tools to help you get started with them.

This section consists of the following chapters:

- Chapter 5, *SQL on Hadoop*

- Chapter 6, *Real-Time Processing Engines*

- Chapter 7, *Widely Used Hadoop Ecosystem Components*

5
SQL on Hadoop

Hadoop is traditionally used as a File System with the capability to process high data volumes using distributed algorithms. However, with its growing popularity among non-programmers and business analysts, there is a need to read and manipulate high volume records using simple, well-known interfaces. SQL is always popular among non-programmers and data analysts because of its simple constructs and easy-to-understand logical syntax. Since Hadoop is used as storage for large volumes of data and because data exploration on top of Hadoop is one of the key use cases, SQL is ideal. Keeping those goals in mind, many SQL engines are developed to process and explore data stored in the Hadoop File System. There are many SQL distributions on Hadoop. Most of them are open source. We will look into those one by one in the following sections.

In this chapter, we will cover the following topics:

- Presto
- Hive
- Impala

Technical requirements

You will be required to have Hadoop 3.0.

The code files of this chapter can be found on GitHub:
https://github.com/PacktPublishing/Mastering-Hadoop-3/tree/master/Chapter05

Check out the following video to see the code in action:
http://bit.ly/2GOVwKt

Presto – introduction

The growing popularity of big data use cases has bought many new technologies and frameworks each of them comes with scalability, high throughput, and low latency in mind. Some companies have very large data warehouses storing hundreds of petabytes of data, and the data is used for various applications such as machine learning, batch analytics, and more. The data is used by technical engineering teams to get insights into businesses, which helps improve the product or services and yields new opportunities to generate more revenue for companies.

The performance of data warehouses plays an important role, as fast results will always help in quicker decision making. Data warehouses should have the ability to run queries in parallel and give results in less time to help businesses increase their productivity and profitability. It is also important to monitor the cost of the warehouse, which will also have an impact on the profitability of the organization. Hadoop came to replace the other legacy warehouse systems with the ability to store huge amounts of data and offer fault-tolerant, scalable, and distributed processing with low infrastructure costs. Facebook has a very large amount of data, which is now more than 400 petabytes. They have built up their Hadoop cluster and use various tools to process and store data such as MapReduce, Hive, Cassandra, and Kafka. However, systems such as Hive are good at processing huge amounts of data but are lacking in the ability to return results with low latency.

Facebook developed Presto to be a low-latency, distributed-processing query engine that can query any source and return results in little time, which means it is an interactive query engine with low latency. Presto is now open source under Apache Licences.

Presto can process data from multiple sources and run low-latency queries. It can scale from gigabytes to petabytes without any downtime for the application. Let's look into its architecture in detail.

Presto architecture

Apache Presto is a distributed query engine that follows a master-slave architecture where the coordinator is the master daemon and the workers are slave daemons. The following diagram shows the Presto architecture:

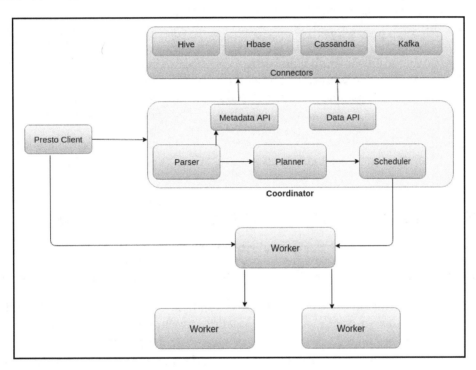

Let's discuss each component in detail:

- **Coordinator**: The **Coordinator** is the master daemon that accepts the request from the **Presto Client**. It has three main components, namely the **Parser**, **Planner**, and **Scheduler**. The **Parser** is responsible for parsing queries submitted by clients and detects syntax errors, if any. The **Planner** makes the execution plan for a query and passes the information to the **Scheduler** for execution. The **Scheduler** is responsible for launching workers on **Worker** nodes and keeping track of each **Worker** node. The **Coordinator** tracks the **Worker** nodes' activities and the execution of the query. The **Coordinator** creates a set of stages for executing the query plan, which is then converted into a series of tasks.

- **Worker**: The **Scheduler** schedules tasks on **Worker** nodes and the responsibility of a **Worker** node is to execute a task for data processing. **Worker** nodes fetch data from source using **Connectors** such as **Hive**, **Kafka**, and **Hbase** and shuffle data across **Worker** nodes. The **Coordinator** fetches the result from the **Worker** nodes and returns the results to the **Presto Client**. This stage can have multiple tasks executing in parallel to complete the stage.

- **Connectors**: Presto provides various **Connectors** to connect and interact with various commonly used data sources such as **Hive**, **HDFS**, and **Kafka**. There are already various in-built **Connectors** available with a Presto distribution, but you can also develop your own connector using the Presto library. The connector provides metadata information and data for queries. The **Coordinator** uses the **Connectors** to get metadata, which helps in building a query plan for execution.

The preceding architecture is simple and easy to understand. The next step is to look at how we install Presto and how to execute queries.

Presto installation and basic query execution

The installation process of Presto is simple and does not have dependencies on any other tool. The Java installation is a prerequisite required by Presto as it uses **Java virtual machine (JVM)** for task execution. Let's look into the installation process step by step:

1. Download the latest tarball of Presto from the Maven repository or the official website and un-tar it to a specific location of your choice on all nodes: `https://repo1.maven.org/maven2/com/facebook/presto/presto-server/`.

2. Presto requires a directory to store logs and other application data. The log directory should be created outside the installation directory, as it may help in preserving this data while upgrading Presto in the future:

```
mkdir /var/presto/
```

3. The next step is to configure the coordinator and worker node. One of the nodes should be configured for the coordinator and work as a master daemon for Presto. The `etc` directory should be created inside the Presto installation directory that contains the configuration file:

```
cd presto-server-0.201
mkdir etc
```

4. Create the following property file and configuration files inside the `etc` folder:

```
node.properties
jvm.config
config.properties
log.properties
```

5. Edit the `node.properties` file and add the following property in the file:

```
node.environment=stage
node.id=39d617c6-022a-4e13-a4cd-9718ad176818
node.data-dir=/var/presto
```

6. We will explain each of the properties as follows:

   - `node.environment`: This is the name of the Presto environment. All Presto nodes in a cluster needs to have the same Presto environment name.
   - `node.id`: The unique identifier for the node in Presto. The value can be obtained by running the `uuid` command on Linux.
   - `node.data-dir`: This is the location (File System path) of the `data` directory. Presto will also store the logs and other data in this directory.

7. Edit the `jvm.config` file and add the following commands. The file contains a list of command-line options, which is used for launching the Java virtual machine. The `heap dump` option will do a thread dump for the heap if it goes into an inconsistent state due to any out-of-memory issue:

```
-server
-Xmx32G
-XX:+UseG1GC
-XX:G1HeapRegionSize=32M
-XX:+UseGCOverheadLimit
-XX:+ExplicitGCInvokesConcurrent
-XX:+HeapDumpOnOutOfMemoryError
-XX:OnOutOfMemoryError=kill -9 %p
-XX:PermSize=150M
-XX:MaxPermSize=150M
-XX:ReservedCodeCacheSize=150M
-Xbootclasspath/p:/home/presto-server-0.60/lib/floatingdecimal-
0.1.jar
```

8. Edit the `config.properties` file, which contains the configuration for a
   coordinator or worker node. A single node in a Presto server can play the role of
   both a coordinator and a worker, but it's always a good practice to have a
   dedicated server to coordinate for better performance and manageability. The
   coordinator's `config.properties` are as follows:

```
coordinator=true
node-scheduler.include-coordinator=false
http-server.http.port=8080
query.max-memory=50GB
query.max-memory-per-node=1GB
discovery-server.enabled=true
discovery.uri=http://10.20.192.167:8080
```

9. We will explain each of the properties as follows:
   - `coordinator`: Enables the Presto server to work as a coordinator. The
     coordinator accepts the query from the client and manages the
     execution.
   - `node-scheduler.include-coordinator`: Enables the coordinator
     node to work as a worker that can handle the task processing work. It
     should be `false` for a larger cluster because it may affect the overall
     performance of a cluster as a coordinator requires more memory for
     parsing, planning, scheduling, and monitoring query execution.
   - `http-server.http.port`: The HTTP port for the Presto server can be
     used for communication between nodes.
   - `query.max-memory`: The maximum amount of memory that a query
     can use for execution.
   - `query.max-memory-per-node`: The maximum amount of memory
     that a query can use for execution on a single machine.
   - `discovery-server.enabled`: Presto nodes will register themselves
     with a discovery service on startup. The coordinator can act as a
     discovery service but it is always good practice to run a dedicated
     machine for the discovery service. It enables a node to act as a
     discovery service.
   - `discovery.uri`: The URI of the discovery server.

- Worker's Config.properties: The following properties should be added in the worker's `config.properties`:

```
coordinator=false
http-server.http.port=8080
query.max-memory=50GB
query.max-memory-per-node=1GB
discovery.uri=http://10.20.192.167:8080
```

10. The next step is to set the log level of Presto. It is very important to set the log level of the Presto application so that we can get the right logs into the correct log file. Edit the `log.properties` file and add the following property. There are four log levels: DEBUG, INFO, WARN, and ERROR. The default level is INFO:

```
com.facebook.presto=INFO
```

11. Create a `Catalog` directory inside the `etc` folder. Presto accesses data from different sources via specific connectors, which are mounted in catalogs. Inside the `catalog` directory, we can have source-specific property files. For example, the `jmx` connector will have the `jmx.properties` file and have the following property inside it:

```
connector.name=jmx
```

12. Launch the Presto application using the following command:

```
bin/launcher start
```

Functions

Database users have been using various function in queries including string functions, date functions, mathematical functions, and so on. Presto is a distributed SQL query engine and contains various built-in functions similar to other databases. We will cover a few commonly used functions in Presto.

Conversion functions

Conversion functions are used to convert one data type to another. They implicitly convert numeric values and character values to their appropriate data types if possible. We need to explicitly call conversion functions to convert between different data types. A query that is expecting the varchar value will not be able to automatically cast an int value into varchar. The different conventions can be seen as follows:

- cast: This converts a value to the specified type. By using this method, we can convert a numeric value to varchar or varchar to a numeric value. The cast function will give an error if it fails to cast the value:

  ```
  select cast((t1*1000 +t2.1000) as varchar) from t1.
  ```

- try_cast: This functions works just like the cast function. The only difference is the query will not fail if cast fails; instead it returns null:

  ```
  select try_cast((t1*1000 +t2.1000) as varchar) from t1.
  ```

- typeof: This function will return dataType for the given expression; for example:

  ```
  Select typeOf('chanchal') ;
  output :-- varchar(8)
  ```

Mathematical functions

Mathematical functions in Presto are very similar to the functions used in other databases such as MySQL and Oracle. We will look into a few commonly used functions as shown:

- abs (n): This function returns the absolute value of n:

  ```
  select abs(-5.65) as abs_value;
  ----------------------------------
  abs_value
  5.65
  ```

- cbrt (n): This method returns the cube root of a given number, which is n:

  ```
  select cbrt(8) as cubic_root;
  ----------------------------------
  cubic_root
  2
  ```

- `ceiling(n)`: This function returns n rounded up to the nearest integer:

```
select ceiling(6.6) as ceil_value;
---------------------------------
ceil_value
7.0
```

- `floor(n)`: This method returns n rounded down to the nearest integer:

```
select floor(6.6) as floor_value;
---------------------------------
floor_value;
6.0
```

- `power(x, y)`: This function returns x raised to the power of y:

```
select power(2,3) as power_value;
---------------------------------
power_value
8
```

String functions

String functions deal with modification, computation, and extraction operations on string columns. Let's look into a few commonly used functions:

- `concat(string1, ..., stringN)`: This function is used to concatenate multiple string into a single string: `select concat('packt','publication') as concat_value;`.
- `length(string)`: This function returns the length of a string.
- `lower(string)`: This function converts a string to lowercase, which means that `lowercase('CHINA')` would return CHINA.
- `ltrim(string)`: This function removes any leading whitespace from a string.
- `rtrim(string)`: This function removes trailing whitespace from a string.
- `replace(sourcestring, search)`: This function removes all instances of a search string from a string.
- `replace(string, searchstring, replace)`: This function replaces all instances of search strings with replace strings in the original string.
- `reverse(string)`: This function reverses the string.

- `split(string, delimiter)`: This `split` function in Presto is similar to the `split` function of Java that splits the string based on `delimiter` and returns the array of string.
- `split(string, delimiter, limit)`: This is an advanced version of the `split` function which splits the string on `delimiter` and returns an array of `string` with limit specified. The last string index in the array always contains everything left in the string.
- `split_part(string, delimiter, index)`: This function splits the string on `delimiter` and returns the string at `index`. The `index` starts with `1` and if the index is greater than the number of fields, then `null` is returned.

Presto connectors

Connectors are used to enable Presto to fetch and process data from specific data sources. Presto allows the user to execute and process data from two different sources in a single query. In this section, we will look into a few commonly used presto connectors and some of their important properties. We will discuss the following connectors in detail:

- Hive connector
- Kafka connector
- MySQL connector
- Redshift connector
- MongoDB connector

Hive connector

Hive is a data warehouse tool to process data stored on a distributed storage system such as HDFS. The default query engine for Hive is MapReduce which processes the data using the MapReduce engine. The MapReduce engine uses disk I/O for reading and writing intermediate output. Presto provides a Hive connector that will process and query data stored in a Hive. Hive data is stored in Hadoop Distributed File System. The metadata information is stored in PostgreSQL or MySQL. Hive also provides metastore service, which can be used to retrieve Hive metadata. The Hive connector allows querying the data stored in the Hive data warehouse.

Presto Hive connector uses the Hive metastore to get information about the file location and table metadata to process the data. The first step is to create a `hive.properties` file inside the catalog directory. Presto works with Hadoop version 2 with a built-in connector. The following properties should be added to the `hive.properties` file that is created:

```
connector.name=hive-hadoop2
hive.metastore.uri=thrift://localhost:9083
```

For example, once the connector is set, we can execute the following queries to test our installation:

```
CREATE SCHEMA hive.test_db
WITH (location = '/home/packt/presto')

CREATE TABLE hive.test_db.test_table (
    id int,
    name varchar,
    email varchar,
    age int
)
WITH (
    format = 'TEXTFILE',
    external_location = '/user/packt/employees'
)

select * from hive.test_db.test_table;
```

Kafka connector

Apache Kafka is a distributed, fault tolerant, and scalable messaging queue that is a part of the data pipeline in many big organizations. A Presto Kafka connector can be used to process data stored in a topic. Each topic will be treated as a separate table in Presto and each record represents a single row in Presto. Presto supports Kafka version 0.8 or later.

To enable Presto to access Kafka topic, create a `kafka.properties` file inside the catalog directory and add the following properties to it:

```
connector.name=kafka
kafka.table-names=topic1,topic2
kafka.nodes=10.20.10.1:9092,10.20.10.2:9092,10.29.10.3:9093
```

Configuration properties

The different configuration properties can be seen as follows:

- `kafka.table-names`: Represents a comma-separated list of all tables. By default, a table name is equivalent to a topic name and therefore each topic can be treated as a table in Presto. A table description file may contain mapping of topic to table name.
- `kafka.nodes`: This is a comma-separated list of Kafka brokers `hostname:port`. At least one broker address should be specified for Presto to work with Kafka.
- `kafka.connect-timeout`: Presto may not be able to connect to Kafka due to a network issue or due to a firewall issue. This property represents the timeout duration, after which presto will throw a connection timeout exception. The default value is 10 seconds, which should be higher in a production cluster.
- `kafka.buffer-size`: Presto acts as a consumer for Kafka and maintains a buffer for data that it reads from Kafka. The default buffer size is 64 KB, which can be increased to improve the performance.

Presto also provides some internal columns along with table columns of the Kafka topic. These columns contain important information such as `partition_id`, `partition_offset`, and message. The Presto CLI with Kafka can be run as follows:

```
./presto-cli --catalog kafka --schema schemaname
```

MySQL connector

The MySQL connector enables Presto to connect to a MySQL instance to query and create tables in an external MySQL database. Presto provides the ability to join tables from two different MySQL databases or between MySQL and other sources.

Like other connectors discussed before, we need to create a `mysql.properties` file inside the `catalog` directory and add the following properties to it:

```
connector.name=mysql
connection-url=jdbc:mysql://localhost:3306
connection-user=test
connection-password=test
```

We will explain this with the help of an example. Once all the configuration and setup is done, we can run presto to use the `mysql` catalog and run the following queries to test it. The first query will list all the schema available in `mysql`. The second query gives us all the tables in the `test_db` schema and the last query describes the table definition with a list of all the columns:

```
SHOW SCHEMAS FROM mysql;
SHOW TABLES FROM mysql.test_db;
DESCRIBE mysql.test_db.test_table;
```

Redshift connector

Amazon Redshift is a fully managed data warehouse service in the cloud. Redshift cluster consists of a set of nodes that have specific configurations to process the queries executed on Redshift. Presto Redshift connector fetches data from a Redshift cluster and processes it on Presto servers.

Create a `redshift.properties` file inside the `catalog` folder and add the following properties into it:

```
connector.name=redshift
connection-url=jdbc:postgresql://redshift.cluster:5439/database
connection-user=test
connection-password=test
```

The query example of Redshift is very much similar to that of MySQL but a few statements such as `alter` table, `delete`, `grant`, and `revoke` are not supported yet.

MongoDB connector

MongoDB is a document storage database that provides scalability, high availability, and high performance. Mongo collections are used as Presto tables and users can execute SQL-like queries over these. To set up the Mongo connector, we must have `mongo.properties` in the `catalog` directory by adding the following properties to it:

```
connector.name=mongodb
mongodb.seeds=host1,hostname:port
```

There are a few other properties that can be set in the catalog properties and they are:

- `mongodb.min-connections-per-host`: The minimum number of connections that can be reserved for the Mongo client. The default is 0, which can be changed if needed.
- `mongodb.max-connections-per-host`: The maximum number of connections allowed for a Mongo client. If more connections are required then they will be put into a waiting queue until the connection is released by any other service in the pool.
- `mongodb.connection-timeout`: Represents connection timeout in milliseconds and the default value is 10000.

Hive

The Hadoop ecosystem has helped organizations to save costs working with large datasets. Most Hadoop implementations use commodity hardware for storage and processing. This helps companies build low-cost infrastructures to provide high availability and scalable processing power. However, Hadoop's MapReduce processing model was mostly written in Java. The existing data storage infrastructure was mostly developed on traditional relational databases that uses SQL for data processing. Thus, it is necessary to have a tool that can provide similar functionality in the Hadoop ecosystem.

Hive is a data warehouse tool that can process huge amounts of data stored over a distributed storage system, like HDFS using SQL-like queries. The user uses Hive query language, which is very much similar to other SQL-like languages. Hive was developed with the purpose of easing the job of data warehouse users who have strong knowledge of SQL queries and who find it difficult to adopt Java or other languages for MapReduce. Users can define tables on top of data stored on HDFS and then can execute queries for transformation or generating reports.

Apache Hive architecture

The simplicity of **Hive query language** (HQL) has helped Hive to gain popularity among a large section of the Hadoop community. It is being used in many projects all over the world. Hive saves development time and for a company and therefore quickens its adoption. Let's discuss Hive architecture in detail. The following diagram shows the Hive architecture:

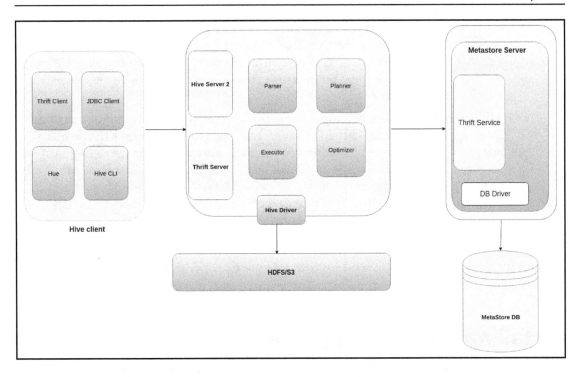

Hive consists of multiple major components and we will discuss a few of them as follows:

- **Hive client**: It is an application that can submit queries to the Hive server for execution. Hive provides a client interface that can be used by clients to make connection with Hive. The **Thrift Server** can connect and serve request to **Thrift Client**. Hive also provides a JDBC and **Hive Server 2** connectivity for clients.

- **Driver**: Driver is responsible for receiving Hive queries submitted by clients. **Driver** creates sessions for executing queries. It has four components called **Parser**, **Planner**, **Executor**, and **Optimizer**. We will discuss each of them in detail:

  - **Parser**: It is responsible for checking queries for any syntax error. The query may have the wrong order of words in a SQL statement or column that is not part of a table. The **Parser** is the first step of query execution and if the statement does not pass the parser check, then an error is returned back to the client via driver.

  - **Planner**: Queries that are successfully parsed are given to the **Planner** who generates plans for query execution by using table and other metadata information from metastore.

  - **Optimizer**: It is responsible for analyzing the plan and generating a new optimized DAG plan. The optimization can be done on joins, reducing shuffling data, and so on to optimize performance.

- **Executor**: Once the **Parser**, **Planner**, and **Optimizer** have finished their jobs, the **Executor** will start the execution of a job in the order of dependencies. The optimized plan is communicated to each task using a file. The **Executor** takes care of the tasks' life cycles and monitors their execution.

- **Metastore Server**: The **Metastore Server** is responsible for providing metadata information about a table to the **Driver**. The **Metastore DB** stores the details about the tables, partitions, schemas, columns, and so on. The database that stores metadata is pluggable and by default, hive uses Derby database but most of the time people prefer using MySQL as a **Metastore DB**. The Metastore provides a **Thrift Service** interface to access metadata information. The **DB Driver** is used to access metadata information from it.

The details of the internals of each component is out of scope for this book. The driver is responsible for managing end-to-end execution of queries and returns results back to the client.

Installing and running Hive

In this section, we will focus on how to install Hive. The Hadoop distribution such as Cloudera, Hortonworks, and MapR comes with software packages such as Hadoop, Hive, Pig, and Kafka. The users use these distributions to run Hive along with other tools. We will cover Hive installation so that you have a basic understanding of how it is set up. Hive is dependent on Hadoop for execution and thus it is important to have Hadoop installed on machines before we install Hive. We will study the installation in different steps as shown:

1. The first step in installation is to check for prerequisites. Hive requires Hadoop and Java 1.7 or later already installed on the machine. The `JAVA_HOME` and `HADOOP_HOME` properties need to be set in the configuration.

2. Download the Hive execution tar from the official website, `https://hive.apache.org/downloads.html`, and un-tar it at the specific location:

```
tar -xvzf apache-hive-2.3.3-bin.tar.gz
```

3. The next step is to set the Hadoop home in the `bashrc` file and add the following properties:

```
export HADOOP_HOME=/home/packt/hadoop3
export HIVE_HOME=/home/packt/hive
export PATH=$PATH:$HIVE_HOME/bin
```

4. Confirm the Hive settings by running the Hive version command and you should see the Hive version and detail as shown:

```
hive --version
```

5. Once the Hive path is set, the next step is to create a directory where the default table data will be stored. The `warehouse` directory will be created by using the following command and permissions will be set for both directories as shown:

```
hdfs dfs -mkdir -p /user/hive/warehouse
hdfs dfs -mkdir /tmp
hdfs dfs -chmod g+w /user/hive/warehouse
hdfs dfs -chmod g+w /tmp
```

6. The Hadoop path should be set in a Hive environment; it can be set in the `hive-env.sh` file:

```
HADOOP_HOME=/home/packt/hadoop3
HADOOP_HEAPSIZE=2048
export HIVE_CONF_DIR=/home/packt/hadoop3/conf
```

7. The next step is to set the configuration properties in `hive-site.xml`. This file contains properties such as the Hive warehouse location and metastore address. Also, add the warehouse location to the file:

```
<property>
    <name>hive.metastore.warehouse.dir</name>
    <value>/user/hive/warehouse</value>
    <description>location of default database for the
                 warehouse</description>
</property>
```

8. Run `hive` and execute queries:

```
hive
```

The Hive CLI can now be used to create databases, tables, and execute queries. Hive queries can be written in a file with the `.hql` extension and can be run using the `hive -f filename` command.

Hive queries

HiveQL is similar to SQL and provides an environment in Hive to work with tables, databases, and queries. Table creation in Hive is different from table creation scripts in RDMS because Hive is not a storage database, it's just an abstraction layer over a file stored on HDFS/S3. In the following section, we will start working with Hive.

Hive table creation

Hive has two types of table: internal or managed table and external table. The internal table deletes the data from a storage system when a table is dropped but an external table only deletes the table metadata and data will be available for further use. The following is an example of creating a table:

- **Table without partition**: The creation script of a Hive table may vary based on the type of file on which the table operates. The table for a text file with line separated record and tab separated columns can be created using the following script:

```
CREATE TABLE IF NOT EXISTS product(
product_id int,
product_name String,
product_catagory
price String,
manufacturer String
)
ROW FORMAT DELIMITED
FIELDS TERMINATED BY '\t'
LINES TERMINATED BY '\n'
STORED AS TEXTFILE
location '/user/packt/products;

CREATE EXTERNAL TABLE IF NOT EXISTS product(
product_id int,
product_name String,
product_catagory
price String,
manufacturer String
)
```

```
ROW FORMAT DELIMITED
FIELDS TERMINATED BY '\t'
LINES TERMINATED BY '\n'
STORED AS TEXTFILE
location '/user/packt/products;
```

- **Table with partition**: Partition table helps in optimizing performance of hive queries by reducing the amount of records that need to be searched to execute queries. The partition table is created as follows:

```
CREATE TABLE IF NOT EXISTS product(
product_id int,
product_name String,
product_catagory
price String,
manufacturer String
)
PARTITIONED BY (manufacturer_country STRING)
ROW FORMAT DELIMITED
FIELDS TERMINATED BY '\t'
LINES TERMINATED BY '\n'
STORED AS TEXTFILE
location '/user/packt/products;
```

The location is optional and if not specified. It will search for data in the Hive warehouse directory and if the directory is not present, then it will create one directory with the table name. The default warehouse directory is /user/hive/warehouse and therefore if the location is not specified the data should be in the /user/hive/warehouse/product directory.

The table description can be seen using the following command:

```
describe formatted product;
```

The output can be seen as follows:

```
hive> describe formatted product;
OK
# col_name              data_type               comment

product_id              int
product_name            string
product_price           double
manufacturer            string

# Detailed Table Information
Database:               default
Owner:                  hadoop
CreateTime:             Mon May 21 08:40:53 UTC 2018
LastAccessTime:         UNKNOWN
Retention:              0
Location:               hdfs://ip-10-254-0-45.ap-south-1.compute.internal:8020/user/hive/warehouse/product
Table Type:             EXTERNAL_TABLE
Table Parameters:
        EXTERNAL                TRUE
        numFiles                1
        numRows                 1
        rawDataSize             22
        totalSize               27
        transient_lastDdlTime   1526894412

# Storage Information
SerDe Library:          org.apache.hadoop.hive.serde2.lazy.LazySimpleSerDe
InputFormat:            org.apache.hadoop.mapred.TextInputFormat
OutputFormat:           org.apache.hadoop.hive.ql.io.HiveIgnoreKeyTextOutputFormat
Compressed:             No
Num Buckets:            -1
Bucket Columns:         []
Sort Columns:           []
Storage Desc Params:
        field.delim             \t
        line.delim              \n
        serialization.format    \t
```

Loading data to a table

Hive tables are abstractions over storage and thus each table has directory locations associated with it. Every time we select from a table, it searches data in this directory and returns the result. If there is no data present in this directory then it would simply return an empty result. The data can be loaded to this directory via two ways. The first way is to copy files to the table's directory location:

```
// for file available on local system
Hadoop fs -copyFromLocal product_2018.tsv /user/packt/product

// for file available on hdfs
hadoop fs -cp /user/packt/product_2018.tsv /user/packt/product
```

The other way to load data to a table is via a query. The following query will load data from a local system to the table:

```
LOAD DATA LOCAL INPATH '/home/packt/product_2018.tsv' OVERWRITE INTO TABLE
product;
```

The data in a partition table can be loaded using the previously mentioned method and if data in partitions are not loaded via the Hive interface, then we must run the msck command to update partition information in the metastore DB that means if data is copied from one location to the target tables partition location using copy command, then we must execute msck as follows:

```
msck repair table product;
```

The select query

The select query in Hive does not have major differences from the select queries of any other databases. Hive provides the ability to use UDF that we discussed previously. The order of different clauses in the statement looks like the following:

```
SELECT [ALL | DISTINCT] select_expr, select_expr2
FROM table_reference
[WHERE where_condition]
[GROUP BY col_list]
[ORDER BY col_list]
[CLUSTER BY col_list
| [DISTRIBUTE BY col_list] [SORT BY col_list]]
[LIMIT [offset,] rows]
```

The following query will get the number of products developed by each manufacturer:

```
Select count(distinct product_id) , manufacturer from product group by
manufacturer;
```

The explain command gives the Hive plan of execution. This is very important when we are debugging queries for optimization. The Explain command along with the query gives the detail plans in stages:

```
Explain Select count(distinct product_id) , manufacturer from product group
by manufacturer;
```

The preceding command will return the detailed execution plan for the query, which looks like the following:

```
hive> explain  Select count(distinct product_id) , manufacturer from product group by manufacturer;
OK
Plan optimized by CBO.

Vertex dependency in root stage
Reducer 2 <- Map 1 (SIMPLE_EDGE)

Stage-0
  Fetch Operator
    limit:-1
    Stage-1
      Reducer 2
      File Output Operator [FS_11]
        Select Operator [SEL_10] (rows=1 width=22)
          Output:["_col0","_col1"]
          Group By Operator [GBY_9] (rows=1 width=22)
            Output:["_col0","_col1"],aggregations:["count(_col0)"],keys:_col1
            Select Operator [SEL_5] (rows=1 width=22)
              Output:["_col0","_col1"]
              Group By Operator [GBY_4] (rows=1 width=22)
                Output:["_col0","_col1"],keys:KEY._col0, KEY._col1
              <-Map 1 [SIMPLE_EDGE]
                SHUFFLE [RS_3]
                  PartitionCols:_col0
                  Group By Operator [GBY_2] (rows=1 width=22)
                    Output:["_col0","_col1"],keys:manufacturer, product_id
                    Select Operator [SEL_1] (rows=1 width=22)
                      Output:["manufacturer","product_id"]
                      TableScan [TS_0] (rows=1 width=22)
                        default@product,product,Tbl:COMPLETE,Col:NONE,Output:["product_id","manufacturer"]

Time taken: 0.108 seconds, Fetched: 29 row(s)
```

Choosing file format

Files are important parts of a data pipeline as data is stored in files. We use different file formats for data management, configuration management, or for other uses. For example, the common files we have been using are XML, JSON, and CSV. Users may require a more lightweight data format and web service for Hadoop. The CPU and memory needed for processing the extra bytes, transporting over the network, and storing using storage are always limited and therefore it is important to choose the right file format and compression techniques. Let's look into how we do it.

Splitable and non-splitable file formats

Hadoop works very well with splitable files as it first splits data and sends it to the MapReduce API to further processing. Since Hadoop is used to store and process the data in blocks, we should begin reading the data at any point within a file to take full advantage of Hadoop's distributed processing system. The file formats that are commonly used are AVRO, ORC, Parquet, and sequences that are splitable files. Hadoop API can easily split these files in these file formats for further processing.

For example, a CSV file is splitable in nature. We can start reading at any line in the file and the data will still make sense. However, an XML file is not splitable as the XML consists of an opening tag at the start and a closing tag at the end, we cannot start processing in the middle of those tags. So Hadoop has to process the entire XML file.

 Compressed files are also non-splitable but we apply compression logic on block level in Hadoop to make sure the entire block is processed by Hadoop at once. This increases performance significantly.

The following factors are important to consider when choosing file formats for tables:

- Query performance
- Disk usage and compression
- Schema change

We will look into each of them in detail.

Query performance

The query in Hadoop is either to read the data from HDFS or to write data to HDFS. The write performance can be increased by choosing a file in a non-compressed format as compression takes more time. The reading performance will be compromised as during processing, compress data can help us process more data at a single mapper. The Hadoop is designed for write once read many, therefore we must always go for compression, as reading from file will happen frequently. The other factor could be the amount of data we are reading, which means we may choose to read the entire row or we only want to read a few columns. A columnar file format such as ORC is a better option for use in case of partial data read.

Disk usage and compression

A large file takes more space in Hadoop and it goes to 3+ times considering the replication factor. Reducing space could be another consideration and we can apply compression on data so that we get the benefits of speed in processing and lower storage space when storing the data. In some cases, AVRO without compression can reduce disk usage by up to 10%, while AVRO with compression can reduce it by up to 40-50%. However, parquet can reduce it to 80% by using specific compression techniques. Compression also helps in reducing network I/O. Hadoop network I/O plays a significant role during shuffling.

Schema change

Data with a flexible structure can have fields added, updated, or deleted over time and even varies amongst concurrently ingested records. Almost all of the file format choices focus on managing flexibly structured data. The AVRO file format provides the ability to deal with schema changes by allowing forward and backward compatibility of schema. The users can focus on data processing and the schema part will be taken care of by AVRO. It also helps in sharing data across two completely different platforms.

Introduction to HCatalog

HCatalog is a table and storage management service. HCatalog enables Hadoop tools such as Pig, MapReduce, and Hive to read table data. HCatalog is built on top of the Hive Metastore service and thus it supports file formats for which Hive SerDe (serialization and deserialization) can be done. HCatalog enables users to view data like relational tables without worrying about where the data is stored and what the format of a file is. The HCatalog supports **Text File**, **ORC File**, **Sequence File**, and RCFile format and Serde can be written for file formats such as AVRO. The following diagram shows the HCatalog architecture:

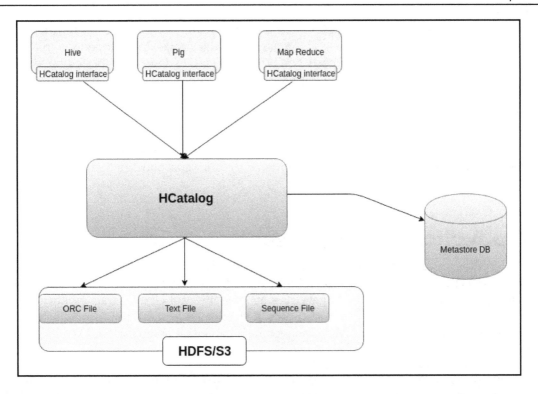

HCatalog provides an interface to use its services. Apache Pig can use `HCatLoader` and `HCatStorer` interfaces to read and write data via **HCatalog**. HCatLoader takes a table as an input, searches metadata for the table in the **Metastore DB**, and reads data from the table. Users can filter out records based on the partition immediately after the load statement:

```
test_table = LOAD 'test_table' using
org.apache.hive.hcatalog.pig.HCatLoader();

test_table_filter = FILTER test_table BY year == '2018' AND month == '07'
and day == '21';
```

Similarly, `HCatStorer` is used to write data to a cluster using HCatalog. The following statement will push data into the `test_filter` table. The table and database should have been created before executing the following statement:

```
store test_table_filter into 'test_db.test_filter' using
org.apache.hive.hcatalog.pig.HCatStorer();
```

The tables in HCatalog are immutable, which means data in the table and the partition are not appendable in nature. In the case of the partition table, data can be appended to a new partition without affecting the old partition, but in the case of a non-partitioned table, table must be deleted before executing the Pig script.

`HCatInputFormat` and `HCatOutputFormat` are the Hcatalog interface for the MapReduce application. `HCatInputFormat` and `HCatOutputFormat` are both implementations of the `InputFormat` and `OutputFormat` classes of Hadoop. The HCatalog is evolving and it will extend more interfaces in future to interact with other components of the Hadoop ecosystem.

Introduction to HiveServer2

HiveServer2 enables clients to execute queries against Hive via JDBC, Thrift-like protocol. HiveServer2 provides support for multi-user concurrency and authentication. It provides better support for open API clients such as JDBC and ODBC. The new thrift RPC interface allows it to handle concurrent clients. It supports advanced popular security features such as Kerberos and LDAP. The metadata can be accessed via JDBC/ODBC clients.

HiveServer2 also provides container resources for the execution engine. It allocates one worker thread per TCP connection. The disadvantage of such a connection is that a thread will be allocated to a connection even if a connection is idle, which leads to a decrease in performance. We hope that in the future release this drawback will be resolved.

Hive UDF

Hive has in-built functions to perform operations on columns with a specific datatype. The date functions can help in dealing with date columns, string functions can help in extracting or modifying the string, and maths functions can do calculations on numerical data. Although Hive provides many in-built functions for users, sometimes users may want to have functions that are not on the list of Hive's in-built functions and therefore Hive provides **user-defined functions** (**UDF**). Hive UDFs provide the ability to build your own functions that are not present in the Hive function library. Hive UDFs are written in Java and they can be created by implementing specific classes provided by the Hive interface.

Let's create one UDF that removes the HTML tags from an input string. One use case is news an API crawled from websites and this data had HTML tags in it, along with other columns.

We had to clean these columns by removing the HTML tags from the data and storing the data in the final table. We create a UDF that removes HTML tags by using a third-party library. Let's see how we created it.

The first step is to create a Maven project and add dependency in the configuration file, which is `pom.xml`:

```xml
<?xml version="1.0" encoding="UTF-8"?>
<project xmlns="http://maven.apache.org/POM/4.0.0"
         xmlns:xsi="http://www.w3.org/2001/XMLSchema-instance"
         xsi:schemaLocation="http://maven.apache.org/POM/4.0.0
http://maven.apache.org/xsd/maven-4.0.0.xsd">
    <modelVersion>4.0.0</modelVersion>

    <groupId>com.packt</groupId>
    <artifactId>masteringhadoop3</artifactId>
    <version>1.0-SNAPSHOT</version>
    <dependencies>
        <!--
https://mvnrepository.com/artifact/org.apache.hadoop/hadoop-client -->
        <dependency>
            <groupId>org.apache.hadoop</groupId>
            <artifactId>hadoop-client</artifactId>
            <version>3.0.0</version>
            <scope>provided</scope>
        </dependency>
        <!-- https://mvnrepository.com/artifact/org.apache.hive/hive-exec -
->
        <dependency>
            <groupId>org.apache.hive</groupId>
            <artifactId>hive-exec</artifactId>
            <version>2.3.3</version>
            <scope>provided</scope>
        </dependency>

        <!-- https://mvnrepository.com/artifact/org.jsoup/jsoup -->
        <dependency>
            <groupId>org.jsoup</groupId>
            <artifactId>jsoup</artifactId>
            <version>1.11.3</version>
        </dependency>

    </dependencies>
    <build>
        <plugins>
            <!-- build for Java 1.8. This is required by HDInsight 3.6  -->
```

```
            <plugin>
                <groupId>org.apache.maven.plugins</groupId>
                <artifactId>maven-compiler-plugin</artifactId>
                <version>3.3</version>
                <configuration>
                    <source>1.8</source>
                    <target>1.8</target>
                </configuration>
            </plugin>
            <plugin>
                <groupId>org.apache.maven.plugins</groupId>
                <artifactId>maven-shade-plugin</artifactId>
                <version>2.3</version>
                <configuration>
                    <transformers>
                        <transformer
implementation="org.apache.maven.plugins.shade.resource.ApacheLicenseResour
ceTransformer">
                        </transformer>
                        <transformer
implementation="org.apache.maven.plugins.shade.resource.ServicesResourceTra
nsformer">
                        </transformer>
                    </transformers>
                    <filters>
                        <filter>
                            <artifact>*:*</artifact>
                            <excludes>
                                <exclude>META-INF/*.SF</exclude>
                                <exclude>META-INF/*.DSA</exclude>
                                <exclude>META-INF/*.RSA</exclude>
                            </excludes>
                        </filter>
                    </filters>
                </configuration>
                <executions>
                    <execution>
                        <phase>package</phase>
                        <goals>
                            <goal>shade</goal>
                        </goals>
                    </execution>
                </executions>
            </plugin>
        </plugins>
    </build>

</project>
```

The HTMLTagRemover is explaines as follows:

HTMLTagRemover: We will create a base class that extends org.apache.hadoop.hive.ql.exec.UDF with an overloaded evaluate method name.

The evaluate method will pass a string containing a HTML tag and will make use of the jsoup date library to remove the HTML tag:

```
package com.packt;

import org.apache.hadoop.hive.ql.exec.UDF;
import org.jsoup.Jsoup;

public class HTMLTagRemover extends UDF {

    public String evaluate(String column) {
        if (column == null)
            return null;
        return Jsoup.parse(column).text();
    }
}
```

The shade plugin will help creating a JAR with all the dependencies. Executing the following command we get the following:

```
mvn clean package
```

Using UDF in hive query: Once the JAR is created, we can use it in a hive queries as follows:

```
hive> ADD JAR /home/packt/htmlremover.jar;
hive> CREATE TEMPORARY FUNCTION removehtml as 'com.packt.HTMLTagRemover';
hive> SELECT source,newstype,removehtml(article) FROM news LIMIT 10;
```

The query will return a result with the HTML tag removed. We can develop other UDFs as per client requirements by changing the return type of the evaluate function. Let's discuss some of the best practices while using HIVE as a data warehouse tool.

Understanding ACID in HIVE

ACID stands for **atomicity, consistency, isolation**, and **durability**. Atomicity means a transaction should complete successfully or else it should fail completely: that is, it should not be left partially. Consistency ensures that any transaction will bring the database from one valid state to another state. Isolation states that every transaction should be independent: that is, one transaction should not affect another. And durability states that if a transaction is completed, it should be preserved in the database even if the machine state is lost or a system failure occurs.

These ACID properties are essential for a transaction and every transaction should ensure that these properties are met:

- **Streaming ingest of data**: Many users have tools such as Apache Flume, Apache Storm, or Apache Kafka that they use to stream data into their Hadoop cluster. While these tools can write data at rates of hundreds or more rows per second, Hive can only add partitions every fifteen minutes to an hour. Adding partitions more often quickly leads to an overwhelming number of partitions in the table. These tools could stream data into existing partitions, but this would cause readers to get dirty reads (that is, they would see data written after they had started their queries) and leave many small files in their directories that would put pressure on the NameNode. With this new functionality, this use case will be supported while allowing readers to get a consistent view of the data and avoiding too many files.

- **Slow changing dimensions**: In a typical star schema data warehouse, dimensions tables change slowly over time. For example, a retailer will open new stores, which need to be added to the stores table, or an existing store may change its square footage or some other tracked characteristic. These changes lead to inserting individual records or updates of records (depending on the strategy chosen). Starting with 0.14, Hive is able to support this.

- **Data restatement**: Sometimes collected data is found to be incorrect and needs correction. Or the first instance of the data may be an approximation (90% of servers reporting) with the full data provided later. Or business rules may require that certain transactions be restated due to subsequent transactions (for example, after making a purchase a customer may purchase a membership and thus be entitled to discount prices, including on the previous purchase). Or a user may be contractually required to remove their customer's data upon termination of their relationship. Starting with Hive 0.14, these use cases can be supported via `INSERT`, `UPDATE`, and `DELETE`.

- Bulk updates using the `SQL MERGE` statement.

BEGIN, COMMIT, and ROLLBACK are not yet supported. All language operations are auto commit. The plan is to support these in a future release. Only the ORC file format is supported in this first release. The feature has been built such that transactions can be used by any storage format that can determine how updates or deletions apply to base records (basically, records that have an explicit or implicit row ID), but so far the integration work has only been done for ORC. By default, transactions are configured to be off. Tables must be bucketed to make use of these features. Tables in the same system not using transactions and ACID do not need to be bucketed. External tables cannot be made ACID tables since the changes on external tables are beyond the control of the compactor (HIVE-13175). Reading/writing to an ACID table from a non-ACID session is not allowed. In other words, the Hive transaction manager must be set to `org.apache.hadoop.hive.ql.lockmgr.DbTxnManager` in order to work with ACID tables.

The LOAD DATA... statement is not supported with transactional tables (this was not properly enforced until HIVE-16732). Transactions in Hive are introduced in Hive 0.13, but they only partially fulfill the ACID properties such as atomicity, consistency, and durability at the partition level. Here, isolation can be provided by turning on one of the locking mechanisms available with ZooKeeper or in memory. But in Hive 0.14, new APIs have been added to completely fulfill the ACID properties while performing any transaction.

Transactions are provided at the row level in Hive 0.14. The different row-level transactions available in Hive 0.14 are as follows:

- Insert
- Delete
- Update

Example

We will consider an example here of understanding ACID in HIVE:

1. Make sure you have a HIVE version that supports ACID. Type the following command on Command Prompt:

    ```
    hive--version
    ```

```
ravion:~ ravishankarnair$ hive --version
Hive 2.3.2
Git git://stakiar-MBP.local/Users/stakiar/Desktop/scratch-space/apache-hive -r 8
57a9fd8ad725a53bd95c1b2d6612f9b1155f44d
Compiled by stakiar on Thu Nov 9 09:11:39 PST 2017
From source with checksum dc38920061a4eb32c4d15ebd5429ac8a
ravion:~ ravishankarnair$
```

The version must be higher than 0.14.

2. Make sure you have set all the following properties to enable transactional capability on HIVE:

    ```
    set hive.support.concurrency = true;
    set hive.enforce.bucketing = true;
    set hive.exec.dynamic.partition.mode = nonstrict;
    set hive.txn.manager =
    org.apache.hadoop.hive.ql.lockmgr.DbTxnManager;
    set hive.compactor.initiator.on = true;
    set hive.compactor.worker.threads = 1;
    ```

```
hive> set hive.support.concurrency = true;
hive> set hive.enforce.bucketing = true;
hive> set hive.exec.dynamic.partition.mode = nonstrict;
hive> set hive.txn.manager = org.apache.hadoop.hive.ql.lockmgr.DbTxnManager;
hive> set hive.compactor.initiator.on = true;
hive> set hive.compactor.worker.threads = 1;
hive>
```

If you want to see any value set, type in `set hive.enforce.bucketing;`.

```
ravishankarnair — java -Xmx256m -Djava.library.path=/Users/ravishankarnair/cdh545/hadoop/lib/native -Djava.net.preferIPv4Stack=true -Dhadoop.log.dir=/Users/ravishankar...
hive> set hive.enforce.bucketing;
hive.enforce.bucketing=true
hive>
```

3. Create a table with the transactional property as `true`. The following is the syntax:

```
create table tschools(school_id int,
                      school_name string, school_loc string)
                      clustered by (school_id) into 5 buckets
stored as ORC TBLPROPERTIES ('transactional'
                      = 'true');
```

```
ravishankarnair — java -Xmx256m -Djava.library.path=/Users/ravishankarnair/cdh545/hadoop/lib/native -Djava.net.preferIPv4Stack=true -Dhadoop.log.dir=/Users/ravishankar...
hive> create table tschools(school_id int, school_name string, school_loc string
) clustered by (school_id) into 5 buckets stored as ORC TBLPROPERTIES ('transact
ional' = 'true');
OK
Time taken: 0.231 seconds
hive>
```

4. Insert values. You may run it twice:

```
insert into tschools values(1, 'abc', 'acb'),
                           (2,'bcd', 'bdc'),
                           (3, 'cde', 'ced'),
                           (4, 'efg','egf'),
                           (5,'fgh', 'fhg');

insert into tschools values(1, 'abc', 'acb'),
                           (2,'bcd', 'bdc'),
                           (3, 'cde', 'ced'),
                           (4, 'efg','egf'),
                           (5,'fgh', 'fhg');
```

Do `select * from tschools` to check:

```
ravishankarnair — java -Xmx256m -Djava.library.path=/Users/ravishankarnair/cdh545/hadoop/lib/native -Djava.net.preferIPv4Stack=true -Dhadoop.log.dir=/Users/ravishankar...
hive> select * from tschools;
OK
5          fgh        fhg
5          fgh        fhg
1          abc        acb
1          abc        acb
2          bcd        bdc
2          bcd        bdc
3          cde        ced
3          cde        ced
4          efg        egf
4          efg        egf
Time taken: 0.298 seconds, Fetched: 10 row(s)
hive>
```

Please observe the HDFS layout in `/user/hive/warehouse/tschools`. You will see delta files and internal representation of transactional tables.

5. Try to update a value based on the bucketed column, that is `school_id`:

```
update tschools set school_id = 10 where school_id = 5;
```

The output for the preceding command is as follows:

```
ravishankarnair — java -Xmx256m -Djava.library.path=/Users/ravishankarnair/cdh545/hadoop/lib/native -Djava.net.preferIPv4Stack=true -Dhadoop.log.dir=/Users/ravishankar...
hive> update tschools set school_id = 10 where school_id = 5;
FAILED: SemanticException [Error 10302]: Updating values of bucketing columns is
 not supported.  Column school_id.
hive>
```

You can't update a bucketing column.

6. Issue the following update and see that the results are updated:

```
update tschools set school_name='MIT' where school_id=5;
```

After the preceding command, run `select * from tschools` as follows to see that relevant rows are updated:

```
ravishankarnair — java -Xmx256m -Djava.library.path=/Users/ravishankarnair/cdh545/hadoop/lib/native -Djava.net.preferIPv4Stack=true -Dhadoop.log.dir=/Users/ravishankar...
hive> select * from tschools;
OK
5       MIT     fhg
5       MIT     fhg
1       abc     acb
1       abc     acb
2       bcd     bdc
2       bcd     bdc
3       cde     ced
3       cde     ced
4       efg     egf
4       efg     egf
Time taken: 0.171 seconds, Fetched: 10 row(s)
hive>
```

7. Issue the following `delete` command and see that the results are as expected:

```
delete from tschools where school_id =5;
```

```
ravishankarnair — java -Xmx256m -Djava.library.path=/Users/ravishankarnair/cdh545/hadoop/lib/native -Djava.net.preferIPv4Stack=true -Dhadoop.log.dir=/Users/ravishankar...
hive> select * from tschools;
OK
1       abc     acb
1       abc     acb
2       bcd     bdc
2       bcd     bdc
3       cde     ced
3       cde     ced
4       efg     egf
4       efg     egf
Time taken: 0.108 seconds, Fetched: 8 row(s)
hive>
```

This way, enabling ACID on HIVE allows users to have more flexibility in managing transactions at row level.

Partitioning and bucketing

This section explains the fundamental concepts of partitioning and bucketing.

Prerequisite

Partitioning data is often used for distributing loads horizontally. This has performance benefits, and helps in organizing data in a logical fashion: for example, if we are dealing with a large `employee` table and often run queries with `WHERE` clauses that restrict the results to a particular country or department. For a faster query response, the Hive table can be `PARTITIONED BY (country STRING, DEPT STRING)`.

Partitioning tables change how Hive structures the data storage and Hive will now create sub-directories reflecting the partitioning structure such as `.../employees/country=ABC/DEPT=XYZ`. If query limits for `employee from country=ABC`, it will only scan the contents of one directory `country=ABC`. This can dramatically improve query performance, but only if the partitioning scheme reflects common filtering.

The partitioning feature is very useful in Hive, however, a design that creates too many partitions may optimize some queries, but be detrimental for other important queries. Another drawback to having too many partitions is the large number of Hadoop files and directories that are created unnecessarily and the overhead to NameNode, since it must keep all metadata for the filesystem in memory. Bucketing is another technique for decomposing datasets into more manageable parts. For example, suppose a table using `date` as the top-level partition and `employee_id` as the second-level partition leads to too many small partitions. Instead, if we bucket the `employee` table and use `employee_id` as the `bucketing` column, the value of this column will be hashed by a user-defined number into buckets. Records with the same `employee_id` will always be stored in the same bucket. Assuming the number of `employee_id` is much greater than the number of buckets, each bucket will have many `employee_id`. While creating table you can specify things such as `CLUSTERED BY (employee_id) INTO XX BUCKETS;`, where XX is the number of buckets. Bucketing has several advantages. The number of buckets is fixed so it does not fluctuate with data. If two tables are bucketed by `employee_id`, Hive can create a logically correct sampling. Bucketing also aids in doing efficient map-side joins and so on.

Partitioning

A partition a divides large amount of data into multiple slices based on the value of a table column. Assume that you are storing information of people in the entire world, spread across 196+ countries spanning around 500 crores of entries. If you want to query people from a particular country (say, Vatican city), in the absence of partitioning, you have to scan all 500 crores of entries even to fetch 1,000 entries of the country. If you partition the table based on country, you can fine tune the querying process by just checking the data for only one country partition. Hive partition creates a separate directory for a column(s) value. Distributing execution load horizontally leads to a faster execution of queries in the case of a partition with low volume of data. That is, it gets the population from Vatican city very quickly instead of searching. There is the possibility of too many small partition creations. It is effective for low volume data for a given partition. But some queries, such as group by high volume of data, still takes a long time to execute. That is, grouping the population of China will take a long time compared to grouping of population of Vatican city. Partition does not solve the responsiveness problem in the case of data skewing towards a particular partition value.

Example: We have a `employee_details` table containing the employee information of a company, such as `employee_id`, `name`, `department`, and `year`. Now, if we want to perform partitioning on the basis of the `department` column, then the information of all the employees belonging to a particular `department` will be stored together in that very partition. Physically, a partition in Hive is nothing but just a sub-directory in the `table` directory. For example, we have data for three departments in our `employee_details` table—`Technical`, `Marketing`, and `Sales`. Thus, we will have three partitions in total for each of the departments. For each department, we will have all the data regarding that very department residing in a separate sub-directory under the table directory.

Bucketing

Bucketing decomposes data into more manageable or equal parts. With partitioning, there is a possibility that you can create multiple small partitions based on column values. If you go for bucketing, you are restricting the number of buckets to store the data. This number is defined during table creation scripts. The advantage of bucketing is that because of equal volumes of data in each partition, joins at map side will be quicker. It also offers a faster query response, like partitioning.

Best practices

The Hadoop ecosystem consists of various tools. Each tool has its specific purpose. As discussed in the previous section, Hive is a data warehouse tool which is used to analyze huge amounts of data. In any processing, the performance of an application is an important consideration. It can be achieved by following standard best practices. Let's look into a few best practices:

- **Execution engine**: Hive uses MapReduce as a default processing engine that runs MapReduce job for executing a query in the background. The high I/O time of MapReduce does not give good latency in terms of query response. We recommend to set the default engine to Tez. Apache Tez is a distributed execution engine that is designed for optimizing Hive query response time. It does not use a MapReduce engine for running Hive queries; instead, it prepares and optimizes a DAG plan and executes queries. It can be set for querying using the following command:

```
set hive.execution.enginer=tez
```

- **Avoid managed table**: Hive has two types of tables: managed tables and external tables. Managed tables can result in data being lost if used in production because, unfortunately, if a user drops the table, the data will be deleted from the target location on which the Hive table was created. We recommend using external tables in production so that the problem of lost data will not occur.

- **Choosing file format**: The file format plays an important role in performance and managing schema evolution. The tables from which reports are generated should use a columnar file format such as ORC, which optimizes the query response time by up to 10 times for some queries using compression on normal text files of greater data size. The columnar file format provides compression on columnar and strip level, which helps in saving storage space without compromising the performance of a query. The AVRO file format provides the ability to deal with schema evolution without breaking the old implementation.

- **Partitioning**: Hive can be used to process terabytes to petabytes of data. The table in Hive should be partitioned whenever required and in most cases we should partition it. The partitioned table helps in optimizing performance by enabling hive to search data in specific partitions only. For example, suppose we have 10 years of data stored on HDFS and a sales table is created on top of it. The user wants to execute a query to get the report of the last 1 year. Imagine if partitioning is not done on the table and Hive executes the query on it: it will search the entire 10 years of data to give the result. In the case of a partitioned table, it will only search the data in the current year partition, assuming the partition is done on the year column.
- **Normalization**: Joining is a costly operation in Hive because it requires data to be shuffled across a network. The tables in Hive should not be in normalization form because to get the report from Hive, we have to do joins that will result in a higher response time. The tables in Hive should be flat and in normalized form so that users can avoid joins as much as possible.

Container optimization and query optimization are some other techniques that can be considered as best practices.

Impala

Impala is a modern, open source **massive parallel processing (MPP)** SQL engine designed to work with a Hadoop environment. It provides the ability to execute queries with low latency. Hive does not meet the expectation for use cases requiring interactive analytics in a multi-user environment. Impala is integrated into the Hadoop environment and uses a number of standard Hadoop components such as Metastore, HDFS, HBase, YARN, and Sentry. Unlike hive, it does not run MapReduce jobs to get results. Hive uses the MapReduce engine for execution and the intermediate output results are stored on disk, which acts as an input to another job.

Impala architecture

Impala is a **massive parallel processing (MPP)** distributed query execution engine. It utilizes the resources of an existing Hadoop cluster. It does not use MapReduce. However, it utilizes the data locality feature of Hadoop processing. Let's discuss the Impala architecture and its components in detail.

The following diagram shows the Impala architecture:

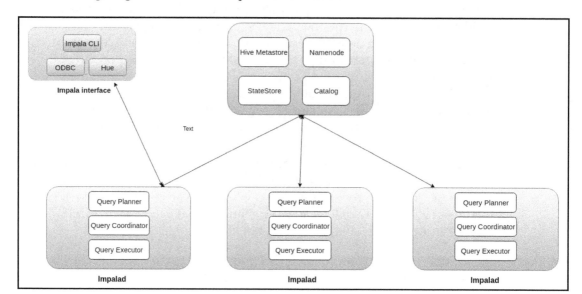

The Impala architecture consists of three major components:

- **Impala daemon (Impalad)**: In a Hadoop cluster, an Impala daemon is deployed on every data node, which helps Impala to take advantage of data locality. The Impala daemon is responsible for accepting query requests from Impala client interfaces and plans the execution of queries across a cluster. The user submits the query to Impalad and this acts as a coordinator for the query. The coordinator distributes the execution work across the cluster. Other Impalad daemons execute the query and transmit the intermediate query results back to the central coordinator node. The coordinator node is responsible for aggregating the result and sending it back to the client.

 In Impala 2.9 or later, we can determine the number of coordinators in advance so that only a few nodes will act as coordinators and others will work as executors. This removes the overhead of reserving RAM for all the Impalads that are not coordinators.

- **StateStore daemon (statestored)**: The Statestore is responsible for checking the health of Impalad in a cluster. If any Impalad node goes down due to any failure, such as a hardware failure, network, or software error, then Statestore informs all other Impala daemons so that future queries will not make any request to the failed node. The Statesstore daemons run on any single machine and are not considered as highly available. If a statestore daemons fails for any reason, the Impala daemons will work as usual and will distribute work among them to complete the user's query. The only disadvantage is that the cluster becomes less robust if Statesstore is not running. The Statesstore re-establishes the connection with other Impala daemons when it comes up again.
- **Catalog daemon (Catalogd)**: This daemon is responsible for providing metadata information to other Impala Daemons using the Statesstore service. The Catalogd pulls information from other metadata stores such as the Hive Metastore and converts it into an aggregated Impala-supported catalog structure. If a new table is created or the schema of a table is updated, we have to refresh the Impalad daemon using the `REFRESH` and `INVALIDATE METADATA` statements. This will send the updated information to all the Impala daemons running on the cluster.

The overall Impala execution is handled by these three components. Let's look into the job execution workflow in Impala.

Understanding the Impala interface and queries

The Impala interface allows users to interact with it for query execution. Users submit queries through the Impala interface; Impala will execute the query and returns the response via the same interface. The following are some commonly used interfaces of Impala:

- **Impala shell**: The Impala shell is a basic and commonly used interface to set up databases and tables, insert data into tables, and issue queries for report generation. There are a few options available that can work with the Impala shell. Users can run an interactive Impala shell by executing the following command:

```
impala-shell
```

`impala-shell` comes with various options and the following are a few of them:

- `-f`: A file containing the Impala queries can be run using the `-f` option. The file may contain multiple Impala SQL statements or statements to create, delete, or modify table structures.
- `-q`: This option can be used to run a single Impala query without opening an Impala interactive query shell.
- `-o`: The option can be used to set the output file location for an Impala query result. Generally, it is used with the `-f` option.

The Hue web interface and JDBC/ODBC interface are explained as follows:

- **Hue web interface**: Hue provides a nice web GUI to users that can be used to run DDL, DML, or `select` queries on Impala. Users do not have to log in to servers and run an Impala shell. They can type their queries on a GUI and run it by clicking the **Run** button. The results of the query will be returned back to the GUI.
- **JDBC/ODBC interface**: The Cloudera JDBC Driver provides the ability to connect to Impala using the JDBC/ODBC port of Impala for query execution. It allows access to Impala from commercial BI tools through software written in JDBC-supported languages. An Impala server creates JDBC connections through port 21050 by default. Users should make sure this port available for communication with other hosts on the network.

The Impala daemon process listens to any requests coming from the previously described interfaces via several ports. The command-line interface and the web-based interface share the same port but JDBC and ODBC use different ports to listen for the incoming queries.

Practicing Impala

This section demonstrates techniques for finding your way around the tables and databases of an unfamiliar (possibly empty) Impala instance. When you connect to an Impala instance for the first time, you use the SHOW DATABASES and SHOW TABLES statements to view the most common types of objects. Also, call the version() function to confirm which version of Impala you are running; the version number is important when consulting documentation and dealing with support issues.

A completely empty Impala instance contains no tables, but still has two databases:

- Default, where new tables are created when you do not specify any other database
- _impala_builtins, a system database used to hold all the built-in functions

The following example shows how to see the available databases, and the tables in each. If the list of databases or tables is long, you can use wildcard notation to locate specific databases or tables based on their names. Type the following in Command Prompt in a Cloudera virtual machine:

```
impala-shell -i localhost --quiet
```

The version() and show databases will give the following output:

Now you can get tables with the `select current_database();` query:

```
                                        cloudera@quickstart:~                    _ □ ×
 File  Edit  View  Search  Terminal  Help

[localhost:21000] > select current_database();
+--------------------+
| current_database() |
+--------------------+
| default            |
+--------------------+
[localhost:21000] > show tables in default;
+-------------+
| name        |
+-------------+
| customers   |
| departments |
| employee    |
| orders      |
| orders1     |
| schools     |
+-------------+
[localhost:21000] > █
```

You can issue a `select` as follows:

```
                                        cloudera@quickstart:~
 File  Edit  View  Search  Terminal  Help
[localhost:21000] > select * from departments;
+-----------------+-------------------+
| department_id   | department_name   |
+-----------------+-------------------+
| 4               | Apparel           |
| 5               | Golf              |
| 2               | Fitness           |
| 3               | Footwear          |
| 6               | Outdoors          |
| 7               | Fan Shop          |
+-----------------+-------------------+
[localhost:21000] > █
```

You can also view the column names with the following command:

```
describe departments;
```

You can even write a `join` condition on two tables, as follows:

```
select word from emp join dept on (emp.deptno = dept.deptno);
```

The USE command can be used to switch databases. For example, if you want to use the database named passion, write `use passion;`.

Loading Data from CSV files

Let's create two subdirectories, `sample1` and `sample2`, in a directory called passion in HDFS. Use the –p option to create parent directories that do not exist. Download data (`data1.csv` and `data2.csv`) from `http://www.forourson.com/passion/impala/data/`. We need to put `data1.csv` into the `passion/sample1` HDFS directory and `data2.csv` into the `passion/sample2` HDFS directory.

The steps are shown as follows:

```
cloudera@quickstart:~
File  Edit  View  Search  Terminal  Help
[cloudera@quickstart ~]$ hadoop fs -mkdir -p passion/sample1
[cloudera@quickstart ~]$ hadoop fs -mkdir -p passion/sample2
[cloudera@quickstart ~]$ hadoop fs -put data1.csv passion/sample1
[cloudera@quickstart ~]$ hadoop fs -put data2.csv passion/sample2
[cloudera@quickstart ~]$
[cloudera@quickstart ~]$


[cloudera@quickstart ~]$
```

Let's create three tables as follows (two are external tables and one is a managed one):

```
CREATE EXTERNAL TABLE table1
(
id INT,
col_1 BOOLEAN,
col_2 DOUBLE,
col_3 TIMESTAMP
)
ROW FORMAT DELIMITED FIELDS TERMINATED BY ','
LOCATION '/user/cloudera/passion/sample1';
CREATE EXTERNAL TABLE table2
(
id INT,
col_1 BOOLEAN,
col_2 DOUBLE
)
ROW FORMAT DELIMITED FIELDS TERMINATED BY ','
LOCATION '/user/cloudera/passion/sample2';
CREATE TABLE table3
(
id INT,
col_1 BOOLEAN,
col_2 DOUBLE,
month INT,
day INT
)
ROW FORMAT DELIMITED FIELDS TERMINATED BY ',' ;
```

Now you can select data from these tables:

```
cloudera@quickstart:~
File  Edit  View  Search  Terminal  Help

[localhost:21000] > select * from table1;
+----+-------+-----------+------------------------------+
| id | col_1 | col_2     | col_3                        |
+----+-------+-----------+------------------------------+
| 1  | true  | 123.123   | 2012-10-24 08:55:00          |
| 2  | false | 1243.5    | 2012-10-25 13:40:00          |
| 3  | false | 24453.325 | 2008-08-22 09:33:21.123000000 |
| 4  | false | 243423.325| 2007-05-12 22:32:21.334540000 |
| 5  | true  | 243.325   | 1953-04-22 09:11:33          |
+----+-------+-----------+------------------------------+
[localhost:21000] > select * from table2;
+----+-------+---------------+
| id | col_1 | col_2         |
+----+-------+---------------+
| 1  | true  | 12789.123     |
| 2  | false | 1243.5        |
| 3  | false | 24453.325     |
| 4  | false | 2423.3254     |
| 5  | true  | 243.325       |
| 60 | false | 243565423.325 |
| 70 | true  | 243.325       |
| 80 | false | 243423.325    |
```

Impala provides a facility to run an external SQL file. For example, if you create a file called `myfile.sql` with your commands, you can execute the following:

```
impala-shell -i localhost -f myfile.sql
```

Best practices

Impala is designed for executing low-latency queries over data stored on a distributed file system like HDFS. The performance of Impala is much faster than Hive using MapReduce. We have identified the best practices that can be followed for achieving good performance. These practices can be seen here:

- **File format**: We have discussed the importance of file formats in the previous sections. Impala performs better with the parquet file format that is a columnar file format. This stores data in columnar format and uses compression technique to minimize storage space. Multiple benchmarks showed Impala with paraquat, which gives 3X better performance than any other file format.

- **Stats computation**: Impala provides the ability to compute table statistics such as the volume of data and the number of rows and columns. Impala uses these stats to optimize queries, especially when there are joins between two or more queries. The Impala query planner uses statistics on entire tables and partitions. The stats include physical characteristics such as the number of rows, number of data files, total size of the data files, and file formats. For partitioned tables, the stats are calculated per partition and as totals for the whole table. This metadata information is stored in the Hive Metastore database. The stats for table computation can be triggered using the following command:

```
compute stats parquet_snappy;
show table stats parquet_snappy;
```

- **Partitioning**: The working of partitioning is very much similar to what we discussed in the Hive best practices section. Partitions help in filtering out records, which means they reduce the amount of records that will be processed by Impala for query execution. Impala reads the partition information from the metadata table and makes a plan to filter out partitions that are not needed for query execution.

- **Avoid small files**: Large numbers of small files can degrade the performance of Impala by up to 100 times. We have run into a situation where we had lots of small files coming from Kafka to HDFS and the query was taking around 15 minutes to process 6 months of data of 200 GB in size. We identified the problem and merged the files in the partition and query time was reduced to 2 minutes. We have also optimized the MapReduce job up to more than 100 times. We recommend using a larger file size and avoiding too many partitions with small file sizes. For example, you can avoid hourly partitions if the data volume is not that big and make partitions up to a year, a month, or a day.

- **Table structure**: We have seen people using the string data type for all the columns in the table and later doing casting at computation. Doing it this way will cause decreased query performance. We recommend using the appropriate data types for columns in the table. The second recommendation regarding table structure is to have a de-normalized table, if possible. As discussed in the previous section, that join is a costly operation that requires shuffling the data, therefore, table structure should be de-normalised.

- **Number of coordinator**: The initial version of Impala forces users to have all the Impalad daemon to work as a coordinator and an executor. But in the latest version, we can configure the number of coordinator and executor nodes. The node can only perform coordinator work and the executor node will utilize resources for query execution. We recommend that you start with two to three coordinator nodes initially so that resources can be utilized in a better way.

Summary

In this chapter, we focused on common SQL components that are used in the Hadoop ecosystem. We also covered the architecture of Hive, Presto, and Impala. Then, we discussed the best practices when using these tools.

In the next chapter, we will focus on the processing engines we use to process huge amounts of data. We will focus more on internal architecture and the in-depth workings of each component. We will also cover a few examples that will help you design your own application.

6
Real-Time Processing Engines

Big data processing has become a priority for companies now, and there are plenty of tools and frameworks available for processing this data. The first distributed framework was MapReduce, and after that there were lots of tools being developed for it, such as Hive and Pig. The requirement of processing a larger dataset quickly resulted in the development of Apache Spark, and to be able to process data in real-time, we had Apache Storm. In this chapter, we will discuss some of the popular processing frameworks, such as Apache Spark, Apache Flink, and Apache Storm.

We are going to cover the following topics:

- Apache Spark architecture and its internal
- Example covering running the Spark application
- Apache Flink architecture and its ecosystem
- Apache Flink APIs
- Apache Storm with Heron as its successor

Technical requirements

You will be required to have Hadoop 3.0.

The code files of this chapter can be found on GitHub:
https://github.com/PacktPublishing/Mastering-Hadoop-3/tree/master/Chapter06

Check out the following video to see the code in action:
http://bit.ly/2H7LWBV

Spark

Hadoop has been used as a processing framework for large datasets for the past decade and it has brought tremendous value and cost saving to organizations. MapReduce has evolved over a time but it is not efficient for a few use cases like near real-time computation, multi-pass computation, which is iterative processing, and so on. Every time the data is processed, it has to be written into the disk and then you have to pick data from disk for further processing. Along with this, if we need to add additional use cases which require libraries such as Mahout and Apache Storm, then it has to be integrated separately in the Hadoop cluster.

Spark is a distributed data processing framework that provides functional APIs for manipulating data at scale, in-memory data caching, and reusability of datasets. Spark utilizes the concept of the **direct acyclic graph** (**DAG**), which is a data lineage graph that helps in recomputing tasks in case of failure. Spark supports a number of file formats and rich sets of APIs to deal with almost any kind of data in distributed mode.

Spark eliminates the drawback of the MapReduce framework by reducing the I/O time and by reducing the cost of shuffling data. The capability of in-memory data storage and near real-time processing makes Spark several times faster than the MapReduce framework. The in-memory storage capability provides an advantage for iterative use cases where the same dataset is used multiple times in different computations. The lazy evaluation feature and rich set of APIs also helps in optimizing job workflow. Let' look into the Spark architecture to see how does it works internally.

Apache Spark internals

Apache Spark is a distributed processing engine and works on the master slave principle. The Apache Spark architecture consists of various components and it is important to have a brief understanding of each component to grab the internals of Spark application execution. The following diagram shows the Spark architecture:

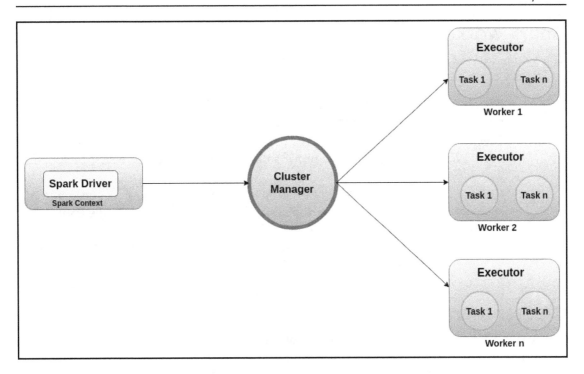

Spark driver

The Spark driver is the master in the Spark architecture. Spark driver is the entry point of the Spark application, and is also responsible for the following tasks:

- **Spark context**: The context of Spark is created in the Spark driver and the context object is responsible for initializing application configuration.
- **DAG creation**: The Spark driver creates lineage based on RDD operations and submits that to the DAG scheduler. Lineage is DAG. The acyclic graph is now submitted to the DAG scheduler.
- **Stage creation**: Spark driver is also responsible for breaking tasks into stages based on a lineage graph.
- **Task schedule and execution**: The task scheduler in the driver schedules the task using a cluster manager such as YARN and Mesos, and controls the execution of each stage.
- **RDD metadata**: The metadata of RDD and its partitions is maintained by Spark driver, which helps in recomputing RDD in case of any failure.

Spark workers

The Spark workers are responsible for managing executors running on their own machine and making communication with the master node. They are listed as follows:

- **Backend process**: The backend processes running on each worker node is responsible for launching the executor.
- **Executors**: Each executor contains a thread pool where each thread executes tasks in parallel. Executors read and process the data from a file and writes data to the target location.
- **Cache:** Executors also contains the cache area, which can be used to persist RDD in-memory. Caching helps in optimizing jobs that require an iterative approach. It may not be necessary that the entire RDD fits in memory, and so we must choose the right caching strategy to make sure that the program execution does not break the executor's memory limit.

Cluster manager

Cluster manager is responsible for receiving job submission requests from Spark driver and managing resources to run the job in Spark cluster. Spark allows to plus any supported type of cluster manager. We will cover different cluster managers and their details later in this chapter. Basically, there are three commonly available cluster managers: Spark standalone cluster manager, Mesos, and YARN.

Spark application job flow

The Spark application life cycle involves various intermediate steps and each step is responsible for handling specific responsibilities. In this section, we will cover the Spark job flow and each step in detail:

1. The first step in any application is to submit the job. The client submits the Spark application using the `Spark-submit` option.
2. The `main` class that's specified during job submission is invoked and the Spark driver program is launched. The driver program is launched on the master node and is responsible for managing the application's life cycle.
3. The driver program requests resources from the cluster manager to launch executors based on application configuration.
4. The cluster manager launches the executor on the worker node on behalf of the Spark driver and the Spark driver now takes ownership of the application life cycle.

5. The Spark driver creates a DAG based on RDD transformation and action. The number of tasks that are created is based on RDD transformation and action. The task is then divided into different stages.
6. Spark driver sends tasks to the executor and the executor executes the task.

> Remember, the executor contains a thread pool, and each thread in the thread pool executes tasks in parallel.

7. The executor sends the task completion request to the driver via the cluster manager. Once all the tasks in all the executors are completed, the driver sends a completion status to the cluster manager.

Deep dive into resilient distributed datasets

Resilient distributed datasets (**RDDs**) are distributed memory abstractions that enable in-memory computation in a fault tolerant manner. The performance bottleneck has been observed in the MapReduce application, which involves an iterative approach that means one dataset is used in multiple computations as the same dataset is read multiple times. The RDD can be computed and persisted intermediate results in memory for iterative processing. Interactive queries where users run multiple ad hoc queries on the same database can also be optimized by using in memory persistence. RDD is partitioned into a collection of records and read only in nature. It can be created by reading data from the storage system or by performing transformations on another RDD. RDDs form a lineage that can be used to compute or recompute its partition from data. Users have control over which RDD to persist and can define a number of partitions for RDD.

RDD features

The different features of RDD are explained as follows:

- **Distributed dataset**: RDD is a distributed collection of datasets that are processed in a distributed set of machines. RDD comes with a rich set of operators that allows users to write optimized and efficient processing code without worrying about its distributed processing, fault tolerance, and data shuffling.

- **Immutable**: RDD is immutable in nature, which means that the transformation cannot affect existing RDDs. Instead, new RDDs will be created. RDDs consist of a number of partitions and each partition contains a logical set of data that is also immutable in nature. The immutable nature helps in achieving consistency, which is very much required in distributed processing.
- **Fault tolerant**: Failure is a common problem in distributed processing and therefore it's very much necessary for applications to handle it. The Spark application forms lineage of RDD, which helps in recovering lost partition in case of failure from the lineage. It's one of the fast ways to handle failure without replicating data across clusters.
- **Lazy evaluations**: The transformation on RDD are lazy in nature, which means until and unless actions are not called on RDD, the execution will not start. Once the `action` operation is called on RDD, the required RDDs in lineage will get computed and the result will be returned to the driver.

RDD operations

RDD operations are divided into two categories, namely:

- **Transformation**: The transformation operation over RDD results in a new RDD, which means that every time you perform a transformation, a new RDD will be created. The transformation over RDD forms a RDD lineage, which indicates a dependency graph of RDD to its parent RDD. Remember, RDD is immutable in nature, thus applying any transformation to RDD will not modify the existing RDD. Instead, it will result in new RDD for which lineage will be formed. All transformations are lazily evaluated, which means they will not be executed until and unless an action is called on any RDD in lineage. Let's look into a few transformation functions:
- `map`: The `map` transformation applies defined changes inside the function to every element in RDD and returns a new RDD dataset. The following RDD returns the RDD of `map` (tuple) with `1` assigned as the value to each record:

```
flatten_data.map(s => (s,1))
```

- `filter`: The `filter` function filter outs the record from input RDD for which function returns a `false` value and returns a new RDD dataset. The following RDD will remove all the records whose length are less than `10`:

```
val filtered_records = input_records.filter(x => x.length < 10)
```

- `flatMap`: The `flatMap` function applies to each record and each record may result in multiple records. The following code is another piece from the word count program. The function splits each record with a space delimiter and thus outputs multiple records from a single record:

```
var flatten_data = input_file.flatMap(s => s.split(" "));
```

- `union`: The `union` function works very much similar to the `set union` operator. The function unions the value of two RDDs and returns another RDD. The following example unions two RDDs and returns a new RDD in which number of elements would need to be equal to sum up the number of elements in both RDDs:

```
val first =
sc.parallelize(List("india","america","nepal","bhutan"))
val second =
sc.parallelize(List("india","australia","russia"))
val result = first.union(second)
```

The other `set` operations such as intersection and subtracts can also be performed in a similar way. These operators work similar to a `set` function:

- **Join**: The `join` operation works very much similar to a database `join`, which joins the table based on the key column. Two RDDs that are RDDs of tuples can be joined together based on a tuple key match.
- **Coalesce**: The partition of RDD is a unit of parallelism in Spark, but making too many partitions does not always help. It may lead to a decrease in performance due to less time being spent in processing and a high time in shuffling records. Coalesce can be used to decrease the number of partitions:

```
val coalesceRDD = input_rdd.coalesce(2)
```

- **Action**: The `action` functions are triggered for RDD execution. The transformation operations are lazy in nature and Spark does not trigger any executions for it. Once an `action` operation is encountered, Spark starts processing RDDs based on DAG and returns the result to drive the program. Let's look into a few commonly used `action` operations:
  - `count`: The `count` operation returns the number of records in RDD. It may be helpful to check the number of records that RDD contains to verify, validate, or compare results:

```
inputRDD.count()
```

- collect: The collect operation returns all the elements of RDD to the driver program. It should be used for testing purposes. Remember that the RDD contains a huge number of records and it should not be collected for the driver because if the size of the data exceeds the machine memory, then the driver will crash:

  ```
  rddResult.collect()
  ```

- take(n): It returns the n numbers of records from RDD. We cannot know which records will be a part of the return result:

  ```
  processedRDD.take(5)
  ```

- saveAsTextFile(Path): The saveAsTextFile saves the RDD records into a text file. Generally, processed final records are saved into a text file:

  ```
  processedRecord.saveAsTextFile("/user/packt/result");
  ```

Installing and running our first Spark job

Before Spark, we used to process data using old Hadoop MapReduce jobs. To run MapReduce programs, we need to have a Hadoop cluster in place. It was a very tedious task for developers to test the MapReduce application without the Hadoop cluster. Spark provides the ability to run the applications in both local and cluster mode. The same application can be run on local and cluster mode by changing the Spark configuration. Let's see how you can use Spark to learn, develop, and test your application.

Spark-shell

Apache Spark provides a quick way to run and test Spark AP's through Spark-shell. Spark-shell is an in-built feature of Apache Spark and it already sets up a SparkContext object for you.

 To download to latest version of the Apache Spark libraries, please visit https://Spark.apache.org/downloads.html.

After downloading the libraries, use the following the command to extract it and run the
`Spark-shell` command:

```
tar -xvf Spark-2.3.1-bin-hadoop2.7.tgz
mv Spark-2.3.1-bin-hadoop2.7.tgz Spark
cd Spark/bin
./Spark-shell
```

The output will be similar to what's shown in the following screenshot. The SparkContext
object `sc` is created by Spark-shell and it's running on local mode with the master as
`local[*]`:

```
exa00077@exa00071:~/Softwares/spark/bin$ ./spark-shell
2018-09-15 20:30:19 WARN  Utils:66 - Your hostname, exa00071 resolves to a loopback address: 127.0.1.1; using 192.168.0.103 instead
ce wlp5s0)
2018-09-15 20:30:19 WARN  Utils:66 - Set SPARK_LOCAL_IP if you need to bind to another address
2018-09-15 20:30:20 WARN  NativeCodeLoader:62 - Unable to load native-hadoop library for your platform... using builtin-java classes
icable
Setting default log level to "WARN".
To adjust logging level use sc.setLogLevel(newLevel). For SparkR, use setLogLevel(newLevel).
Spark context Web UI available at http://192.168.0.103:4040
Spark context available as 'sc' (master = local[*], app id = local-1537023626092).
Spark session available as 'spark'.
Welcome to



      ____              __
     / __/__  ___ _____/ /__
    _\ \/ _ \/ _ `/ __/  '_/
   /___/ .__/\_,_/_/ /_/\_\   version 2.3.1
      /_/

Using Scala version 2.11.8 (Java HotSpot(TM) 64-Bit Server VM, Java 1.8.0_181)
Type in expressions to have them evaluated.
Type :help for more information.
```

Once we are logged in to Spark-shell, we can test the Spark API. Let's run a word count
program on Spark-shell. The output is saved to the output directory, as shown here:

```
scala> var input_file = sc.textFile("/home/packt/india.txt");
input_file: org.apache.Spark.rdd.RDD[String] = /home/hduser/india.txt
MapPartitionsRDD[1] at textFile at <console>

scala> var flatten_data = input_file.flatMap(s => s.split(" "));
flatten_data: org.apache.Spark.rdd.RDD[String] = MapPartitionsRDD[2] at
flatMap at <console>

scala> var number_assigned_words = flatten_data.map(s => (s,1))
number_assigned_words: org.apache.Spark.rdd.RDD[(String, Int)] =
MapPartitionsRDD[3] at map at <console>

scala> var word_count_sum = number_assigned_words.reduceByKey((a, b) => a +
b)
word_count_sum: org.apache.Spark.rdd.RDD[(String, Int)] = ShuffledRDD[4] at
reduceByKey at <console>

word_count_sum.saveAsTextFile("/home/packt/wordcount")
```

Spark submit command

Spark-shell is good for quick code testing and learning Spark at a beginner level, but when it comes to a production application or a long-running Spark streaming application, we have to make use of the `Spark-submi` script.

Let's develop and run our first Spark word count application. We will be developing a Spark Maven project that will package the application into a .jar file. We will then submit this to the Spark cluster using the `Spark-submit` script.

Maven dependencies

The only dependency that we need to develop a Spark word count program is Spark core. The `build` plugin helps us package our application into a JAR:

```xml
<?xml version="1.0" encoding="UTF-8"?>
<project xmlns="    http://maven.apache.org/POM/4.0.0"
         xmlns:xsi="http://www.w3.org/2001/XMLSchema-instance"
         xsi:schemaLocation="http://maven.apache.org/POM/4.0.0
http://maven.apache.org/xsd/maven-4.0.0.xsd">
    <modelVersion>4.0.0</modelVersion>
    <parent>
        <artifactId>mastering-hadoop-3</artifactId>
        <groupId>com.packt</groupId>
        <version>1.0-SNAPSHOT</version>
    </parent>

    <artifactId>chapter6</artifactId>

<dependencies>
        <!-- https://mvnrepository.com/artifact/org.apache.Spark/Spark-core
-->
        <dependency>
            <groupId>org.apache.Spark</groupId>
            <artifactId>Spark-core_2.11</artifactId>
            <version>2.3.1</version>
        </dependency>

</dependencies>
    <build>
        <plugins>
            <plugin>
                <groupId>org.apache.maven.plugins</groupId>
                <artifactId>maven-compiler-plugin</artifactId>
                <version>2.0.2</version>
                <configuration>
```

```
                    <source>1.8</source>
                    <target>1.8</target>
                </configuration>
            </plugin>
            <plugin>
                <groupId>org.apache.maven.plugins</groupId>
                <artifactId>maven-jar-plugin</artifactId>
                <configuration>
                    <archive>
                        <manifest>
                            <addClasspath>true</addClasspath>
                            <classpathPrefix>lib/</classpathPrefix>
<mainClass>com.packt.masteringhadoop3.Spark.wordcount.SparkWordCount</mainClass>
                        </manifest>
                    </archive>
                </configuration>
            </plugin>
            <plugin>
                <groupId>org.apache.maven.plugins</groupId>
                <artifactId>maven-dependency-plugin</artifactId>
                <executions>
                    <execution>
                        <id>copy</id>
                        <phase>install</phase>
                        <goals>
                            <goal>copy-dependencies</goal>
                        </goals>
                        <configuration>
<outputDirectory>${project.build.directory}/lib</outputDirectory>
                        </configuration>
                    </execution>
                </executions>
            </plugin>
        </plugins>
    </build>
</project>
```

`SparkWordCount`: The word count program start by defining the Spark configuration and creating a SparkContext object. SparkContext is the starting point of our Spark application and RDD creation will start with the context object. Let's have a look at the following word count program:

```
import java.util.Arrays;
import java.util.Iterator;
import java.util.regex.Pattern;

import org.apache.Spark.api.java.*;
import org.apache.Spark.api.java.function.*;
import org.apache.Spark.SparkConf;
import scala.Tuple2;

public class SparkWordCount {

 private static final Pattern SPACE = Pattern.compile(" ");

 public static void main(String[] args) throws Exception {

 if (args.length < 1) {
 System.err.println("Usage: JavaWordCount <file>");
 System.exit(1);
 }

 SparkConf sparkConf = new SparkConf().setAppName("JavaWordCount");
 JavaSparkContext javaSparkContext = new JavaSparkContext(sparkConf);
 JavaRDD<String> lines = javaSparkContext.textFile(args[0], 1);

 JavaRDD<String> wordsRDD = lines.flatMap(new FlatMapFunction<String,
String>() {
 @Override
 public Iterator<String> call(String s) throws Exception {
 return Arrays.asList(SPACE.split(s)).iterator();
 }
 });


 JavaPairRDD<String, Integer> numberedAssignedRDD = wordsRDD.mapToPair(new
PairFunction<String, String, Integer>() {
 @Override
 public Tuple2<String, Integer> call(String s) {
 return new Tuple2<>(s, 1);
 }
 });

 JavaPairRDD<String, Integer> wordCountRDD =
```

```
numberedAssignedRDD.reduceByKey(new Function2<Integer, Integer, Integer>()
{
@Override
public Integer call(Integer i1, Integer i2) {
return i1 + i2;
}
});

wordCountRDD.saveAsTextFile(args[1]);
javaSparkContext.stop();
}
}
```

`Building package`: The following Maven command will help us create a JAR file:

`mvn clean install`

`Spark-submit`: The following Spark submit command runs the Spark application in local mode with three cores. Remember, `--master` has to be changed with a cluster address or YARN:

```
# Run application locally on three cores
./bin/Spark-submit \
 --class com.packt.masteringhadoop3.Spark.wordcount.SparkWordCount \
 --master local[3] \
 /home/packt/wordcount-1.0-SNAPSHOT.jar inputdir outputdir

#Running Spark in client mode
./bin/Spark-submit \
 --class com.packt.masteringhadoop3.Spark.wordcount.SparkWordCount \
  --master Spark://ipadress:port \
  --executor-memory 4G \
  --total-executor-cores 10 \
  /home/exa00077/wordcount-1.0-SNAPSHOT.jar inputdir outputdir

#Running in yarn cluster mode
./bin/Spark-submit \
 --class com.packt.masteringhadoop3.Spark.wordcount.SparkWordCount \
  --master yarn \
  --deploy-mode cluster \
  --executor-memory 4G \
  --num-executors 10 \
  /home/exa00077/wordcount-1.0-SNAPSHOT.jar inputdir outputdir
```

There are many options available with `Spark-submit` and we suggest that you to explore all of these options through the Spark documentation, which is available at `https://Spark.apache.org`.

Accumulators and broadcast variables

Spark is a distributed processing framework where datasets are being processed in parallel. The values of the variables used in the program are not shareable and its scope is limited to that machine only. Think about a use case where you want to track the count of a particular record that occurs in a dataset without performing any RDD aggregation operation, or if you want to create central variables that can be modified by a Spark program. In such cases, there has to be a way to share variables across different workers. Spark provides two special types of shared variables:

- **Broadcast variable**: Broadcast variables are shared throughout the cluster, which means that a program running on a worker node can read a broadcast variable. The only limitation is about memory. Remember, if a worker node does not have sufficient memory available that can fit the broadcast variables in memory, then the program will fail. The broadcast variables are immutable in nature, which means its value cannot be modified. Broadcast variables are generally used in use cases where any kind of lookup is required during RDD computation:

```
Broadcast<String[]> broadcastVar = sc.broadcast(new String[]
  {"Delhi", "Mumbai", "Kolkata"});

broadcastVar.value();
```

- **Accumulators**: Accumulators are very much similar to counters in MapReduce. It is a type of variable that has two operations called add and reset. Spark provides in-built support for the numeric accumulator, but also allows you to use custom accumulators.

For example, we can create and use a double accumulator, as shown in the following code, and then use that in a RDD operation. The result of accumulator count is 4 as we have 4 values in the array:

```
val accum = sc.doubleAccumulator("double counters")

sc.parallelize(Array(1.444, 2.6567, 3.8378, 4.93883)).foreach
  (x => accum.add(x))

accum.count;

======================
4
```

In some cases, we may want to built our custom accumulator, which can be created by extending `AccumulatorV2`. The custom accumulator then has to be registered with the Spark context, as follows:

```
sc.register(myCustomAcc, "MyCustomAcc")
```

- The update on the accumulator should be done inside an RDD action operation, which guarantees that each task will make an update to the accumulator only once. The value of the accumulator is only updated when there is any action on RDD, otherwise it will return 0 as a result.

  The shared variable makes it easy for the programmer to track count and provides an in-memory lookup service without making any separate implementation effort.

Understanding dataframe and dataset

RDD is the core of the Spark framework. Everything starts with it and ends with it, which means that you start loading data to RDD and finish saving the RDD to a file or external system such as a database.

Dataframes

Spark introduced dataframes in version 1.3 to store structured data in distributed mode, just like RDDs. Dataframes were introduced as an extension to existing RDDs with named columns. The concept of a dataframe was taken from Python (pandas) and R.

A dataframe is a distributed collection of organized data, similar to a table in a relational database with a rich set of features for optimization. As it is also a type of RDD, it has immutability, in-memory computation, and lazy evaluation, just like RDDs. Let's look into a few features of dataframes:

- **Schema:** A dataframe is a distributed collection of data that is organized into a named column. You can assume that they are database tables for which the processing is internally optimized. A dataframe is a distributed collection of data that's organized into named columns.
- **Immutability**: Dataframes are abstractions of RDD and have named columns. They also have immutable feature similar to RDD, which means a transformation over a dataframe will result in another dataframe.

- **Flexibility API**: Dataframes can process a wide range of file formats including CSV, AVRO, ORC, and paraquat. It can also read data from storage systems such as HDFS, Hive, and so on.
- **Catalyst optimizer**: Dataframes use the Spark catalyst optimizer for performance optimization. There are different sets of rules that are applied to all four sets of query execution steps, namely analysis, logical optimization, physical planning, and code generation to compile parts of queries into Java bytecode.
- **Memory management**: The schema for the data is already defined, and so it avoids Java serialisation and stores data off heap in a binary format, which helps in saving memory and improving garbage collection.

Apart from the rich set of features that dataframes provide, they do have a few limitations such as they do not guarantee the type-safe operation, which means your program execution may fail if there is a type mismatch. Let's look into a few programming interface examples:

- **Creating dataframe**: The dataframe can be created by reading data from a file or by applying a transformation over a RDD. The following example shows dataframe creation from a file and another dataframe that was created by transforming it:

```
val rawDF = Spark.read.json("/user/packt/author.json")
salaryFiltered = rawDF.filter(rawDF.salary > 30000)
```

- **Registering dataframe as table**: A dataframe can be registered as a temporary table in Spark and the user can then execute an SQL-like query on top of it:

```
rawDF.createOrReplaceTempView("author")
val selectDF = sparkSession.sql("SELECT * FROM author");
selectDF.show()
```

- **Saving dataframe result**: The processed dataframe result can be saved to table or external filesystem. The save mode can be set to append, overwrite and so on:

```
salaryFiltered.write.bucketBy(10,
"name").sortBy("salary").saveAsTable("author_salary")

salaryFiltered.write.partitionBy("age").format(
"parquet").save("salary_filtered.parquet")
```

We would recommend that you refer to the Spark dataframe API for more in-depth information about its rich set of APIs as you will be able to understand its concepts further.

Dataset

Spark dataframes have some limitations such as type-safety and therefore the dataset APIs were introduced in version 1.6. The dataset is nothing but an advanced version of a dataframe and is a collection of strongly typed JVM objects. These are represented in tabular format using an encoder. The RDD features such as immutability, fault tolerance, lazy evaluation, and so on are also available with a dataset. The encoder is responsible for the serialization and deserialization of data. It helps in translating data from a JVM object into Spark internal binary format and vice versa. Let's look into a few features of a dataset:

- **Processing capabilities**: A dataset can operate on both structure and unstructured datasets. It can also work as a dataframe, which is also known as untyped dataset operation, but at the same time can provide type-safety with a strongly typed schema definition.
- **Optimization**: The dataset also takes advantage of the Spark query catalyst optimizer and Tungsten. The optimization is applied to various levels based on a set of rules, and it has been observed that in a few cases it gives multiple performance benefits over normal RDD.
- **Strongly type safe**: The dataset has the ability to bind data with Java objects, which helps in identifying any wrong operation or syntax error at compile time itself. Unlike dataframe, it helps in avoiding any runtime exception like invalid operation and type casting errors.
- **Convertibility**: The dataset API has the ability to convert a dataset into a dataframe by using its conversion API. The RDD can also be converted into dataset or dataframe using this API. However, in the last version of Spark, the dataframe APIs are merged with the dataset and all the operations can be achieved through the dataset APIs.

Now, let's look into how we can create a dataset in Spark and what some of the commonly used transformation and actions are that can be applied to a dataset:

- **Creating a dataset**: Creating a dataset is very much similar creating a dataframe. In the latest version of Spark, we only get a dataset as output instead of a dataframe, as the dataframe APIs are merged with the dataset:

```
case class Author(name: String, salary:
  Long, email: String,age: String)

val authorDataset= sparkSession.read.json(
"/user/packt/author.json").as[Author]
```

- **Transformation**: The dataset API also provides functional APIs similar to RDD such as map, filter, groupby, and so on. Let's look at the word count example through a dataframe:

```
import org.apache.Spark.sql.SparkSession

object WordCountWithDataset {

    def main(args: Array[String]) {

        val sparkSession = SparkSession.builder.
                    master("local[*]")
                    .appName("wordcount")
                    .getOrCreate()

        import sparkSession.implicits._
        val inputDataset =
        sparkSession.read.text("/home/packt/test.data").as[String]

        val workdsDataset =
        inputDataset.flatMap(value => value.split("\\s+"))

        val groupedWordsDataset =
        workdsDataset.groupByKey(_.toLowerCase)

        val wordcountsDataset =
        groupedWordsDataset.count()
        wordcountsDataset.show()
    }
}
```

Remember that untyped datasets are nothing but dataframes, and typed datasets are actual datasets that provide rich functionality. There are a lot of other functions that you can use with datasets such as sort, partition, and save dataset. For a detailed use of every method, please refer to http://Spark.apache.org/.

Spark cluster managers

The Spark driver in Spark interacts with the cluster manager to submit and schedule tasks. Spark supports a pluggable policy for the cluster manager, which means that we can use different cluster managers in different Spark clusters as per our application requirements. The challenge is to decide which cluster manager will be the right fit for your use case. We will look into a few common principles that can help us solve this problem. The execution of the Spark application is managed by the Spark driver. The Spark driver coordinates with the cluster manager for resources and job scheduling.

In a Spark cluster, we have a master node and many worker nodes. We have already discussed that the driver program runs tasks into executors running on worker nodes. These executors interact with the driver for status updates and resource needs. The cluster manager has the responsibility of scheduling and resource allocation. The basic functionality is available in all types of cluster manager, but how do we know and decide which cluster manager to use? We came up with a few principles that can help us choose the right cluster manager:

- **High availability**: The Spark standalone cluster manager supports high availability of the master via Zookeeper. The Standby master takes over the failed master in case of any failure. We need to run a failover controller on the master, which sends a signal to Zookeeper about its active status. If for a period of time Zookeeper does not get any signal from `FailOverController`, then it makes a standby master node active and kills the connection to the failed node from all the worker nodes. If we are not running any other services apart from Spark, then it is a good option to go with Spark cluster manager initially.
  The **Apache Mesos** cluster manager is similar to the standalone cluster manager and is as resilient for master failure. In case of master failover, the existing tasks will continue their execution. **Apache YARN** supports both manual recovery and automatic recovery using a command-line utility and Zookeeper, respectively. The Resource manager has `ActiveStandByElector`, which elects a new master in case the current active master goes down.

- **Security**: Spark standalone cluster manager security can be enabled using a shared secret key, SSL, and an **access control list** (**ACL**). The shared secret key is configured on each node of the Spark cluster. The data encryption can be done by enabling SSL, and access to a web UI can be restricted using ACL. Mesos provides authentication for all the entities interacting with the cluster. The default authentication module is Cyrus SASL, which can be replaced by any custom authentication module. The data encryption for data on the wire can be done using SSL/TSL and access to the UI can be controlled by ACL.

  YARN has a rich set of functionalities on terms of security such as Kerberos for authentication and authorization. It also provides service-level authorization to ensure that the users are authorized to use services that the user wants to use. The data on the wire can be encrypted using the SSL protocol.

- **Monitoring**: Almost all cluster managers have a UI for monitoring Spark jobs. The web UI displays various information such as the currently running Spark jobs, number of executors used, storage and memory utilization, failed task, access to their logs, and so on. The completed application details can be accessed via the Spark application history server. Apache Mesos and YARN have different metrics that can be used for monitoring and debugging.

- **Scheduling capability**: The important thing is to consider how the cluster manager schedules jobs. The Spark standalone cluster uses a FIFO scheduler for job scheduling and execution. By default, the Spark applicatio uses all the nodes for execution, but we can limit the amount of CPU, executors, and resources through configuration.

In the case of Mesos, it makes a resource offer to an application and the application can either accept or reject the request based on its requirements. It offers both fine-grained and course-grained allocation of resources simultaneously, which means in a single cluster one application can use a fine - rained approach while another can be chosen to use a course=grained allocation of resources.

YARN provides a pluggable scheduler policy and by default uses the capacity scheduler, which allows multiple users to securely share a large cluster so that their applications are allocated resources under constraints of allocated capacities. It also provides implementation for a fair scheduler, which ensures a fair distribution of resources across the application queue.

Best practices

Spark is now one of the most widely used applications in data processing because of its integrated ecosystem and ability to process large datasets quickly. We have identified a few basic practices that can be used to make our Spark application robust, efficient, and less error-prone. Let's look into a few of them:

- **Avoid sending large datasets to driver**: The memory allocated to Spark driver is limited and can be configured while running the Spark job. The operation used on RDD such as `collect()` copies the entire resultant dataset to the driver machine and if the size of the dataset exceeds the memory available on the driver machine, then it will throw a memory exception. We recommend taking only a sample dataset by using the `take()` operation, which will limit the amount of records that are taken from the dataset.

- **Avoid GroupByKey**: The shuffling operation is a major issue in performance optimization. The more you reduce the amount of data traversal, the better your application performance will be. The `GroupByKey` is an aggregation operation that causes data to be shuffled across the worker node without any aggregation at the partition level. It is similar to the reduce operation in MapReduce, but without a combiner.
  The alternative is to use `reducebykey`, which will also give a similar result but provides an added advantage by reducing the amount of data that needs to be shuffled. It is similar to that of the combiner, which is called **mini reducer**, as it does aggregation operation at the partition level before shuffling the data.

- **Using the broadcast variable correctly**: Broadcast variables are shared variables that can be used for lookup operations. Broadcast variables are available on every worker node before the actual execution of RDD starts. This can be used for doing map side joining if one of the datasets is small enough to fit into memory. We can convert the small dataset into a broadcast variable and use it to join with a larger dataset.
  The second use case could be any dataset that is not big enough to fit into memory, but the key of a smaller dataset can fit into memory. In such a case, we can filter out records from the bigger dataset by performing a filter operation based on the key of the smaller dataset. In this way, we will only have records in the bigger dataset for which there is at least one key in the smaller dataset.

- **Memory tuning**: The correct use of cluster resources always helps in increasing the performance of an application. Spark provides the ability to set a driver's and executor's memory configuration. Spark applications should be debugged for their resource utilization and based on their stats, we should increase or decrease the executor's memory.

- **Parallelism**: The partitions are units of parallelism in Spark. By default, Spark creates as number of partitions equal to the number of blocks of the input file. We can set the partition for any RDD based on the stats collected for the job. Spark can process a maximum number of partitions in parallel, which is equal to the number of cores available on the worker node. If there are 10 CPU cores, then it can process 10 RDD partitions in parallel. Each individual should not take more then 150 ms to execute and if this is happening, then we must increase the number of partitions.
- **Caching RDD**: Spark provides an ability to cache RDD in memory, but this does not mean that we should cache each and every RDD in memory. A rule of thumb is that if RDD is being used more than once in the transformation operation, then it must persist and we should not go for `memory_only` caching if we are unsure whether the RDD will fit into memory because Spark has to do recomputation on the fly to get the partition of RDDs which were not cached.

The code level practice and configuration level recommended changes should always be part of your best practice while working with an Apache Spark application.

Apache Flink

We have a huge number of data processing tools available in the market. Most of them are open sourced and a few of them are commercial. The question is, how many processing tools or engines do we need? Can't we have just one processing framework that can fulfill the processing requirement of each and every use case that has different processing patterns? Apache Spark was built for the purpose of solving these problem and came up with a unified system architecture where use cases ranging from batch, near-real-time, machine learning models, and so on can be solved using the rich Spark API.

Apache Spark was not suitable for real-time processing use cases where event-by-event processing is needed. Apache Flink came up with a few new design models to solve similar problems that Spark was trying to solve in addition to its real-time processing capability.

Apache Flink is an open source distributed processing framework for stream and batch processing. The dataflow engine is the core of Flink and provides capabilities such as distribution, communication, and fault tolerance. Flink is very much similar to Spark but has an API for custom memory management, real-time data processing, and so on, which makes it a little different from Spark, which works on micro batches instead of real time.

Flink architecture

Like other distributed processing engines, Apache Fink also follows the master slave architecture. The **Job manager** is a master and the **Task Manager** are worker processes. The following diagram shows the Apache Flink architecture:

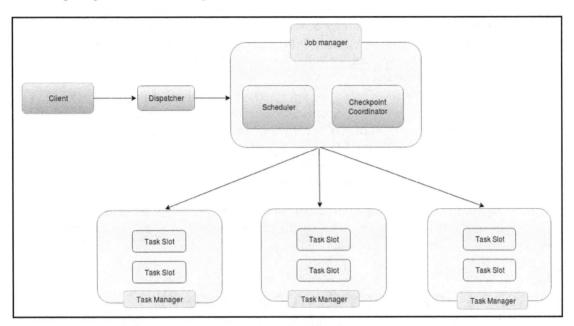

- **Job manager**: The **Job manager** is the master process of the Flink cluster and works as a coordinator. The responsibility of the **Job manager** is not only to manage the entire life cycle of data flow but also track the progress and state of each stream and operator. It also coordinates the dataflow execution in distributed environments. The **Job manager** maintains the checkpoint metadata in fault-tolerant storage systems so that if an active **Job manager** goes down, the standby **Job manager** can use the checkpoint to recover the dataflow execution state.

- **Task Manager**: These are workers in the Flink cluster who are responsible for executing task that are assigned by the **Job manager**. The Flink cluster consists of multiple worker nodes and **Task Manager** is available on each worker node. Each **Task Manager** contains multiple task slots that are responsible for executing tasks. Each **Task Manager** can execute a number of tasks, which is equal to the number of slots it has. The slots are registered with the Resource Manager so that the Resource Manager knows which slots have to be assigned to a task if they are asked by the **Job manager**. The **Task Manager** executing the tasks of the same application can also communicate with each other to exchange information if required.

- **Dispatcher**: The dispatcher provides a REST interface that the client can use to submit an application for execution. Upon receiving any such request, it sends the same to the **Job manager**, which then actually carries out the execution of the application using a **Task Manager**. Once it receives an application, it starts a **Job manager** and hands the application over. It also runs a web dashboard where you can see previously executed applications.

We just talked about a few major components of the Apache Flink architecture. There are other minor components that also play a significant role in the architecture. Covering every component in detail is outside the scope of this book.

Apache Flink ecosystem component

Apache Flink is an emerging data processing framework that comes with multiple capabilities for its unified ecosystem architecture. If you have been working with big data ecosystems, then you would have experienced the following scenarios:

- **Multiple frameworks**: Since data has started growing rapidly in the last 10 years, companies started exploring data processing frameworks for quick business reporting. MapReduce took the market for batch processing, Apache Storm for real-time processing, Apache Mahout for distributed machine learning, and so on. For every new type of data processing, we had to configure a new cluster for the framework, depending on its architecture and system requirements. It became a tedious task for companies managing the infrastructure.

- **Development and testing**: The data processing frameworks that were built initially were not designed to run on local mode, which means that without setting up a cluster, you cannot just test your application. Quick development and testing was very much a tedious task. We still remember mocking up the MapReduce framework to test the MapReduce application.

- **Source and target connectors**: Fetching data from the source system and pushing it to the target system required extra development effort.

The following diagram represents the Apache Flink ecosystem and its components:

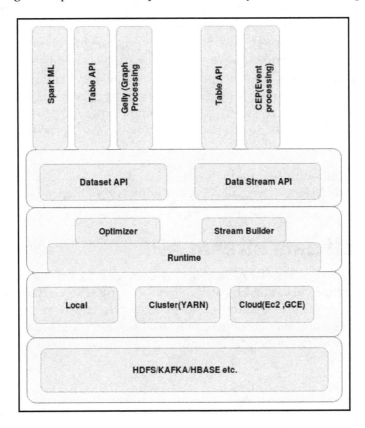

The preceding diagram can be explained as follows:

- **Storage layer**: Every processing framework is designed with a storage system, but Apache Flink does not have any storage system with it. Apache Flink can read and write data to and from any storage or streaming source. It provides an API to write data to HDFS, Kafka, RabbitMQ, and so on.
- **Deployment mode**: The Apache Flink application can run on multiple modes, which means that your application can run on local, standalone, YARN, or the cloud by just changing configuration. This provides you with ability to develop and test applications on a local machine without setting up any Flink cluster, which helps in saving significant development time.

- **Runtime**: Apache Flink's runtime layer consists of multiple smaller components, which helps in preparing an execution graph and optimizing the graph. It is the kernal of Apache Flink that provides features like fault tolerance, distributed processing, iterative processing, and so on.

- **DataSet and dataStream API**: Apache Flink provides a dataset and data stream API to process batch and stream data, respectively. Dataset APIs are available in three languages, namely Java, Scala, and Python, while streaming APIs are only available in Java and Scala. We will talk about this in detail in the next section.

- **Apache Flink tools**: Apache Flink provides a unified platform for data processing applications. For graph processing, it provides a graph processing library called Gelly. Similarly, for a machine learning use case, it provides FlinkML. These unified system designs provide less overhead for infrastructure and maintenance.

The Apache Flink community is rapidly working on adding more features and processing capabilities. In the next section, we will cover the Flink API in brief.

Dataset and data stream API

Apache Flink provides two special APIs to deal with batch and stream data. The dataset API provides capabilities to deal with batch data processing wherein you can perform operations such as map, filter join, group, and so on whereas the data stream API provides capabilities to hand stream events, which can be useful for event processing applications such as fraud detection, recommendation, and so on. Let's look into each of them one by one with an example.

Dataset API

The Dataset APIs in Flink are used to develop batch processing applications. The dataset can be created from reading data from a file, distributed storage system, collections, and so on. Similar to Apache Spark, the transformation operation on a dataset such as `map`, `flatMap` also returns a new dataset. Let's have a look at a few commonly used dataset operations.

Transformation

The transformation dataset API transforms one dataset into another dataset. Operations such as filtering data based on condition, joining two datasets, grouping the records in a dataset, union, are a few commonly used transformations. Let's take a look at them in brief:

- `map`: The transformation applies a defined function to each record in the dataset and exactly one element will be returned after the transformation. The following map function converts each record in the dataset into upper case:

```
DataStream<String> parsed = input.map(new MapFunction<String,
   String>() {
      @Override
      public String map(String value) {
         return value.toUpperCase();
      }
   });
```

- `flatmap`: Unlike the `map` function, `flatmap` returns multiple values from a single record transformation. The `flatmap` transformation applies to each record in the dataset. The following `flatmap` function splits each line based on space and converts each word of the line into uppercase. The return type is collection:

```
public class RecordSplitter implements FlatMapFunction<String,
   String> {
      @Override
      public void flatMap(String value, Collector<String> out) {
         for (String word : value.split(" ")) {
            out.collect(word.toUpperCase());
         }
      }
   }
```

- `filter`: The `filter` transformation applies to each element in the dataset and removes all those records for which the function returns a `false` value. The following `filter` function filters out all the record whose length is more than 100:

```
public class RecordLenthFilter implements FilterFunction<String>
   {
      @Override
      public boolean filter(String record) {
         return record.length() >= 100;
      }
   }
```

- `distinct`: The `distinct` transformation removes all the duplicate entries from dataset operations:

  ```
  dataset.distinct();
  ```

- `join`: The `join` transformation joins two datasets and returns record based on the matching condition. The following `join` transformation joins `dataset1` and `dataset2` based on equal conditions:

  ```
  outputdataset = dataset1.join(dataset2)
          .where(0)
          .equalTo(1);
  ```

> There are a number of transformation functions available in Flink. We recommend that you explore Flink to get more information on the same.

Data sinks

The data sink in dataset operations consumes the transformed dataset and saves it to a file or returns it to the console:

- `writeAsText()`: This function saves the dataset as a string to a file:

  ```
  transformmedData.writeAsText("path_to_outputfile");
  ```

- `writeAsCsv()`: This function separates the tuples as delimited separated files. The following function separates the tuple based on #:

  ```
  transformmed.writeAsCsv("file:///path/to/the/result/file", "\n",
      "#");
  ```

- `print()`: This data sink operation prints the output to the console. It is a good idea to print the small output for testing during development:

  ```
  transformmed.print()
  ```

Data streams

The data streams API in Flink helps you deal with event-based streaming data. The stream datasets are created from various sources such as a messaging queue like Kafka, log streaming, click streams, and so on. The real-time streaming use cases such as recommendation engines, fraud detection, sensor, and alerting requires that the event is proceeded without any delay of time. Unlike Spark, where it processes the event in micro batches, Flink provides the ability to process data on a per event basis, which means that once the data is received, it will be immediately processed, but it can also process events based on window time.

The operations on event data are very much similar to the transformation API. Apache Flink also provides window functions to deal with streaming data. There are three parts of the stream processing, namely:

- **Source**: Apache Flink provides a number of commonly used source connector libraries such as Kafka, Cassandra, Amazon Kinesis data streams, Apache Nifi, Twitter stream, and so on. The following is an example of connecting Flink with Kafka as a source:

```
Properties kafkaProperties = new Properties();
    kafkaProperties.setProperty("bootstrap.servers",
"localhost:9092");
    kafkaProperties.setProperty("zookeeper.connect",
"localhost:2181");
    kafkaProperties.setProperty("group.id", "test");
    DataStream<String> kafkaStream = env
            .addSource(new FlinkKafkaConsumer08<>("topic",
    new
SimpleStringSchema(), kafkaProperties));
```

- **Event processing:** Once the event is received, the next step is to perform an operation on it such as a lookup operation. For example, if you have developed a fraud IP detection Flink application, then you want to check the event data, filter out the IP, and look this up in the fraud database for a match. You may want to just filter out records that are not eligible for fraud checks and so on. We can perform map, filter, reduce, and many other transformation operations on the event stream as well.
- **Sink**: Similar to source, Apache Flink has commonly used sink connectors. The sink connector helps in storing processed or filtered events to a target system such as Kafka, Cassandra, HBase, or filesystem.

Apache Flink has a rich set of APIs for dealing with real-time or near-real-time data. The community is continuously working on adding more connectors and simplifying the APIs.

Exploring the table API

The table API provides you with the ability to deal with data in a SQL-like language. It can work with both batch and stream processing. The table API is currently available for Scala and Java. The SQL-like query processing helps developers as they just have to write queries instead of complex processing algorithms. The table in Flink can be created by using a dataset or data stream. Once the table is created, it can be registered for further use. Every table is bound to a specific table environment. The most commonly used table operators include `select`, `where`, `groupBy`, `Intersect`, `Union`, `join`, `LeftOuterJoin`, `RightOuterJoin`, and so on.

The following example shows how we can read data from a CSV file, assign a named column to it, and then perform SQL operations to data:

```
public class FlinkTableExample{
public static void main(String args()){
    // set up execution environment
        val env = StreamExecutionEnvironment.getExecutionEnvironment
        val tEnv = TableEnvironment.getTableEnvironment(env)

    // configure table source
        val employee_records = CsvTableSource.builder()
                .path("employee_monthly.csv")
                .ignoreFirstLine()
                .fieldDelimiter(",")
                .field("id", Types.LONG)
                .field("name", Types.STRING)
                .field("last_update", Types.TIMESTAMP)
                .field("salary", Types.LONG)
                .build()

    // name your table source
        tEnv.registerTableSource("employee", employee_records)

    // define your table program
        val table = tEnv
                .scan("employee")
                .filter('name.isNotNull && 'last_update > "2018-30-01
00:00:00".toTimestamp)
                .select('id, 'name.lowerCase(), 'prefs)

  val ds = table.toDataStream[Row]
    ds.print()
    env.execute()
}
}
```

Let's look into a few commonly used table operations and when to use them:

- `select`: The `select` operators are used when you want to extract records from registered Flink tables. This works very much similar to SQL `select` statements:

```
Table tablename = tableEnv.scan("tableName");
Table result = tablename.select("column1, column2 as col");

// * will fetch all the columns of registered table.
Table tablename = tablename.select("*")
```

- `where`: The `where` operator is used to filter out records based on a filter condition. It works in the same way as SQL `where` clause:

```
Table tablename = tableEnv.scan("tablename");
Table result = orders.where("columnname === 'value'");
```

- `GroupBy`: The `groupBy` operator is used to group the records based on grouping key. This is very much similar to how `groupBy` works in SQL:

```
Table tablename = tableEnv.scan("tablename");
Table result =
orders.groupBy("column1").select("column1, column2.max as
maxsal");
```

- `join`: The `join` operator can join tables based on the join condition and fetch records from the tables whose prediction returns `true`. The two tables should have distinct field names and at least one join condition:

```
Table table1 = tableEnv.fromDataSet(dataset1, "col1, col2,
  col3");
Table table2 = tableEnv.fromDataSet(dataset2, "col4, col5,
col6");

Table result = table1.join(table2).where("col1 = col4").
              select("col1, col5, col6");
```

`fullOuterJoin`, `leftOuterJoin`, and `rightOuterJoin` can also be used similar to the preceding script by just changing the function name.

- **Set operations**: The set operators can be used to perform set operation on two tables. The commonly used set operators are `union`, `intersect`, `union all`, `minus`, and so on:

```
Table table1 = tableEnv.fromDataSet(dataset1, "col1, col2, col3");
Table table2 = tableEnv.fromDataSet(dataset2, "col4, col5, col6");
Table result = table1.union(table2);
```

The `Table` API comes with specific windows functions that can be applied to a window-level operation.

Best practices

The best practices of development and coding should be followed everywhere, irrespective of languages or frameworks. The common best practices such as naming standards, comments, module structure, functions, and so on are applicable everywhere, but there are a few language and framework-specific best practices. Let's talk about few of them that are related to Apache Flink:

- **Using parameter tool**: One of the API features that Flink provides is the `ParameterTool` class. If you are a programmer, you would have experienced that most of the time when you forget to add few properties into the `Properties` object, this modifies the program and rebuilds packages. `ParameterTool` provides you with the ability to add any number of properties through command-line arguments. For setting up properties in Flink, we should use the `ParameterTool` object feature, which helps in dealing with dynamic properties:

```
ParameterTool parameterTool = ParameterTool.fromArgs(args);
```

The `ParameterTool` should be registered with the environment globally:

```
env.getConfig().setGlobalJobParameters(parametersTool);
```

- **Avoid large TupleX types**: The idea of passing more arguments to a function apply here. It is always recommended to use the Java `POJO` function to return more than one value or accept more than four values. Using a tuple with more arguments may lead to less readable code and will be very difficult to debug:

```
//Initiate MultiArgumentTuple Tuple
        MultiArgumentTuple multiArgumentTuple =
        new MultiArgumentTuple(val0, val1,
```

```
        val2, val3, val4, val5, val6, val7,cal8,val9,val10);

// Define MultiArgumentTuple which can be used instead of Tuple11
        public static class MultiArgumentTuple extends Tuple11<String,
        String, Integer, String, Integer, Integer, Integer,
        Integer,String,String,String> {

            public MultiArgumentTuple() {
                super();
            }

            public MultiArgumentTuple(String val0,
            String val1, Integer val2, String val3,
            Integer val4, Integer val5,
            Integer val6, Integer val7,String val8,String
val9,String val10) {
                super(val0, val1, val2, val3, val4, val5, val6,
val7,val8,val9,val10);
            }
        }
```

- **Monitoring**: The performance of an application can be tuned by observing different parameters at runtime. It is always a good idea to configure monitoring of an application for Apache Flink. For example , you may want to handle back pressure scenario where consuming an operator works slower than a producer operator. Remember that situations like back pressure may lead to wrong output or failure of jobs—even Flink has the ability to handle this internally, but it's not always true in every situation.

Configuration tuning and writing optimized code with the help of rich APIs should always be on your radar as a best practice.

Storm/Heron

Apache Storm is a distributed real-time computing system that processes a large volume of high velocity data. Unlike Spark, it does not create micro batches instead, it gives us the ability to process events in real-time mode. Applications where even a delay of seconds can cause a big loss could not go with a near real-time processing engine like Spark. There are a large number of companies that are using Apache Storm for processing events in real time for use cases such as fraud detection, recommendation engines, identifying suspicious activity, and so on.

Apache Storm is a distributed real-time processing engine that provides the ability to process events as quick as they arrive to the node. It is super fast and can process millions of events per machine. Storm is reliable in processing both bounded and unbounded streams of event.

Deep dive into the Storm/Heron architecture

Like other distributed processing engines, Apache Storm is also built using the master-slave architecture, where Nimbus is the master node and supervisors act as the slave nodes:

- **Nimbus:** Nimbus is the master node that plays the same role as JobTracker, which is used in initial versions of Hadoop. Basically, it acts as the major communication point between the Storm cluster and the user:
    - The user submits the topology as a part of the application build. Upon receiving the topology submission request as part of the submitted application, the code is stored at the Nimbus local disk and topology is stored on Zookeeper as a thrift object.
    - The supervisors send periodic heartbeats to Nimbus and these heartbeat requests also contain some other information such as resources available to run tasks, detailed state of the topology they are running, and so on. Since Nimbus has all the details about supervisors, it can simply schedule pending typologies to those supervisors.
    - Remember that both Nimbus and Supervisor are stateless and they maintain all their states on Zookeeper. Workers will continue working even if Nimbus goes down and will keep updating their states to Zookeeper. All coordination between Nimbus and the supervisors is done using Zookeeper. If workers fail, the supervisors restarts them.
    - But if Nimbus is down, then no users can submit any topologies. Nimbus keeps track of each worker and in case of failure it reassigns tasks to some other worker node, which means that if Nimbus is down and the machine running the worker task goes down as well, then there is no way it can be reassigned to another worker node.

- **Supervisors**: The supervisors are slave nodes and run on each worker node. Nimbus sends assignment to supervisors and supervisors, and then launches the worker on its machine. It also keeps track of each worker and restarts them in case of any failure. The supervisor sends a heartbeat to Nimbus at regular intervals, which by default is every 15 seconds to tell Nimbus that it is alive:

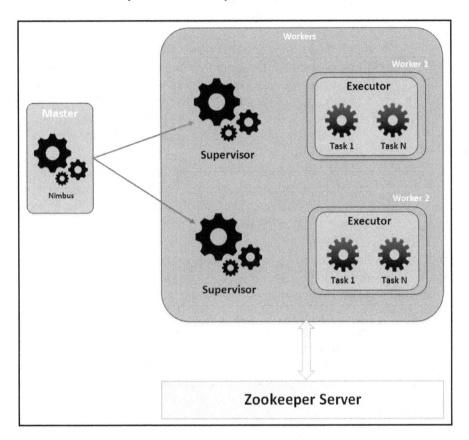

Remember that we said that Storm is stateless; both Nimbus and Supervisor save its state on Zookeeper. Whenever Nimbus receives a Storm application execution request, it asks for the available resources from Zookeeper and then schedules the task on the available supervisors. It also saves progress metadata to Zookeeper, so in the case of failure, if Nimbus restarts, it knows where to start again.

Concept of a Storm application

An Apache Storm application consists of three components:

- **Spout**: Spout is responsible for reading the streams of events from an external source system and emit it to the topology for further processing. There are basically two types of spout: reliable and unreliable. Let's look into each in little detail:

  - **Reliable spout**: Reliable spout has the ability to replay data in the case that data fails. How this works is the spout emits a message and waits for acknowledgement before dropping out the event. The process of guaranteeing the event processing can cause some increase in latency time, but it is useful and must have functionality for a streaming application like credit card fraud detection and so on.

  - **Unreliable spout**: Unreliable spouts are super fast and do not wait for acknowledgement because they do not replay the spout to re-emit the event in case of event failure. An unreliable spout is useful if loss of some event can be tolerated and does not cause serious business issues.

- **Bolt**: The record emitted by spout is proceed by bolt. All the operations such as filtering , grouping, lockups, and other business calculations are done under bolt. Processed results are then stored in fast write supported storage systems such as HBase.

- **Topology**: Topology is an DAG representation of spouts and bolts. The topology is nothing but the representing flow of an application that bounds spout and bolt together to achieve business objective. The topology is created inside the Spark application and submitted to the cluster. Each topology that's submitted is by default bound to run forever until killed forcefully or handled in the application.

The following diagram gives a better representation of topology:

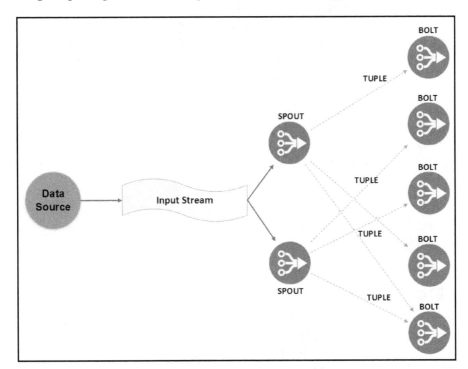

One spout can emit data to multiple bolts at a time and can track for an acknowledgement for all bolts.

Introduction to Apache Heron

Apache Heron is a new generation real-time processing engine that provides backward compatibility for Apache Storm. There are some major improvements in Apache Heron that provide a better trade-off between throughput, latency, and processing speed. Twitter has adopted Apache Storm for its streaming use cases and at the time they felt that Apache Storm had some bottleneck in design. They also thought of having a new stream processing engine that can still support all of Apache Storm applications that are already written by them. Let's look into some of the bottlenecks of Storm:

- **Harder to Debug**: The major challenge with the Apache Storm application was to debugging code errors, hardware failures, application errors, and so on. This is because there is no clear mapping of logical units of computation and physical processing.

- **On Demand Scaling**: The Scaling on demand is currently a requirement of every application. We understand that Apache Storm needs separate dedicated cluster resources with hardware to run the Storm topology. Because everything is manually set up and there is no design implementation to scale the storm cluster on demand, it was difficult to deal with the situation. Remember that the resources used by a storm cluster cannot be shared by other applications like Spark, which restrict the ability of sharing resources.
- **Managing Cluster:** Running a new Storm topology requires manual isolation of machines. Also, killing the topology requires decommissioning machines that are allocated to that topology. Think about doing this in a production environment. It will cost you more in terms of infrastructure cost, manageability cost, and productivity for users.

Keeping all these limitations as an preference, Twitter decided to build a new stream processing engine, which could overcome these limitations and also run an old Storm production topology efficiently.

Heron architecture

The limitation of Apache Storms helped them build Apache Heron. Now, the major consideration was that all the applications that are built using Apache Storm should still work on Heron and therefore compatibility with Apache Storm was always a priority during Apache Heron development. Heron uses the Aurora scheduler where typologies are submitted for execution. The Aurora scheduler launches multiple containers to run the topology, where the topology consists of multiple tasks or jobs. The following diagram is a representation of the Heron architecture:

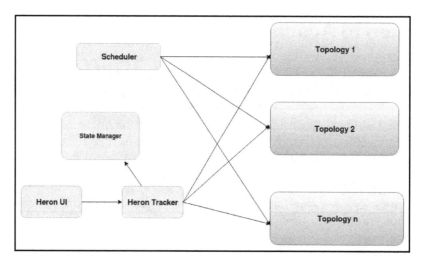

The Heron topology looks similar to the topology of Storm, which consists of two important components: spout and bolt. Spout is responsible for consuming events from the source system and then passes these on for further processing. On the other hand, bolt actually processes the events that are consumed and emitted by spout. The following diagram represents the core component of Apache Heron:

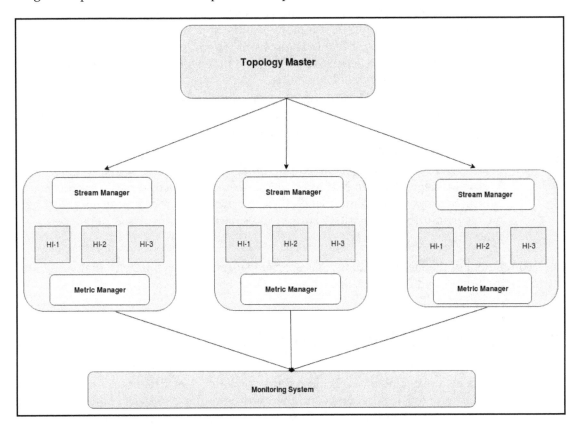

The Apache Heron components are as follows:

- **Topology Master:** If we recall what we learned in the Chapter 3, *YARN Resource Management in Hadoop*, the Resource Manager launches application master for application when a job is submitted to it for execution and then the application manager manages the life cycle of the application. Similarly, Heron also launches the **Topology Master** (**TM**) when new topology requests are submitted to it. Now ,TM is responsible to managing the entire life cycle of the application. There is entry created in Zookeeper by TM with detail so that no other TM exists for the same topology it is managing.

- **Containers:** The concept of a container is similar to that of YARN where one machine can have multiple containers running on their own JVM. Each container has a single **Stream Manager (SM)**, single **Metric Manager**, and multiple **Heron Instances (HI)**. Each container communicates with TM to ensure correctness of topology.

- **Stream Manager:** The name itself indicates its functionality; it manages the routing of streams within the topology. All the stream managers are connected with each other to ensure that back pressure is handled efficiently. If it finds that any bolt is processing streams very slowly, it manages spout serving data to that bolt and cuts off input to bolt.

- **Heron Instance:** Each Heron instance in a container is connected to a **Stream Manager**, and they are responsible for running the actual spout and bolt of topology. It helps in making the debugging process very easy, as each Heron instance is a JVM process.

- **Metric Manager:** As we discussed previously, each container contains one **Metric Manager**. **Stream Manager** and all Heron instances report their metrics to **Metric Manager**, which then sends these metrics to the monitoring system. This makes monitoring of topology simple and saves lots of effort and development time.

Each component of the Heron topology has special features. We recommend that you go to the following link to find out more: `https://apache.github.io/incubator-heron/`.

Understanding Storm Trident

Storm Trident is a layer that's built on top of Apache Storm. Unlike Apache Storm, which processes events on a real-time basis, Trident works on batches of streams, which means it collects the tuples for a few milliseconds and then processes these tuples in batches. The concept of Trident is equivalent to the concept of transaction where each transaction has a list of statements and the transaction is considered as successful only when all statements are executed successfully.

Trident provides functionality like joins, aggregations, grouping, functions, and filters. It is very difficult to achieve exactly one semantic in storm topology, but due to its micro batch processing ability, Trident makes it easy to achieve exactly one semantic, which is very useful for a few use cases:

- **Trident topology**: Trident topology is another type of Apache Storm topology that consists of two major components: trident spouts and trident bolts. Trident spouts consume the event from the source and emits it while bolts are responsible for performing operations on tuples such as filter, aggregation, and so on:

  ```
  TridentTopology topology = new TridentTopology();
  ```

- **State**: Trident maintains the state of every transaction and therefore it is easy to achieve exactly one semantic process. The topology can store the state information but the user can also choose to save a store in a separate database. The state helps in reprocessing the tuple in case it fails for any reason. Trident provides multiple mechanisms to maintain the state of the topology. The one way is to store state information in the topology itself, and other way could be to store the state in some persistence database. The State information helps in achieving guaranteed processing of event as if processing of tuple fails because of some reason, then it can be retried by using the state information. These is another problem when we do a retry – what if a tuple failed after updating the state information and then because of a retry it has again updates the state and increases the count there? It will again make the state unstable. It is important to make sure that the tuple only updates information once. The following are some recommendations to make sure that an event or tuple is process exactly once:

  - Use small batches to process the tuple.

  - Use a unique ID to assign each batch, that is `BatchID`. If the batch is failed and retried, then it will be assigned with the same `BatchID`.

  - The updating of state should be order by batches, that is, if the first batch is failed and has not updated the state, then it won't be possible for the first batch to update the state.

Storm integrations

Every processing engine has source and target systems and most of them provide connectors for integration with these systems. Apache Storm can connect to a variety of source systems and target systems such as Kafka, HBase, HDFS, and so on. Let's have a look at how to use a few of them:

- **Kafka integration**: Apache Kafka is being used as a common source for nearly all the processing system. Due to its capability to persist data for duration and provide replay-ability, `KafkaSpout` helps Storm connect to any Kafka topic. The configuration for Kafka is passed through the `SpoutConfig` object. Kafka can also act as target system for Apache Storm and `KafkaBolt` can be used for the same:

  ```
  KafkaSpout kafkaSpout = new KafkaSpout(spoutConfig);
  ```

- **HBase integration**: Apache base is widely used as target system in Storm applications because of its random read write capabilities. Most of the application requires fast read, write, and update for processed data and HBase fulfills the need in terms of throughput and latency. The HBase bolt API can be used to integrate HBase with Storm. Remember that good throughput and latency can be achieved by using the micro batch approach of pushing data to HBase. If you do HBase read and write for every record, then you have to compromise with throughput and latency:

  ```
  HBaseBolt hbase = new HBaseBolt("appname", HbaseMapperobject)
  ```

- **HDFS integration**: We have discussed before that Storm can be integrated with multiple sources and target systems, but it also comes with a set of already built connectors. Apache Storm provides HDFS bolt to write data to a HDFS-like distributed filesystem. We recommend that you consider the following cases when using HDFS bolt:

  - **File format**: The HDFS bolt that's used in storm does not come up with a rich set of functionalities. The older version only supports text and sequence files, and later AVRO file support was introduced. We recommend that you check file format support for a version before using HDFS bolt.

- **Failure handling**: The processed tuple is flushed to HDFS based on a configured period of time. For example, if you set 10 seconds as the configured time, then every 10 seconds the data will be flushed to the HDFS filesystem. Remember that when your bolt fails before it writes data to HDFS, then there is a possibility of data loss and you must handle this case in your application.

There are many spouts and bolt already built for Storm, you can check it out before writing your custom spout or bolt.

Best practices

Apache Storm has been used widely as a real-time stream processing engine, since its capability of processing millions of events per second in parallel has made significant impact on business performance. The best practices are as follows:

- **Failure handling**: The failure of event processing is common when there are millions of events landing per second. The loss of event processing may lead to huge losses for businesses. At least processing or exactly one processing pattern should be followed wherever required. The acknowledgement should only be sent to an event producing system when processing is done for the event. This may increase latency time up to some extent but will help us get business value.
- **Using checkpoint**: The Storm application may also fail due to any reason—it may be machine failure, unexpected topology kill, and so on. What will happen if, when attempting recovery, you didn't know where you needed to see how much data had been processed. The checkpoint plays an important role in handling such cases. Storm provides a default checkpoint interval but you should change `topology.state.checkpoint.interval.ms` based on your application.
- **Managing throughput and latency**: Everybody wants to achieve low latency and high throughput for their applications, but the fact is that you have to make a correct trade-off between these two. Remember that it's not always good to compromise on latency for throughput for some latency critical application such as fraud detection. If only latency is no concern for your application then we must choose a micro batch approach to process the events. Trident topology in Spark provides features so that you can micro batch an event and then process the events together. Remember that micro batching can be based on time and size, but you must choose the right one based on your requirements.

- **Logging**: The data traverses through spout to bolt in the storm topology, and adding the appropriate logging into an application helps in tracing the application logic and debugging it if there are any errors in the topology flow. The appropriate logging level should be configured from the external log configuration file so that you can make changes easily.

Summary

In this chapter, we covered three popular frameworks: Apache Spark, Apache Flink, and Apache Storm. We briefly covered their architecture, internal working, and the set of APIs that's provided by them. We also covered best practices for all processing engines and studied their importance.

In the next chapter, we will talk about a few widely used components such as Apache Pig, Apache Kafka, Apache Flume, and Apache HBase. We will go though the internals of each component and walk you through certain examples. The primary area of focus would be to understand when to use which component and what the best practices to be followed are with these applications.

7
Widely Used Hadoop Ecosystem Components

Since the invention of Hadoop, many tools have been developed around the Hadoop ecosystem. These tools are used for data ingestion, data processing, and storage, solving some of the problems Hadoop initially had. In this section, we will be focusing on Apache Pig, which is a distributed processing tool built on top of MapReduce. We will also look into two widely used ingestion tools, namely Apache Kafka and Apache Flume. We will discuss how they are used to bring data from multiple sources. Apache Hbase will be described in this chapter. We will cover the architecture details and how it fits into the CAP theorem. In this chapter, we will cover the following topics:

- Apache Pig architecture
- Writing custom **user-defined functions** (UDF) in Pig
- Apache HBase walkthrough
- CAP theorem
- Apache Kafka internals
- Building producer and consumer applications
- Apache Flume and its architecture
- Building custom source, sink, and interceptor
- Example of bringing data from a Twitter source

Technical requirements

You will be required to have basic knowledge of Linux and Apache Hadoop 3.0.

The code files of this chapter can be found on GitHub:
`https://github.com/PacktPublishing/Mastering-Hadoop-3/tree/master/Chapter07`

Check out the following video to see the code in action:
`http://bit.ly/2NyN1DX`

Pig

Hadoop had MapReduce as a processing engine when it first started and Java was the primary language that was used for writing MapReduce jobs. Since Hadoop was mostly used as an analytics processing framework, large chunks of use cases involved data mining on legacy data warehouses. These data warehouse applications were migrated to use Hadoop. Most users using legacy data warehouses had SQL and that was their core expertise. Learning a new programming language was time-consuming. Therefore, it is better to have a framework that can help SQL skilled people to write MapReduce jobs in an SQL-like language. Apache Pig was invented for this purpose. It also solved the complexity of writing multiple MapReduce pipeline jobs where output of one job becomes the input to another. the

Apache Pig is a distributed processing tool that is an abstraction over MapReduce and is used to process large datasets representing data flows. Apache Pig on Apache Spark is also an option that the open source community is working on. It has been tested for a few use cases.

Apache Pig basically consists of two components, namely Pig Latin and the Pig execution Engine. Pig Latin is a language that's used for writing Pig applications and Pig Execution Engine is responsible for the execution of Pig applications.

Apache Pig architecture

Apache Pig uses Pig Latin as a programming language and also provides an SQL-like API to write your MapReduce program. Pig consists of four major components, which are represented in the following diagram:

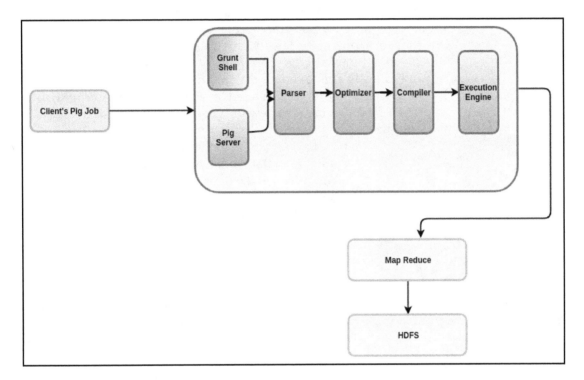

The preceding diagram can be explained as follows:

- **Parser**: The **Parser** is responsible for accepting Pig scripts and doing the necessary validations for the script. It first checks whether the script is syntactically correct or not, and if there is any syntax error in the script then it immediately throws an error. It also does type checking and a few other checks to make sure everything passes the test so that it can generate the DAG for the script. Once the DAG is generated, the nodes represents the logical operators and the Edge that connects the two nodes represents the data flow.

- **Optimizer**: The DAG that is created by the parser represents the logical plan for Pig script, which is passed to the logical optimizer. The optimizer is responsible for making an optimized plan for execution by using different optimization techniques. Pig's optimizer is rule-based and does not use a cost-based optimizer. Apache Pig basically has two layers of optimizer, which are as follows:

  - **Logical layer**: We discussed that the Pig script, once successfully parsed, is converted into a logical plan known as a DAG. Pig applies various optimization rules to split, merge, reorder, and transform operators. Finally, this optimized logical plan is converted into a MapReduce plan. The logical layer optimization rules mostly aim to reduce the amount of data in the shuffle phase or the temporary files generated between consecutive MapReduce jobs. The following are a few techniques that are used for logical optimization:

    - `PushUpFilter`: Applying push up filter reduces the amount of data in the pipeline. If there are multiple conditions in the filter found and the filters are splittable, then Pig splits the conditions and pushes up each condition separately.

    - `PushDownForEachFlatten`: It tries to apply operations such as FLATTEN, which produces more records from single large tuples and keeps the number of records low in the pipeline.

    - `ColumnPruner`: Selecting fewer numbers of columns is always the good idea for optimization; `ColumnPruner` omits the columns that are no longer needed in a logical plan.

    - `MapKeyPruner`: It omits the map keys that are never used.

    - `LimitOptimizer`: The operator applies the limit operator as soon as it can for a given logical plan because it limits the number of records that can be traversed across the network.

  - **MapReduce layer**: It aims to optimize the MapReduce job properties such as the number of MapReduce jobs in the pipeline, selecting Combiner, and so on. The MapReduce plan is converted to a more efficient plan with respect to the optimization rules.

- **Compiler**: The compiler is responsible for compiling the optimized logical plan into a series of MapReduce jobs. The output of one map reduce job may become the input to another MapReduce job in the pipeline.
- **Execution Engine**: The Apache Pig execution engine is responsible for the actual execution of MapReduce jobs that are created by the compiler. The default MapReduce engine for Pig is map reduce. Apache Pig can now use Tez and Spark as execution engines for job execution, which will make Pig faster than using its legacy execution engine.

Installing and running Pig

Apache Pig runs as a client-side application and requires Hadoop and Java as prerequisite for execution.

> Please make sure that you have Hadoop and Java already setup on your Linux machine.

The installation of Apache Pig is simple and requires fewer steps given that the prerequisite is already done. The steps are as follows:

1. The first step is to make sure you have HADOOP_HOME and JAVA_HOME already set on your Linux system. If HADOOP_HOME is not set, then Apache Pig will run within an embedded version of Hadoop.
2. The next step is to download the Apache Pig stable release from http://pig.Apache.org/releases.html and unpack the tarball to a specific location, as follows:

```
mkdir /opt/pig
tar xvf pig-0.17.0.tar.gz
mv pig-0.17.0/* /opt/pig
```

3. The final step is to set PIG_HOME and configure it to a system classpath, as follows:

```
export PIG_HOME=/opt/pig
export PATH=$PATH:$PIG_HOME/bin
```

Now, we are done with the installation of Apache Pig. Next, we will check whether it has installed properly or not. The following command will show the version of `pig` installed in the system:

```
pig -version
```

To see Pig usage, use the `-help` command, as follows:

```
pig -help
```

Once the installation is verified, you can start the execution of your Pig script or run a Grunt shell to execute and test the Pig commands and functions. There are different ways we can run and execute Pig programs, which are as follows:

- **Grunt Shell**: Grunt shell is an interactive shell for running Pig commands and functions. Generally, it is used for debugging and testing your program logic, or learning Pig from scratch.
- **Embedded mode**: Apache Pig provides `PigServer` class to run Pig from Java programs and executes our Pig logic from there.
- **Script**: The most widely used technique is to write a Pig program to a script file and execute it from the command line using Pig command `pig testscript.pig`. The `-e` option can be used to execute a Pig script specified as a string from the command line.

Introducing Pig Latin and Grunt

Pig Latin is a programming language that was originally developed at Yahoo Research. Pig Latin provides an SQL-like syntax along with a low-level procedural language syntax. Users can write a program using Pig Latin that is similar to writing a query plan.

An Apache Pig program consists of a series of statements that are responsible for applying some transformation on data. Each statement can be considered as a single command. Each statement needs to be terminated by a semicolon and the statement can be split into multiple lines without any additional syntax or symbol. Pig will read a statement until it finds a semicolon, which acts as an indicator of the end of the statement.

Let's look into a few important pillars of the Pig Latin language:

- **Data type**: Like every programming language, Apache Pig does have a defined set of inbuilt data types and each data type has its own uses. We can categorize the data types into two categories namely, simple and complex. The simple data type includes `Boolean`, `int`, `float`, `double`, `long`, `biginteger`, `bigdecimal`, `chararray`, `bytearray`, and `datetime` while complex data types are `tuple`, `bag`, and `map`.

- **Statement**: The Pig Program executes the Pig statements and parses each statement sequentially. If the Pig parser finds any syntax or semantic error in the Pig script then it will straight away throw an error message. If the statement is successfully parsed then it will be added to the logical plan step and then the interpreter will move to the next statement. Until and unless all the statements in the script are added to the execution plan, no execution will happen. Apache Pig statements can also be categorized into different categories, they are:

  - **Load and store statements**: Load, store, dump
  - **Filter statements**: Filter, generate, distinct
  - **Group and join statements**: Join, group, co-group, cross, cube
  - **Sort statements**: Order, rank, limit
  - **Combining and splitting**: Union, split
  - **Other operator**: Describe, explain, register, define, and so on

- **Expression**: Pig Latin provides a set of expressions to use with statements to perform some operations on data, such as comparing two values using relational operator, applying arithmetic operation over a set of values, and so on. Let's look at following the example:

```
youngPeople= Filter population BY age>18;
youngMalePeople = Filter youngPeople where gender=='male';
```

Expression can also be a function, UDF function, or relational operation, which results in some value.

- **Schema**: We mentioned earlier that Pig uses an SQL-like syntax and to do this there has to be some schema associated with the data. Pig Latin provides you the ability to define a schema for the dataset loaded in the Pig script. If you do not provide any schema, Pig creates a default schema for you with all fields defined with `charaaray` type, as follows:

```
input_records = LOAD 'employee.csv' USING PigStorage(',')
AS (employee_id:int, age:int, salary:int);
DESCRIBE input_records;
```

The output of the describe statement will give us the following result:

```
input_records: {employee_id:int, age:int, salary:int}
```

If you do not define a column name then Pig assigns a default name, such as $0, $1, and so on, with the datatype as chararray.

- **Functions**: Pig Latin has a set of commonly used functions built in with it and also provides the user an ability to build custom user-defined functions, which can be applied to records in the dataset. There are different types of functions available, such as eval, filter, load, store, and so on.

Writing UDF in Pig

Apache Pig comes with a wide range of functions and operators, but most of the time the user requires custom functions to deal with data. Apache Pig provides an API to write our own custom user-defined functions. Apache Pig provides you an ability to write UDFs in different languages, such as Java, Python, Groovy, and so on. Java is a widely used language for writing custom Pig UDF due to its extensive support by the Pig community. There are different types of UDF functions available in Pig and we will look into few of them.

If your project is a Maven project, then add the following Maven dependency into the project:

```
<dependency>
    <groupId>org.Apache.pig</groupId>
    <artifactId>pig</artifactId>
    <version>0.17.0</version>
</dependency>
```

Eval function

Eval function is responsible for iterating through each tuple in a dataset and applies eval type functions over tuple. Some of the built-in eval functions are min, max, count, sum, avg, and so on.

All eval functions extend the Java class EvalFunc. The class uses Java generic and is parameterized by return type of UDF. The custom UDF class will extend the function and implement the exec method, which takes a single record and returns a single result.

The following is a sample template for writing an `eval` function. If you run the following program, the return type of the exec function is the same as the parameter passed to the `EvalFunc` in class definition, as follows:

```
import org.Apache.pig.EvalFunc;
import org.Apache.pig.data.Tuple;

import java.io.IOException;

public class CustomEvalUDF extends EvalFunc<String> {

    @Override
    public String exec(Tuple tuple) throws IOException {

        //Logic to extract or modify tuple here
        return null;
    }
}
```

An `eval` function UDF can be created using the preceding template. Let's create a UDF that can trim white spaces and convert a string to upper case, as follows:

```
import org.Apache.pig.EvalFunc;
import org.Apache.pig.data.Tuple;
import java.io.IOException;

public class UpperCaseWithTrimUDF extends EvalFunc<String> {
    @Override
    public String exec(Tuple tuple) throws IOException {

        if (tuple == null || tuple.size() == 0)
            return null;

        try {
            String inputRecord = (String) tuple.get(0);
            inputRecord = inputRecord.trim();
            inputRecord = inputRecord.toUpperCase();
            return inputRecord;
        } catch (Exception ex) {
            throw new IOException("unable to trim and convert to upper case
", ex);

        }
    }
}
```

Filter function

The filter function is used to filter out the record based on conditions defined in the `exec` function of the user-defined function. The `FilterFunc` class is extended to build any custom filter function. The following template can be used to build any custom filter function:

```
import org.Apache.pig.FilterFunc;
import org.Apache.pig.data.Tuple;

import java.io.IOException;

public class CustomFilterFuncUDF extends FilterFunc {
    @Override
    public Boolean exec(Tuple tuple) throws IOException {
        //condition to filter the record
        return null;
    }
}
```

Let's look at how we can build and use a filter function that can filter out all the records with length less then 50, as follows:

```
import org.Apache.pig.FilterFunc;
import org.Apache.pig.data.Tuple;

import java.io.IOException;

public class IsLengthGreaterThen50 extends FilterFunc {
    @Override
    public Boolean exec(Tuple tuple) throws IOException {

        if (tuple == null || tuple.size() == 0)
            return false;

        String inputRecord = (String) tuple.get(0);

        return inputRecord.length()>=50;
    }
}
```

How to use custom UDF in Pig

To use any custom UDF in Pig we have to register the UDF with Pig or put the UDF in an Apache pig class path so that Apache Pig can search the UDF class in the path. Remember that the UDF class name will act as a function name inside the Pig script, for example:

```
Register  udfname.jar;

filtered_records = FILTER records BY IsLengthGreaterThen50(recordcolumn);
```

Pig with Hive

In most of the use cases, Apache Pig is used along with Apache Hive, where Apache Pig acts as a processing engine and Apache Hive acts as a database system for data warehouse over Hadoop. Apache Pig provides an API to integrate Apache Hive using the Hive metastore called HCatalog. There are basically two major operations that perform over Hive using Apache pig, which are as follows:

- **Read/load record from Hive table**: Apache Pig can load data from the Hive table for further processing. The HCataLoader function can be used to load data from Apache Hive tables into Pig relation. Remember that if the Hive metastore does not contain information about the table, then we won't be able to load data from Hive as it will result in a table not found exception. Load the employee table from dev database into relation employeeRecord relation, as follows:

    ```
    employeeRecrods = LOAD 'dev.employee' USING
    org.Apache.HCatalog.pig.HCatLoader();
    ```

    The preceding statement will load the employee table from dev database into employeeRecord relation. The datatype and column name will be read from the Hive metastore and can be used in further processing.

- **Storing Records to Hive Table**: The processed or transformed record can finally be loaded into the Hive table for performing some analytics queries. The datatype and number of columns in relation should match with the Hive tables. In simple terms, if you have 10 columns in the Hive table then the Pig relation should also contain the same number of columns with compatible data types. HCatStorer can be used to store data to Hive using a Pig script, for example:

    ```
    STORE filteredEmployeeStats INTO 'default.employeeStats' USING
    org.Apache.HCatalog.pig.HCatStorer();
    ```

The preceding statements are just sub parts of a Pig script and to use HCatLoader and HCatStorer we must run the Pig script file using the following command:

```
pig -useHCatalog employeeprocess.pig
```

If you do not use the -useHCatalog option then Pig will go through an exception of not recognizing HCatLoader or HCatStorer. Remember that the function names are case sensitive in nature and will go through exception in case of mismatch.

Best practices

Apache Pig does have a lot of scope for optimization but it depends on the use case you are trying to solve and how the Pig Latin script looks for it. But there are still common best practices that we can follow to boost performance, which are as follows:

- **Filter records**: The group and join operation involves lots of data shuffling across data nodes, which results in adding more processing time that slows up the overall execution time. It is always recommended to filter out records that do not make any sense in the data, for example, you may want to join records for only a few categories or you may not want to consider records with null values, and so on. Filtering records reduces the data size and helps in speeding up the process.

- **Avoid too many small files**: We should always avoid processing too many small files because it may result in too many MapReduce jobs, which makes no sense as most of the time they will just start and stop the mapper and reduce the processes. It is always recommended to avoid too many small files or to run a compaction job that will convert these small files into a single or multiple large file.

- **Explicit data type declaration**: Apache Pig has a way of loading the data and defining the schema for it. If we do not specify the type declaration, Pig automatically assigns default datatypes for columns, which may take extra memory space and reduce performance. We should always define schema and column types explicitly while loading data, which reduces processing time up to 20% and in some cases up to two times.

- **Sampling data**: Apache Pig has lazy evaluation and if you want to just dump the data for verifying the output or for any other debugging purpose then always use limit operator with your statement, which will only get you few records instead of dumping all the records to terminal.
- **Compression**: In most cases, compression has resulted in better performance. Apache Pig scripts may involve a chain of MapReduce operations and in such cases the intermediate result of each job is written to temporary storage, which is then shuffled across the network. The `pig.tmpfilecompression` function should be turned on to use compression for intermediate MapReduce results, which helps in saving space and increasse read time when used for further processing by downstream systems.

HBase

Although Hadoop was getting popular after its invention, it was still only suitable for batch processing use cases where a huge set of data could be processed in a single batch. Hadoop came from the Google research paper called **Hadoop Distributed File System** (**HDFS**) from the Google File System Research paper and MapReduce from the Google MapReduce research paper. Google has one more popular product, which is Big Table, and to support random read/write access over large sets of data, HBase was discovered. HBase runs on top of Hadoop and uses the scalability of Hadoop by running its daemon—HDFS, with real-time data access as a key/value store.

 Apache HBase is an open source, distributed, NoSQL database that provides real-time random read/write access to large datasets over HDFS.

HBase architecture and its concept

Apache HBase is a distributed column storage database that also follows the master/slave architecture. Below is a picture representation of HBase architecture and its components:

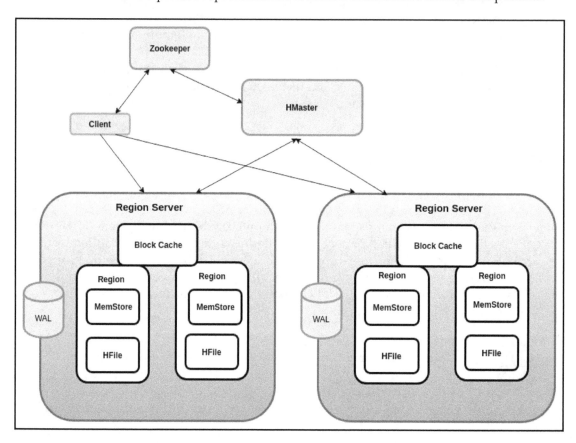

The HBase architecture has four major components, which are as follows:

- **HMaster**: HMaster is a process that is responsible for assigning region to region servers in the Hadoop cluster for load balancing. HMaster is responsible for monitoring all **Region Server** instances in the HBase cluster, and acts as the interface for all metadata changes. The master typically runs on Namenode in a distributed system. Now the question is, what happens when the master goes down? In a distributed HBase cluster there are other masters that are on standby mode and available to take over the current master and the ZooKeeper takes care of this if the leader is elected. But it is possible that the master goes down for some time and the HBase cluster has to work without the master for some time. This is possible because a client directly interacts with the region servers and clusters can function in steady state. But it is always good to have the master up and running as soon as possible, because it handles some critical functionality, such as:
  - Manages and monitors the Hadoop cluster
  - Assigns regions to region servers on startup and re-assigns regions for recovery or load balancing to region servers
  - Monitors all the region servers in the cluster and takes action on their failure
  - All Data Definition Language (DDL) operations from client are handled by the HMaster
- **Region Server**: The region server in HBase contains multiple regions that are assigned by HMaster. It is responsible for handling client communication and performing all data-related operations. Any read or write request to regions are handled by the region server that contains the region. Region servers run on every data node in the HBase cluster and have the following components:
  - **Block Cache**: Block cache resides in the top of the region server and is responsible for storing frequently accessed data in the memory, which helps in performance boosting. The block cache follows the least recently used (LRU) cache concept, which means records that were least recently used will be removed from the block cache.
  - **MemStore**: MemStore acts as a temporary storage for all the incoming data. The data is then committed to the permanent storage system. There are multiple MemStores in the HBase cluster. In simple terms it acts as a write cache for all incoming data.

- **HFile**: HFiles are actual files or cells in which data is written. When the MemStore memory gets full, it writes data to an HFile over disk. HFiles are stored on HDFS.
- **Write ahead log** (**WAL**): WAL is used to recover the data in case of any failure. It stores the new data that is not yet committed to the disk.

- **Regions**: HBase tables are divided by row key range into regions. All the rows between the region start key and region end key will be available in the region. Each region is assigned to one region server, which manages the read/write request for that region. Regions are basic blocks of scalability in HBase. It is always recommended to have a low number of regions per region server to ensure high performance.
- **Zookeeper**: ZooKeeper is a distributed coordination service that is responsible for region assignments to region servers and also responsible for recovering regions in case of region server crash by loading them onto other region servers. If a client wants to share or exchange with regions, they have to approach the ZooKeeper first. The master service HMaster and all the region servers are registered with the ZooKeeper service. The client accesses ZooKeeper quorum to connect with region servers and HMaster. In case of any node failure in HBase cluster, ZooKeeper's ZKquoram will activate error messages and then start to repair failed nodes.

The ZooKeeper service is responsible for keeping track of all the region servers in the HBase cluster and collecting the information such as the number of region servers, data nodes attached to region servers, and so on. HMaster connects to ZooKeeper to get the details of region servers. It is also responsible for establishing client communication with region servers, keeping track of server failure and network partitions, maintaining the configuration information, and so on.

CAP theorem

If you have been using NoSQL databases for your application then somewhere down the line you would have heard about CAP theorem, which says that any database cannot achieve all three features, which are consistency, availability, and partition tolerance. They will have to compromise with two of them at a time.

Let's understand first what is consistency, availability, and partition tolerance:

- **Availability**: Availability indicates that every client who submits the query request must get a response, regardless of the individual node state in the system. It is only possible when your system remains operational all the time. If we have to put this in more simple words then availability guarantees that every request to the database will get a response, regardless of guaranteeing that result has the latest write to the database included in it.

- **Consistency**: Consistency guarantees that every node in a distributed system must return a same data as result. The system can only be in a consistence state when a transaction started by a client is completed successfully, which means the transaction is applied to all the nodes in system. If any error occurs during the transaction, then the entire transaction will be rolled back. In simple words, the system is said to be in a consistent state if every non-failure node in the system can return the data with the most recent write to the database system.

- **Partition tolerance**: The partition tolerance tells that your system will continue to run even if there is any delay in the number of messages between nodes due to network issues. The partition tolerance network can sustain any number of network failures given that the entire network does not fail. All the records are replicated across a sufficient number of nodes, which helps in serving client requests, even if one or two nodes go down. In all the modern distributed systems, partition tolerance is a necessity and you have to compromise between availability and consistency.

A system is said to be in partition tolerance when isolation of one or more nodes does not affect the system consistency for serving client requests.

Since partition tolerance is always a part of NoSQL modern databases, each database falls into two categories, availability and partition tolerance, and consistency and partition tolerance. The following diagram initiates a few commonly-used databases and their features with respect to CAP theorem:

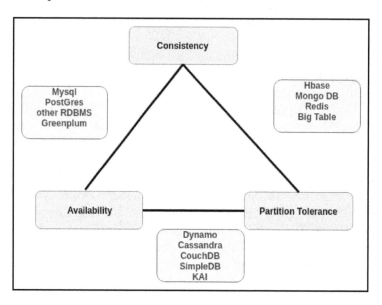

Consistency and partition tolerance (CP): CP indicates that a system can have two features, namely consistency and partition tolerance at a time but not availability. If we try to add availability in the system with CP property, then partition tolerance needs to be eliminated for at least one node and it needs to correctly address the query that receives the most recent writes from all the nodes in the system if any link is broken.

Availability and partition tolerance (AP): AP indicates that the system will have availability and partition tolerance property but not consistency. If we try to add consistency in the AP system, then availability needs to be eliminated because the system has to wait and does NOT have to answer any query until ALL nodes in the system are synced up on the latest write.

Availability and consistency (**AC**): The AC indicates that the system will have availability and consistency at the same time but not partition tolerance, because if we try to add partition tolerance to it, then consistency needs to be eliminated because the most recent writes cannot be sent to ALL nodes when links between them are broken.

HBase operations and its examples

Every database has some set of basic operations that are generally referred as **create**, **read**, **update**, and **delete** (**CRUD**) operations. Since most of the time HBase is used with applications that are built using different programming languages, we will look at how CRUD operations are done using programming APIs.

The first step in any database is table creation. In HBase the table creation syntax shown as follows:

```
create '<table name>','<column family>'
```

Taking the following as an example:

```
create 'testtable', 'colfamily1', 'colfamily2'
```

Now let's look into few commonly used operations executed over HBase using *JAVA API*.

Put operation

The insertion of a record into HBase can be done using the Put object. You have to provide a row to create a `Put` instance. A row is identified by a unique row key and is the case with most values in HBase—it is a Java `byte[]` array, as follows:

```
import org.Apache.Hadoop.conf.Configuration;
import org.Apache.Hadoop.hbase.HBaseConfiguration;
import org.Apache.Hadoop.hbase.client.HTable;
import org.Apache.Hadoop.hbase.client.Put;
import org.Apache.Hadoop.hbase.util.Bytes;

import java.io.IOException;

public class HBasePutExample {

    public static void main(String[] args) throws IOException {
        Configuration conf = HBaseConfiguration.create();
        HTable table = new HTable(conf, "testtable");
        Put recordPuter = new Put(Bytes.toBytes("samplerow"));
        recordPuter.addColumn(Bytes.toBytes("colfamily1"),
```

```
Bytes.toBytes("col1"),
                Bytes.toBytes("val1"));
        recordPuter.addColumn(Bytes.toBytes("colfamily1"),
Bytes.toBytes("col2"),
                Bytes.toBytes("val2"));
        table.put(recordPuter);
    }
}
```

There are multiple ways of putting a record into the HBase table using the put method; we have just covered the basic one. You can also create a list of put instances and insert batch records into HBase tables.

Get operation

The Get call is used to retrieve data that's already stored in the HBase table that is reading the data from HBase tables. We have to provide a row key that is the row you want to access from HBase table, as follows:

```
import org.Apache.Hadoop.conf.Configuration;
import org.Apache.Hadoop.hbase.HBaseConfiguration;
import org.Apache.Hadoop.hbase.client.Get;
import org.Apache.Hadoop.hbase.client.HTable;
import org.Apache.Hadoop.hbase.client.Result;
import org.Apache.Hadoop.hbase.util.Bytes;

import java.io.IOException;

public class HBaseGetExample {

    public static void main(String[] args) throws IOException {
        Configuration conf = HBaseConfiguration.create();
        HTable table = new HTable(conf, "testtable");
        Get get = new Get(Bytes.toBytes("samplerow"));
        get.addColumn(Bytes.toBytes("colfamily1"), Bytes.toBytes("col1"));
        Result result = table.get(get);
        byte[] val = result.getValue(Bytes.toBytes("colfamily1"),
                Bytes.toBytes("col2"));
        System.out.println("Value: " + Bytes.toString(val));
    }
}
```

Similar to Put, HBase also provides the ability to get data in batches. We just need to provide a list of Get instance and our job should be done.

Delete operation

Deleting the record from the HBase table is also likely in some use cases. The `Delete` call can be used to delete a row or column family. You can also delete multiple rows or a column family by passing list of `Delete` object to table delete method, as follows:

```
import org.Apache.Hadoop.conf.Configuration;
import org.Apache.Hadoop.hbase.HBaseConfiguration;
import org.Apache.Hadoop.hbase.client.Delete;
import org.Apache.Hadoop.hbase.client.HTable;
import org.Apache.Hadoop.hbase.util.Bytes;
import java.io.IOException;
import java.util.ArrayList;
import java.util.List;

public class HBaseDeleteExample {

    public static void main(String[] args) throws IOException {

        Configuration conf = HBaseConfiguration.create();
        HTable table = new HTable(conf, "testtable");
        List<Delete> deletes = new ArrayList<Delete>();
        Delete delete1 = new Delete(Bytes.toBytes("samplerow"));
        delete1.setTimestamp(4);
        deletes.add(delete1);

        Delete delete2 = new Delete(Bytes.toBytes("row2"));
        delete2.addColumn(Bytes.toBytes("colfam1"), Bytes.toBytes("col1"));
        delete2.addColumn(Bytes.toBytes("colfam2"), Bytes.toBytes("col3"),
5);
        deletes.add(delete2);
        Delete delete3 = new Delete(Bytes.toBytes("row3"));
        delete3.addFamily(Bytes.toBytes("colfamily1"));
        delete3.addFamily(Bytes.toBytes("colfamily1"), 3);
        deletes.add(delete3);
        table.delete(deletes);

    }
}
```

Batch operation

Now you should be comfortable with basic HBase APIs and can add, retrieve, and delete records from HBase tables. Remember, `Row` is a parent interface for `Get`, `Put`, and `Delete` objects and thus you can perform all three operations in a batch by passing the list of row object operation to table API, shown as follows:

```
List<Row> batchOperation = new ArrayList<Row>();
batchOperation.add(put);
batchOperation.add(get);
batchOperation.add(delete);
Object[] results = new Object[batch.size()];
table.batch(batchOperation, results);
```

Installation

The HBase installation can be done in different modes namely, local mode, pseudo-distributed mode, and distributed mode. In this section, we will be focusing on local mode and distributed mode setup for HBase cluster.

Local mode Installation

The local mode does not require any Hadoop path setup and it is easier to install and test the application. Let's begin step by step:

1. Download stable tar balls from `http://www.Apache.org/dyn/closer.lua/hbase/` and keep it in the stable folder

2. Untar the stable HBase tarball and put all the files in new `hbase` directory, as follows:

```
tar -xvf hbase-2.1.1-bin.tar.gz
mkdir /opt/hbase
mv hbase-2.1.1/* /opt/hbase
```

3. Set `JAVA_HOME` in `conf/hbase-env.sh` file and save it, as follows:

```
# Set environment variables here.

# This script sets variables multiple times over the course of starting an hbase process,
# so try to keep things idempotent unless you want to take an even deeper look
# into the startup scripts (bin/hbase, etc.)

# The java implementation to use.  Java 1.8+ required.
 export JAVA_HOME=/opt/java/jdk1.8.0/

# Extra Java CLASSPATH elements.  Optional.
# export HBASE_CLASSPATH=

# The maximum amount of heap to use. Default is left to JVM default.
# export HBASE_HEAPSIZE=1G

# Uncomment below if you intend to use off heap cache. For example, to allocate 8G of
# offheap, set the value to "8G".
# export HBASE_OFFHEAPSIZE=1G

# Extra Java runtime options.
# Below are what we set by default.  May only work with SUN JVM.
# For more on why as well as other possible settings,
# see http://hbase.apache.org/book.html#performance
export HBASE_OPTS="$HBASE_OPTS -XX:+UseConcMarkSweepGC"

# Uncomment one of the below three options to enable java garbage collection logging for the server-side processes.

# This enables basic gc logging to the .out file.
# export SERVER_GC_OPTS="-verbose:gc -XX:+PrintGCDetails -XX:+PrintGCDateStamps"

# This enables basic gc logging to its own file.
# If FILE-PATH is not replaced, the log file(.gc) would still be generated in the HBASE_LOG_DIR .
# export SERVER_GC_OPTS="-verbose:gc -XX:+PrintGCDetails -XX:+PrintGCDateStamps -Xloggc:<FILE-PATH>"

# This enables basic GC logging to its own file with automatic log rolling. Only applies to jdk 1.6.0_34+ and 1.7.0_2+.
# If FILE-PATH is not replaced, the log file(.gc) would still be generated in the HBASE_LOG_DIR .
# export SERVER_GC_OPTS="-verbose:gc -XX:+PrintGCDetails -XX:+PrintGCDateStamps -Xloggc:<FILE-PATH> -XX:+UseGCLogFileRotation -XX:NumberO
```

4. The next step is to add `HBASE_HOME` to classpath, considering the Ubuntu system addthe following line to the `~/.bashrc` file, as follows:

```
export HBASE_HOME=/opt/hbase
export PATH= $PATH:$HBASE_HOME/bin
```

5. Modify `hbase-site.xml` and add `hbase.root` and the `hbase.zookeeper.property.dataDir` property to it and set their respective values, as follows:

```
<property>
        <name>hbase.rootdir</name>
        <value>file:///home/packt/hbase</value>
</property>

<property>
        <name>hbase.zookeeper.property.dataDir</name>
        <value>/home/packt/zookeeper</value>
</property>
```

6. Now you can run the `hbase shell` command and verify the installation.

Distributed mode installation

Distributed mode setup requires little changes in the way we configured the HBase in local mode. The steps for setting up HBASE_HOME will be the same in the distributed mode setup—the only difference will come on the master and slave configuration. Let's look at each configuration in little detail.

Master node configuration

The master node, also known as HMaster, is responsible for managing slave nodes, which are region server. The following details need to be added to master hbase-site.xml:

```
<configuration>
<property>
    <name>hbase.rootdir</name>
    <value>hdfs://Namenode-ip:9000/hbase</value>
</property>
<property>
    <name>hbase.cluster.distributed</name>
    <value>true</value>
 </property>
<property>
    <name>hbase.zookeeper.property.dataDir</name>
    <value>hdfs://Namenode-ip:9000/zookeeper</value>
</property>
 <property>
    <name>hbase.zookeeper.quorum</name>
    <value>Namenode-ip, Datanode1, Datanode2</value>
 </property>
<property>
    <name>hbase.zookeeper.property.clientPort</name>
    <value>2181</value>
</property>
</configuration>
```

Once the details are added, we also need to add all the slave node information to conf/resgionservers file, as follows:

```
Namenode-ip
Datanode1
Datanode2
```

Slave node configuration

Region servers act as a slave node in the HBase cluster and all the nodes are hosted on the data nodes. Each HBase slave node must have the following information in their `hbase-site.xml` file. Make sure you set the `hbase.cluster.distributed` property to true on every slave node so that it acts as `hbase` daemon node, as follows:

```
<configuration>
<property>
    <name>hbase.rootdir</name>
    <value>hdfs://Namenode-NN:9000/hbase</value>
 </property>
<property>
    <name>hbase.cluster.distributed</name>
    <value>true</value>
</property>
</configuration>
```

Once the master and slave nodes are set up we can run the `start-hbase.sh` script on the master node and it will do the rest of the job for us. Now you have your own distributed HBase cluster, where you can create HBase tables and use it with your application.

Best practices

There are some common best practices that we can follow to boost performance, which are as follows:

- **Selecting number of region**: While creating the table in HBase, you can explicitly define the number of regions for a table. If you don't define it, HBase will calculate it for you based on some algorithm that might not be fit for your table. It is always good to explicitly assign the number of the regions for the table and it helps in achieving good performance.

- **Choosing number of column family**: In most cases, we have a row key and one column family but sometimes you may choose to put an important column in one column family and another to anther column family; whatever the case may be we should not have more than 10 column family per table in HBase. Try to keep the number as low as you can.

- **Balanced cluster**: A HBase cluster is said to be a balanced cluster when almost every region server has an equal number of regions in them. You may want to turn on the balancer, which will balance the cluster every 5 minutes.

- **Avoiding running other job on HBase cluster**: People have been using some integrated framework for HBase setup, such as Cloudera, Hortonworks, BigInsight, and so on. The integrated framework also comes up with other tools such as Hive, Pig, Spark, and so on. HBase is CPU and memory intensive with sporadic large sequential I/O access and therefore running other jobs will result in a significant decrease in performance.

- **Avoid major compaction and do splitting**: HBase has two types of compaction one being minor compaction, which compacts well-defined default configured files and helps in increasing performance. The other is major compaction, which takes all the files in a region and combines them into one. As compaction can be time consuming, you cannot perform any write to region until a compaction job completes. Therefore, it is a good idea to avoid major compaction as much as you can. We must also split the region once it reaches a defined size, maybe 4–5 GB, based on region capacity.

Kafka

LinkedIn portal will be the most used portal in your professional career. The Kafka system was first introduced by the LinkedIn technical team. LinkedIn built a software metrics tool using custom in-house components with minor support from existing open source tools. The system collected user activity data on the data portal. It also used this activity data to show relevant information to each user on the web portal. The system was originally built as a traditional XML-based logging service, that was processed with different **extract transform load** (ETL) tools. However, as this arrangement did not work, they started running into various problems. To solve these problems, they built a system called Kafka. LinkedIn built Kafka as a distributed, fault-tolerant, publish/subscribe system. It records messages organized into topics. Applications can produce or consume messages from topics. All messages are stored as logs to persistent file systems. Kafka is a WAL system that writes all published messages to log files before making them available for consumer applications. Subscribers/consumers can read these written messages as required in an appropriate time frame. Kafka was built with the following goals in mind:

- Loose coupling between message producers and message consumers
- Persistence of message data to support a variety of data consumption scenarios and failure handling
- Maximum end-to-end throughput with low latency components
- Managing diverse data formats and types using binary data formats

While we will introduce Kafka in more detail in the upcoming sections, you should understand that one of the common uses of Kafka is in its stream processing architecture. With its reliable message delivery semantics, it helps in consuming high rates of events. Moreover, it provides message replaying capabilities along with support for different types of consumer.

This further helps in making streaming architecture fault-tolerant and supports a variety of alerting and notification services.

Apache Kafka architecture

All messages in the Kafka topics are a collection of bytes which is represented as an array. The Producers are the main applications which stores information in Kafka queues and sends messages to Kafka topics that stores all types of messages. All the topics are further categorised into partitions in which each partition stores messages in the sequence that they arrive. Basically, there are two major operations that Producers and Consumers can perform in Kafka, the Producers append to the end of the write-ahead log files and Consumers fetch messages from these log files belonging to a given topic partition. Physically, each topic is spread over different Kafka brokers, which host one or two partitions of each topic. Ideally, Kafka pipelines should have a uniform number of partitions per broker and all topics on each machine. Consumers are applications or processes that subscribe to a topic or receive messages from these topics.
The following diagram shows you the conceptual layout of a Kafka cluster:

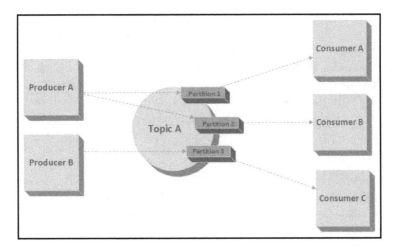

The preceding paragraphs explain the logical architecture of Kafka and how different logical components coherently work together. While it is important to understand how Kafka architecture is divided logically, you also need to understand what Kafka's physical architecture looks like. This will help you in later chapters as well. A Kafka cluster is basically composed of one or more servers (nodes). The following diagram depicts how a multi-node Kafka cluster looks:

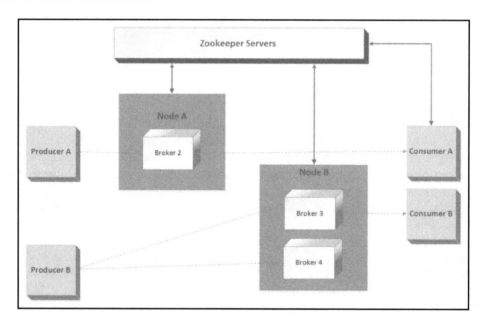

A typical Kafka cluster consists of multiple brokers. It helps in load balancing message reads and writes to the cluster. Each of these brokers is stateless. However, they use ZooKeeper to maintain their states. Each topic partition has one of the brokers as a leader and zero or more brokers as followers. The leaders manage any read or write requests for their respective partitions. Followers replicate the leader in the background without actively interfering with the leader's working. You should think of followers as a backup for the leader and one of those followers will be chosen as the leader in the case of leader failure.

 Each server in a Kafka cluster will either be a leader for some of the topic's partitions or a follower for others. In this way, the load on every server is equally balanced. Kafka broker leader election is done with the help of ZooKeeper.

ZooKeeper is an important component of a Kafka cluster. It manages and coordinates Kafka brokers and consumers. ZooKeeper keeps track of any new broker additions or any existing broker failures in the Kafka cluster. Accordingly, it will notify the producer or consumers of Kafka queues about the cluster state. This helps both producers and consumers in
coordinating work with active brokers. ZooKeeper also records which broker is the leader for which topic partition and passes on this information to the producer or consumer to read and write the messages. At this juncture, you must be familiar with producer and consumer applications with respect to the Kafka cluster. However, it is beneficial to touch on this briefly so that you can verify your understanding. Producers push data to brokers. At the time of publishing data, producers search for the elected leader (broker) of the respective topic partition and automatically send a message to that leader broker server. Similarly, the consumer reads messages from brokers. The consumer records its state with the help of ZooKeeper as Kafka brokers are stateless. This design helps in scaling Kafka well. The consumer offset value is maintained by ZooKeeper. The consumer records how many messages have been consumed by it using partition offset. It ultimately acknowledges that message offset to ZooKeeper. It means that the consumer has consumed all prior messages.

Installing and running Apache Kafka

Apache Kafka installation is very different from any other setup that we have looked at previously. Apache Kafka is an independent, distributed, fault tolerant, and scalable messaging system that does not have any dependency on Hadoop. Today Apache Kafka is not only being used in Big Data ecosystem, but also for building various micro service applications because of its high throughput read and write capability. It easily solves the producer/consumer problem and helps the producer and consumer perform their work independently.

In this section, we will look at how to install Kafka in local and distributed modes. Let's start with setting it up in local mode.

Local mode installation

Installing and running Kafka in local mode requires only 5-10 minutes, if you follow these steps. Make sure you have Java installed on your system before you start:

1. The first step is to download the latest Kafka tarball from this link `https://kafka.Apache.org/downloads`

2. Once the tarball is downloaded, we have to untar it using following command:

```
tar -xvf kafka_2.11-2.0.0.tgz
```

3. Create a Kafka directory at some common location and copy all the Kafka files into the directory, as follows:

```
mkdir /opt/kafka
mv kafka_2.11-2.0.0/* opt/kafka
```

4. Now the next step is to start ZooKeeper using the already available property file, which will run ZooKeeper at port 2181, as follows:

```
bin/zookeeper-server-start.sh config/zookeeper.properties
```

5. Once the ZooKeeper is up and running, you can now set up the Kafka broker server. In a single machine you can run multiple Kafka servers by providing different configuration files. The `config/server.properties` contains the broker property and the default port is `9092`. Each broker also has a unique ID associated with it and the default is `0`. Run the broker as follows:

```
bin/kafka-server-start.sh config/server.properties
```

To create another server property file, change `broker-id`, port, and log directory and run the new broker on same machine.

6. Now the Kafka cluster is up and running. We can create a topic and push data to it. Let's create the topic, as follows:

```
bin/kafka-topics.sh --create --topic testtopic --zookeeper
localhost:2181 --partitions 1 --replication-factor 1
```

7. Use console producer and consumer to quickly test the setup. Producers should run in one console and consumers should run in another console. Console 1 should be as follows:

```
bin/kafka-console-producer.sh --broker-list localhost:9092
  --topic testtopic
```

Console 2 should be as follows:

```
bin/kafka-console-consumer.sh --bootstrap-server localhost:9092
--topic testtopic --from-beginning
```

Now type the messages in the producer console and you will see the messages in the consumer console immediately. You can also write producer and consumer programming using APIs such as Java.

Distributed mode

The setup of a Kafka cluster involves running two major components, ZooKeeper and Kafka brokers. All Kafka brokers must be in sync with the ZooKeeper server and thus the only change that is required to get your distributed multi-node Kafka cluster to work is to change the ZooKeeper and Kafka server configuration:

- Make sure you have Kafka tarball on every node and have untared it
- Make changes in the `zookeeper.properties` file and add all the following three entries of ZooKeeper server:

```
# zoo servers
server.1=broker1ip:2888:3888
server.2=broker2ip:2888:3888
server.3=broker3ip:2888:3888
```

Some other properties that have to be changed are `clientPortAddress` and `datadir`.

- Now make changes in `server.properties` of each broker machine and add ZooKeeper client address to it as follows:

```
zookeeper.connect=broker1ip:2181,broker2ip:2181,broker3ip:2181
```

Also make sure that each broker has a unique ID, which you can set by changing `broker.id` in `server.properties`. Make sure that the `log.dirs` value is set as a unique location, for example on `broker1  ir` it can be `/tmp/kafka-logs-1`, on `broker2` it can be `/tmp/kafka-logs-2`, and so on.

- Once everything is set up, run the following command on each node:

  `./bin/zookeeper-server-start.sh –daemon config/zookeeper.properties`

  `./bin/kafka-server-start.sh –daemon config/server.properties`

- Verify the setup using the `jps` command on each node and start working with the distributed Kafka cluster.

Internals of producer and consumer

In this section, we will cover the different responsibilities of Kafka producer and consumer in detail.

Producer

When we write the Producer applications, we use Producer APIs that expose methods at an abstract level. Before we send any data, there are a lot of steps are performed by these APIs. Hence, it is important to understand the internal steps to gain knowledge about the Kafka producers. We will cover these in this section.

First, we need to understand the responsibilities of Kafka producers besides publishing messages. Let's look at them one by one:

- **Bootstrapping Kafka broker URLs**: The producer connects to at least one broker to fetch metadata about the Kafka cluster. It may happen that the first broker to which the producer wants to connect may be down. To ensure a failover, the producer implementation takes a list of more than one broker URL to bootstrap from. The producer iterates through a list of Kafka broker addresses until it finds the one to connect to fetch cluster metadata.

- **Data serialization**: Kafka uses a binary protocol to send and receive data over TCP. This means that while writing data to Kafka, producers need to send the ordered byte sequence to the defined Kafka broker's network port. Subsequently, it will read the response byte sequence from the Kafka broker in the same ordered fashion. The Kafka producer serializes every message data object into ByteArrays before sending any record to the respective broker over the wire. Similarly, it converts any byte sequence received from the broker as a response to the message object.

- **Determining topic partition**: It is the responsibility of the Kafka producer to determine which topic partition data needs to be sent. If the partition is specified by the caller program, then the producer APIs do not determine topic partition and send data directly to it. However, if no partition is specified, then the producer will choose a partition for the message. This is generally based on the key of the message data object. You can also code for your custom partitioner in case you

- **Determining the leader of the partition**: Producers send data to the leader of the partition directly. It is the producer's responsibility to determine the leader of the partition to which it will write messages. To do so, producers ask for metadata from any of the Kafka brokers. Brokers answer the request for metadata about active servers and leaders of the topic's partitions at that point of time.

- **Failure handling/retry ability**: Handling failure responses or number of retries is something that needs to be controlled through the producer application. You can configure the number of retries through the producer API configuration, and this has to be decided as per your enterprise standards. Exception handling should be done through the producer application component. Depending on the type of exception, you can determine different data flows.

- **Batching**: For efficient message transfers, batching is a very useful mechanism. Through producer API configurations, you can control whether you need to use the producer in asynchronous mode or not. Batching ensures reduced I/O and optimum utilization of producer memory. While deciding on the number of messages in a batch, you have to keep in mind the end-to-end latency. End-to-end latency increases with the number of messages in a batch.

Publishing messages to a Kafka topic starts with calling producer APIs with appropriate details such as messages in string format, topic, partitions (optional), and other configuration details such as broker URLs, and so on. The producer API uses the passed on information to form a data object in a form of a nested key-value pair. Once the data object is formed, the producer serializes it into byte arrays. You can either use an in-built serializer or you can develop your custom serializer. Avro is one of the commonly used data serializers. Serialization ensures compliance to the Kafka binary protocol and efficient network transfer.

Next, the partition to which data needs to be sent is determined. If partition information is passed in API calls, then producer would use that partition directly. However, in case partition information is not passed, then the producer determines the partition to which data should be sent. Generally, this is decided by the keys that are defined in data objects. Once the record partition is decided, the producer determines which broker to connect to in order to send messages. This is generally done by the bootstrap process of selecting the producers and then, based on the fetched metadata, determining the leader broker. Producers also need to determine supported API versions of a Kafka broker. This is accomplished by using API versions exposed by the Kafka cluster. The goal is that producers will support different versions of producer APIs. While communicating with the respective leader broker, they should use the highest API version supported by both the producers and brokers. Producers send the used API version in their write requests. Brokers can reject the write request if a compatible API version is not reflected in the write request. This kind of setup ensures incremental API evolution while supporting older versions of APIs.

Once a serialized data object is sent to the selected broker, the producer receives a response from those brokers. If they receive metadata about the respective partition along with new message offsets, then the response is considered successful. However, if error codes are received in the response, then the producer can either throw the exception or retry as per the received configuration.

Consumer

As mentioned previously, consuming messages from Kafka is different than other messaging systems. However, when we write consumer applications using consumer APIs, all the details are abstracted and most of the internal work is done by the Kafka consumer libraries that are used by your application. We need to consider not to code for most of the consumer internal work and understand the internal workings. These concepts will help in debugging consumer applications and make the right application decision choices.

As seen in the previous section on Kafka producers, we will understand the different responsibilities of Kafka consumers. We will see them in the following points below:

- **Subscribing to a topic**: The Consumer operations initializes by subscribing to a topic and if the consumer is part of a consumer group, it will be assigned a subset of partitions from that topic. The consumer process will read data from the assigned partitions and we can think of the topic subscription as a registration process to read data from topic partitions.
- **Consumer offset position**: Kafka does not maintain message offsets and all the consumer is responsible for maintaining its own consumer offset. Consumer offsets are maintained by consumer APIs and you do not have to do any additional coding for this. However, in some use cases, where you may want to have more control over offsets, you can write custom logic for offset commits. We will cover such scenarios in this chapter.
- **Replay/rewind/skip messages**: Kafka consumer has full control over starting offsets to read messages from a topic partition. Using consumer APIs, any consumer application can pass the starting offsets to read messages from topic partitions. They can choose to read messages from the beginning or from some specific integer offset value irrespective of what the current offset value of a partition is. In this way, consumers have the capability of replaying or skipping messages as per specific business scenarios.

- **Heartbeats**: It is the consumer's responsibility to ensure that it sends regular heartbeat signals to the Kafka broker (consumer group leader) to confirm their membership and ownership of designated partitions. If heartbeats are not received by the group leader in a certain time interval, then the partition's ownership would be reassigned to some other consumer in the consumer group.
- **Offset commits**: Kafka does not track positions or offsets of the messages that are read from consumer applications. It is the responsibility of the consumer application to track their partition offset and commit it. This has two advantages—it improves broker performance as they do not have to track each consumer offset and this gives flexibility to consumer applications in managing their offsets as per their specific scenarios. They can commit offsets after they finish processing a batch or they can commit offsets in the middle of very large batch
processing to reduce side effects of rebalancing.
- **Deserialization**: Kafka producers serialize objects into byte arrays before they are sent to Kafka. Similarly, Kafka consumers deserialize these Java objects into byte arrays. Kafka consumers use the deserializers that are the same as serializers used in the producer application.

In consumer work flows, the first step toward consuming any messages from Kafka is topic subscription. Consumer applications first subscribe to one or more topics. After that, consumer applications poll Kafka servers to fetch records. In general terms, this is called poll loop. This loop takes care of server co-ordinations, record retrievals, partition rebalances, and keeps alive the heartbeats of consumers.

For new consumers that are reading data for the first time, poll loop first registers the consumer with the respective consumer group and eventually receives partition metadata. The partition metadata mostly contains partition and leader information of each topic.

Consumers, on receiving metadata, would start polling respective brokers for partitions assigned to them. If new records are found, they are retrieved and deserialized. They are finally processed, and after performing some basic validations, they are stored in some external storage systems. In very few cases, they are processed at runtime and passed to some external applications.

Finally, consumers commit offsets of messages that are successfully processed. The poll loop also sends periodic keep-alive heartbeats to Kafka servers to ensure that they receive messages without interruption.

Writing producer and consumer application

Kafka provides a rich set of APIs to write your own producer or consumer application. Kafka does has a few commonly used producer and consumers in the form of connectors, which you can run by changing the configuration. In this section, we will see how to write producer and consumer application using the Kafka API.

Let's see how we can write our own producer and consumer application. The following are a few prerequisites before we jump into coding:

- **IDE:** We recommend that you use a Java and Scala-supported IDE, such as IDEA, NetBeans, or Eclipse. We have used JetBrains IDEA. You can get more details from the following link: `https://www.jetbrains.com/idea/`
- **Build Tool**: We have used Maven as the build tool for the project. You may choose Gradle or any other tool that you are comfortable with
- **Maven Project**: Create a new Maven project using Intellij
- **Kafka Dependency**: Add Maven dependency to your `pom.xml`

The following code shows the Maven dependency:

```
<dependency>
    <groupId>org.Apache.kafka</groupId>
    <artifactId>kafka_2.11</artifactId>
  <version>1.1.0</version>
</dependency>
```

Producer example: The producer application can push the data to Kafka topic using a `KafkaProducer` class API that accepts the configure Kafka property object and send data to the configured topic on Kafka brokers. The `Future` object contains the response code for each message that's sent to the Kafka broker and you can use response to check if a message was delivered successfully or not, and can then resend message to guarantee the delivery in case of failure, as follows:

```java
import java.util.Properties;
import java.util.concurrent.Future;

import org.Apache.kafka.clients.producer.KafkaProducer;
import org.Apache.kafka.clients.producer.ProducerRecord;
import org.Apache.kafka.clients.producer.RecordMetadata;


public class CustomProducer {

    public static void main(String[] args) {
        Properties producerProps = new Properties();
```

```
        producerProps.put("bootstrap.servers", "localhost:9092");
        producerProps.put("key.serializer",
 "org.Apache.kafka.common.serialization.StringSerializer");
        producerProps.put("value.serializer",
 "org.Apache.kafka.common.serialization.StringSerializer");
        producerProps.put("acks", "all");
        producerProps.put("retries", 1);
        producerProps.put("batch.size", 20000);
        producerProps.put("linger.ms", 1);
        producerProps.put("buffer.memory", 24568545);
        KafkaProducer<String, String> producer = new KafkaProducer<String,
 String>(producerProps);

        for (int i = 0; i < 2000; i++) {
            ProducerRecord data = new ProducerRecord<String,
 String>("test1", "Hello this is record " + i);
            Future<RecordMetadata> recordMetadata = producer.send(data);
        }
        producer.close();
    }
}
```

Consumer application: Kafka consumer uses the `KafkaConsumer` class API to consume data from Kafka topics. The consumer applications are responsible for committing messages back to the Kafka, which indicates that the consumer has successfully read the message up to the committed offset and then Kafka advances its offset for the consumer to serve the next set of messages. Remember its up to the consumer how they want to consume and process the message, therefore message semantic, such as at list one, exactly-one, at most-one, are all dependent on consumer implementation, as follows:

```
import org.Apache.kafka.clients.consumer.*;
import org.Apache.kafka.common.TopicPartition;
import java.util.*;

public class CustomConsumer {

    public static void main(String[] args) throws Exception {

        String topic = "test1";
        List<String> topicList = new ArrayList<>();
        topicList.add(topic);
        Properties consumerProperties = new Properties();
        consumerProperties.put("bootstrap.servers", "10.200.99.197:6667");
        consumerProperties.put("group.id", "Demo_Group");
        consumerProperties.put("key.deserializer",
 "org.Apache.kafka.common.serialization.StringDeserializer");
        consumerProperties.put("value.deserializer",
```

```
"org.Apache.kafka.common.serialization.StringDeserializer");

        consumerProperties.put("enable.auto.commit", "true");
        consumerProperties.put("auto.commit.interval.ms", "1000");
        consumerProperties.put("session.timeout.ms", "30000");

        KafkaConsumer<String, String> customKafkaConsumer = new
KafkaConsumer<String, String>(consumerProperties);

        customKafkaConsumer.subscribe(topicList);
        int i = 0;
        try {
            while (true) {
                ConsumerRecords<String, String> records =
customKafkaConsumer.poll(500);
                for (ConsumerRecord<String, String> record : records)
                    //TODO : Do processing for data here
                    customKafkaConsumer.commitAsync(new
OffsetCommitCallback() {
                        public void onComplete(Map<TopicPartition,
OffsetAndMetadata> map, Exception e) {

                        }
                    });

            }
        } catch (Exception ex) {
            //TODO : Log Exception Here
        } finally {
            try {
                customKafkaConsumer.commitSync();

            } finally {
                customKafkaConsumer.close();
            }
        }
    }

}
```

The preceding code shows basic examples of the Kafka producer and consumer application. You can write more complex producer and consumer application by changing this code.

Kafka Connect for ETL

The ETL is the processing of extracting data from the source system, doing some transformation, and loading data to the target system. In the last couple of years, development around Kafka has been moving fast and there has been effort to make Kafka a unified model for building your ETL pipeline. Kafka Connect and Kafka Streams are two of them, which can help you build your ETL pipeline. Kafka Connects are of two types; one is the Source connector and other one is the Sink connector. The source connector is responsible for bringing data to Kafka and the Sink connector is used to move data out of Kafka. Let's look at the following diagram for more information:

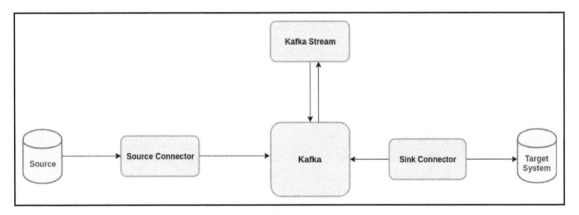

This diagram indicates the three major steps involved in any ETL process. Let's look into how Kafka can help us in each of the ETL steps:

- **Extracting**: Kafka provides some pre-built connectors that can connect to a few commonly used source systems and extract data from these source systems before pushing it to Kafka topics. Kafka Source connectors do provide APIs to build custom source connectors in order to extract data from custom sources. The following are few examples of connectors:
  - **JDBC Source Connector**: The JDBC connector can fetch data from JDBC compatible databases, such as mysql, postgres, and so on. We will be using `sqlite3` for this example. Let's see how to use it:
  - Install TRMMJUF:

    ```
    sudo apt-get install sqlite3
    ```

  - Start Console:

    ```
    sqlite3 packt.db
    ```

- Create a database table, and insert records, as follows:

```
sqlite> CREATE TABLE authors(id INTEGER PRIMARY KEY
                             AUTOINCREMENT NOT NULL,
                             name VARCHAR(255));

sqlite> INSERT INTO authors(name) VALUES('Manish');

sqlite> INSERT INTO authors(name) VALUES('Chanchal');
```

  - Create `sqlite-source-connector.properties` and add, as follows:

```
name=test-source-sqlite-jdbc-autoincrement
connector.class=
io.confluent.connect.jdbc.JdbcSourceConnector
tasks.max=1
connection.url=jdbc:sqlite:packt.db
mode=incrementing
incrementing.column.name=id
topic.prefix=test-
```

- Run the source connector to get the data to kafka topics, as follows:

```
./bin/connect-standalone etc/schema-
registry/connect-avro-standalone.properties
etc/sqlite-source-connector.properties
```

- Confirm by running the consumer on topic test-authors, as follows:

```
bin/kafka-avro-console-consumer --new-consumer
--bootstrap-server localhost:9092 --topic test-authors
--from-beginning
```

The output of the preceding code is as follows:

```
SLF4J: Class path contains multiple SLF4J bindings.
SLF4J: Found binding in [jar:file:/home/chanchal/projects/confluent-3.2.2/share/
StaticLoggerBinder.class]
SLF4J: Found binding in [jar:file:/home/chanchal/projects/confluent-3.2.2/share/
aticLoggerBinder.class]
SLF4J: See http://www.slf4j.org/codes.html#multiple_bindings for an explanation.
SLF4J: Actual binding is of type [org.slf4j.impl.Log4jLoggerFactory]
{"id":1,"name":{"string":"Manish"}}
{"id":2,"name":{"string":"Chanchal"}}
```

- **Transforming**: The Kafka Streams can be used to transform the data available in Kafka topics and can push back a transformed result in another topic. However Kafka Stream is used to process the stream of events but you can also use it as a batch processing application if developed correctly. Kafka Stream applications do not require any special cluster to run, they can run on any machine where any Java application can run. Kafka Streams pushes the processed data back to the Kafka topic from where it is available to consume by another process such as Kafka Sink connector, which can then push data to the target system.

- **Loading**: Loading is the process of loading transform data into a target system from where it is available for further consumption. The Kafka Sink connector can help you load data from Kafka topics to some commonly used target system such as RDBMS, HDFS, and so on. Let's use the JDBC Sink connector for further loading data pushed to a Kafka topic into a new sqlite3 table.

JDBC Sink connector: Ths JDBC sink connector can load data from Kafka topics to any `jdbc` compatible databases. The following are the steps for running `jdbc` Sink connector:

1. First step is to set up `jdbc-sqlite-sink-connector.properties` and add following details to it, as follows:

   ```
   connector.class=io.confluent.connect.jdbc.JdbcSinkConn
   ector
   tasks.max=1
   topics=authors_sink
   connection.url=jdbc:sqlite:packt_author.db
   auto.create=true
   ```

2. The next step is to run Sink connector using the following command:

   ```
   ./bin/connect-standalone etc/schema-registry/connect-
   avro-standalone.properties etc/jdbc-sqlite-sink-
   connector.properties
   ```

3. If you have a custom producer to push data to a topic then use that custom producer or use the following console producer for testing:

   ```
   ./bin/kafka-avro-console-producer \
   --broker-list localhost:9092 --topic authors_sink \
   --property value.schema='{"type":"record",
                             "name":"authors","fields":
   [{"name":"id","type":"int"},{"name":"author_name",
     "type": "string"}, {"name":"age", "type": "int"},
    {"name":"popularity_percentage", "type": "float"}]}'
   ```

4. Once the producer is up, paste the following record to the Kafka producer console:

```
{"id":1,"author_name":"Chanchal",
 "age":"26", popularity_percentage":60)

{"id":1,"author_name":"Manish", "age":"33",
 popularity_percentage":80)
```

5. Check record in `sqlite3` database table, as follows:

```
sqlite3 packt_authors.db;
select * from author_sink;
```

The output of the preceding code is as follows:

```
sqlite> select * from authors_sink;
Chanchal|60.0|1|26
Manish|80.0|2|32
sqlite>
```

Kafka connect is not an ETL framework in itself, but it can be part of an ETL pipeline where Kafka is being used. Our intention was to focus on how Kafka Connect can be used in the ETL pipeline and how you can use it to import or export data from Kafka.

Best practices

Apache Kafka has different components such as producer, consumer, and brokers. It is important to follow best practices at each component level, for example:

- **Data validation**: The main aspect in data validation while writing a producer system is to perform basic data validation tests on the data which is to be written on the Kafka cluster. The examples could be conformation to the schema and not null values for Key fields. By not doing data validation, you are risking breaking downstream consumer applications and affecting the load balancing of brokers as data may not be partitioned appropriately.

- **Exception handling**: It is the sole responsibility of producer and consumer programs to decide on program flows with respect to exceptions. While writing a producer or consumer application, you should define different exception classes and as per your business requirements, decide on the actions that need to be taken. Clearly defining exceptions not only helps you in debugging but also in proper risk mitigation. For example, if you are using Kafka for critical applications such as fraud detection, then you should capture relevant exceptions to send email alerts to the Ops team for immediate resolution.

- **Number of retries**: In general, there are two types of errors that you get in your producer application. The first type are errors that producer can retry, such as network timeouts and leader not available. The second type are errors that need to be handled by producer programs, as mentioned in the preceding section. Configuring the number of retries will help you in mitigating risks related to message losses due to Kafka cluster errors or network errors.

- **Number of bootstrap URLs**: You should always have more than one broker listed in your bootstrap broker configuration of your producer program. This helps producers to adjust to failures because if one of the brokers is not available, producers try to use all the listed brokers until it finds the one it can connect to. An ideal scenario is that you should list all your brokers in the Kafka cluster to accommodate maximum broker connection failures. However, in case of very large clusters, you can choose a lesser number that can significantly represent your cluster brokers. You should be aware that the number of retries can affect your end-to-end latency and cause duplicate messages in your Kafka queues.

- **Avoid adding new partitions to existing topics**: You should avoid adding partitions to existing topics when you are using key-based partitioning for message distribution. Adding new partitions would change the calculated hash code for each key as it takes the number of partitions as one of the inputs. You would end up having different partitions for the same key.

- **Handling rebalances**: Whenever any new consumer joins consumer groups or any old consumer goes down, a partition rebalance on the Kafka cluster is triggered. Whenever a consumer is losing its partition ownership, it is imperative that they should commit the offsets of the last event that they have received from Kafka. For example, they should process and commit any in-memory buffered datasets before losing the ownership of a partition. Similarly, they should close any open file handles and database connection objects.

- **Commit offsets at the right time**: If you are choosing to commit offset for messages, you need to do it at the right time. An application processing a batch of messages from Kafka may take more time to complete the processing of an entire batch; this is not a rule of thumb but if the processing time is more than a minute, try to commit the offset at regular intervals to avoid duplicate data processing in case the application fails. For more critical applications where processing duplicate data can cause huge costs, the commit offset time should be as short as possible if throughput is not an important factor.

Flume

The first step in any data pipeline is data ingestion, which brings data from the source system for necessary processing. There are different types of source systems available and to bring data from these source systems there are different specific tools available. Big Data ecosystem has its own setup of tools to bring data from these systems, for example, sqoop can be used to bring data from relational databases, Gobblin can bring data from relational databases, REST API, FTP server, and so on.

Apache flume is a Java-based, distributed, scalable, fault tolerant system to consume data from a streaming source, such as Twitter, log server, and so on. At one time it was a widely used application in different use case and still large numbers of pipeline use Flume (specifically as a producer to Kafka).

Apache Flume architecture

The producer and consumer problem was there even before Hadoop. The common problem that the producer/consumer faces is the producer producing data faster than the consumer can consume. Messaging systems have been used for a long time to tackle this problem, but due to the massive amount of data being generated in businesses, there was a necessity for a system that can consume data from the producer and deliver to the target system with negligible effect on throughput. In this section, we will discuss more about the Apache Flume architecture and how it handles massive amounts of streaming data with its scalable, distributed, and fault tolerant pattern. The following diagram explains the Flume architecture:

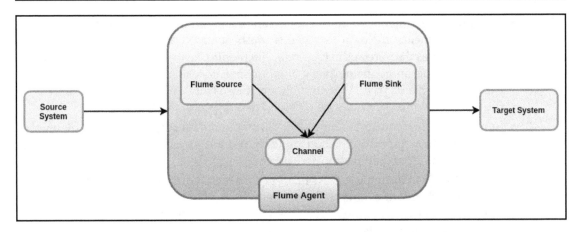

In this diagram, we see the three components of the Apache Flume agent but Flume also consists of a few other subcomponents. Let's look at few of them:

- **Event**: A single row or record is termed as an event, which is also known as a singular unit of data. Flume transports events from source to sink. Every event consists of a header and a body where the header contains metadata information and the body contains the actual record. Flume is written in Java so you can consider the body as a ByteBuffer.

- **Source**: The source component in Flume is responsible for receiving event data from the source system and pushing the event to a channel. There are two types of sources in Flume, namely:

  - **Pollable source**: Pollable source requires an external driver to poll events to determine whether there are events that are available to ingest from the source. The sequence generator example is a common example of a pollable source that generates integer value in an increasing order.

  - **Event-driven sources**: Event-driven source enables the push based data ingestion approach that controls the rate in which events can be pushed to the channel. The example could be an HTTP source, which enables the user to make HTTP API calls when required, and provides the ability to have control over concurrency and latency.

- **Sink**: It corresponds to the source in which is a destination for data in Flume NG. Some built-in sinks are the Hadoop Distributed File System sink, that writes events to HDFS, the logger sink, which simply logs all events received, and the null sink, which is Flume NG's version of /dev/null. Sinks are a user accessible API extension point.

- **Channel**: A channel is an intermediate buffer for events between source and sink, which means the data received from the source is pushed to a channel and sink consumes data from the channel. The memory can be used as a channel but it does not guarantee the delivery of a message in case of unexpected failure, and we may lose the data. It is recommended to use fully durable channels such as file channel, which provides guaranteed delivery against data loss.
- **Source and sink runners**: The source runner and sink runner are used by Flume NG. The runners are internal components and are invisible to the end user. They are responsible for driving source and sink.
- **Agent**: Agent in Flume is a JVM process that hosts components such as source, channel, and sink to enable the end-to-end flow of events. Agents can run any number of sources, channels, and sink if it has a sufficient amount of resources to hosts these components.
- **Configuration provider**: Flume NG provides a pluggable configuration system called the configuration provider. By default, Flume NG comes with a Java property file-based configuration system which gets easily generated programatically. The Flume old generation has a centralised configuration system with a master and ZooKeeper for coordination, which was seen to be an overhead for most of the user. Users also implements arbitrary plugins to integrate with any type of configuration systems, namely JSON files, a shared RDBMS, a central system with ZooKeeper, and so forth.
- **Client**: The client is responsible for sending the data to a Flume source. It may or may not be a Flume component; we may refer it as anything that sends data to a Flume source component is a client. It can be log4j appnder, twitter streams, and so on.

Deep dive into source, channel, and sink

Flume agent consists of three major components namely, source, channel, and sink. Source is responsible for pulling data from the source system and pushing it to a configured channel. Channel is a temporary storage in Flume where it stores the data that is pushed from the source until and unless sink reads out the data from it and acknowledges the successful read. Sink is responsible for reading data from channel and pushes it to the target system. In this section, we will look into each component in detail.

Sources

Sources are responsible for consuming data from a client and pushing it to Flume channels. Flume already has common source built in but also provides the capability to build your own source. Source can consume data from the log generating system, messaging system, or from Flume sink, which can send data via an RPC call to another Flume agent. To be concise, sources can receive events from two types of client, external systems and from other Flume agents.

The `ConfigurationProvider` is responsible for providing configuration for the Flume source system. Every source requires at least one channel to be configured with it where the source will write data. The following are a few properties that are required while configuring the source:

- `type`: The source type defines the client that will send data to the Flume sources. The source can be defined as a fully qualified class name or alias that's been defined for it. The alias is already defined for a few built-in sources and fully qualified names can be used for custom sources.
- `channel`: The channels are responsible for buffering events that are written by source. It is mandatory to configure at least one channel with source so that source can write data to it. You can also specify multiple channels separated by commas in the configuration and source will write data to channels to a specified configuration.

There are few optional parameters that can be used with all the sources, which we will discuss later in this section. Before we move ahead, we will walk through two different types of sources.

Pollable source

The external system drives the pollable source, which means source does not run on any server but instead polls the external system to receive the data. Let's look into building custom pollable source.

Pollable source implements the `PollableSource` class and implements a configurable interface to accept a system or external configuration. The following is an example template for custom pollable source:

```
import org.Apache.flume.Context;
import org.Apache.flume.EventDeliveryException;
import org.Apache.flume.FlumeException;
import org.Apache.flume.source.AbstractPollableSource;
```

```
public class CustomPollableSource extends AbstractPollableSource {

    @Override
    protected Status doProcess() throws EventDeliveryException {

      // Logic to generate or convert stream to flume event here
        return Status.READY;
    }

    @Override
    protected void doConfigure(Context context) throws FlumeException {
     // read and set external configuration here
    }

    @Override
    protected void doStart() throws FlumeException {
     //initialise the external connection for client here
    }

    @Override
    protected void doStop() throws FlumeException {
      / Close any connection open in start method here
    }
}
```

This template can be used to create a custom pollable source. Look at the Jmx source code https://github.com/Apache/flume/blob/trunk/flume-ng-sources/flume-jms-source/src/main/java/org/Apache/flume/source/jms/JMSSource.java, which gives details about how you can built your own custom connector using this template. Remember, source runs on its own thread called SourceRunner and PollableSourceRunner runs a pollable source. The thread repeatedly calls the doprocess() and every time the doprocess method is called, a new set of events are generated and passed to the channel processor.

In either case, if source is able to generate an event successfully, or not able to generate an event successfully, it returns a status to the Flume framework and upon receiving the event status Flume acts accordingly. The status READY should be returned in case the event generation was successful and BACKOFF should be returned in case the event generation failed. Once the process returns the READY status, the runner immediately calls the process method. In case of BACKOFF status, the runner calls the backoff and the runner method will be only called after configured timeout.

Event-driven source

Event-driven source controls the rate of events being pushed to channels and also controls the concurrency and latency. The event-driven source implements the EventDrivenSource interface, which acts as a marker interface in selecting the appropriate SourceRunner. Event-driven sources are run by the EventDrivenSourceRunner

There are two ways to write your own custom event-driven source, which are as follows:

- Implementing the EventDrivenSource interface
- Extending the AbstractEventDrivenSource class

Instead of using a template for the first approach of creating an event-driven source, we would like to take the following example of TwitterSource class, which can be found at: https://github.com/Apache/flume:

```
import java.io.ByteArrayOutputStream;
import java.io.IOException;
import java.text.DecimalFormat;
import java.text.SimpleDateFormat;
import java.util.ArrayList;
import java.util.Arrays;
import java.util.List;

import org.Apache.avro.Schema;
import org.Apache.avro.Schema.Field;
import org.Apache.avro.Schema.Type;
import org.Apache.avro.file.DataFileWriter;
import org.Apache.avro.generic.GenericData.Record;
import org.Apache.avro.generic.GenericDatumWriter;
import org.Apache.avro.generic.GenericRecord;
import org.Apache.avro.io.DatumWriter;
import org.Apache.flume.Context;
import org.Apache.flume.Event;
import org.Apache.flume.EventDrivenSource;
import org.Apache.flume.annotations.InterfaceAudience;
import org.Apache.flume.annotations.InterfaceStability;
import org.Apache.flume.conf.BatchSizeSupported;
import org.Apache.flume.conf.Configurable;
import org.Apache.flume.event.EventBuilder;
import org.Apache.flume.source.AbstractSource;
import org.slf4j.Logger;
import org.slf4j.LoggerFactory;

import twitter4j.MediaEntity;
import twitter4j.StallWarning;
```

```java
import twitter4j.Status;
import twitter4j.StatusDeletionNotice;
import twitter4j.StatusListener;
import twitter4j.TwitterStream;
import twitter4j.TwitterStreamFactory;
import twitter4j.User;
import twitter4j.auth.AccessToken;

/**
 * Demo Flume source that connects via Streaming API to the 1% sample
twitter
 * firehose, continuously downloads tweets, converts them to Avro format
and
 * sends Avro events to a downstream Flume sink.
 *
 * Requires the consumer and access tokens and secrets of a Twitter
developer
 * account
 */

@InterfaceAudience.Private
@InterfaceStability.Unstable
public class TwitterSource
    extends AbstractSource
    implements EventDrivenSource, Configurable, StatusListener,
BatchSizeSupported {

  private TwitterStream twitterStream;
  private Schema avroSchema;

  private long docCount = 0;
  private long startTime = 0;
  private long exceptionCount = 0;
  private long totalTextIndexed = 0;
  private long skippedDocs = 0;
  private long batchEndTime = 0;
  private final List<Record> docs = new ArrayList<Record>();
  private final ByteArrayOutputStream serializationBuffer =
      new ByteArrayOutputStream();
  private DataFileWriter<GenericRecord> dataFileWriter;

  private int maxBatchSize = 1000;
  private int maxBatchDurationMillis = 1000;

  // Fri May 14 02:52:55 +0000 2010
  private SimpleDateFormat formatterTo =
      new SimpleDateFormat("yyyy-MM-dd'T'HH:mm:ss'Z'");
  private DecimalFormat numFormatter = new DecimalFormat("###,###.###");
```

```
private static int REPORT_INTERVAL = 100;
private static int STATS_INTERVAL = REPORT_INTERVAL * 10;
private static final Logger LOGGER =
    LoggerFactory.getLogger(TwitterSource.class);

public TwitterSource() {
}

@Override
public void configure(Context context) {
  String consumerKey = context.getString("consumerKey");
  String consumerSecret = context.getString("consumerSecret");
  String accessToken = context.getString("accessToken");
  String accessTokenSecret = context.getString("accessTokenSecret");

  twitterStream = new TwitterStreamFactory().getInstance();
  twitterStream.setOAuthConsumer(consumerKey, consumerSecret);
  twitterStream.setOAuthAccessToken(new AccessToken(accessToken,
                                                    accessTokenSecret));
  twitterStream.addListener(this);
  avroSchema = createAvroSchema();
  dataFileWriter = new DataFileWriter<GenericRecord>(
      new GenericDatumWriter<GenericRecord>(avroSchema));

  maxBatchSize = context.getInteger("maxBatchSize", maxBatchSize);
  maxBatchDurationMillis = context.getInteger("maxBatchDurationMillis",
                                              maxBatchDurationMillis);
}

@Override
public synchronized void start() {
  LOGGER.info("Starting twitter source {} ...", this);
  docCount = 0;
  startTime = System.currentTimeMillis();
  exceptionCount = 0;
  totalTextIndexed = 0;
  skippedDocs = 0;
  batchEndTime = System.currentTimeMillis() + maxBatchDurationMillis;
  twitterStream.sample();
  LOGGER.info("Twitter source {} started.", getName());
  // This should happen at the end of the start method, since this will
  // change the lifecycle status of the component to tell the Flume
  // framework that this component has started. Doing this any earlier
  // tells the framework that the component started successfully, even
  // if the method actually fails later.
  super.start();
}
```

```java
@Override
public synchronized void stop() {
  LOGGER.info("Twitter source {} stopping...", getName());
  twitterStream.shutdown();
  super.stop();
  LOGGER.info("Twitter source {} stopped.", getName());
}

public void onStatus(Status status)  {
  Record doc = extractRecord("", avroSchema, status);
  if (doc == null) {
    return; // skip
  }
  docs.add(doc);
  if (docs.size() >= maxBatchSize ||
      System.currentTimeMillis() >= batchEndTime) {
    batchEndTime = System.currentTimeMillis() + maxBatchDurationMillis;
    byte[] bytes;
    try {
      bytes = serializeToAvro(avroSchema, docs);
    } catch (IOException e) {
      LOGGER.error("Exception while serializing tweet", e);
      return; //skip
    }
    Event event = EventBuilder.withBody(bytes);
    getChannelProcessor().processEvent(event); // send event to the flume
sink
    docs.clear();
  }
  docCount++;
  if ((docCount % REPORT_INTERVAL) == 0) {
    LOGGER.info(String.format("Processed %s docs",
                              numFormatter.format(docCount)));
  }
  if ((docCount % STATS_INTERVAL) == 0) {
    logStats();
  }
}

private Schema createAvroSchema() {
  Schema avroSchema = Schema.createRecord("Doc", "adoc", null, false);
  List<Field> fields = new ArrayList<Field>();
  fields.add(new Field("id", Schema.create(Type.STRING), null, null));
  fields.add(new Field("user_friends_count",
                       createOptional(Schema.create(Type.INT)),
                       null, null));
  fields.add(new Field("user_location",
                       createOptional(Schema.create(Type.STRING)),
```

```
                              null, null));
    fields.add(new Field("user_description",
                         createOptional(Schema.create(Type.STRING)),
                         null, null));
    fields.add(new Field("user_statuses_count",
                         createOptional(Schema.create(Type.INT)),
                         null, null));
    fields.add(new Field("user_followers_count",
                         createOptional(Schema.create(Type.INT)),
                         null, null));
    fields.add(new Field("user_name",
                         createOptional(Schema.create(Type.STRING)),
                         null, null));
    fields.add(new Field("user_screen_name",
                         createOptional(Schema.create(Type.STRING)),
                         null, null));
    fields.add(new Field("created_at",
                         createOptional(Schema.create(Type.STRING)),
                         null, null));
    fields.add(new Field("text",
                         createOptional(Schema.create(Type.STRING)),
                         null, null));
    fields.add(new Field("retweet_count",
                         createOptional(Schema.create(Type.LONG)),
                         null, null));
    fields.add(new Field("retweeted",
                         createOptional(Schema.create(Type.BOOLEAN)),
                         null, null));
    fields.add(new Field("in_reply_to_user_id",
                         createOptional(Schema.create(Type.LONG)),
                         null, null));
    fields.add(new Field("source",
                         createOptional(Schema.create(Type.STRING)),
                         null, null));
    fields.add(new Field("in_reply_to_status_id",
                         createOptional(Schema.create(Type.LONG)),
                         null, null));
    fields.add(new Field("media_url_https",
                         createOptional(Schema.create(Type.STRING)),
                         null, null));
    fields.add(new Field("expanded_url",
                         createOptional(Schema.create(Type.STRING)),
                         null, null));
    avroSchema.setFields(fields);
    return avroSchema;
}

private Record extractRecord(String idPrefix, Schema avroSchema, Status
```

```
status) {
    User user = status.getUser();
    Record doc = new Record(avroSchema);

    doc.put("id", idPrefix + status.getId());
    doc.put("created_at", formatterTo.format(status.getCreatedAt()));
    doc.put("retweet_count", status.getRetweetCount());
    doc.put("retweeted", status.isRetweet());
    doc.put("in_reply_to_user_id", status.getInReplyToUserId());
    doc.put("in_reply_to_status_id", status.getInReplyToStatusId());

    addString(doc, "source", status.getSource());
    addString(doc, "text", status.getText());

    MediaEntity[] mediaEntities = status.getMediaEntities();
    if (mediaEntities.length > 0) {
      addString(doc, "media_url_https",
mediaEntities[0].getMediaURLHttps());
      addString(doc, "expanded_url", mediaEntities[0].getExpandedURL());
    }

    doc.put("user_friends_count", user.getFriendsCount());
    doc.put("user_statuses_count", user.getStatusesCount());
    doc.put("user_followers_count", user.getFollowersCount());
    addString(doc, "user_location", user.getLocation());
    addString(doc, "user_description", user.getDescription());
    addString(doc, "user_screen_name", user.getScreenName());
    addString(doc, "user_name", user.getName());
    return doc;
  }

  private byte[] serializeToAvro(Schema avroSchema, List<Record> docList)
      throws IOException {
    serializationBuffer.reset();
    dataFileWriter.create(avroSchema, serializationBuffer);
    for (Record doc2 : docList) {
      dataFileWriter.append(doc2);
    }
    dataFileWriter.close();
    return serializationBuffer.toByteArray();
  }

  private Schema createOptional(Schema schema) {
    return Schema.createUnion(Arrays.asList(
        new Schema[] { schema, Schema.create(Type.NULL) }));
  }

  private void addString(Record doc, String avroField, String val) {
```

```
    if (val == null) {
      return;
    }
    doc.put(avroField, val);
    totalTextIndexed += val.length();
  }

  private void logStats() {
    double mbIndexed = totalTextIndexed / (1024 * 1024.0);
    long seconds = (System.currentTimeMillis() - startTime) / 1000;
    seconds = Math.max(seconds, 1);
    LOGGER.info(String.format("Total docs indexed: %s, total skipped docs:
%s",
                numFormatter.format(docCount),
numFormatter.format(skippedDocs)));
    LOGGER.info(String.format("    %s docs/second",
                numFormatter.format(docCount / seconds)));
    LOGGER.info(String.format("Run took %s seconds and processed:",
                numFormatter.format(seconds)));
    LOGGER.info(String.format("    %s MB/sec sent to index",
                numFormatter.format(((float) totalTextIndexed / (1024 *
1024)) / seconds)));
    LOGGER.info(String.format("    %s MB text sent to index",
                numFormatter.format(mbIndexed)));
    LOGGER.info(String.format("There were %s exceptions ignored: ",
                numFormatter.format(exceptionCount)));
  }

  public void onDeletionNotice(StatusDeletionNotice statusDeletionNotice) {
    // Do nothing...
  }

  public void onScrubGeo(long userId, long upToStatusId) {
    // Do nothing...
  }

  public void onStallWarning(StallWarning warning) {
    // Do nothing...
  }

  public void onTrackLimitationNotice(int numberOfLimitedStatuses) {
    // Do nothing...
  }

  public void onException(Exception e) {
    LOGGER.error("Exception while streaming tweets", e);
  }
```

```
    @Override
    public long getBatchSize() {
      return maxBatchSize;
    }
  }
```

This class does not contain any process or do-process method. Instead, the start method has code to start the source to consume events from Twitter stream. The configuration initialises the configure method where all authentication and required fields are set for the `TwitterStream` class.

The second approach is to simply extend `AbstractEventDrivenSource`, which internally implements configurable, `EventDrivenSource`, and other interfaces, and provides an ability to override `dostart()`, `dostop()`, and `doConfigure()`. The following is a sample template for creating class using `AbstractEventDrivenSource`:

```
import org.Apache.flume.Context;
import org.Apache.flume.FlumeException;
import org.Apache.flume.source.AbstractEventDrivenSource;

public class CustomEventDrivenSource extends AbstractEventDrivenSource {
    @Override
    protected void doConfigure(Context context) throws FlumeException {

    }

    @Override
    protected void doStart() throws FlumeException {

    }

    @Override
    protected void doStop() throws FlumeException {

    }
}
```

In the start of this section, we discussed a few required configurations for agent configuration that included type and channel property. The following are a few optional configurations that can be used with source:

- `Interceptors`: Interceptors can be used to filter or modify events while they reach the channel or after being consumed from the channel. The chain of interceptors can be attached with source using this property.
- `selector`: Selector can be used to select a target channel for source. By default, the replicating selector is used if no selector is specified.

Considering this, the source configuration would now as follows:

```
agent.sources = testsource
agent.channels = memorychannel

//requied
agent.sources.testsource.type =
com.packt.flumes.sources.CustomPollableSource

agent.sources.testsource.channels = memorychannel

//intercptor
agent.sources.testsource.interceptors = filterinterceptor
agent.sources.testsource.interceptors.filterinterceptor.type =
com.packt.flumes.interceptor.Filterinterceptor

agent.sources.testsource.selector.type = multiplexing
agent.sources.testsource.selector.header = priority
agent.sources.testsource.selector.mapping.1 = memorychannel
```

Channels

Channels acts as a buffer for events generated by Flume source. Source produces events to channels and sink consumes those events from channels. Channel enables source to produce events at its own rate and consumer to consume events at its own rate. This is possible because events are buffered into temporary storage and do not get removed until any sink removes them from channel. In simple terms, once the data is buffered to channel, it is ready to be consumed by sink, and events are removed from channel once successfully consumed by sink. If sink fails to consume the data from channel, it is rolled back to channel again for further consumption by same or other sink.

 Each event can only be consumed by a single sink, which means the same event from the same channel cannot be consumed by two sinks.

There are different types of channels available in Flume. Let's now look at few widely used channels and their configuration.

Memory channel

The memory channel keeps the event in heap memory. Since events are buffered in the memory, it provides the ability to achieve high throughput but increases the risk of data loss in the case of memory channel failure. As all of its events are buffered in memory, any cause of system or memory failure may result in data loss. If data loss is not a big concern for you, then you may use memory channel, but in most of the production Flume use cases, memory channels are not the preferred option.

The channel configuration for previously discussed source is given as follows:

```
agent.channels.memorychannel.type = memory
agent.channels.memorychannel.capacity = 1000
agent.channels.memorychannel.transactionCapacity = 100
agent.channels.memorychannel.byteCapacity = 800000
```

The capacity indicates the amount of events the channel can hold at a given time. If the difference between the event produced by source and event consumed by sink exceeds the configured capacity limit, then Flume will throw `ChannelException`. The `transactionCapacity` denotes the amount of events that can be committed to a channel at one time.

File channel

The file channel is considered as a durable buffer for Flume. The events are written to disk and thus any failure, such as process failure, machine shutdown failure, or system crash may result in data loss. The durable file channel ensures that any events committed to it are not removed from channel until and unless sinks consumes the event and sends an acknowledgement to channel.

The file system can have multiple disks attached to it, which is abstract to channel, meaning that channel does not have direct information about it. The disks are mounted at different mount points and channels are configured to write data to directories on these disks in a round robin fashion, for example:

```
agent.channels.testfilechannel.type = file
agent.channels.testfilechannel.checkpointDir=/etc/flume-file/checkpoint
agent.channels.testfilechannel.dataDirs=/etc/flume-file/data,=/etc/flume-
file/data2,=/etc/flume-file/data3
agent.channels.testfilechannel.transactionCapacity=100000
agent.channels.testfilechannel.capacity=500000
agent.channels.testfilechannel.checkpointInterval=500000
agent.channels.testfilechannel.checkpointOnClose=true
agent.channels.testfilechannel.maxFileSize=1036870912
```

Kafka channel

Apache Kafka is a distributed messaging system that can be used as a durable channel for Apache Flume. The fault tolerant, distributed, replication, and many other features of Apache Kafka enables Kafka channel to provide durability and event persistent. Even if Flume does not have any sink to consume data, normal consumer applications can be used to consume the data from the Kafka channel, which also enables channel data to be consumed by multiple sinks, which was not possible with in memory or file channels. The basic configuration for Kafka channel looks as follows:

```
agent.channels.testkafkachannel.type =
org.Apache.flume.channel.kafka.KafkaChannel
agent.channels.testkafkachannel.kafka.bootstrap.servers =
broker1:9092,broker2:9092,broker3:9092
agent.channels.testkafkachannel.kafka.topic = testtopic
agent.channels.testkafkachannel.kafka.consumer.group.id = flume-channel-
consumer
```

Sinks

Sinks are responsible for consuming events available on channels and removing them after successful reads. Sink writes events to external systems or passes events to another agent in the pipeline. There are a few common built-in sinks that are already available, but the user can write their own sinks by using Flume's sink API.

The reading of data from channels happens in batches and each batch is one transaction that sink reads. The channel reads events in batches and commits the transaction back to the channel to remove the successfully read events. Each sink can consume data from exactly one channel and if that channel is not configured then the agent ignores the sink. The SinkRunner is responsible for running the sink process and calls the process method of the sink class. Once the events are successfully read and written to the target system, method returns `Status.READY`, which indicates that sink is ready to consume another batch, or it returns `Status.BACKOFF`, which backs off the process for a configured period of time before calling the process method again.
The following template can be used to create custom flume sink:

```
import org.Apache.flume.*;
import org.Apache.flume.conf.Configurable;
import org.Apache.flume.sink.AbstractSink;

public class CustomFlumeSink extends AbstractSink implements Configurable {

    @Override
    public synchronized void start() {
```

```
        super.start();
    }

    @Override
    public void configure(Context context) {

    }

    @Override
    public Status process() throws EventDeliveryException {
        Status status = null;
        Channel sourceChannel = getChannel();
        Transaction transaction = sourceChannel.getTransaction();
        transaction.begin();
        try {
            // logic to process event here

            Event event = sourceChannel.take();

            transaction.commit();
            status = Status.READY;
        } catch (Throwable tx) {
            transaction.rollback();
            status = Status.BACKOFF;
            if (tx instanceof Error) {
                throw (Error) tx;
            }
        }
        return status;

    }

    @Override
    public synchronized void stop() {
        super.stop();
    }
}
```

When creating a custom sink, you also have as a process() that is called by SinkRunner repeatedly based on status received from the method. The external configuration can be read in configure() and connection or object intialization can be done in start().

Flume interceptor

Flume interceptors are intermediate components between Flume source and channel. The events that are produced by Flume can be modified or filtered by the interceptor. The number of events as output will always be equal or less than the number of events consumed by the interceptor.

You can have a chain of interceptors to modify or filter out original events before each reaches to the target channel. You can also use interceptor to select channels for events coming from the same source based on certain conditions. Apache Flume already has a few common interceptors built in. Let's look into few of them one by one. Later in this section, we will also cover how you can write your customize interceptor using Apache Flume APIs. You can add interceptor for source events as follows:

```
agent.sources.testsource.interceptors = testInterceptor
agent.sources.testsource.interceptors.testInterceptor.type =
interceptorType
```

Timestamp interceptor

Adding creation timestamp for records is the most common practice we have been using for data warehouse applications. The creation timestamp helps us trace different metrics in the future. In most of cases with Flume, event does not have timestamp attached to it by default from source. The timestamp interceptor provides us with the ability to add timestamps for events into the header with timestamp as key. Remember if timestamp is already in the header, interceptor will override the value until and unless the preserveExisting property is set to true, for example:

```
agent.sources.testsource.interceptors = testInterceptor
agent.sources.testsource.interceptors.testInterceptor.type = timestamp
```

Universally Unique Identifier (UUID) interceptor

Most applications do require a unique key to deal with events ingested by Flume sinks. UUID interceptor can be used to generate a unique identifier key for each event generated by Flume source. The following is a sample template that can be used for UUID interceptor:

```
agent.sources.testsource.interceptors = uuidInterceptor
agent.sources.testsource.interceptors.uuidInterceptor.type = \
org.Apache.flume.sink.solr.morphline.UUIDInterceptor$Builder
agent.sources.testsource.interceptors.uuidInterceptor.headerName = uuid
agent.sources.testsource.interceptors.uuidInterceptor.prefix = test-
```

Regex filter interceptor

In a few cases, the event generated by source may not be useful for down stream systems attached to Flume sink; those events may slow up the processing at a later stage if they are large in numbers. It is always a good idea to exclude or include the event based on a data and filtering condition. The regex interceptor provides us with the ability to filter out events and gives us features to either include them or drop them right away.

The following template can be used for the regex filtering interceptor. The `excludeEvent` parameter is responsible for passing the event to a channel or the next Flume component. If set to false, it will include the matching regex event and passes the event to a channel or the next flume event component. If set to true, it will drop out all the event matching the regex pattern, for example:

```
agent.sources.testsource.interceptors = testFilterInterceptor
agent.sources.testsource.interceptors.testFilterInterceptor.type =
regex_filter
agent.sources.testsource.interceptors.testFilterInterceptor.regex =
.*cricket.*
agent.sources.testsource.interceptors.testFilterInterceptor.excludeEvents =
false
```

There are other built-in interceptors as well as Host interceptor, which can be used to add host detail to the event header. Let's now look into how we write our own interceptor and use it with Apache Flume.

Writing a custom interceptor

Apart from all the built-in interceptors available in Apache Fume library, sometime these interceptors are not sufficient for the use case. Apache Flume provides APIs to write your own custom interface, which can modify/filter events based on custom logic. The custom `interceptor` class should implement an interceptor interface that has `initialize`, `intercept`, and `close` method, for example:

```
import org.Apache.flume.Event;
import org.Apache.flume.interceptor.Interceptor;
import java.util.ArrayList;
import java.util.List;
import java.util.Map;
import org.Apache.flume.Context;

public class CustomEventInterceptor implements Interceptor {

    public CustomEventInterceptor(Context context) {
```

```
    }

    @Override
    public void initialize() {

    }

    @Override
    public Event intercept(Event event) {
        Map<String, String> eventHeaders = event.getHeaders();
        byte[] eventBody = event.getBody();

        //Add Modify or Filter logic here

        return null;
    }

    @Override
    public List<Event> intercept(List<Event> eventList) {
        List processedEvent = new ArrayList(eventList.size());
        for (Event event : eventList) {
            event = intercept(event);
            if (event != null) {
                processedEvent.add(event);
            }
        }
        return processedEvent;
    }

    @Override
    public void close() {

    }

    public static class Builder implements Interceptor.Builder {

        private Context context;

        public Builder() {
        }

        @Override
        public CustomEventInterceptor build() {
            return new CustomEventInterceptor(context);
        }

        @Override
        public void configure(Context context) {
```

```
        this.context = context;
    }

  }
}
```

This template can be used to write a custom interface. Each event is going through the intercept method. There are two intercept methods shown; one is accepting the event and the other is accepting the list of events. The intercept method with a list of events also calls the other intercept method with a single event. The builder class is necessary to initialize and build the interceptor class and provide the context object to interceptor.

The reference code for `UUIDInterceptor` from the Apache Flume source code can be accessed at: `https://github.com/Apache/flume` and is shown as follows:

```
package org.Apache.flume.sink.solr.morphline;

import java.util.ArrayList;
import java.util.List;
import java.util.Map;
import java.util.UUID;

import org.Apache.flume.Context;
import org.Apache.flume.Event;
import org.Apache.flume.interceptor.Interceptor;

/**
 * Flume Interceptor that sets a universally unique identifier on all
events
 * that are intercepted. By default this event header is named "id".
 */
public class UUIDInterceptor implements Interceptor {

  private String headerName;
  private boolean preserveExisting;
  private String prefix;

  public static final String HEADER_NAME = "headerName";
  public static final String PRESERVE_EXISTING_NAME = "preserveExisting";
  public static final String PREFIX_NAME = "prefix";

  protected UUIDInterceptor(Context context) {
    headerName = context.getString(HEADER_NAME, "id");
    preserveExisting = context.getBoolean(PRESERVE_EXISTING_NAME, true);
    prefix = context.getString(PREFIX_NAME, "");
  }
```

```
@Override
public void initialize() {
}

protected String getPrefix() {
  return prefix;
}

protected String generateUUID() {
  return getPrefix() + UUID.randomUUID().toString();
}

protected boolean isMatch(Event event) {
  return true;
}

@Override
public Event intercept(Event event) {
  Map<String, String> headers = event.getHeaders();
  if (preserveExisting && headers.containsKey(headerName)) {
    // we must preserve the existing id
  } else if (isMatch(event)) {
    headers.put(headerName, generateUUID());
  }
  event.setHeaders(headers);
  return event;
}

@Override
public List<Event> intercept(List<Event> events) {
  List results = new ArrayList(events.size());
  for (Event event : events) {
    event = intercept(event);
    if (event != null) {
      results.add(event);
    }
  }
  return results;
}

@Override
public void close() {
}

public static class Builder implements Interceptor.Builder {

  private Context context;
```

```
public Builder() {
}

@Override
public UUIDInterceptor build() {
  return new UUIDInterceptor(context);
}

@Override
public void configure(Context context) {
  this.context = context;
}

  }
}
```

Use case – Twitter data

The social media sentiment analysis is a very common use case that has been implemented by various companies to understand the sentiment of people on different social sites and then target them to increase their revenue. Twitter is the most popular social networking site to express your feeling related to products, news, and many more things. In this section, we will talk about how you can bring in Twitter data using Flume and perform batch or real-time analysis on top of the data. The following flow diagram shows the architecture for Twittter sentiment analysis:

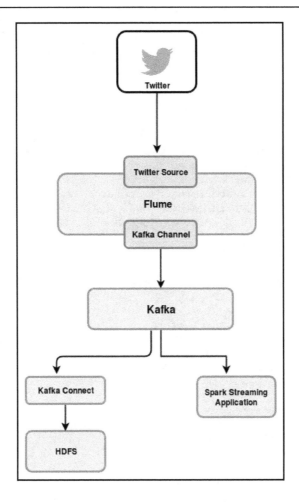

This diagram is a representation of the general architecture for **Twitter** sentiment analysis, which can be changed on a requirement basis. Let's look into the **Flume** agent configuration to bring **Twitter** data to **HDFS**. The first step is to register over `https://dev.twitter.com/apps/` and then generate the corresponding keys:

- `consumerKey`
- `consumerSecret`
- `accessToken`
- `accessTokenSecret`

Once you have keys available, use the following Twitter configuration and make sure the class `com.cloudera.flume.source.TwitterSource` is available in your `flume` library, as follows:

```
TwitterAgent.sources = Twitter
TwitterAgent.channels = MemChannel
TwitterAgent.sinks = HDFS

TwitterAgent.sources.Twitter.type = com.cloudera.flume.source.TwitterSource
TwitterAgent.sources.Twitter.channels = MemChannel
TwitterAgent.sources.Twitter.consumerKey = <consumerKey>
TwitterAgent.sources.Twitter.consumerSecret = <consumerSecret>
TwitterAgent.sources.Twitter.accessToken = <accessToken>
TwitterAgent.sources.Twitter.accessTokenSecret = <accessTokenSecret>

TwitterAgent.sources.Twitter.keywords = samsung,apple, LG, sony, MI

TwitterAgent.sinks.HDFS.channel = MemChannel
TwitterAgent.sinks.HDFS.type = hdfs
TwitterAgent.sinks.HDFS.hdfs.path = hdfs://yourPath
TwitterAgent.sinks.HDFS.hdfs.fileType = DataStream
TwitterAgent.sinks.HDFS.hdfs.writeFormat = Text
TwitterAgent.sinks.HDFS.hdfs.batchSize = 1000
TwitterAgent.sinks.HDFS.hdfs.rollSize = 0
TwitterAgent.sinks.HDFS.hdfs.rollCount = 10000

TwitterAgent.channels.MemChannel.type = memory
TwitterAgent.channels.MemChannel.capacity = 100000
TwitterAgent.channels.MemChannel.transactionCapacity = 1000
```

You can use Apache Kafka as a channel for your application, which will persist data to Kafka topics and then it can be used for real-time analytics and batch analytics on the same data, as described in preceding diagram. There is no need to configure Flume sink if you configure Apache Kafka as a channel because you can use Kafka consumer to consume data from channels on a need basis.

Best practices

Apache Flume has been widely used across many uses cases and in all the use cases people have followed a few best practices that we should also take into consideration before using it.

The best practices can be seen as follows:

- **Avoid the memory channel**: The memory channel is not recommended for use while you use Flume in production; there is always a chance of machine failure and, in such cases, the data stored in memory would be lost. It's obvious that the memory channel is faster than any other channel in Flume, but in most cases, data is more important than achieving a faster speed.
- **Use batching**: Using batch to write or read chunks of data is always a good option to boost throughput and performance. Apache Flume also provides an ability to read data from a channel in batches, and sink can define in the configuration how many records it wants to read in a single batch.
- **Filter events**: In some cases we may not require all the events to be processed or some event has to be ignored because of a policy or security issue; in such cases it is important to filter out events before even writing them to the Flume channel. Apache Flume interceptor can be used to achieve this objective. Interceptor can filter out events that are not required and will only push those events that pass the filter condition.

Summary

In this chapter, we learned about detailed architecture and uses of a few widely used Hadoop components, such as Apache Pig, Apache HBase, Apache Kafka, and Apache Flume. We have covered a few examples around writing custom UDF in Apache Pig, writing custom source, sink, and interceptor in Apache Flume, writing producer and consumer in Apache Kafka, and so on. Our focus was also to see how we can install and set up these componentS for practical use.

In the next chapter, our focus will be to look into some advanced topics in Big Data and cover some useful fundamental techniques and concepts, such as compression, file format serialization techniques, and some important pillars of data governance.

Section 3: Hadoop in the Real World

3

This section assumes that you have a good understanding of the Hadoop ecosystem and the components we introduced in the previous chapters. This section covers real-world problems faced by customers and the possible solutions to these problems. This section also covers machine learning, data governance, cluster profiling, and the cloud.

This section consists of the following chapters:

- Chapter 8, *Designing Applications in Hadoop*
- Chapter 9, *Real-Time Stream Processing in Hadoop*
- Chapter 10, *Machine Learning in Hadoop*
- Chapter 11, *Hadoop in the Cloud*
- Chapter 12, *Hadoop Cluster Profiling*

8
Designing Applications in Hadoop

In the previous chapter, we talked about multiple widely used components in data processing. We focused on a batch processing framework, Apache Pig, and talked about its architecture. We discussed a distributed columnar store database, HBase, and also covered the distributed messaging system, Kafka, which gives you ability to store and persist real-time events. Apache Flume was also the focus of the last chapter, which can help in pulling some real-time logs for further processing.

In this chapter, we will talk about some of the design considerations for application processing semantic. The following will be some of the focus points of this chapter:

- Different file formats available
- Advantage of using compression codecs
- Best data ingestion practices
- Design consideration for applications
- Data governance and its importance

Technical requirements

You will be required to have basic knowledge of Linux and Apache Hadoop 3.0.

The code files of this chapter can be found on GitHub:
https://github.com/PacktPublishing/Mastering-Hadoop-3/tree/master/Chapter08

Check out the following video to see the code in action:
http://bit.ly/2IICbMX

File formats

Files have been in data processing for decades. A file acts as a persistent storage for data, and programmers have been using files for exchanging or storing data for a long time now. There are formats associated with each file that tell you how data is being written and read from the file. For example, if we consider the `.csv` file, we may assume that each record is separated by a line and each column is separated by a delimiter. If the writer does not put data in the specific agreed format, then the reader may read data wrongly or processing logic may break. Each file format has a specific way of storing the data and there are different parameters that can help you decide which file format is best suited for your application. In this section, we will walk you through some of the widely used file formats and their internals.

Understanding file formats

Before we dive into the details of different big data formats, we need to establish a method that we can use to evaluate when to use what. In this section, we will use a different parameter that we can take into consideration when selecting a file format. We have chosen four parameters that are specific to each file format that's available today.

Row format and column format

It is one of the most important factors when selecting a file format that indicates if a row or column-based format is something that is best suited to our objectives. The column-based storage file format gives better performance when we perform analytic queries that require only a subset of columns to be analysed over large datasets.

In columnar formats, data is stored sequentially by column from left to right, top to bottom. If data is grouped by column, then it makes it more efficient to easily focus computation on specified columns of data. Accessing relevant columns of data will save significant amounts of compute costs because unwanted columns are ignored. Column-based storage is also well-suited for sparse datasets where we may have lots of empty values.

If it is done row-wise, then it will gather all the rows and all the columns in each row. It would be an unwanted overhead of fetching columns that are not required as a part of final result. When we need to analyze only a few selected columns in the data, the columnar file format is the clear choice.

Schema evolution

Schema evolution refers to changes in the schema of underlying data over some intervals of time. The schema stores the detail of each attribute and its type. Unless we are confident that the schema is guaranteed to never change, we will need to consider schema evolution, or how the schema of data changes over time. How will specific file formats handle the fields that are added, modified, or deleted?

One of the important design considerations when selecting a file format for data is how it manages schema evolution.

Splittable versus non-splittable

Today, data size is growing rapidly and each dataset consists of millions of records and thousands of files. To process these files using the capability of distributed computing, it is required to have these files splittable into multiple chunks and to send them across different machines for processing. All file formats are not splittable in nature, which restricts the ability to achieve effective parallelism when using a distributed processing engine like MapReduce. For example, XML or JSON record files are not splittable, which means they cannot be broken into smaller records that can be handled independently.

We will look at all the file formats that support splittability, and all of them play a significant role in the Hadoop ecosystem, which needs to break large chunks of data into smaller, more processable chunks.

Compression

Data compression provides the ability to reduce the amount of data needed for the storage or transmission of a given set of data across a network that indirectly saves processing time and storage cost. Compression uses the technique of encoding on frequently repeating data at the source of the data before it is stored on the disk or transmitted over the network. Columnar data has the ability to achieve better compression rates than row-based data because it stores the column values next to each other. While compression may save on storage costs, it is important to also consider other parameters such as compute costs and resources. Data decompression also takes a significant amount of processing time, which results in compute costs. It is always advisable to choose better trade-offs between storage and compute performance.

Text

The main use case of Hadoop is the storage and analysis of the two main logs, namely web logs and server logs. This text data comes in many other forms, like CSV files or emails. The main consideration while storing text data in Hadoop is the arrrangement of the files in the filesystem, which we will discuss more in the section called *HDFS Schema Design*. We will need to select a compression format for the files, since text files can take in considerable space on your Hadoop cluster. Also, keep in mind that there is an overhead of type conversion associated with storing the data in textual context. For example, storing `1234` in a text file and using it as an integer will require a string-to-integer conversion during reading, and the other way around during writing. This overhead will add up when you do many such conversions and when storing large amounts of data.

The selection of the compression format will be based on how the data will be used. For archival purposes, we will choose the most compact compression available, but if the data is used in processing jobs such as MapReduce, we will want to select a splittable format. These splittable formats will enable Hadoop to split the files into chunks for processing, which will be critical for efficient parallel processing.

Sequence file

A `sequence` file is a container format that contains binary key-value pairs. Each record in a `sequence` file contains a key and its associated value. The common use of the `sequence` file is to combine small files into a single large file so that the small file problem that can cause significant performance problems can be avoided. Since it is in container file format, there is support for the compression of data using rich compression codec, such as snappy or LZO.

Each record in the `sequence` file contains record related metadata, such as the record length and key lengths, followed by key and value bytes. When record compression is enabled for a sequence file, the value bytes are compressed using the configured codec without any change to the record structure. Compression can also be applied at block level, which is block compression—the size of block can be configured by setting the property `io.seqfile.compress.blocksize`. In record level compression, keys are not compressed but in block level compression, keys will be compressed. The following are examples of how we read or write to the `sequence` file.

The following code shows writing to the `sequence` file:

```
package com.packt.hadoopdesign;

import java.io.File;
```

```
import java.io.IOException;

import org.apache.commons.io.FileUtils;
import org.apache.hadoop.conf.Configuration;
import org.apache.hadoop.fs.FileSystem;
import org.apache.hadoop.fs.Path;
import org.apache.hadoop.io.IntWritable;
import org.apache.hadoop.io.SequenceFile;
import org.apache.hadoop.io.SequenceFile.Writer;
import org.apache.hadoop.io.Text;
import org.apache.hadoop.io.compress.GzipCodec;
public class PacktSequenceFileWriter {
    public static void main(String[] args) {
        Configuration conf = new Configuration();
        int i =0;
        try {
            FileSystem fs = FileSystem.get(conf);
            File file = new File("/home/packt/test.txt");
            Path outFile = new Path(args[0]);
            IntWritable key = new IntWritable();
            Text value = new Text();
            SequenceFile.Writer sequneceWriter = null;
            try {
                // creating sequneceQriter
                sequneceWriter = SequenceFile.createWriter(fs, conf,
outFile,
                        key.getClass(), value.getClass());
                for (String line : FileUtils.readLines(file)) {
                    key.set(i++);
                    value.set(line);
                    sequneceWriter.append(key, value);
                }
            }finally {
                if(sequneceWriter != null) {
                    sequneceWriter.close();
                }
            }

        } catch (IOException e) {
            // TODO Auto-generated catch block
            e.printStackTrace();
        }
    }
}
```

The following code shows the `reading` file in Hadoop:

```
package com.packt.hadoopdesign;

import org.apache.hadoop.conf.Configuration;
import org.apache.hadoop.fs.Path;
import org.apache.hadoop.io.IOUtils;
import org.apache.hadoop.io.SequenceFile;
import org.apache.hadoop.io.Writable;
import org.apache.hadoop.util.ReflectionUtils;

import java.io.IOException;

public class PacktSequenceFileReader {
    public static void main(String[] args) throws IOException {


    String uri = args[0];
    Configuration conf = new Configuration();
    Path path = new Path(uri);
    SequenceFile.Reader sequenceReader = null;
    try {
        sequenceReader = new SequenceFile.Reader(conf,
SequenceFile.Reader.file(path), SequenceFile.Reader.bufferSize(4096),
SequenceFile.Reader.start(0));
        Writable key = (Writable)
ReflectionUtils.newInstance(sequenceReader.getKeyClass(), conf);
        Writable value = (Writable)
ReflectionUtils.newInstance(sequenceReader.getValueClass(), conf);
        while (sequenceReader.next(key, value)) {
            String syncSeen = sequenceReader.syncSeen() ? "*" : "";
            System.out.printf("[%s]\t%s\t%s\n", syncSeen, key, value);
        }
    } finally {
        IOUtils.closeStream(sequenceReader);
    }
}
}
```

Avro

Apache Avro is a serialized file format that was developed to remove the language dependency of Hadoop writable. Apache Avro provides the ability of cross language portability, which means data written in one language can be easily read and processed by other formats. We will see some of the high-level features that Avro provides as follows:

- **Language portability**: The Avro data has an attached schema with it that is language independent in nature, and therefore it is easy for the user to read it without worrying about who has written it. Cross language communication is something that most of the application requires where one microservice may be written in Java and another in Python, and they need to communicate with each other using some data.

- **Schema evolution**: Schema evolution is one of the important features that most of the use cases look for. It may be possible that the source schema changes many times and you may end up with a new data structure in the next ingestion run. The schema change could be either the addition or deletion of data that can impact your processing pipeline or queries being fired on a table. The schema evolution feature allows you to use different versions of the schema while reading and writing the data, and the new field or deleted file will be ignored during reading.

- **Splitable and compression**: One of the important requirements of a distributed processing systems like Hadoop is that a file should be splittable so that it can be processed in parallel by splitting the larger file into some configured size of manageable chunks. Avro is splittable and allows compression. By using a better compression codec with Avro compression, we can achieve better performance during processing and reasonable cost savings during storage.

The following code shows an example of writing an `avro` file:

```
package com.packt.hadoopdesign.avro;
import java.io.File;
import java.io.IOException;

import org.apache.avro.file.DataFileWriter;
import org.apache.avro.io.DatumWriter;
import org.apache.avro.specific.SpecificDatumWriter;
import packt.Author;

public class PacktAvroWriter {
    public static void main(String args[]) throws IOException{

        Author author1=new Author();
```

```
            author1.setAuthorName("chanchal singh");
            author1.setAuthorId("PACKT-001");
            author1.setAuthorAddress("Pune India");

            Author author2=new Author();

            author2.setAuthorName("Manish Kumar");
            author2.setAuthorId("PACKT-002");
            author2.setAuthorAddress("Mumbai India");

            Author author3=new Author();

            author3.setAuthorName("Dr.Tim");
            author3.setAuthorId("PACKT-003");
            author3.setAuthorAddress("Toronto Canada");


            DatumWriter<Author> empDatumWriter = new
    SpecificDatumWriter<Author>(Author.class);
            DataFileWriter<Author> empFileWriter = new
    DataFileWriter<Author>(empDatumWriter);

            empFileWriter.create(author1.getSchema(), new
    File("/home/packt/avro/author.avro"));

            empFileWriter.append(author1);
            empFileWriter.append(author2);
            empFileWriter.append(author3);

            empFileWriter.close();

            System.out.println("Succesfully Created Avro file");
        }
    }
```

The following shows an example of reading an `avro` file:

```
    package com.packt.hadoopdesign.avro;

    import org.apache.avro.file.DataFileReader;
    import org.apache.avro.io.DatumReader;
    import org.apache.avro.specific.SpecificDatumReader;
    import packt.Author;

    import java.io.File;
    import java.io.IOException;

    public class PacktAvroReader {
```

```
    public static void main(String args[]) throws IOException{

        DatumReader<Author> authorDatumReader = new
SpecificDatumReader<Author>(Author.class);

        DataFileReader<Author> authorFileReader = new
DataFileReader<Author>(new
            File("/home/packt/avro/author.avro"), authorDatumReader);
        Author author=null;

        while(authorFileReader.hasNext()){

            author=authorFileReader.next(author);
            System.out.println(author);
        }
    }
}
```

Optimized Row Columnar (ORC)

The development of **Optimized Row Columnar** (ORC) started at Hortonworks to optimize storage and performance in Hive, a data warehouse for summarization, query, and analysis that lives on top of Hadoop. Hive is designed for queries and analysis, and uses the query language HiveQL (similar to SQL). ORC files are designed for high performance when Hive is reading, writing, and processing data. ORC stores row data in columnar format. This row-columnar format is highly efficient for compression and storage. It allows for parallel processing across a cluster, and the columnar format allows for the skipping of unnecessary columns for faster processing and decompression. ORC files can store data more efficiently without compression than compressed text files. Like Parquet, ORC is a good option for read-heavy workloads.

This advanced level of compression is possible because of its index system. ORC files contain *stripes* of data, or 10,000 rows. These stripes are the data building blocks and are independent of each other, which means that queries can skip to the stripe that is needed for any given query. Within each stripe, the reader can focus only on the columns that are required. The footer file includes descriptive statistics for each column within a stripe such as count, sum, min, max, and if null values, if they are present.

ORC is designed to maximize storage and query efficiency.

> *"Facebook uses ORC to save tens of petabytes in their data warehouse and demonstrated that ORC is significantly faster than RC File or Parquet."*

– *Apache Foundation*

Similar to Parquet, schema evolution is supported by the ORC file format, but its efficacy is dependent on what the data store supports. Recent advances have been made in Hive that allow for appending columns, type conversion, and name mapping.

Parquet

Launched in 2013, Parquet was developed by Cloudera and Twitter (and inspired by Google's Dremel query system) to serve as an optimized columnar data store on Hadoop. Because data is stored in columns, it can be highly compressed and splittable (for the reasons we noted previously). Parquet is commonly used with Apache Impala, an analytics database for Hadoop. Impala is designed for low latency and high concurrency queries on Hadoop. The column metadata for a `Parquet` file is stored at the end of the file, which allows for fast, one-pass writing. Metadata can include information such as, data types, compression/encoding scheme used (if any), statistics, element names, and more. Parquet is especially adept at analyzing wide datasets with many columns. Each Parquet file contains binary data organized by *row group*.

For each row group, the data values are organized by column. This enables the compression benefits that we described previously. Parquet is a good choice for read-heavy workloads. Generally, schema evolution in the Parquet file type is not an issue and is supported. However, not all systems prefer Parquet support schema evolution optimally. For example, consider a columnar store such as Impala. It is hard for that data store to support schema evolution, as the database needs to have two versions of the schema (old and new) for a table.

Data compression

Many of us have been working on many big data projects and have used a wide range of frameworks and tools to solve customer problems. Bringing the data to distributed storage is the first step of data processing. If you have ever observed that in the case of **Extract, Transform, Load** (**ETL**) or **Extract, Load, Transform** (**ELT**), the first step is to extract the data and bring it in for processing. A storage system has a cost associated with it and we always want to store more data in less storage space. The big data processing happens over massive amounts of data, which may cause I/O and network bottlenecks. The shuffling of data across the network is always a painful, time-consuming process that burns significant amounts of processing time.

Here is how compression can help us in different ways:

- **Less storage**: A storage system comes with a significant amount of cost associated with it. Companies are moving toward the cloud, and even if we have to pay less for storage over the cloud, it is a good practice to compress the data so that you pay less for storage. In some of the cases, it is observed that compression helped gigabytes of data to become megabytes.

- **Reduce processing time**: You must be thinking how compression can reduce processing time because there will be time involved in uncompromising the data before processing. This must be true when the data size is small and there is not much shuffling required across a distributed cluster. Think about a scenario where gigabytes or terabytes of data need to be shuffled across a network and then used for processing. There will be lot of I/O and network bandwidth involved, which may cause significant performance problems and thus compression will give a significant boost in such cases.

- **CPU and I/O trade-off**: The compression reduces the significant amount of time consumed in I/O but at the same time it has to process more data, which will be the result of the decompression operation. In many cases where data size is significant, it has been found that the overall job processing time has been increased significantly.

- **Block compression in Hadoop**: Hadoop has a concept of splittable and non-splittable file formats, and in most of cases, splittable file formats are preferred as they allow each block to be processed in parallel, which improves processing time. In a splittable file format, it is not advisable to compress one big file and then use it for processing; in such cases, block compression can be a useful option. In block compression, data stored on HDFS blocks are compressed and then will be used by MapReduce or any other tool for processing at a later stage.

Types of data compression in Hadoop

The Hadoop framework supports many compression formats for both input and output data. A compression format or a **coder-decoder** (**codec**) is a set of compiled, ready-to-use Java libraries that a developer can invoke programmatically to perform data compression and decompression in a MapReduce job. Each of these codecs implements an algorithm for compression and decompression and also has different characteristics.

Among the different data compression formats, some are splittable, which can further enhance performance when reading and processing large compressed files. So, when a single large file is stored in HDFS, it is split into many data blocks and distributed across many nodes. If the file has been compressed using the splittable algorithms, data blocks can be decompressed in parallel by using several MapReduce tasks. However, if the file has been compressed by a non-splittable algorithm, Hadoop must pull the blocks together and use a single MapReduce task to decompress them. Some of these compression techniques are explained in the following sections.

Gzip

Gzip is a compression utility by the GNU project; the details of the project are available at `https://www.gnu.org/software/gzip/`. It generates compressed files. The implementation of Gzip is based on the DEFLATE algorithm, which is a combination of Huffman Coding and LZ77. Gzip provides a higher compression ratio, which results in more CPU resource usage. Gzip is mostly a good choice for cold data. Cold data is the data that is not accessed frequently. The compression performance of Gzip is more than two times that of Snappy in most cases. Here is how we can set compression with map reduce job execution:

```
hadoop jar mapreduce-example.jar sort "-
Dmapreduce.compress.map.output=true"
      "-
Dmapreduce.map.output.compression.codec=org.apache.hadoop.io.compress.GzipC
odec"
    "-Dmapreduce.output.compress=true"
      "-
Dmapreduce.output.compression.codec=org.apache.hadoop.io.compress.GzipCodec
" -outKey
      org.apache.hadoop.io.Text -outValue org.apache.hadoop.io.Text input
output
```

BZip2

The BZip2 file compression program is implemented based on the Burrows-Wheeler algorithm that was developed by Julian Seward and launched on the 18th of July in 1996. The program can compress files but cannot archive them, and it works on nearly all major operating systems. The functions for BZip2 are as follows:

- **Filename extension**: bz2
- **Media Type**: application/x-bzip2 on internet
- **Uniform type identifier**: public.archive.bzip2

BZip2 provides better compression performance, but in terms of processing performance, it can be significantly slower than Snappy. A simple rule is that the more we get better compression, the less we get to read and write performance, and anything that takes more read and write time than expected is not an ideal codec for Hadoop storage, unless the primary requirement is to reduce the storage footprint. These could be good choices for archiving infrequently accessed data.

Lempel-Ziv-Oberhumer

The **Lempel-Ziv-Oberhumer** (**LZO**) compression format provides a modest compression ratio. It provides fast speed for compression and decompression and is composed of many small blocks of compressed data, allowing jobs to be divided along the block boundaries. It is one of the file formats that supports splittable compression, which helps in the parallel processing of compressed text file splits by distributed processing jobs, such as MapReduce. LZO creates an index when it compress the file, which tells the distributed process, such as MapReduce, from where to split the file.

LZO is optimized for better compression and decompression speed, which helps in improving processing time. LZO has a licence that does not allow it to be directly used with Hadoop, and has to be separately installed, but most of the integrated platform already comes up with the installation and they have taken care of the licencing part. The following are examples of configuration changes so that you can use LZO compression:

- `core-site.xml`:

```
<property>
    <name>io.compression.codecs</name>
    <value>org.apache.hadoop.io.compress.GzipCodec,org.apache.hadoop
.io.compress.DefaultCodec,com.hadoop.compression.lzo.
LzoCodec,com.hadoop.compression.lzo.LzopCodec,org.apache.
hadoop.io.compress.BZip2Codec</value>
</property>
<property>
    <name>io.compression.codec.lzo.class</name>
    <value>com.hadoop.compression.lzo.LzoCodec</value>
</property>
```

- `mapred-site.xml`:

```xml
<!-- Add LZO Codecs details -->
<property>
    <name>mapreduce.map.output.compress</name>
    <value>true</value>
</property>
<property>
    <name>mapreduce.map.output.compress.codec</name>
    <value>com.hadoop.compression.lzo.LzoCodec</value>
</property>
```

- `hadoop-env.sh`:

```sh
export
HADOOP_CLASSPATH="$HADOOP_HOME/lib/hadoop-
lzo.jar:$HADOOP_CLASSPATH:$CLASS_FILES"

# For 32-bit machines
export
JAVA_LIBRARY_PATH=$HADOOP_HOME/lib/native/Linux-i386-32:
$HADOOP_HOME/lib/native
# For 64-bit machines
export
JAVA_LIBRARY_PATH=$HADOOP_HOME/lib/native/Linux-amd64-64:
$HADOOP_HOME/lib/native
```

It is a compression technique that creates a splittable, compressed file in Hadoop. There is no need for external indexing when using this compression. It can be used at any level of speed/compression-ratio in Hadoop, from fast mode reaching 500 MB/s compression speed up to high/ultra modes providing increased compression ratio, almost comparable with Gzip.

Snappy

Snappy is another compression and decompression technique that does not target maximum compression, nor does it target compatibility with any other compression technique. Snappy is designed for very high speeds and reasonable compression. The compression speed of Snappy is around 250 MBP/s and decompression speed is around double the compression speed on Core i7 64 bit processor machines.

Snappy is not CPU intensive, which ensures that map and reduce processes running at the same time will not be reduced or affected because of the CPU time. Please note that Snappy is inherently splittable and intended to be used with a container file format such as Sequence Files, Avro, Paraquat, and so on. The following shows the property for Snappy:

```
<property>
    <name>mapred.compress.map.output</name>
     <value>true</value>
 </property>
<property>
    <name>mapred.map.output.compression.codec</name>
    <value>org.apache.hadoop.io.compress.SnappyCodec</value>
</property>
```

We will explain these compression techniques in the following table:

Codec	Splittable	Degree of compression	Compression speed
Gzip	No	Medium	Medium
BZip2	Yes	High	Slow
Snappy	No	Medium	Fast
LZO	No, unless indexed	Medium	Fast

Compression format consideration

We have been discussing the Hadoop objective from the beginning of this book, which is to process large datasets in parallel, and it is important to take advantage of compression to achieve a higher processing performance. The choice of compression completely depends on what is the objective of the use case and what tools are being used for processing.

The following are a few points that we can take into consideration when selecting a compression format:

- **Use the container file format**: The container file formats that are splittable and support compression are a good choice for the application. Along with the container file format, fast compression algorithms such as Snappy, LZ4, and so on should be used.
- **Compressed file size**: The primary feature of a distributed storage system like HDFS is to split the file into a configured block size. S, a compressed chunk size of files should be approximately equal to or less than the HDFS block. It will help in achieving better read performance as a single mapper will be able to process more decompressed data.

- **Non-splittable file**: There is no point in applying compression over a file that is not splittable in nature because the whole file will be processed by a single mapper and we will lose data locality in such cases.

Serialization

Serialization is the process of converting structured objects into a byte stream that will be transferred over a network or will be written to a persistent storage. Deserialization is the process of converting a byte stream back into structured objects.

The basic question that some of us always have is, why do we need serialization? Let us understand it in simple terms. Every language or application has its own way of representing data, for example, Java has objects to represent data, Spark has RDD to represent data, MapReduce has writable objects to represent data, and so on. These representations are only known to frameworks that can be processed in memory, but this data cannot be shared between different processes or applications that have a different way of representing data. Now, we are clear that data needs some common representation when it is written to the storage system or shared across networks to be used by different applications. In most cases, writing data into a serialized file format helps with these issues. The file formats such as AVRO, ORC, RC, Paraquat, and so on are common serialized formats that are used across big data processing pipelines.

The serialization process can take place in the following two types of communications in a distributed data processing:

- **Inter-process communication**: The distributed processing system has multiple intermediate process communications involved, where one process may communicate with the other using **Remote Procedure Calls** (**RPCs**). The serialization format that should be used with the RPC protocol should make use of better network bandwidth that is fast enough to serialise or deserialise the data.

- **Persistent storage**: The final stage of most of processing pipeline is to write data to the persistent storage system where object representation needs to be converted into some common data representation that can be easily read by other systems. File formats that have recently evolved, such as AVRO, have added value to the processing time.

Data ingestion

The data ingestion is the process of bringing data from one or more sources to a target data storage layer for processing. It is the first step of building any data pipeline. If you think about the two processes, which are **Extract, Transform, and Load** (ETL) and **Extract, Load, and Transform** (ELT), the first process is the extraction of data from the source system. In big data processing, the ingestion process has been categorized into multiple types. We will look into some of the design considerations while following these design patterns across the implementation.

Batch ingestion

Batch ingestion is the process of extracting the data from the source system in longer duration intervals, for example, configuring the ingestion process to run on a daily basis at 5 am. The source of batch ingestion is generally the persistent storage such as database systems, persistent filesystems, and so on, where data is already available. The following diagram shows the design considerations of batch ingestion:

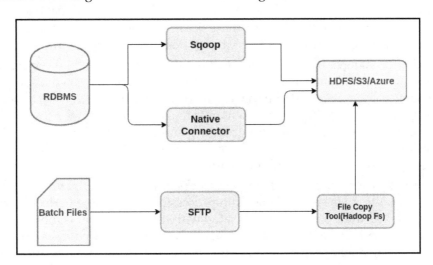

The following are the different design considerations of batch ingestion:

- **Batch size**: There are multiple ways of increasing the performance of ingestion. Configuring the optimized batch size for an application is always helpful. Please take into consideration that configuring a larger batch size requires more memory to be allocated to the task containers.

- **Parallelism**: Distributed systems available today for extracting data from the source system have a capability to extract data in parallel. It is obvious that for extracting larger datasets, the amount of time taken by one node will always be greater than when it is done by multiple nodes in parallel. For example, parallelism in Sqoop is controlled by increasing or decreasing the number of mappers that are dependent on how many parallel connections the source system allows for the application.

- **Incremental ingestion**: Full extraction of data does not make any sense if you already have most of the data present for processing. In most cases, you only need records that are either new, updated, or deleted from the system in the second batch run. The incremental ingest is only possible if the source system has some fields to identify when a record was created, updated, or deleted, such as `date_created`, `date_modified`, and so on. Sometimes, we have also come across sources that do not have these fields that restrict the ability to do incremental extraction, and full extraction has to be done for further processing.

- **Schema changes**: The source system and the data pipeline in the system are loosely coupled and therefore it is possible that something on the source system changes and it breaks down the downstream system, which is the processing step. There are multiple ways to handle this problem; one way could be only extracting the required column from the source, and the other way could be using a schema evaluation file format such as AVRO to deal with such scenarios using a backward compatibility feature.

- **Access pattern, file format, and compression codec**: The file format plays an important role in storage space and processing speed. How to decide which file format has multiple factors associated with it, such as what is the access pattern that's used in the data ingestion, what is the primary objective, saving space or increasing query performance, or better trade-off between both, and so on. We have observed better performance, that is, increase in speed by more than 60% based on the file format used with a specific compression codec.

Macro batch ingestion

Macro batch ingestion is the process of bringing data to the target system in shorter duration of intervals, such as 30 minutes, 1 hour, and so on. One of the use cases that is common across the industry is offloading data from streaming messaging storage, such as Kafka to HDFS on an hourly basis, and then doing batch processing on top of it, or doing micro batch processing. These types of ingestion are being adopted very rapidly as people are looking forward to building batch and real-time use cases using Kafka, like distributed messaging systems. There can be other sources for micro batch ingestion, as represented in the following diagram:

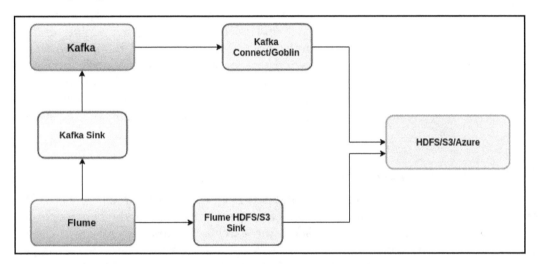

Macro batch ingestion also explains the following:

- **Data loss or duplicate data**: The major challenge in micro batch ingestion is how do we avoid data loss or deal with duplicate data during ingestion? For sources such as Kafka or Flume, it is common to have these challenges in place. Guaranteed consumption of data from these sources has to be there but also controlling duplicates is required to give up throughput and latency. It is always better to deal with data loss first and remove duplicates once the data has landed on your storage system.

- **Small file problem**: The data ingested in micro batches will sometimes have multiple smaller files in hourly or minute-based directories/partitions which may cause major performance bottleneck during processing. The file size should at least match the default block size. The first step in such cases should be the merging of smaller files into bigger ones.
- **Ingestion throughput**: Throughput of ingesting micro batch data should be good enough to finish the ingestion process before the next macro ingestion batch triggers. It is always good to configure and give fair amounts of resources for the macro data ingestion process to avoid any further issues to the downstream system.
- **History data**: It is always a good practice to maintain the history of ingested data and it is applicable for both batch and macro batch processing. It gives us the flexibility to avoid further ingestion processes if we have to rebuild the data pipeline because of some bugs or errors in the processing stage. We can maintain the date partition at first stage of directory and move very infrequently used data to some low-cost storage system. Maintaining history data also enables you to use the same dataset in multiple other business use cases in the organization.

Real-time ingestion

Real-time ingestion is the process of bringing data from the source immediately after it is generated. For example, consider the click events generated per second when people across the world are searching something on Google or searching products on Amazon. These events have to be captured as soon as possible to get data for some real-time use case, such as building a recommendation system or detecting any fraudulent activity. The source systems that generate real-time events are generally application logs, click stream events, sensor data, and so on.

The target system where this real-time data will be ingested must be capable enough to handle huge amounts of load coming into the system. The system must also be distributed and easy to scale in nature. There are systems like Kafka, AWS Kinesis, Apache Flume, and so on that are available to be used as a storage layer for real-time data. A system such as Flume deletes the data immediately after the downstream system consumes and acknowledges the data, which is not applicable and desirable for the use case. In the use cases, Flume and Kafka are used together to maintain the data for some time. The following diagram shows the real-time ingestion:

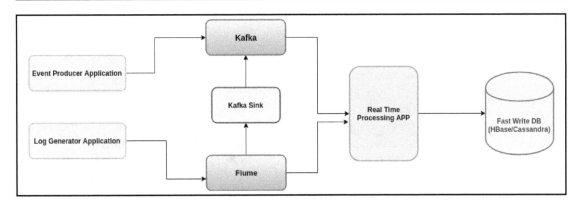

The different features for real-time ingestion are mentioned as follows:

- **Avoid data loss**: For some of the use cases such as credit card fraud detection, even a single event of a loss may cause trouble for the business. The producer system should not drop out a message until and unless it has received acknowledgement from the storage system like Kafka for the successful commit of data.
  It may happen that you get a commit timeout from Kafka or another system, and you can always re-send the events to the target system. It is also important to write failed producer events to some other local filesystem to avoid data loss because of target system failure, and alert the users if the numbers are really high.
- **Retention period**: The data is continuously ingested to the target system and it grows at a rapid speed, which may cause a system like Kafka to run out of disk space or force users to add more machines. The proper capacity planning and design of use cases may avoid such problems. The retention period is the amount of time we want to keep the real-time events on these storage systems, and then if the data is not being used for real-time processing, we should offload it to some distributed file system, like HDFS or S3 for further use.
- **Capturing bad events**: It is sometimes obvious that the events getting generated may fail due to any reason, such as a parsing exception, casting exception, or so on. These events must be captured in some bad event file where at a later stage someone can take a look to see what happened at the producer side and if there is something that needs to be changed.
- **Monitoring storage system**: System monitoring is an important aspect in real-time ingestion. Because everything is live all the time, we can not accommodate the node failures for a longer duration to avoid data loss. A monitoring and alerting system helps in avoiding any data loss because of disk space, system failure, or any other failure.

Data processing

Data processing is a next step after the ingestion stage is successful. Each ingestion type we discussed previously has an equivalent data processing type. When we refer to data processing here, we generally talk about distributed data processing and there are a lot of scenarios that must be taken into consideration during the processing of data. It is also important to understand that a distributed system is designed to reduce the data processing time and we must take all the best practices into consideration before we start implementing a data processing application. In this section, we will walk you through each of the data processing types and some of the best practices that need to be taken into consideration.

Batch processing

Batch processing is the type of data processing where data elements are processed in a group of batches. For example, if we consider data to be arriving on a daily basis for processing, then we can consider a day as one batch and process the entire data for the single batch. Batch processing is triggered on a scheduled time interval; you may have a daily extraction job, which extracts data from RDBMS and then does some processing on this daily extracted data. The amount of data that is generally processed in batch processing is relatively large in number.

Hadoop was first discovered to process data in batches, and distributed batch processing helps in processing terabytes of data in a very reduced time compared to some legacy data processing frameworks. In batch processing system like MapReduce, the data is accumulated before it is processed, which leads to a larger turnaround time. It increases storage system usage, memory usage, and the compute resources of the system.

If we do not have on demand a cluster setup for processing, then batch processing does not utilize the cluster resources efficiently, because during data extraction/ingestion, the cluster compute resources and memory are idle. There are some design considerations that should be taken into consideration in batch processing, as follows:

- **Maintaining history data with partition**: We always recommend using history data at the incoming and gold layer so that, if required, all the intermediate stage data can be recreated using the same application logic over all data. Maintaining history data with a partition also enables fast data processing and usability of data in some other use case.

- **On demand cluster**: Cloud technologies have enabled the launching of new clusters within a time frame of a few minutes, which gives us the ability to launch clusters as and when required. We should make it a provision of cluster to launch only when required for data processing. It can save a huge cost.
- **File format and compression**: Storing and processing huge amounts of data is always costly and time-consuming. It is always advisable to use a file format that gives a better trade-off between compression ratio and processing speed. In frameworks like MapRreduce, we should also consider compressing intermediate output to speed up the process by enabling compression over intermediate results.
- **Avoid shuffling of data**: A distributed system involves shuffling as one of the essential phases in which data is traversed across the network to some other node for further processing. Operations such as Join, Group by, and so on, involve the huge movement of data and, therefore, we must filter out and apply logic to avoid less data bring traversed across the network.
- **Data quality**: Data quality plays a major role in eliminating a record that does not make any sense in processing because it has column values that do not pass the data quality check. It is recommended to run a data quality check so that if the data quality threshold is not met, then we can conclude whether to run the batch or not run the batch.
- **Effective use of resources**: In most cases, either for MapReduce or Apache Spark, it has been observed that cluster resources have not been used efficiently. The best idea is to analyse the MapReduce program or Spark program and decide how many mappers or partitions we really need for the batch processing.

Micro batch processing

Micro batch processing is type of data processing where data is processed in groups of micro batches, which means batches of a few seconds or minutes. Micro batch processing frameworks like Apache Spark provide the ability to group stream events into a micro batch and process it to get the desired results. For example, you may want to have a business result saying the number of successful transactions happening per minute or the number of transaction failures in a few minutes or seconds.

Micro stream processing is dependent on some stream source that has the ability to replay a batch exactly the same way it was played before. Replayability enables the ability to recompute and calculate things in case of any processing failure. We talked about Apache Kafka as a source for stream events in the previous chapters, which helps us achieve the desire result. The consumer, that is, the micro batch processing application, has to maintain offset of read messages and then can replay from the same point in case of any failure. Although the high-level approach of micro batch looks simple, there are some best practices and challenges that we should follow when building or designing such applications, which are as follows:

- **Avoid unreliable processing**: The micro batch application has an acknowledgement mechanism to tell the source stream that it has successfully consumed the messages. It is important to note that the reliability of the message depends on when we choose to send the acknowledgement. Sometimes, sending an acknowledgement too early may result in data loss if the processing application fails before the event processing is successful. The acknowledgement to a source stream system like Kafka should be sent after the successful processing of an event if we don't want to lose data as part of the processing design.
- **Data duplication**: Data duplication refers to the duplicate processing of events. Think about a scenario where data is successfully processed and before sending an acknowledgement back to the source stream provider like Kafka, the application processing event went out of service. In such a case, when the application restarts, it will consume the data from the same offset, which will result in duplicate processing.
- **Increased latency**: Sometimes, it may happen that we receive more events in some batches and less events in other batches. This may happen because of peak hours of business and non-peak hours of business. If event batches are too small, then it may result in the decrease of performance, and event batches that are too large can slow down the processing speed.
- **Batch with size and time**: To overcome the problems we discussed in the increase latency step, the batches should be configured by both tuple size and time. This will ensure that even if a batch does not have a configured batch size, it will go for processing if the waiting time has reached the timeout. Even if the timeout has not been reached and the batch size is reached, the processing of the batch will trigger.

- **Choosing right framework**: Throughput and latency plays an important role in micro batch processing and therefore it is important to choose the right framework for building and executing the application. Apache Spark has emerged as a market leader in dealing with batch and micro batch use cases today, but we cannot ignore the popularity of Apache Flink and some other frameworks. Before choosing a framework, evaluate the different parameters, like your team expertise, application requirements, pros and cons of the framework, already solved use cases and benchmarks, and so on.

Real-time processing

Real-time processing is a type of processing in which a stream event is immediately processed without waiting for any other event to arrive. This enables the use cases where even the delay of milliseconds or a second may cause business loss. For example, consider the credit card fraud detection application where the card is first used in one country and then immediately, or in an hour, in the second country, it has to trigger fraud alert to the customer or block the transaction before the event transaction completes.

The major challenges of real-time processing solutions are how do we ingest data, process the data, and store processed data in real time, especially at high volumes. The processing of events must not block the ingestion of the events that indicate that everything should be loosely coupled. The target data store must have support for high-volume writes. The different features for real-time processing are as follows:

- **Enable checkpointing**: Checkpointing is the process of maintaining the metadata of the current state of the application. It helps in building fault tolerant applications where the application can use checkpoint metadata to recompute the application logic where it left at last failure. The new generation stream processing framework like Apache provides integrated checkpoints, which we can use to checkpoint required information.

- **Loosely coupled ingestion and processing**: The system that's generating events in real time should not be directly integrated with the processing application. Imagine if some processing application goes down for sometime, we may end up losing events that are generated during that time. The event that was generated should be pushed to a distributed messaging system like Kafka, where data will be persisted from some time and can be replayed whenever required.

- **Multiple event producer**: In real use cases, there will be scenarios where multiple applications are generating the same or different events, which have to be processed by the same streaming application. If both applications are not loosely coupled, then the chances of losing the data are even higher, and it will also increase the latency of the application.

- **Parallelism**: New generation stream processing frameworks enable the ability to process real-time events in parallel, which gives better latency and throughput. But parallelism in most cases, depends on how the source system has been configured. In most cases where the stream source is Kafka, parallelism depends on how many partitions a particular topic has. We must carefully plan the amount of parallelism we need by considering various factors, such as event rate, cluster capacity, complexity of processing, and so on.

- **Target system capability**: A real-time processed event goes into some target system for decision-making. For example, the recommendation system we built sometime back has HBase as the target system, which helped us in achieving fast lookup and high write throughput. Similarly, in some cases, people also use Cassandra as a target system or push processed events back to Apache Kafka. Finally, the point is, the target system should not become a bottleneck for the stream processing application.

- **Data duplication and data loss**: Data duplication and data loss are common things we should avoid in design consideration. In some cases, duplicate event processing may result in incorrect reports that may further cause some serious business issues. Data loss is obviously something that no one wants to consider as part of the design. The application should have reliable and efficient logical implementation to handle these two scenarios by keeping latency and throughput into consideration.

Common batch processing pattern

Batch processing has been used for many years and there has been some common design problems encountered during batch processing implementation. People have some common design patterns to solve such problems. In this section, we will basically discuss some of the common design patterns and how we solve design problems using common techniques.

Slowly changing dimension

Slowly Changing Dimension (**SCD**) refers to the concept where some or most part of the data changes at irregular intervals. There are multiple SCD types available and each have different implementations in Hadoop. We will talk about each type and how to deal with it. We will look into *Type 1* and *Type 2*, which are commonly used *slowly changing dimensions*.

Slowly changing dimensions – type 1

Slowly changing dimensions type 1 implementation overwrites all the old data with new and updated records. It does not maintain history of old data, meaning we will not be able to track the changes if we want to at some later stage. The approach for the solution is very simple, and the following diagram is a simple representation of SCD type-1:

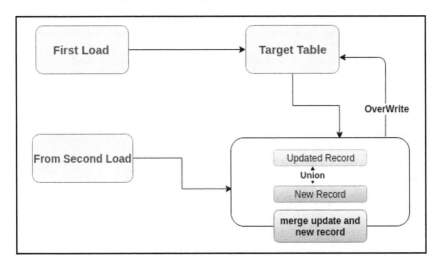

In programming terms, if we have to solve this problem, there are two approaches, with the database supporting a merge statement, it is easy to run the update and insert in single run using the following sample query:

```
merge into
 targetTable
using
 incoming_table as incoming
on
 incoming.id = targetTable.primarykey_column
when matched then
 update set col1 = value1, col2 = value2, col3 = value3, col4 = value4
when not matched then
 insert values (incoming_table.primarykey_column, incoming_table.col1,
incoming_table.col2, incoming_table.col3,incoming_table.col4);
```

In the case of Hive, which is used as a warehouse engine like Hadoop, update is a very costly operation. Cloud providers like AWS offer managed services like Redshift, which provides better speed with update statements. If you have to apply the implementation in any procedural or programming language or framework, use the approach represented in the SCD type-1 diagram.

Slowly changing dimensions - type 2

The slowly changing dimensions type 2 is very similar to SCD type 1, with the difference that it maintains the history of records. The history record keeps versions of past representations of the original table and current record keeps the current version of the table with the latest update. The approach for SCD type 2 is shown in the following diagram:

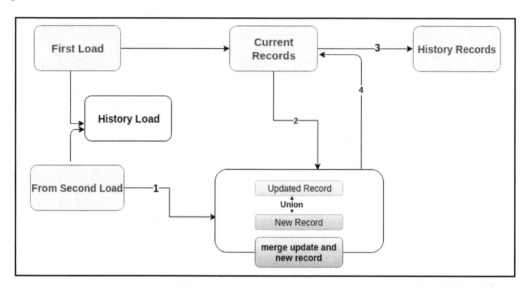

The only difference is that we need to first copy the current record to the history record before we overwrite it to the current table. If you are maintaining a file system over HDFS like storage, then copy the current data to the history directory in the current date partition.

Duplicate record and small files

The other common processing patterns that we normally come across is small file problem or duplicate records. Small file problem is common where data is ingested in near real-time into hourly or half hourly buckets and then later used for batch processing. Similarly, duplicate record is also common in stream ingestion or the duplicate copy of records from the source system.

In the previous chapters, we discussed what problems small files or duplicate records may cause. In this section, we will talk about how we can solve these two problems using Hive and Apache Spark.

With Hive it is simple to use a distinct query and then load the record into a new table, which will remove the duplicate records. Now, to deal with the small file problem, there are a few approaches that we can follow, as follows:

- **Number of mapper and reducer**: The simple approach is to make the number of mapper or reducer 1, depending upon what type of job it is. This will ensure that at the end of the Hive query we have one output file as a result in a partition or directory where the Hive query is writing to. But with a huge number of records, this is not a feasible solution.

- **Map task merge**: If you want to merge files at the end of each map task, then set `hive.merge.mapfiles` to true and set `hive.merge.size.per.task` to the desired per file size in bytes, or set `hive.merge.smallfiles.avgsize` to some desired `threshhold` value, which will ensure that if the file size is less than the configured value, Hive will run additional jobs to merge the files into a bigger one.

- **MapReduce task merge**: Similar to map task merge, there is another property `hive.merge.mapredfiles`, which when set to true, will merge files at the end of the map reduce tasks. It is used with `hive.merge.size.per.task` and `hive.merge.smallfiles.avgsize`.

- **QUERY**: The following alter query can also be used to merge small files in a partition table:

```
ALTER TABLE tablename [PARTITION partition_detail] CONCATENATE;
```

With Spark, the simplest way to merge small files is to reparation the RDD when writing the output to disk. The method `coalesce(numPartitions)` can be used to define the number of files you need at the end of the Spark job. But remember, calculating the number of partitions to pass to the coalesce function is little tricky. We found some repository over Git created by some cool developers to ease community work, which gives a good idea about how we go with the approach for calculating the number of partitions. In most cases, you can reuse code written by them. The repository can be found at the following: `https://github.com/imduffy15/spark-avro-compactor`.

Real-time lookup

Realtime lookup is the process of making a lookup during the processing of records. For example, you may want to lookup if a record belongs to a certain category or if the IP is available in an abuse report, or whether a person has an aadhar number, and so on. We have also come across many applications that have such requirements during data processing. You may be wondering why we need to do lookup when we can load data and join between datasets. What about the scenario where you are not allowed to access a dataset for lookup and need to make an API call to check if data exists in the system? What about if there is any database like Redis, which is updated every few minutes or seconds, and data is there in the Redis system?

The following diagram represents real-time lookup:

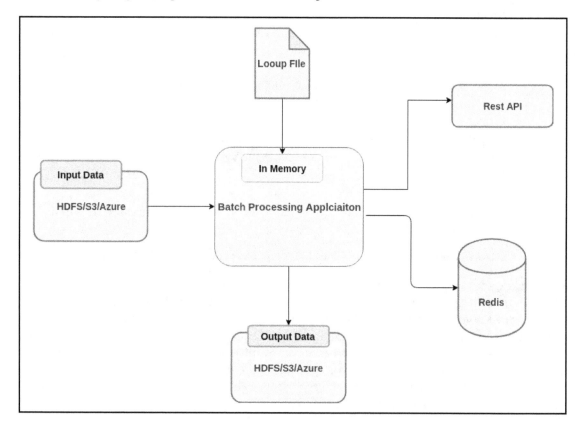

There are multiple ways to do lookups in the system when doing batch processing:

- **In memory lookup**: If the dataset that has to be used for lookup is available and the size is just a few megabytes, it is always recommended to use in memory lookup for such use cases. In MapReduce, we have a distributed cache to make such files available to mapper to do either in memory lookup or map side join.
- **Rest API**: Sometimes, we may not have permission to get data from the same system in which we have to do a lookup to get some results. In such cases, there are some REST APIs made available by data owners to do lookups or make REST calls to get results. These processes may slow down processing time, but it is still an option we can go for.
- **Redis or database lookup**: Sometimes, it may happen that we need a shared lookup system because the lookup dataset is huge or it is getting updates every few minutes or seconds. In such cases, having a fast lookup by using a database like Redis is recommended, where the latency of response is fair enough to not slow down the performance of batch processing.

Airflow for orchestration

Orchestration is the process of automating the workflow/pipeline that is to manage the task of scheduling the tasks, making coordination between tasks, and managing the created workflow. There are multiple tools available for automating the workflow such as Oozie, Azkaban, Jenkins, and so on.

We have observed that people don't spend much time on workflow orchestration and the impact of scheduling failure or rerun. This causes big problems in later stages and then it will be difficult to manage the kind of problem it creates. In this section, we will learn about Airflow, which is the new generation orchestration tool for Hadoop applications.

The user interface of Airflow is simple and easy to manage, and gives user's the flexibility to use and manage the workflows. The pipelines in Airflow are represented by **DAG** (**Direct Acyclic Graph**), where one task is dependent on another until the end of the pipeline.

The following screenshot shows the Airflow UI:

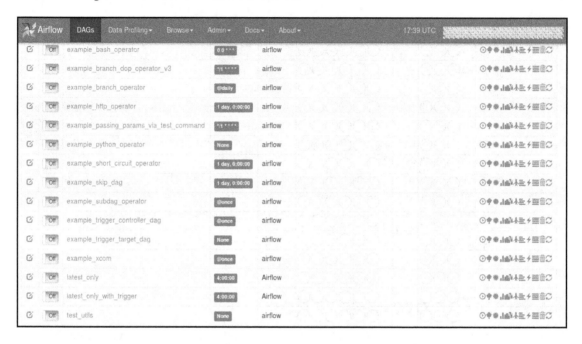

More details about the Airflow architecture and examples can be referred to at `https://airflow.apache.org/`. Airflow has multiple inbuilt operators, which can be used to schedule jobs of different types. For example, a Python operator can be used to submit Python tasks, a bash operator for bash jobs, and so on. You can also write your own custom operator using the Python API.

All the Python DAG modules placed under `$AIRFLOW_HOME/plugins` will be auto-imported by Airflow and will be visible on the UI.

Data governance

Data governance is the process of ensuring high quality, high availability, usability, integrity, and security of the data that's used across the organization. Data governance helps the organization to efficiently manage the data it has and get more value from that data, along with making the important value of that data visible to users.

Data governance enables and encourages good behavior about data and also limits any behavior that create risks. This objective is similar, irrespective of whether we are in a big data environment or a traditional data management environment. It helps the organization identify who is responsible for the data, collaborate to set policies and decisions, analyse how the data is used and what it is for, understand how and where metrics and information are derived, and determines the impact of any change in data on the business.

Data governance pillars

There are multiple definitions you will find about data governance pillars; we have defined three important pillars of data governance, and the following diagram is a representation of them:

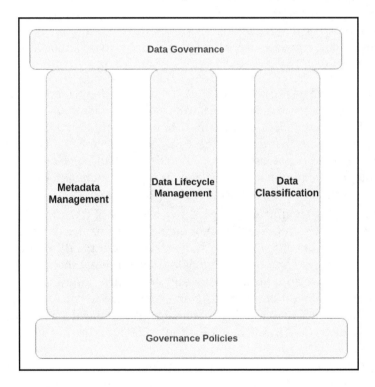

Metadata management

Use of data grows rapidly within the organization and, at some point in time, it is important to identify, define, and classify the data using subject areas, which helps managing the context of the data in the system. Metadata of data helps in achieving this objective by providing details of data flow within or outside the organization.

 The basic definition of metadata is "data about data" that gives the detailed information about data.

Metadata enables policy-based access to the organization data and policies, addresses concerns regarding data definition, data security, data lineage, data usage, and so on. The data governance and policies define the appropriate actions to be applied to data, which has to be applied to physical, which means actual storage of data, as well. It is a very powerful feature of data governance that enables both business and technical teams to make important decisions. The different features of metadata are as follows:

- **Capture metadata**: To have effective metadata management as part of the data governance policy, it is important to capture the metadata of all the data at the time of its creation. It is always important to identify all the external and internal metadata sources that the business is trying to use for decision-making. There are some metadata management tools already available such as Apache Atlas, which has integration and features available to capture metadata from various data sources, such as Hive Metastore, Apache Spark, and so on.
- **Data lineage**: Data lineage shows the entire flow of data from the time of its creation. A visual representation of data lineage enables organizations to track data from its source to its target. It also talks about the different intermediate processes or steps involved in the data flow and what their dependencies are. Some tools have advanced functionality to capture column lineage of tables, which gives a broad perspective to analyse where sensitive data is flowing in the organization and who is using it. It also helps technical teams to understand the improvement areas in the data pipeline or data model that are generating this lineage.
- **Metadata storage**: It's important to store the captured metadata into some persistent storage, keeping the access restricted based on the configured policy. The central metastore storage also removes the possibility of keeping duplicate data and allows metadata to be used by multiple applications.

- **Data security and access control**: It is always important to control the access of data to the user to meet security compliance. It is also important to take care that all the PII, PHI, or PCI data has been protected using masking, encryption, and that other security measures are in place. This data must not be downloaded or sent across a network without ensuring security compliance has been taken into consideration.

Data life cycle management

Data life cycle management is the concept of managing data from the start of its creation until it is destroyed or archived:

Data life cycle management (**DLM**) is a policy-based approach of managing the flow of data within an organization throughout its life cycle. In simple terms, managing data from the time of its creation, initial storage, to the time when it becomes obsolete and is deleted or archived. The DLM process automates the different processes involved, typically putting the data into separate layers according to configured policies, and automating data migration from one layer to another layer by certain criteria.

- **Data creation**: The data creation process describes when the data is created in the organization. The data might come from different places, such as sensors, click stream events, application logs, website visitors, or other sources. Some of this data must have some security policies associated with it, such as PII data, PHI data, or PCI data. At the time of creation, the security measures may not have been applied to this data, such as masking encryption or so on.
- **Data storage management**: The data that's created has to be stored in some persistent storage system and you must ensure that the data that's stored is protected. The data must not be easily accessible by anyone within or outside the organization.
- **Controlling data access**: The data will go through different processes of transformation, analysis, and be viewed at some stage. The data that is not supposed to be accessed or viewed by users should be protected based on security policies. All the user's activities are monitored and controlled to prevent data leak.

- **Data sharing**: Data is constantly being shared between different stockholders in the company, including employees, customers, and partners, which requires the securing and monitoring of sensitive data. At this stage, data may move between different storage systems, applications, or tools and platforms, which makes it important to implement the right security control strategy at the right time.
- **Archive**: At some point, old data may be very infrequently used which puts unnecessary cost and performance issue on the primary layer. This type of data is then archived and stored in a low cost storage system with protection and availability in mind. Some countries or organizations also have data storage compliancies, which restricts storing data after a certain amount of time.
- **Permanently removing data or purging data**: At some point in time, archived data grows at a rapid speed, resulting in additional cost and compliance issues. It is not feasible or compliant to store such data in archived layers for a longer duration. We can configure policies to auto-delete such data once the required policy conditions are met.

Data classification

Data classification is the process of classifying data in an effective way to ensure an effective level of data protection. Each organization who uses data governance usually defines a data classification policy, which tells us about where the data falls in multiple level of classification and how that data will be protected. There are few prerequisites for data classification such as defining roles and responsibilities for classifying data, all the business processes should be identified and documented, identification of risks associated with confidential information, policies and procedures for data classification should be defined and so on.

Data classification is the classification of data based on defining the level of sensitivity and the impact to the business should that data be disclosed, altered, or destroyed without authorization.

The different features of data classification can be explained as follows:

- **Identify the type of data**: The first step in the classification process is identifying the type of data, and there are basically three categories in which data is classified:

    - **Sensitive data**: Data should be classified as Sensitive/Restricted when breach, alteration, or destruction of the data causes a significant level of risk to the business. If this kind of data is disclosed to an unauthorized person, it may cause the violation of security laws of the country, domain, state, or specific organization. All PHI, PCI, and PII compliance data falls into this category.

    - **Internal data**: Data that is classified as internal data that, if breached or compromised, would have a low impact on the business and this data must be protected from unauthorized access due to proprietary, ethical, or privacy considerations. These policies are defined internally by the organization.

    - **Public data**: Data which is open to the public and does not have any significant impact on the the business. Sometime organizations can also define copyright or some other policies that the public user must agree on before using it.

- **Defining the data classification procedure**: Once the identification of the data type is done, it is important to define the classification procedures for effective data management:

    - **Identify owner**: It is important to define the owner of the data that was classified in first step. This owner must define the authorized and unauthorized users who can access the data. Each data owner must classify the information asset and guide its control within the organization.

    - **Identify and analyse data vulnerabilities/risks**: Identify the risk assessment and the attribute to each information asset. The points that should be given consideration include data control, data encryption, and the process to take if a security breach happened.

    - **Define and apply control**: The policy/principle should be defined and applied to control the access of data to only those users who have authorization to use it. The policy should also ensure that unauthorized users are not able to access any information through electronic material, networks, or by accessing the system. The data deletion and archived policy must be retained and followed to meet security compliance.

- **Maintaining audit logs**: Audit logs help in maintaining the confidentiality and integrity of classified information assets. Audit log should be able to capture all user or system activity so that in the case of any security breach, it must be able to provide enough evidence to the legal team. It can also help in tracking what changes have been made to any system, who made the changes, and at what time.

Summary

Now that you're at the end of this chapter, you should have a better understanding of file formats and the deciding factors of choosing the right one. We covered the different types of ingestion processes and the design considerations for them. We also focused on different types of data processing processes and some of the best practices of those processing systems. Data governance was our major area of focus, and we talked about its importance and what the important pillars of data governance are.

In the next chapter, we will study real-time stream processing in Hadoop.

Real-Time Stream Processing
in Hadoop

9

All industries have started adopting big data technology, as they have seen the advantages that companies are gaining after implementing it into their existing business model. Traditionally, companies were more focused on batch job implementation, and there has always been a lag of several minutes, or sometimes hours, between the arrival of data and it being displayed to the user. This leads to a delay in decision making, which in turn leads to revenue loss. This is where real-time analytics comes into the picture.

Real-time analytics is a methodology in which data is processed immediately after the system receives it and processed data gets available for use. Spark Streaming helps in achieving such objectives very efficiently. This chapter will cover a brief introduction to the following topics:

- Spark Streaming
- Integration of Apache Kafka with Apache Spark Streaming
- Common stream data patterns
- Streaming design considerations
- Case studies

This chapter is intended to help all developers and business analysts to understand the overall integration strategy, the advantages of different integration APIs, and what scenarios to keep in mind during project implementation.

Technical requirements

You will be required to have basic knowledge of Linux and Apache Hadoop 3.0.

The code files of this chapter can be found on GitHub:
https://github.com/PacktPublishing/Mastering-Hadoop-3/tree/master/Chapter09

Check out the following video to see the code in action:
`http://bit.ly/2T3yYfz`

What are streaming datasets?

Streaming datasets are about doing data processing, not on bounded data, but on unbounded data. Typical datasets are bounded. That means they are complete. At the very least, you will process data as if it were complete. Realistically, we know that there will always be new data, but as far as data processing is concerned, we will treat it as if it were a complete dataset. In the case of bounded data, data processing is done in phases and until and unless one phase is complete, other phases of data processing do not start. Another way to think about bounded data processing is that we will be done analyzing the data before new data comes in. Bounded datasets are finite in size. The following diagram represents how bounded data is processed using a typical MapReduce batch processing engine:

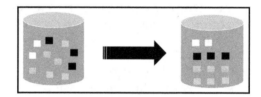

On the other hand, if you have an unbounded dataset (also known as an **infinite dataset**), it is never complete; there is always new data coming in, and typically, data is coming in even as you are analyzing data. So, we tend to think about analysis on unbounded datasets, as this is a temporary thing, carried out many times. It is valid only at a particular point in time. So, streaming is essentially data processing on unbounded data. Bounded data is data at rest. Stream processing is how you deal with data that is not at rest with unbounded data. But, more broadly, people often talk about streaming as an execution engine. An important feature of stream data processing is that it is highly unsettled with regard to event times, which means you need some kind of time-based shuffles in your pipeline to analyze the data against the background. The following diagram represents unbounded infinite datasets:

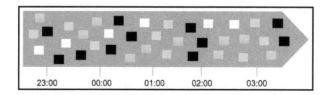

Stream data ingestion

Data ingestion represents a mechanism in which data is moved from a specific type of source to destination storage, where it can be further used for advanced analytics. Where there are very large data volumes, data is generally streamed to the destination storage, but only on the condition that the source and destination systems are capable of handling continuous streams of data. Stream data ingestion can be of one of two types: one is event-based and another one uses message queues.

Flume event-based data ingestion

Flume is a highly available distributed system that is used for streaming data ingestion. It collects, aggregates, and processes streaming data on the fly and stores it on disk for reliability. The following diagram shows the flume architecture:

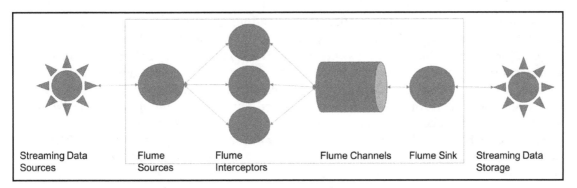

The preceding diagram represents the architecture components of the flume components, the details of which are mentioned in the following points:

- **Flume Sources**: These grasp events from external sources and pass them to channels via interceptors. These external sources are streaming sources that generate events like machine logs and message queues.
- **Flume interceptors**: Interceptors allow events from **Flume Sources** to be intercepted and modified on the fly. This could be transforming the events or enriching the events. These can be implemented using Java programming languages.

- **Flume Channels**: Channels store events until a sink is consumed. The memory channel and the file channel are two types of frequently used channels. The memory channel stores memory events and therefore delivers the best performance between the channels. However, it is also less reliable, since events are lost when the flume agent process or the flume agent host goes down. The disk channel that provides more durable storage for events by remaining on the disk is, therefore, more commonly used. Choosing right channel is an important architectural decision that needs performance and durability to be balanced.
- **Flume Sink**: This removes events from a channel and delivers them to a destination. The destination could be the final target system for events, or it could feed into further flume processing. An example of a common **Flume Sink** is the HDFS sink, which, as its name implies, writes events into HDFS files.

Kafka

In this section, we will introduce Kafka, a widely adopted scalable, performant, and distributed messaging platform. Initially, the LinkedIn technical team built the Kafka system. LinkedIn built a collecting system of software metrics with custom components in-house, supported by open source tools. The system was used to collect data on your portal for user activity. You use this data to display necessary information on your web portal for each user. The system was first developed as a traditional XML logging service and was subsequently processed with different ETL tools for extract-transforming loads. But for a long time, this framework didn't work well. They began to face several problems. They built a system called Kafka to solve these problems. Kafka is a **write-forward logging** (**WAL**) system that writes all messages published to log files before they are made available to consumer applications. Subscribers may, in a suitable time frame, read these written messages. Kafka was built with the following goals in mind:

- Loose coupling between message producers and message consumers
- Persistence of message data to support a variety of data consumption scenarios and failure handling
- Maximum end-to-end throughput with low latency components
- Managing diverse data formats and types using binary data formats
- Scaling servers linearly without affecting the existing cluster setup

Kafka further helps in making streaming architecture fault-tolerant and supports a variety of alerting and notification services. Each message is a collection of bytes in Kafka topics. The array is presented as this collection. Producers store data in Kafka queues in applications. They send Kafka messages, which are able to store all kinds of messages. Each subject is further distinguished into partitions. In the sequence in which they come, each partition stores messages.

Two major operations in Kafka can be carried out by producers/consumers. Producers add log files to the end of the writing forward. Consumers fetch messages from these log files that are part of a particular topic partition. Physically, each topic is spread over different Kafka brokers, which host one or two partitions of each topic. Ideally, Kafka pipelines should have a uniform number of partitions per broker, and all topics on each machine. Consumers are applications or processes that subscribe to a topic or receive messages from topics. The following diagram shows the Kafka logical architecture:

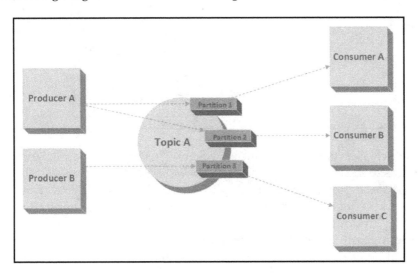

The preceding paragraph explains the logical architecture of Kafka and how different logical components coherently work together. While it is important to understand how Kafka architecture is divided logically, you also need to understand what Kafka's physical architecture looks like. This will help you in the later chapters as well. A Kafka cluster is basically composed of one or more servers (nodes).

The following diagram depicts what a multi-node Kafka cluster looks like:

A typical Kafka cluster consists of multiple brokers. This helps in load-balancing message reads and writes to the cluster. Each of these brokers is stateless. However, they use Zookeeper to maintain their states. Each topic partition has one of the brokers as a leader and zero or more brokers as followers. The leaders manage any read or write requests for their respective partitions. Followers replicate the leader in the background, without actively interfering with the leader's working. You should think of followers as a backup for the leader, and one of those followers will be chosen as the leader in the event of leader failure.

Common stream data processing patterns

In this section, we will talk about various processing patterns for unbounded data. Unbounded data patterns differ from bounded or fixed width data. As with every data stream, the context in which old records were processed changes. Therefore, stream processing is continuous and only true at a given time. In this section, we will cover some of the patterns common to any type of stream processing. Let's look at them one by one.

Unbounded data batch processing

You can always process unbounded data in batch mode. You can achieve this by slicing or converting unbounded data to bounded data. A common technique for performing that is called windowing or tumbling windowing. In this process, unbounded data is processed in a window of fixed length, mostly separated by a time frame, repeatedly. The following diagram shows batch stream processing windowing:

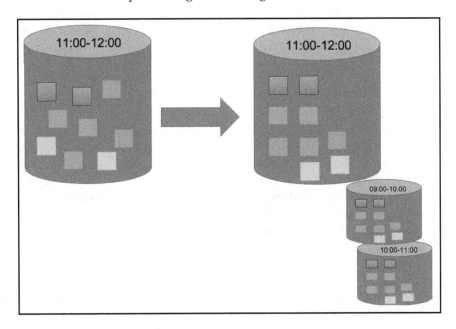

Another approach to batch unbounded data processing is using sessions. The following diagram represents how sessions are organized across time windows:

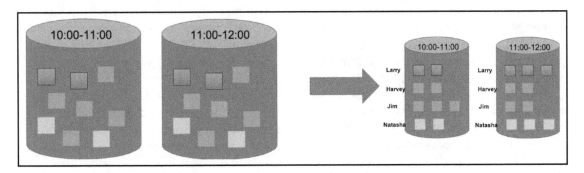

Streaming design considerations

Streaming is always an important pillar for large-scale organizations. More and more organizations rely on a massive data pool, and they have a need for faster actionable insights. You should understand the long-lasting profitability impact of timely data and appropriate actions based on such timely insights into data. In addition to in-time activities, streaming opens up channels to capture massive, unbounded data from various business groups throughout an organization. This section focuses on the factors that should be taken into account when designing a streaming application. The end results of such designs are driven by the business objectives of the organization.

Latency

The processing of incoming data from several sources and the production of an immediate result is one of the fundamental features of any streaming application. The initial considerations for the desired feature are latency and throughput. In other words, latency and throughput are measured for the performance of any streaming application. Any streaming application expects results to be achieved as soon as possible and high input rates to be handled. Both factors affect the selection of technology and hardware for streaming solutions. Let's first understand the meanings of both terms before we understand their impact in detail. In milliseconds, latency is defined as the time unit that the streaming application takes when an event or group of events is processed and when the result is produced. Average latency, best latency, or worst cases latency can be expressed. Sometimes the amount of events that occur in each window is also represented. For example, 2 ms for 85% of messages received in the last 24 hours can be defined. The performance is defined as the number of results produced by streaming apps at each time unit. In general, the number of events that a streaming application can process at each time unit derives throughput. Usually, you consider the maximum output that the system can handle when designing a streaming application, keeping end-to-end latency within the agreed SLAs. If the system is at the highest level of performance, all system resources are utilized fully, and events are waiting until resources are released. Now that latency and performance are clear with the definitions, it is easy to understand that they are not separated from each other. High latency means more time for processing an event and generating a result. This also means that system resources will be used for an event for a longer period of time and thus less parallel events can be processed at a time. High latency will, therefore, lead to reduced performance if the system capacity is limited. There are multiple factors to remember when striking a balance between your streaming application throughput and latency. The load distribution in several nodes is one such factor. Low latency per node can be ensured by the load distribution in the optimal use of every system resource. The mechanism is a built-in standard for most stream processing engines.

However, you must sometimes ensure it prevents too much data shuffling during runtime and that data partitions are properly defined. You have to plan your cluster accordingly to achieve the desired output and frequency. Some important factors that affect your application streaming performance include the number of CPUs, RAM, page cache, and so forth. It is imperative that you program your streaming application appropriately in order to keep your streaming performance at the desired level. Choice of programs and algorithms affect garbage collection, data shuffling, and so on. Finally, your latency and output will also be affected by factors such as bandwidth.

Data availability, integrity, and security

Data integrity, security, and accessibility are some of the key requirements of any solution that successfully streams. When you think about these factors, you should understand that persistence plays an important role in ensuring integrity, safety, and availability. For example, for any streaming solution, it is absolutely essential that its state continues, and we often call it a checkpoint. The control system allows streaming applications to persist over a period of time in their states and ensures recovery in the event of failure. State persistence also assures high consistency, which is essential for data accuracy and precisely message delivery semantics. You must now understand why it is important to have a continuing state. The results of data processing or raw unprocessed events are another aspect of persistence. This is a dual purpose. It allows us to replay messages and to compare existing information with historical data. It also allows us to retry messages if failures occur. At peak times, it helps us also deal with the back pressure on the source system. The storage medium used to retain the data must be carefully considered. Certain factors driving a storage media for streaming applications include a low read/write latency, hardware default tolerance, horizontal scalability, and optimized data transfer protocol that supports both synchronous and asynchronous operations.

Unbounded data sources

The main fundamental requirements for any streaming application is that sources need to have the ability to get unbounded data in terms of streams. Even if system sources have support for such data streams then streaming solutions are great but if not, then either you must build or use pre-built custom components that build data streams out of those data sources. Either way, the major takeaway is that streaming solutions should have data stream producing data sources. This is one of the major important design decisions that is present in any streaming applications.

Data lookups

The first question to be considered is why we need external data surveys in the pipeline for stream processing. The answer is that, sometimes, operations such as enhancement, validation of data, or filtering of data are necessary on the basis of some often changing external system data. However, these data surveys pose certain challenges in the streaming design context. These data searches could lead to increased end-to-end latency because calls to external systems are frequently made. Not all external reference data can be stored, because such external datasets are too large to fit in the memory. They change too often, which makes it difficult to refresh your memory. If these external systems are down, they will become a streaming solution bottleneck. In keeping with these challenges, three important factors are performance, scalability, and tolerance when designing solutions with external data surveys. All these can, of course, be achieved and trade-offs between the three always exist. One of the criteria for data lookups is that the impact on the processing time should be minimized. In fact, the millisecond response time for stream solutions is not even acceptable within seconds. Some solutions use caching systems, such as Redis, to cache all external data in order to comply with these requirements. For data searches, Redis uses streaming systems. You should also be aware of the latency of the network. As such, your streaming solutions usually serve in the Redis cluster. You choose fault tolerance and scalability by caching everything.

Data formats

Data formats serve as an integration platform as one of the important characteristics of any streaming solution. It collects events from various sources and processes these various events in order to achieve the desired results. Different data formats are among the relevant problems with such integration platforms. Every source type has a format of its own. Some support JSON or Avro formats and XML formats. A solution for all formats is difficult to design. In addition, when more and more data sources are added, support must be added to the newly added source for support of data formats. This is clearly buggy and a nightmare of maintenance. Ideally, you should support one data format with your streaming solution to which key/value model the events should be. The data format should be one agreed format for these key/value events. For your application, you should select a single data format. It is important to select a single data format to ensure compliance with all data sources and integration points while designing and implementing solutions for streaming.

One of the common solutions used is to develop a message format conversion layer for stream processing in one common data format. The REST APIs are exposed to various data sources for this message conversion layer. These data sources push events to this conversion layer using REST APIs in their respective formats and later they are converted into one common data format. Converted events are switched to streaming. This layer is sometimes also used to validate basic data on incoming events. You should separate stream processing logic, and have the data format conversion.

Serializing your data

Nearly all streaming technologies are serialized. The serialization technique used, however, is the key to any streaming application performance. Should the serialization be slow, your streaming application latency will be affected. In addition, it may be that serialization of your choice is not supported if you integrate with an old legacy system. The number of CPU cycles required, the time needed for serialization/deserialization, and support from all integrated systems are the key factors in selecting any serialization technique for your streaming application.

Parallel processing

Every stream processing engine of your choice offers ways to parallel stream processing. The parallel level needed for your application should always be taken into consideration. One key point here is that you must make maximum use of your existing cluster for low latency and high performance. Parameters are default, depending on the current capacity of your cluster. Therefore, you should always achieve your latency and throughput SLAs by designing your cluster with the desired degree of parallelism. Moreover, the auto-determination of the maximum number of parallels limits most motors. Take the example of Spark's processing engine and see how parallelism can be achieved. You have to increase the number of parallel execution tasks in very simple terms. Every task is run on a single data partition in Spark. If you want to increase the number of parallel tasks, the number of partitions should also be increased. You can re-partition the data with the desired number of partitions or increase the number of source splits. Parallel levels are also dependent on your cluster's number of cores. You should ideally plan your parallel level for two to three tasks per CPU core.

Out-of-order events

This is one of the most important issues with any unbound data stream. Sometimes, an event comes so late that, after that, out-of-order events are first processed. Different distant, discrete sources may produce events simultaneously, and some of them are delayed due to latency in a network or other problem. As they arrive very late, data searches on relevant datasets are part of the challenge with non-order events. In addition, the conditions to help you decide whether an event is a non-organized event are very difficult to determine. In other words, whether all the events in each window were received or not is difficult to determine. In addition, it is a risk of resource dispute to handle these out-of-order events. Other impacts on latency and system degradation overall could be increased. Factors such as latency, easy maintenance, and accurate results are important for the processing of out-of-order events, in order to take these challenges into account. You can drop these events according to company requirements. If an event drops, you will not have to handle additional processing components and your latency will not be affected. However, the accuracy of treatment results is affected. Another option is to wait and process it if all events are received in each window. Your latency will be hit and additional software components must be maintained. Another common technique is the processing of such data events by batch processing at the end of the day. Factors such as latency are therefore moot. However, accurate results will be delayed.

Message delivery semantics

Precisely once delivery is the sacred grail of streaming analytics; it is uncomfortable and often unwanted to handling duplicates of processes in a streaming job is undesirable, based on how the application is coded. For example, if applications fail to bill an event or process an event twice, customers could lose income. It is never difficult to guarantee these scenarios; any project that seeks such an estate must make certain choices regarding availability and consistency. One major challenge is that a streaming pipeline can have several stages and delivery needs to take place exactly once at each stage. Another challenge is that intermediate calculations may affect the final calculation. The retraction of these results causes difficulties once exposed. It is useful to provide guarantees exactly once because they are required in many situations. For instance, the unintentional processing of an event twice is bad in financial cases, such as credit card transactions. Everyone guarantees to process once with Spark Streaming, Flink, and Apex. Storm operates with delivery at least once. With the use of a Trident extension, it can be done exactly once with Storm, but this can reduce performance somewhat. Deduplication is one way to prevent multiple operations and achieve precise semantics. De-duplication is possible if a database update is an application action. Some other measures, such as a call to web services, can be considered.

Micro-batch processing case study

This section covers a small case study that is used to detect an IP default with Kafka and Spark Streaming, and the IP has attempted to hit the server many times. We will cover the following use cases:

- **Producer**: The Kafka producer API will be used to read a log file and publish documents on the topic of Kafka. In a real case, however, we could use the flume or producer application, which records in real time directly and publishes on Kafka.
- **Fraud IPs list**: We will keep a list of predefined IP frauds to identify the IPs for fraud. We use an in-memory IP list for this application, which can be substituted by fast key-based searching, such as HBase.
- **Spark Streaming**: Spark Streaming applications can read Kafka records and detect suspicious IPs and domains.

Maven is a tool for building and managing projects and we will build this project using Maven. Eclipse or IntelliJ are recommended for project creation. Add to your pom.xml the following adjustments and plugins:

```
<?xml version="1.0" encoding="UTF-8"?>
<project xmlns="http://maven.apache.org/POM/4.0.0"
         xmlns:xsi="http://www.w3.org/2001/XMLSchema-instance"
         xsi:schemaLocation="http://maven.apache.org/POM/4.0.0
http://maven.apache.org/xsd/maven-4.0.0.xsd">
    <modelVersion>4.0.0</modelVersion>

    <groupId>com.packt</groupId>
    <artifactId>ip-fraud-detetion</artifactId>
    <version>1.0-SNAPSHOT</version>
    <packaging>jar</packaging>

    <name>kafka-producer</name>

    <properties>
        <project.build.sourceEncoding>UTF-8</project.build.sourceEncoding>
    </properties>


    <dependencies>
        <!--
https://mvnrepository.com/artifact/org.apache.spark/spark-streaming-kafka_2
.10 -->
        <dependency>
            <groupId>org.apache.spark</groupId>
```

```xml
            <artifactId>spark-streaming-kafka_2.10</artifactId>
            <version>1.6.3</version>
        </dependency>


        <!--
https://mvnrepository.com/artifact/org.apache.hadoop/hadoop-common -->
        <dependency>
            <groupId>org.apache.hadoop</groupId>
            <artifactId>hadoop-common</artifactId>
            <version>2.7.2</version>
        </dependency>

        <!--
https://mvnrepository.com/artifact/org.apache.spark/spark-core_2.10 -->
        <dependency>
            <groupId>org.apache.spark</groupId>
            <artifactId>spark-core_2.10</artifactId>
            <version>2.0.0</version>
            <scope>provided</scope>

        </dependency>
        <!--
https://mvnrepository.com/artifact/org.apache.spark/spark-streaming_2.10 -
->
        <dependency>
            <groupId>org.apache.spark</groupId>
            <artifactId>spark-streaming_2.10</artifactId>
            <version>2.0.0</version>
            <scope>provided</scope>

        </dependency>


        <dependency>
            <groupId>org.apache.kafka</groupId>
            <artifactId>kafka_2.11</artifactId>
            <version>0.10.0.0</version>
        </dependency>
    </dependencies>

    <build>
        <plugins>
            <plugin>
                <groupId>org.apache.maven.plugins</groupId>
                <artifactId>maven-shade-plugin</artifactId>
                <version>2.4.2</version>
                <executions>
```

```
                    <execution>
                        <phase>package</phase>
                        <goals>
                            <goal>shade</goal>
                        </goals>
                        <configuration>
                            <filters>
                                <filter>
                                    <artifact>junit:junit</artifact>
                                    <includes>
<include>junit/framework/**</include>
                                        <include>org/junit/**</include>
                                    </includes>
                                    <excludes>
<exclude>org/junit/experimental/**</exclude>
<exclude>org/junit/runners/**</exclude>
                                    </excludes>
                                </filter>
                                <filter>
                                    <artifact>*:*</artifact>
                                    <excludes>
                                        <exclude>META-INF/*.SF</exclude>
                                        <exclude>META-INF/*.DSA</exclude>
                                        <exclude>META-INF/*.RSA</exclude>
                                    </excludes>
                                </filter>
                            </filters>
                            <transformers>
                                <transformer
implementation="org.apache.maven.plugins.shade.resource.ServicesResourceTra
nsformer"/>

                                <transformer
implementation="org.apache.maven.plugins.shade.resource.ManifestResourceTra
nsformer">
<mainClass>com.packt.streaming.FraudDetectionApp</mainClass>
                                </transformer>
                            </transformers>
                        </configuration>
                    </execution>
                </executions>
            </plugin>
            <plugin>
                <groupId>org.codehaus.mojo</groupId>
                <artifactId>exec-maven-plugin</artifactId>
                <version>1.2.1</version>
                <executions>
                    <execution>
```

```xml
                        <goals>
                            <goal>exec</goal>
                        </goals>
                    </execution>
                </executions>
                <configuration>
<includeProjectDependencies>true</includeProjectDependencies>
<includePluginDependencies>false</includePluginDependencies>
                    <executable>java</executable>
                    <classpathScope>compile</classpathScope>
<mainClass>com.packt.streaming.FraudDetectionApp</mainClass>
                </configuration>
            </plugin>


            <plugin>
                <groupId>org.apache.maven.plugins</groupId>
                <artifactId>maven-compiler-plugin</artifactId>
                <configuration>
                    <source>1.8</source>
                    <target>1.8</target>
                </configuration>
            </plugin>
        </plugins>
    </build>
</project>
```

To build a producer application, you can use IntelliJ or Eclipse. This producer reads an Apache project log file containing detailed records, such as the following:

```
10.0.0.153 - - [12/Mar/2004:12:23:18 -0800] "GET /cgi-
bin/mailgraph.cgi/mailgraph_0_err.png HTTP/1.1" 200 6324
10.0.0.153 - - [12/Mar/2004:12:23:18 -0800] "GET /cgi-
bin/mailgraph.cgi/mailgraph_1.png HTTP/1.1" 200 8964
10.0.0.153 - - [12/Mar/2004:12:23:18 -0800] "GET /cgi-
bin/mailgraph.cgi/mailgraph_0.png HTTP/1.1" 200 6225
10.0.0.153 - - [12/Mar/2004:12:23:18 -0800] "GET /cgi-
bin/mailgraph.cgi/mailgraph_2_err.png HTTP/1.1" 200 7001
10.0.0.153 - - [12/Mar/2004:12:23:18 -0800] "GET /cgi-
bin/mailgraph.cgi/mailgraph_2.png HTTP/1.1" 200 9514
10.0.0.153 - - [12/Mar/2004:12:23:18 -0800] "GET /cgi-
bin/mailgraph.cgi/mailgraph_1_err.png HTTP/1.1" 200 6949
10.0.0.153 - - [12/Mar/2004:12:23:18 -0800] "GET /cgi-
bin/mailgraph.cgi/mailgraph_3.png HTTP/1.1" 200 6644
10.0.0.153 - - [12/Mar/2004:12:23:18 -0800] "GET /cgi-
bin/mailgraph.cgi/mailgraph_3_err.png HTTP/1.1" 200 5554
10.0.0.153 - - [12/Mar/2004:12:23:41 -0800] "GET /dccstats/stats-
spam.1day.png HTTP/1.1" 200 2964
```

```
10.0.0.153 - - [12/Mar/2004:12:23:41 -0800] "GET /dccstats/stats-spam-
ratio.1day.png HTTP/1.1" 200 2341
10.0.0.153 - - [12/Mar/2004:12:23:41 -0800] "GET /dccstats/stats-spam-
ratio.1week.png HTTP/1.1" 200 2346
10.0.0.153 - - [12/Mar/2004:12:23:41 -0800] "GET /dccstats/stats-
spam.1week.png HTTP/1.1" 200 3438
10.0.0.153 - - [12/Mar/2004:12:23:41 -0800] "GET /dccstats/stats-
hashes.1week.png HTTP/1.1" 200 1670
10.0.0.153 - - [12/Mar/2004:12:23:41 -0800] "GET /dccstats/stats-
spam.1month.png HTTP/1.1" 200 2651
```

You can have a single record in the test file and the producer is able to generate records by random IPs. We will, therefore, have millions of separate records with unique IP addresses. The columns of the records are separated by space boundaries that we change into producer commas. The first column shows the IP address or domain name used to detect whether the request was from a fraud customer.

A producer application is designed to be like a manufacturer in real time, where the producer runs every 3 seconds with random IP addresses and generates a new record. The IP LOG.log file contains some records, and the producer is responsible for producing millions of records that have unique characteristics. We have also made auto-creation possible, so before running your producer application, you don't need to create a theme. In the streaming.properties file, as mentioned, you can change the theme name. The following is the producer of Java Kafka that recalls logs:

```
package com.packt.producer;

import org.apache.kafka.clients.producer.KafkaProducer;
import org.apache.kafka.clients.producer.ProducerRecord;
import org.apache.kafka.clients.producer.RecordMetadata;
import java.io.File;
import java.io.IOException;
import java.util.Properties;
import java.util.Scanner;
import java.util.concurrent.Future;


public class IPLogProducer {
    private File readfile() {
        ClassLoader classLoader = getClass().getClassLoader();
        File file = new
File(classLoader.getResource("IP_LOG.log").getFile());
        return file;

    }
```

```
public static void main(final String[] args) {
    IPLogProducer ipLogProducer = new IPLogProducer();
    Properties producerProps = new Properties();

    //replace broker ip with your kafka broker ip
    producerProps.put("bootstrap.servers", "localhost:9092");
    producerProps.put("key.serializer",
"org.apache.kafka.common.serialization.StringSerializer");
    producerProps.put("value.serializer",
"org.apache.kafka.common.serialization.StringSerializer");
    producerProps.put("auto.create.topics.enable","true");

    KafkaProducer<String, String> ipProducer = new
KafkaProducer<String, String>(producerProps);

    try (Scanner scanner = new Scanner(ipLogProducer.readfile())) {
        while (scanner.hasNextLine()) {
            String line = scanner.nextLine();
            ProducerRecord ipData = new ProducerRecord<String,
String>("iplog", line);
            Future<RecordMetadata> recordMetadata =
ipProducer.send(ipData);
        }
        scanner.close();

    } catch (IOException e) {
        e.printStackTrace();
    }
    ipProducer.close();
}


}
```

As a search service, the following classes will assist us in identifying whether a request comes from a fraud IP. Before implementing the classes, we use the interface to add more NoSQL databases or any rapid search services. This service can be implemented and the service is added via HBase or any other quick key search service. We've just added a fraud IP to the cache with an input memory survey. Fill your project with the following code:

```
package com.packt.streaming;

public interface IIPScanner {

    boolean isFraudIP(String ipAddresses);

}
```

CacheIPLookup is the implementation for the IIPScanner interface, which does an in-memory lookup:

```
package com.packt.streaming;

import scala.util.parsing.combinator.testing.Str;

import java.io.Serializable;
import java.util.HashSet;
import java.util.Set;


public class CacheIPLookup implements IIPScanner, Serializable {

    private Set<String> fraudIPList = new HashSet<>();

    public CacheIPLookup() {
        fraudIPList.add("212.92");
        fraudIPList.add("10.100");
    }


    @Override
    public boolean isFraudIP(String ipAddresses) {
        return fraudIPList.contains(ipAddresses);
    }
}
```

We will create a hive table over base directory, where a streaming record is getting pushed on HDFS. This will help us track the number of fraud records being generated over time, as shown here:

```
create database packt;
create external table packt.teststream (iprecords STRING) LOCATION
<external_log_file_location>;
```

You can also show hive tablets in addition to the input data, which will be taken to the Kafka topic to track fraud in the overall record for the percentage of IPs. Create another table and add the following line to the streaming application:

```
ipRecords.dstream().saveAsTextFiles("<hdfs_location>","");
```

Note that `SqlContext` can also be used to hive data, but we did it very simply for this use. In our code, we did not concentrate much on modularization. The IP fraud scans each record and filters those records that qualify as records based on the fraud-related IP scanning service. You can change the search services to use any quick search database. For this application, we'll use an in-memory search service:

```java
package com.packt.streaming;

import org.apache.spark.SparkConf;
import org.apache.spark.api.java.function.Function;
import org.apache.spark.streaming.api.java.JavaStreamingContext;
import java.util.Set;
import java.util.regex.Pattern;
import java.util.HashMap;
import java.util.HashSet;
import java.util.Arrays;
import java.util.Map;
import org.apache.spark.streaming.dstream.DStream;
import scala.Tuple2;
import kafka.serializer.StringDecoder;
import org.apache.spark.streaming.api.java.*;
import org.apache.spark.streaming.kafka.KafkaUtils;
import org.apache.spark.streaming.Durations;

public class FraudDetectionApp {
    private static final Pattern SPACE = Pattern.compile(" ");

    public static void main(String[] args) throws Exception {

        String brokers = "localhost:9092";
        String topics = "iplog";
        CacheIPLookup cacheIPLookup = new CacheIPLookup();
        SparkConf sparkConf = new SparkConf().setAppName("IP_FRAUD");
        JavaStreamingContext javaStreamingContext = new
JavaStreamingContext(sparkConf, Durations.seconds(2));

        Set<String> topicsSet = new
HashSet<>(Arrays.asList(topics.split(",")));
        Map<String, String> kafkaConfiguration = new HashMap<>();
        kafkaConfiguration.put("metadata.broker.list", brokers);
        kafkaConfiguration.put("group.id", "ipfraud");
        kafkaConfiguration.put("auto.offset.reset", "smallest");

        JavaPairInputDStream<String, String> messages =
KafkaUtils.createDirectStream(
                javaStreamingContext,
                String.class,
```

```
                    String.class,
                    StringDecoder.class,
                    StringDecoder.class,
                    kafkaConfiguration,
                    topicsSet
        );

    JavaDStream<String> lines = messages.map(Tuple2::_2);

    JavaDStream<String> fraudIPs = lines.filter(new Function<String,
Boolean>() {
        @Override
        public Boolean call(String s) throws Exception {
            String IP = s.split(" ")[0];
            String[] ranges = IP.split("\\.");
            String range = null;
            try {
                range = ranges[0] + "." + ranges[1];
            } catch (ArrayIndexOutOfBoundsException ex) {

            }
            return cacheIPLookup.isFraudIP(range);

        }
    });

    DStream<String> fraudDstream = fraudIPs.dstream();
    fraudDstream.saveAsTextFiles("FraudRecord", "");

    javaStreamingContext.start();
    javaStreamingContext.awaitTermination();
    }
}
```

In this section, we focused on various ways to integrate Kafka with Spark, and its pros and cons. We covered an IP fraud detection case for a small micro batch using the log file and the search service. Now you can build a Spark Streaming application with your own micro batch. We will study a case on real-time processing in the next section.

Real-time processing case study

In this section, for the IP fraud detection case mentioned in the preceding section, we will use Apache Storm for the same log processing. Apache Storm is used for very sensitive applications in which even a 1 second delay could cause enormous losses. There are many enterprises that use Storm to detect fraud, develop recommendation engines, trigger suspicious activity, and so on. It uses Zookeeper for coordination purposes and maintains significant metadata information. Apache Storm is stateless. It is a distributed real-time processing framework that can handle one event at a time with the processing of millions of records per second per node. Streaming data can be limited or unlimited; Storm can reliably process it in both situations. The Maven app is as follows:

```xml
<?xml version="1.0" encoding="UTF-8"?>
<project xmlns="http://maven.apache.org/POM/4.0.0"
        xmlns:xsi="http://www.w3.org/2001/XMLSchema-instance"
        xsi:schemaLocation="http://maven.apache.org/POM/4.0.0
http://maven.apache.org/xsd/maven-4.0.0.xsd">
    <modelVersion>4.0.0</modelVersion>

    <groupId>com.packt</groupId>
    <artifactId>chapter6</artifactId>
    <version>1.0-SNAPSHOT</version>

    <properties>
        <project.build.sourceEncoding>UTF-8</project.build.sourceEncoding>
    </properties>

    <dependencies>

        <!-- https://mvnrepository.com/artifact/org.apache.storm/storm-hive
-->
        <dependency>
            <groupId>org.apache.storm</groupId>
            <artifactId>storm-hive</artifactId>
            <version>1.0.0</version>
            <exclusions>
                <exclusion><!-- possible scala confilict -->
                    <groupId>jline</groupId>
                    <artifactId>jline</artifactId>
                </exclusion>
            </exclusions>
        </dependency>


        <dependency>
            <groupId>junit</groupId>
```

```xml
            <artifactId>junit</artifactId>
            <version>3.8.1</version>
            <scope>test</scope>
        </dependency>

        <dependency>
            <groupId>org.apache.hadoop</groupId>
            <artifactId>hadoop-hdfs</artifactId>
            <version>2.6.0</version>
            <scope>compile</scope>
        </dependency>

        <!--
https://mvnrepository.com/artifact/org.apache.storm/storm-kafka -->
        <dependency>
            <groupId>org.apache.storm</groupId>
            <artifactId>storm-kafka</artifactId>
            <version>1.0.0</version>
        </dependency>
        <!-- https://mvnrepository.com/artifact/org.apache.storm/storm-core
-->
        <dependency>
            <groupId>org.apache.storm</groupId>
            <artifactId>storm-core</artifactId>
            <version>1.0.0</version>
            <scope>provided</scope>
        </dependency>
        <dependency>
            <groupId>org.apache.kafka</groupId>
            <artifactId>kafka_2.10</artifactId>
            <version>0.8.1.1</version>
            <exclusions>
                <exclusion>
                    <groupId>org.apache.zookeeper</groupId>
                    <artifactId>zookeeper</artifactId>
                </exclusion>
                <exclusion>
                    <groupId>log4j</groupId>
                    <artifactId>log4j</artifactId>
                </exclusion>
            </exclusions>
        </dependency>

        <dependency>
            <groupId>commons-collections</groupId>
            <artifactId>commons-collections</artifactId>
            <version>3.2.1</version>
        </dependency>
```

```xml
            <dependency>
                <groupId>com.google.guava</groupId>
                <artifactId>guava</artifactId>
                <version>15.0</version>
            </dependency>

    </dependencies>

    <build>
        <plugins>

            <plugin>
                <groupId>org.apache.maven.plugins</groupId>
                <artifactId>maven-shade-plugin</artifactId>
                <version>2.4.2</version>
                <executions>
                    <execution>
                        <phase>package</phase>
                        <goals>
                            <goal>shade</goal>
                        </goals>
                        <configuration>
                            <filters>
                                <filter>
                                    <artifact>junit:junit</artifact>
                                    <includes>
<include>junit/framework/**</include>
                                        <include>org/junit/**</include>
                                    </includes>
                                    <excludes>
<exclude>org/junit/experimental/**</exclude>
<exclude>org/junit/runners/**</exclude>
                                    </excludes>
                                </filter>
                                <filter>
                                    <artifact>*:*</artifact>
                                    <excludes>
                                        <exclude>META-INF/*.SF</exclude>
                                        <exclude>META-INF/*.DSA</exclude>
                                        <exclude>META-INF/*.RSA</exclude>
                                    </excludes>
                                </filter>
                            </filters>
                            <transformers>
                                <transformer
implementation="org.apache.maven.plugins.shade.resource.ServicesResourceTra
nsformer"/>
```

```xml
                        <transformer
implementation="org.apache.maven.plugins.shade.resource.ManifestResourceTra
nsformer">
<mainClass>com.packt.storm.ipfrauddetection.IPFraudDetectionTopology</mainC
lass>
                            </transformer>
                        </transformers>
                    </configuration>
                </execution>
            </executions>
        </plugin>
        <plugin>
            <groupId>org.codehaus.mojo</groupId>
            <artifactId>exec-maven-plugin</artifactId>
            <version>1.2.1</version>
            <executions>
                <execution>
                    <goals>
                        <goal>exec</goal>
                    </goals>
                </execution>
            </executions>
            <configuration>
<includeProjectDependencies>true</includeProjectDependencies>
<includePluginDependencies>false</includePluginDependencies>
                <executable>java</executable>
                <classpathScope>compile</classpathScope>
<mainClass>com.packt.storm.ipfrauddetection.IPFraudDetectionTopology</mainC
lass>
            </configuration>
        </plugin>
        <plugin>
            <groupId>org.apache.maven.plugins</groupId>
            <artifactId>maven-compiler-plugin</artifactId>
            <configuration>
                <source>1.6</source>
                <target>1.6</target>
            </configuration>
        </plugin>
    </plugins>
  </build>
</project>
```

For certain key values, such as a topic and Kafka broker URL, we chose to use a property file. If you want to read more values in the file, you can change it in the code. The following is the structure of the streaming.properties file:

```
topic=fraudip2
broker.list=52.88.50.251:6667
appname=fraudip
group.id=Stream
log.path=/user/packtuser/teststream/FraudRecord
iplog.path=/user/packtuser/iprecrods/FraudRecord
```

The following code represents the property reader Java class:

```
package com.packt.storm.reader;

import java.io.FileNotFoundException;
import java.io.IOException;
import java.io.InputStream;
import java.util.Properties;

public class PropertyReader {

  private Properties prop = null;

  public PropertyReader() {

  InputStream is = null;
  try {
  this.prop = new Properties();
  is = this.getClass().getResourceAsStream("/streaming.properties");
  prop.load(is);
  } catch (FileNotFoundException e) {
  e.printStackTrace();
  } catch (IOException e) {
  e.printStackTrace();
  }
  }

  public String getPropertyValue(String key) {
  return this.prop.getProperty(key);
  }
}
```

Main code

Our producer application is designed like a real-time log producer, which produces a new record with random IP addresses also in which the producer runs every three seconds. You can add a few records in the IP_Log.log file and producing millions of unique records from those three records will be taken care of by the producer.

We have also enabled the auto-creation of topics, so you need not create a topic before running your producer application. You can change the topic name in the streaming.properties file, mentioned previously:

```java
package com.packt.storm.producer;

import com.packt.storm.reader.PropertyReader;
import org.apache.kafka.clients.producer.KafkaProducer;
import org.apache.kafka.clients.producer.ProducerRecord;
import org.apache.kafka.clients.producer.RecordMetadata;

import java.io.BufferedReader;
import java.io.File;
import java.io.IOException;
import java.io.InputStreamReader;
import java.util.*;
import java.util.concurrent.ExecutionException;
import java.util.concurrent.Future;


public class IPLogProducer extends TimerTask {
    static String path = "";

    public BufferedReader readFile() {
        BufferedReader BufferedReader = new BufferedReader(new
InputStreamReader(
                this.getClass().getResourceAsStream("/IP_LOG.log")));
        return BufferedReader;

    }

    public static void main(final String[] args) {
        Timer timer = new Timer();
        timer.schedule(new IPLogProducer(), 3000, 3000);
    }

    private String getNewRecordWithRandomIP(String line) {
        Random r = new Random();
        String ip = r.nextInt(256) + "." + r.nextInt(256) + "." +
r.nextInt(256) + "." + r.nextInt(256);
```

```
        String[] columns = line.split(" ");
        columns[0] = ip;
        return Arrays.toString(columns);
    }

    @Override
    public void run() {
        PropertyReader propertyReader = new PropertyReader();

        Properties producerProps = new Properties();
        producerProps.put("bootstrap.servers",
propertyReader.getPropertyValue("broker.list"));
        producerProps.put("key.serializer",
"org.apache.kafka.common.serialization.StringSerializer");
        producerProps.put("value.serializer",
"org.apache.kafka.common.serialization.StringSerializer");
        producerProps.put("auto.create.topics.enable", "true");

        KafkaProducer<String, String> ipProducer = new
KafkaProducer<String, String>(producerProps);

        BufferedReader br = readFile();
        String oldLine = "";
        try {
            while ((oldLine = br.readLine()) != null) {
                String line =
getNewRecordWithRandomIP(oldLine).replace("[", "").replace("]", "");
                ProducerRecord ipData = new ProducerRecord<String,
String>(propertyReader.getPropertyValue("topic"), line);
                Future<RecordMetadata> recordMetadata =
ipProducer.send(ipData);

                System.out.println(recordMetadata.get().toString());
            }
        } catch (IOException e) {
            e.printStackTrace();
        } catch (InterruptedException e) {
            e.printStackTrace();
        } catch (ExecutionException e) {
            e.printStackTrace();
        }
        ipProducer.close();
    }
}
```

The next classes help us to determine whether requests are from a fraudulent IP. Before we implemented the class, we used the interface to add additional NoSQL databases or quick search services. You can use HBase or any other key quick search service to implement this service and to add a search service.

We are using InMemoryLookup and have just added the fraud IP range in the cache. Add the following code to your project:

```
package com.packt.storm.utils;

public interface IIPScanner {

    boolean isFraudIP(String ipAddresses);

}
```

CacheIPLookup is using the IIPScanner interface, which does an in-memory lookup. The code is as follows:

```
package com.packt.storm.utils;

import java.io.Serializable;
import java.util.HashSet;
import java.util.Set;


public class CacheIPLookup implements IIPScanner, Serializable {

    private Set<String> fraudIPList = new HashSet<>();

    public CacheIPLookup() {
        fraudIPList.add("212");
        fraudIPList.add("163");
        fraudIPList.add("15");
        fraudIPList.add("224");
        fraudIPList.add("126");
        fraudIPList.add("92");
        fraudIPList.add("91");
        fraudIPList.add("10");
        fraudIPList.add("112");
        fraudIPList.add("194");
        fraudIPList.add("198");
        fraudIPList.add("11");
        fraudIPList.add("12");
        fraudIPList.add("13");
        fraudIPList.add("14");
        fraudIPList.add("15");
```

```
        fraudIPList.add("16");
    }


    @Override
    public boolean isFraudIP(String ipAddresses) {

        return fraudIPList.contains(ipAddresses);
    }
}
```

The `Ipfrauddetection` class will build the topology that indicates how spout and bolts are connected together to form the storm topology. This is the main class of our application and we will use it while submitting our topology to the Storm cluster, as shown in the following code:

```
package com.packt.storm.ipfrauddetection;


import com.packt.storm.example.StringToWordsSpliterBolt;
import com.packt.storm.example.WordCountCalculatorBolt;
import org.apache.log4j.Logger;
import org.apache.storm.Config;
import org.apache.storm.LocalCluster;
import org.apache.storm.StormSubmitter;
import org.apache.storm.generated.AlreadyAliveException;
import org.apache.storm.generated.AuthorizationException;
import org.apache.storm.generated.InvalidTopologyException;
import org.apache.storm.hive.bolt.HiveBolt;
import org.apache.storm.hive.bolt.mapper.DelimitedRecordHiveMapper;
import org.apache.storm.hive.common.HiveOptions;
import org.apache.storm.kafka.*;
import org.apache.storm.spout.SchemeAsMultiScheme;
import org.apache.storm.topology.TopologyBuilder;
import org.apache.storm.tuple.Fields;

import java.io.FileInputStream;
import java.io.IOException;
import java.io.InputStream;
import java.util.Properties;


public class IPFraudDetectionTopology {

    private static String zkhost, inputTopic, outputTopic, KafkaBroker,
consumerGroup;
    private static String metaStoreURI, dbName, tblName;
    private static final Logger logger =
```

```
Logger.getLogger(IPFraudDetectionTopology.class);

    public static void Intialize(String arg) {
        Properties prop = new Properties();
        InputStream input = null;

        try {
            logger.info("Loading Configuration File for setting up input");
            input = new FileInputStream(arg);
            prop.load(input);
            zkhost = prop.getProperty("zkhost");
            inputTopic = prop.getProperty("inputTopic");
            outputTopic = prop.getProperty("outputTopic");
            KafkaBroker = prop.getProperty("KafkaBroker");
            consumerGroup = prop.getProperty("consumerGroup");
            metaStoreURI = prop.getProperty("metaStoreURI");
            dbName = prop.getProperty("dbName");
            tblName = prop.getProperty("tblName");

        } catch (IOException ex) {
            logger.error("Error While loading configuration file" + ex);

        } finally {
            if (input != null) {
                try {
                    input.close();
                } catch (IOException e) {
                    logger.error("Error Closing input stream");

                }
            }
        }

    }

    public static void main(String[] args) throws AlreadyAliveException,
InvalidTopologyException, AuthorizationException {
        Intialize(args[0]);
        logger.info("Successfully loaded Configuration ");


        BrokerHosts hosts = new ZkHosts(zkhost);
        SpoutConfig spoutConfig = new SpoutConfig(hosts, inputTopic, "/" +
KafkaBroker, consumerGroup);
        spoutConfig.scheme = new SchemeAsMultiScheme(new StringScheme());
        spoutConfig.startOffsetTime =
kafka.api.OffsetRequest.EarliestTime();
        KafkaSpout kafkaSpout = new KafkaSpout(spoutConfig);
```

```
        String[] partNames = {"status_code"};
        String[] colNames = {"date", "request_url", "protocol_type",
"status_code"};

        DelimitedRecordHiveMapper mapper = new
DelimitedRecordHiveMapper().withColumnFields(new Fields(colNames))
                .withPartitionFields(new Fields(partNames));


        HiveOptions hiveOptions;
        //make sure you change batch size and all paramtere according to
requirement
        hiveOptions = new HiveOptions(metaStoreURI, dbName, tblName,
mapper).withTxnsPerBatch(250).withBatchSize(2)
                .withIdleTimeout(10).withCallTimeout(10000000);

        logger.info("Creating Storm Topology");
        TopologyBuilder builder = new TopologyBuilder();

        builder.setSpout("KafkaSpout", kafkaSpout, 1);

        builder.setBolt("frauddetect", new
FraudDetectorBolt()).shuffleGrouping("KafkaSpout");
        builder.setBolt("KafkaOutputBolt",
                new IPFraudKafkaBolt(zkhost,
"kafka.serializer.StringEncoder", KafkaBroker, outputTopic), 1)
                .shuffleGrouping("frauddetect");

        builder.setBolt("HiveOutputBolt", new IPFraudHiveBolt(),
1).shuffleGrouping("frauddetect");
        builder.setBolt("HiveBolt", new
HiveBolt(hiveOptions)).shuffleGrouping("HiveOutputBolt");

        Config conf = new Config();
        if (args != null && args.length > 1) {
            conf.setNumWorkers(3);
            logger.info("Submiting topology to storm cluster");

            StormSubmitter.submitTopology(args[1], conf,
builder.createTopology());
        } else {
            // Cap the maximum number of executors that can be spawned
            // for a component to 3
            conf.setMaxTaskParallelism(3);
            // LocalCluster is used to run locally
            LocalCluster cluster = new LocalCluster();
            logger.info("Submitting topology to local cluster");
            cluster.submitTopology("KafkaLocal", conf,
```

```
builder.createTopology());
                // sleep
                try {
                    Thread.sleep(10000);
                } catch (InterruptedException e) {
                    // TODO Auto-generated catch block
                    logger.error("Exception ocuured" + e);
                    cluster.killTopology("KafkaToplogy");
                    logger.info("Shutting down cluster");
                    cluster.shutdown();
                }
                cluster.shutdown();

        }

    }
}
```

The fraud detector bolt will read the tuples emitted by Kafka spout and will detect which record is fraud by using an in-memory IP lookup service. It will then emit the fraud records. The following code explains the fraud detector bolt:

```
package com.packt.storm.ipfrauddetection;

import com.packt.storm.utils.CacheIPLookup;
import com.packt.storm.utils.IIPScanner;
import org.apache.storm.task.OutputCollector;
import org.apache.storm.task.TopologyContext;
import org.apache.storm.topology.IRichBolt;
import org.apache.storm.topology.OutputFieldsDeclarer;
import org.apache.storm.topology.base.BaseRichBolt;
import org.apache.storm.tuple.Fields;
import org.apache.storm.tuple.Tuple;
import org.apache.storm.tuple.Values;

import java.util.Map;

public class FraudDetectorBolt extends BaseRichBolt {
    private IIPScanner cacheIPLookup = new CacheIPLookup();
    private OutputCollector collector;


    @Override
    public void prepare(Map map, TopologyContext topologyContext,
OutputCollector outputCollector) {
        this.collector = outputCollector;
    }
```

```
        @Override
        public void execute(Tuple input) {
            String ipRecord = (String) input.getValue(0);
            String[] columns = ipRecord.split(",");

            String IP = columns[0];
            String[] ranges = IP.split("\\.");
            String range = null;
            try {
                range = ranges[0];
            } catch (ArrayIndexOutOfBoundsException ex) {

            }
            boolean isFraud = cacheIPLookup.isFraudIP(range);

            if (isFraud) {
                Values value = new Values(ipRecord);
                collector.emit(value);
                collector.ack(input);
            }
        }


        @Override
        public void declareOutputFields(OutputFieldsDeclarer
    outputFieldsDeclarer) {
            outputFieldsDeclarer.declare(new Fields("fraudip"));
        }
    }
```

The `IPFraudHiveBolt` call will process the records emitted by the fraud detector bolt and will push the data to Hive using a thrift service, as shown in the following code:

```
    package com.packt.storm.ipfrauddetection;

    import com.packt.storm.utils.CacheIPLookup;
    import com.packt.storm.utils.IIPScanner;
    import org.apache.log4j.Logger;
    import org.apache.storm.task.OutputCollector;
    import org.apache.storm.task.TopologyContext;
    import org.apache.storm.topology.OutputFieldsDeclarer;
    import org.apache.storm.topology.base.BaseRichBolt;
    import org.apache.storm.tuple.Fields;
    import org.apache.storm.tuple.Tuple;
    import org.apache.storm.tuple.Values;

    import java.util.Map;
```

```
public class IPFraudHiveBolt extends BaseRichBolt {
    private static final long serialVersionUID = 1L;
    private static final Logger logger =
Logger.getLogger(IPFraudHiveBolt.class);
    OutputCollector _collector;
    private IIPScanner cacheIPLookup = new CacheIPLookup();

    public void prepare(Map stormConf, TopologyContext context,
OutputCollector collector) {
        _collector = collector;
    }

    public void execute(Tuple input) {
        String ipRecord = (String) input.getValue(0);
        String[] columns = ipRecord.split(",");
        Values value = new Values(columns[0], columns[3], columns[4],
columns[5], columns[6]);
        _collector.emit(value);
        _collector.ack(input);


    }

    public void declareOutputFields(OutputFieldsDeclarer ofDeclarer) {
        ofDeclarer.declare(new Fields("ip", "date", "request_url",
"protocol_type", "status_code"));
    }
}
```

`IPFraudKafkaBolt` uses the Kafka Producer API to push the processed fraud IP to another Kafka topic:

```
package com.packt.storm.ipfrauddetection;

import com.packt.storm.utils.CacheIPLookup;
import com.packt.storm.utils.IIPScanner;
import org.apache.kafka.clients.producer.KafkaProducer;
import org.apache.kafka.clients.producer.Producer;
import org.apache.kafka.clients.producer.ProducerRecord;
import org.apache.kafka.clients.producer.RecordMetadata;
import org.apache.log4j.Logger;
import org.apache.storm.task.OutputCollector;
import org.apache.storm.task.TopologyContext;
import org.apache.storm.topology.OutputFieldsDeclarer;
import org.apache.storm.topology.base.BaseRichBolt;
import org.apache.storm.tuple.Fields;
import org.apache.storm.tuple.Tuple;
```

```java
import java.util.HashMap;
import java.util.Map;
import java.util.Properties;
import java.util.concurrent.Future;


public class IPFraudKafkaBolt extends BaseRichBolt {
    private static final long serialVersionUID = 1L;
    private Producer<String, String> producer;
    private String zkConnect, serializerClass, topic, brokerList;
    private static final Logger logger =
Logger.getLogger(IPFraudKafkaBolt.class);
    private Map<String, String> valueMap = new HashMap<String, String>();
    private String dataToTopic = null;
    OutputCollector _collector;
    private IIPScanner cacheIPLookup = new CacheIPLookup();


    public IPFraudKafkaBolt(String zkConnect, String serializerClass,
String brokerList, String topic) {
        this.zkConnect = zkConnect;
        this.serializerClass = serializerClass;
        this.topic = topic;
        this.brokerList = brokerList;
    }

    public void prepare(Map stormConf, TopologyContext context,
OutputCollector collector) {
        logger.info("Intializing Properties");
        _collector = collector;
        Properties props = new Properties();
        props.put("zookeeper.connect", zkConnect);
        props.put("serializer.class", serializerClass);
        props.put("metadata.broker.list", brokerList);
        KafkaProducer<String, String> producer = new KafkaProducer<String,
String>(props);


    }

    public void execute(Tuple input) {

        dataToTopic = (String) input.getValue(0);
        ProducerRecord data = new ProducerRecord<String, String>(topic,
this.dataToTopic);
        Future<RecordMetadata> recordMetadata = producer.send(data);
        _collector.ack(input);
```

```
    }

    public void declareOutputFields(OutputFieldsDeclarer declarer) {
        declarer.declare(new Fields("null"));
    }
}
```

Executing the code

You need to first make permission-related changes on HDFS, as follows:

```
sudo su - hdfs -c "hdfs dfs -chmod 777 /tmp/hive"
sudo chmod 777 /tmp/hive
```

You have to run the following command to submit Storm jobs that run in cluster mode:

```
Storm jar /home/ldap/chanchals/kafka-Storm-integration-0.0.1-SNAPSHOT.jar
com.packt.Storm.ipfrauddetection.IPFraudDetectionTopology
iptopology.properties TopologyName
```

Alternatively, for small unit testing, you can run the same job in Storm local mode:

```
Storm jar kafka-Storm-integration-0.0.1-SNAPSHOT.jar
com.packt.Storm.ipfrauddetection.IPFraudDetectionTopology
iptopology.properties
```

Summary

In this chapter, we have learned some basics of stream processing, including stream data ingestion and some of the stream processing patterns. We also had a look at micro-batch stream processing using Spark Streaming and real-time processing using Storm processing engines.

In the next chapter, we will learn about machine learning in Hadoop.

Machine Learning in Hadoop

10

This chapter is about how to design and architect machine learning applications in the Hadoop platform. It addresses some of the common machine learning challenges that you can face in Hadoop and how to solve these. In this chapter, we will walk through different machine learning libraries and processing engines. This chapter also covers some of the common steps involved in machine learning and further elaborates on this with a case study.

In this chapter, we will cover the following topics:

- Machine learning steps
- Common machine learning challenges
- Spark machine learning
- Hadoop and R
- Mahout
- Case study in Spark

Technical requirements

You will be required to have basic knowledge of Linux and Apache Hadoop 3.0.

Check out the following video to see the code in action:
http://bit.ly/2VpRc7N

Machine learning steps

We will look at the different features of machine learning in the following steps:

1. **Gathering data**: Well, this step you have seen and heard of many times. It is about ingesting data from multiple data sources for your machine learning steps to use. For machine learning, quality of data and quantity of data both matter. Therefore, this step is crucial.

2. **Preparing the data**: In this step, after performing the previous step of gathering data, we load our data into a suitable place and prepare it for use in our machine learning processes.

3. **Choosing a model**: In this step, you get to decide which algorithm to choose and what kind of problem you are trying to solve. So, you decide whether a particular class of problems belongs to classification, regression, or forecasting. The type of algorithm you choose to apply will be based on trail and tuning basis.

4. **Training**: In this step, we actually train our models on bulk data. Here, you first perform data sampling (downsample or upsample), then divide the records into an 80% to 20% ratio. You train your model based on 80% of the divided sample and then test the trained model with 20% of the remaining data. Based on the model accuracy threshold, you can decide to keep the model or refine it by repeating the process.

5. **Evaluation**: Evaluation is basically done on the set of data that comprises the 20% portion of the training samples that were never used in model training. Based on your organization's expectations and other business factors, you can come up with a threshold of model accuracy beyond which is acceptable.

6. **Hyperparameter tuning**: Hyperparameter tuning is basically tuning certain machine learning models for accuracy. Some examples could be the degree of the polynomial features that can be used for linear regressions or the depth of the decision tree. These tuning parameters are basically used to improve the accuracy of your machine learning models iteratively.

7. **Prediction**: This is the process where you use machine learning models to predict the outcome. This is the final step.

The following diagram represents the high-level steps that are involved in most of the machine learning:

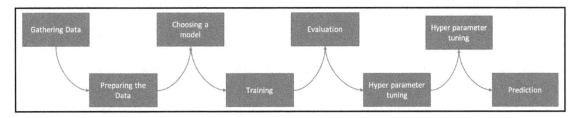

Common machine learning challenges

The following are some of the common challenges that you will face while running your machine learning application:

- **Data quality**: Data from sources is, most of the time, not suitable for machine learning. It has to be cleaned or checked for data quality first. Data has to be in the format that is suitable for the machine learning processes that you want to run. One such example would be removing nulls. The popular machine learning algorithm Random Forest does not support nulls.

- **Data scaling**: Sometimes, your data is comprised of attributes that vary in magnitude or scale. So, to prevent machine learning algorithms from being unbiased to re-scaling, under-scaled or over-scaled, attributes of the same scale is helpful. This helps machine learning optimization algorithms like gradient descent a great deal. Algorithms that iteratively weigh inputs, like regression and neural networks, or algorithms that are based on distance measures, like k-nearest neighbors, also benefit from this technique.

- **Feature selection**: Feature selection or dimensionality reduction is another critical component of your machine learning process. There are problems with high dimensions of data. They take more time to train and it increases exponentially because of the iterative nature of most machine learning algorithms. Another problem that can occur with high dimensions is the risk of overfitting. Feature selection methods help these problems by reducing the dimensions without much loss of total information. It also helps make sense of the features and their importance.

Spark machine learning

Spark is the distributed in-memory processing engine that runs machine learning algorithms in distributed mode by using abstract APIs. Using a Spark machine learning framework, machine learning algorithms can be applied on large volumes of data, represented as resilient distributed datasets. Spark machine learning libraries come with a rich set of utilities, components, and tools that let you write in-memory, processed, distributed code in an efficient and fault-tolerant manner. The following diagram represents the Spark architecture at a high level:

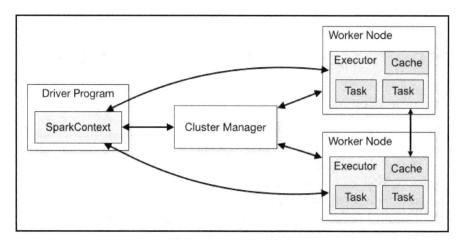

There are three **Java virtual machine** (**JVM**) based components in Spark: they are Driver, Spark executor, and **Cluster Manager**. These explained as follows:

- **Driver**: The **Driver Program** runs on a logically or physically segregated node as a separate process and is responsible for launching the Spark application, maintaining all relevant information and configurations about launched Spark applications, executing the DAG application according to user code and schedules, and distributing tasks to variously available executors. To coordinate all Spark cluster activity, the **Driver Program** uses a **SparkContext** or SparkSession object that's created by user code. **SparkContext** or SparkSession is a point of entry to execute any code using a Spark-distributed engine. The driver program converts a logical DAG into a physical plan and divides user code into a set of tasks to schedule any tasks. Each of these tasks is then scheduled to run on executors by schedulers that run in Spark driver code. The driver is a central part of any Spark application and runs the Spark application throughout its lifetime. If the driver fails, the whole application fails. The driver thus becomes a single failure point for the Spark application.

- **Spark executor**: Spark executor processes are responsible for the performance of the tasks assigned to them by the driver processes, the storage of data in memory data structures called **Resilient Distributed Datasets** (**RDDs**), and the reporting of its code execution to the driver processes. The key point to remember here is that the driver does not terminate executor processes by default, even if they are not used or performed. This behavior can be explained by the fact that the RDDs follow a lazy design pattern for evaluation. Even if executors are accidentally killed, however, the Spark application does not stop and the driver processes can restart those executors.

- **Cluster Manager**: It is the process responsible for physical machines and the allocation of resources to any Spark application. The cluster manager processes even launch driver code. The cluster manager is a plugin component and is cynical with the Spark user code for data processing. The Spark processing engine supports three types of cluster managers: Standalone, YARN, and Mesos.

Spark MLlib is a library of algorithms and utilities for machine learning that were designed to facilitate and run machine learning in parallel. This includes regression, filtering, classification, and clustering in collaboration. Spark MLlib provides two types of APIs that sre included in the packages, namely `spark.mllib` and `spark.ml`, where `spark.mllib` is built on top of the RDD and `spark.ml` is built on top of the DataFrame. Spark's primary machine learning API is now the `spark.ml` package API based on the DataFrame. The use of `spark.ml` with the DataFrame API is more versatile and flexible, and we can benefit from DataFrame, such as the catalyst optimizer and `spark.mllib`, which is an API based on RDD, which is expected to be removed in the future. Machine learning applies to different types of data, including text, images, structured data, and vectors. Spark ML includes the Spark SQL DataFrame to support these data types under a unified dataset concept. Various algorithms can be easily combined in a single workflow or pipeline. The following sections will give you a detailed overview of the Spark ML API's key concepts.

Transformer function

This can transform one data frame into another. For example, an ML model can transform a data framework with features into a predicted data framework. A transformer contains the transformer feature and the model that's being learned. This uses the `transform()` method to transform one DataFrame into another. The following is the sample code:

```
import org.apache.spark.ml.feature.Tokenizer
val df = spark.createDataFrame(Seq( ("This is the Transformer", 1.0),
    ("Transformer is pipeline component", 0.0))).toDF( "text", "label") val
tokenizer = new Tokenizer().setInputCol("text").setOutputCol("words") val
tokenizedDF = tokenizer.transform(df)
```

Estimator

An estimator is another algorithm that can create a transformer by attaching a data framework. For example, a learning algorithm can train and produce a model on a dataset. By learning an algorithm, this produces a transformer. It uses the `fit()` method to produce a transformer. For instance, the Naïve Bayes learning algorithm is an estimator that calls the `fit()` method and trains a Naïve Bayes model, which is a transformer. The following is an example:

```
import org.apache.spark.ml.classification.NaiveBayes
val nb = new NaiveBayes().setModelType("multinomial")
val model = nb.fit(Training_DataDF)
```

Spark ML pipeline

The Spark ML pipeline is a sequence of stages in which each stage is a transformer or an estimator. All of these stages are in order and the input dataset is changed as it passes through each stage. For the stages of transformers, the `transform()` method is used, while for the stages of estimators, the `fit()` method is used to create a transformer. Every DataFrame that is output from one stage is input for the next stage. The pipeline is also an estimator. Therefore, it produces the `PipelineModel` once the `fit()` method is run. A transformer is a `PipelineModel`. The `PipelineModel` includes the same number of stages as the original pipeline. `PipelineModel` and pipelines ensure that test and training data take similar steps in the processing of features. For example, consider a three-stage pipeline:

- **Stage 1**: Tokenizer, which tokenizes the sentence and converts it into a word using `Tokenizer.transform()`
- **Stage 2**: HashingTF, which is used to represent a string in a vector form, since all ML algorithms only understand vectors and not strings, using the `HashingTF.transform()` method
- **Stage 3**: Naive Bayes, an estimator that's used for prediction

We can save the model at `HDFSlocation` using the `save()` method, so we can load it in the future using the loading method and use it to predict the new dataset. This loaded model will work on the `newDataset` feature column, and the predicted column will also pass through all of the stages of the pipeline with this `newDataset`. The following is an example of this:

```
import org.apache.spark.ml.{Pipeline, PipelineModel}
import org.apache.spark.ml.feature.{HashingTF, Tokenizer}
import org.apache.spark.ml.classification.NaiveBayes
```

```
val df = spark.createDataFrame(Seq(
    ("This is the Transformer", 1.0),
    ("Transformer is pipeline component", 0.0)
  )).toDF( "text", "label")
  val tokenizer = new
Tokenizer().setInputCol("text").setOutputCol("words")
val
HashingTF=newHashingTF().setNumFeatures(1000).setInputCol(tokenizer.getOutp
utCol).setOutputCol("features")
  val nb = new NaiveBayes().setModelType("multinomial")
  val pipeline = new Pipeline().setStages(Array(tokenizer, hashingTF, nb))
  val model = pipeline.fit(df)
  model.save("/HDFSlocation/Path/")
  val loadModel = PipelineModel.load(("/HDFSlocation/Path/")
  val PredictedData = loadModel.transform(newDataset)
```

Hadoop and R

R is a data science programming tool for analyzing statistical data on models and translating analytical results into colorful graphics. R without the doubt is the most preferred programming tool for statisticians, data scientists, data analysts, and data architects, but when working with large datasets, it is short. One major disadvantage of the R programming language is that all objects are loaded into a single machine's main memory. Large petabyte size datasets cannot be loaded into the RAM. Hadoop is an ideal solution when it is integrated with R language. Data scientists must limit their data analysis to a sample of data from the large dataset to adapt to the single machine limitation of the R programming language in memory. When dealing with big data, this limitation of the R programming language is a major obstacle. Since R is not very scalable, only limited data can be processed by the core R engine. Its data processing capacity is limited to one node memory. This limits the amount of data that can be processed with R. So, when you try to work on large datasets, R runs out of memory. On the contrary, distributed processing frameworks such as Hadoop can be scaled for complex operations and tasks in large datasets (petabyte range), but do not have strong analytical statistical capabilities. Since Hadoop is a popular big data processing framework, the next logical step is to integrate R with Hadoop. The use of R on Hadoop provides a highly scalable data analysis platform that can be scaled according to the dataset size. Integrating Hadoop with R allows data scientists to run R on a large dataset in parallel, as none of the R-language data science libraries work on a dataset larger than their memory.

This memory problem can be solved using SparkR. In conjunction with R, Apache Spark offers a range of APIs for Python, Scala, Java, SQL, and other languages. These APIs serve as a bridge when they are connected to Spark. Spark offers distributed data sources and data structures memory to process engines. R provides dynamic surroundings, interactivity, packages, and views. SparkR brings together the benefits of Spark and R.

The R programming language with Hadoop (RHadoop) is by far the most widely used open source analysis solution. With Revolution Analytics developed, RHadoop allows users to directly ingest HBase database subsystems and HDFS file systems data. Because of its practicality and cost advantages, the RHadoop package is the go to solution for R on Hadoop. RHadoop has five different packages that allow Hadoop users to use the R programming languages to manage and analyze data. RHadoop, the Hadoop Open Source Package supports Hadoop, as well as the popular Cloudera, Hortonworks, and MapR distributions.

ORCH is Hadoop's Oracle R Connector. It is a compilation of R packages that provide the useful interfaces for working with tables from Hive, the computer infrastructure from Apache Hadoop, local R, and database tables from Oracle. ORCH provides also predictive methodologies that could be used in HDFS files for data.

The **R and Hadoop integrated programming environment** (**RHIPE**) package uses the big data analysis divide and recombine technique. Data is split into subsets, the calculation is performed by specific R-analytics operations over the subsets, and the results are combined. You can carry out a thorough analysis of both large and small data using RHIPE. Users can also conduct analytical operations in R using a lower language. RHIPE has a number of features to support the **Hadoop Distributed File System** (**HDFS**) and the operation of MapReduce using a simple R console.

Hadoop Streaming is another tool that enables users to add and run jobs as mapper or reducer using any executables. You can create working Hadoop jobs with sufficient knowledge of Java using the streaming system to write two shell scripts working in tandem. The combination of R and Hadoop is a must for people with statistical and large data and large datasets. However, some enthusiasts of Hadoop made a red flag when dealing with huge fragments of big data. They say that R's advantage is not its syntax, but an extensive library of visual and statistical elements. The basically unauthorized distribution of these libraries makes data collection a time-consuming business. This is an inherent contradiction with R, as R and Hadoop can still perform wonders if you want to overlook this.

Mahout

Mahout is the Apache library for open source learning. Mahout mainly uses, but is not limited to, the classification and dimensional algorithms of clustering recommend engines (collaborative filtering and classification). Mahout's objective is to provide the usual machine learning algorithms with a highly scalable implementation. If the historical data to be used is large, then Mahout is the machinery of choice. We generally find that it is not possible to process the data on a single device. With large data becoming an important area of focus, Mahout meets the need for a machine learning tool that can extend beyond a single computer. Mahout is different from other tools such as R, Weka, and so on, as its emphasis on scalability. The Mahout learning implementations are written in Java, and most but not all of them are compiled using the MapReduce paradigm on Apache's distributed Hadoop calculation project. Mahout will be built using Scala DSL on Apache Spark, and programs written on Scala DSL will be parallel to Apache Spark and automatically optimized. MapReduce's commitments for new algorithms have been stopped, and now support the current MapReduce execution. In 2008, Mahout started life as an Apache's Lucene project subproject, the same name's a well-known open source search engine. Lucene provides advanced search, text mining, and data recovery technology deployments. These concepts are adjacent to machine learning methods such as clustering and, to an extent, classification as found in the world of computer science. As a consequence, some of the work of Lucene's engaged people who fell into these areas was expanded to their own subproject. Mahout soon took up the collaborative filtering open source project, taste.

Machine learning case study in Spark

In this section, we will look into how to implement text classification using the Spark ML and Naive Bayes algorithms. The classification of text is one of NLP's most common cases of use. Text classification can be used to detect email spam, identify retail product hierarchy, and analyze feelings. This process is typically a problem of classification in which we try to identify a specific subject from a natural language source with a large volume of data. We can discuss several topics within each of the data groups and it is therefore important to classify the article or textual information in logical groups. The techniques of text classification help us to do this. These techniques require a lot of computing power if the data volume is large and a distributed computing framework for text classification is recommended. For example, if we want to classify legal documents in a knowledge repository on the internet, text classification techniques can be used to logically separate different types of documents.

The following illustration represents a typical text classification process that is done in two phases:

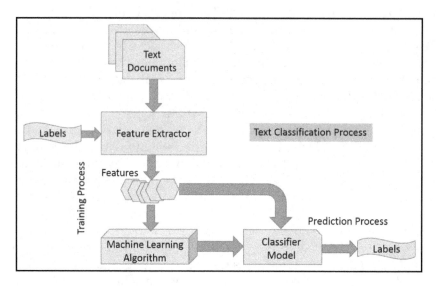

Now, let's see how text can be classified using Spark. We divide our code into the following four parts:

- Text preprocessing
- Feature extraction
- Model training
- Prediction verification

We will use the **Naive Bayes** (**NB**) algorithm for model training and prediction. But let's see how NB works before we go deep into the code. We'll also give you a brief overview of another algorithm, Random Forest, which can be used for text classification.

The classifier of **Naive Bayes** (**NB**) is a very powerful classification algorithm. If we use natural language processing for text analysis, NB is very good. Like the name Naive means independent or no relationship, the NB algorithm assumes that features are not related. As the name suggests, it works on the theorem of Bayes. So what is the theorem of Bayes? The theorem of Bayes finds out the likelihood of an event in the future based on previous events. This type of probability is also called the probability of condition. This probability is context-based and context is determined by knowledge of previous events. For any given two events, A and B, Bayes' theorem calculates $P(A|B)$ (the probability of event A occurring when event B has happened) from $P(B|A)$ (the probability of event B occurring, given that event A has already occurred). Naive Bayes attempts to classify data points in classes. It calculates the likelihood of each class data point. Each probability is then compared to the highest probability and the second highest probability is determined. The highest class of probability is considered the primary class and the second highest class is determined. If you have multiple classes, for example, we are classify fruit like apple, banana, orange, or mango, then we have more than two classes in which we classify a fruit, then this is known as **multinomial Naive Bayes**, and if we only have two classes, email as spam or non-spam, for example, it would be Binomial multinomial Naive Bayes. The following is the Naive Bayes' example in Spark ML:

```
import org.apache.spark.ml.{Pipeline, PipelineModel}
import org.apache.spark.ml.classification.{NaiveBayes, NaiveBayesModel}
import org.apache.spark.ml.feature.{StringIndexer, StopWordsRemover,
HashingTF, Tokenizer, IDF, NGram}
import org.apache.spark.ml.linalg.Vector
import org.apache.spark.sql.Row
//Sample Data
val exampleDF = spark.createDataFrame(Seq(
(1,"Samsung 80 cm 32 inches FH4003 HD Ready LED TV"),
(2,"Polaroid LEDP040A Full HD 99 cm LED TV Black"),
(3,"Samsung UA24K4100ARLXL 59 cm 24 inches HD Ready LED TV Black")
)).toDF("id","description")
exampleDF.show(false)
//Add labels to dataset
val indexer = new StringIndexer()
  .setInputCol("description")
  .setOutputCol("label")
val tokenizer = new Tokenizer().setInputCol("description")
  .setOutputCol("words")
val remover = new StopWordsRemover()
  .setCaseSensitive(false)
  .setInputCol(tokenizer.getOutputCol)
  .setOutputCol("filtered")
val bigram = new
NGram().setN(2).setInputCol(remover.getOutputCol).setOutputCol("ngrams")
val hashingTF = new HashingTF()
```

```
        .setNumFeatures(1000)
        .setInputCol(bigram.getOutputCol)
        .setOutputCol("features")
    val idf = new
IDF().setInputCol(hashingTF.getOutputCol).setOutputCol("IDF")
    val nb = new NaiveBayes().setModelType("multinomial")
    val pipeline = new
    Pipeline().setStages(Array(indexer,tokenizer,remover,bigram,
    hashingTF,idf,nb))
    val nbmodel = pipeline.fit(exampleDF)
    nbmodel.write.overwrite().save("/tmp/spark-logistic-regression-model")
    val evaluationDF = spark.createDataFrame(Seq(
    (1,"Samsung 80 cm 32 inches FH4003 HD Ready LED TV")
    )).toDF("id","description")
    val results = nbmodel.transform(evaluationDF)
    results.show(false)
```

Sentiment analysis using Spark ML

We have carried out sentiment analysis in the following code snippet based on the NLP theory we discussed in this chapter. It uses Tweeter JSON records and Spark libraries to train models to identify feelings such as happy or unhappy. In the Twitter messages, it looks for keywords like happy and then flags them with a value of 1, indicating that this message is a happy feeling. Finally, the TF-IDF algorithm is applied to train the models. The following is the code for the same:

```
import org.apache.spark.ml.feature.{HashingTF, RegexTokenizer,
    StopWordsRemover, IDF}
    import org.apache.spark.sql.functions._
    import org.apache.spark.ml.classification.LogisticRegression
    import org.apache.spark.ml.Pipeline
    import org.apache.spark.ml.classification.MultilayerPerceptronClassifier
    import org.apache.spark.ml.evaluation.MulticlassClassificationEvaluator
    import scala.util.{Success, Try}
    import sqlContext.implicits._
    val sqlContext = new org.apache.spark.sql.SQLContext(sc)
    var tweetDF = sqlContext.read.json("hdfs:///tmp/sa/*")
    tweetDF.show()
    var messages = tweetDF.select("msg")
    println("Total messages: " + messages.count())
    var happyMessages =
messages.filter(messages("msg").contains("happy")).withColumn("label",lit("
    1"))
    val countHappy = happyMessages.count()
    println("Number of happy messages: " + countHappy)
    var unhappyMessages = messages.filter(messages("msg").contains("
```

```
      sad")).withColumn("label",lit("0"))
      val countUnhappy = unhappyMessages.count()
      println("Unhappy Messages: " + countUnhappy)
      var allTweets = happyMessages.unionAll(unhappyMessages)
      val messagesRDD = allTweets.rdd
      val goodBadRecords = messagesRDD.map(
        row =>{
            val msg = row(0).toString.toLowerCase()
            var isHappy:Int = 0
            if(msg.contains(" sad")){
          isHappy = 0
        }else if(msg.contains("happy")){
          isHappy = 1
        }
        var msgSanitized = msg.replaceAll("happy", "")
        msgSanitized = msgSanitized.replaceAll("sad","")
        //Return a tuple
        (isHappy, msgSanitized.split(" ").toSeq)
} )
val tweets = spark.createDataFrame(goodBadRecords).toDF("label","message")
// Split the data into training and validation sets (30% held out for
validation testing)
val splits = tweets.randomSplit(Array(0.7, 0.3))
val (trainingData, validationData) = (splits(0), splits(1))
val tokenizer = new
RegexTokenizer().setGaps(false).setPattern("\\p{L}+").setInputCol("msg").se
tOutputCol("words")
val hashingTF = new
HashingTF().setNumFeatures(1000).setInputCol("message").setOutputCol("featu
res")
val idf = new IDF().setInputCol(hashingTF.getOutputCol).setOutputCol("IDF")
val layers = Array[Int](1000, 5, 4, 3)
val trainer = new MultilayerPerceptronClassifier().setLayers(layers)
val pipeline = new Pipeline().setStages(Array(hashingTF,idf,trainer))
val model = pipeline.fit(trainingData)
val result = model.transform(validationData)
val predictionAndLabels = result.select("message","label","prediction")
predictionAndLabels.where("label==0").show(5,false)
predictionAndLabels.where("label==1").show(5,false)
```

Summary

In this chapter, we studied the different machine learning steps and the common ML challenges that we face. We also covered the Spark ML algorithms and how they can be applied on large volumes of data, represented as resilient distributed datasets. This chapter also covered R as the most preferred programming tool for statisticians, data scientists, data analysts, and data architects. We learned about Mahout, which provides the usual machine learning algorithms with a highly scalable implementation, along with a case study on Spark.

In the next chapter, we will get an overview of Hadoop on the cloud.

11
Hadoop in the Cloud

In the previous chapters, we focused on a few basic concepts of machine learning, case studies for machine learning, how to stream data ingestion, and so on. Until now, we have walked you through the different components of data ingestion and data processing, some advanced concepts of the big data ecosystem, and a few best design practices that have to be taken into consideration while designing and implementing Hadoop applications. For any data pipeline that requires infrastructure setup to execute the data pipeline, the infrastructure can either be set up on premises or on the cloud. In this chapter, we will cover the following topics:

- Logical view of Hadoop in the cloud
- How a network setup looks on the cloud
- Resource management made easy
- How to make data pipelines on the cloud
- Cloud high availability

Technical requirements

You will be required to have basic knowledge of AWS Services and Apache Hadoop 3.0.

Check out the following video to see the code in action:
http://bit.ly/2tGbwWz

Logical view of Hadoop in the cloud

The usability of infrastructure in the cloud has been increasing at a rapid speed. The companies who were worrying about adopting the cloud for its computing and storage needs due to security and availability now have enough confidence as there have been lots of improvements on the architecture and features being made by different cloud service providers. Apache Hadoop started with on premises deployment and during the initial years of the Hadoop foundation, the Hadoop infrastructure was mainly set up using self-managed infrastructure. But over the last few years, cloud service providers have given focus to the Hadoop infrastructure and now we have everything that's needed for a big data/Hadoop setup. Today, almost every company moving to big data adaptability is using the cloud for their data storage and infrastructure needs. In this section, we will talk about how the logical architecture for Hadoop looks over the cloud:

- **Ingestion layer**: Data ingestion has always been given priority in all the data processing pipelines and thus it has been important to put thought into building robust ingestion process pipelines. There has always been some basic questions, such as the rate of data ingestion, data size, ingestion frequency, file format, directory structure, and so on. The ingestion of data to cloud storage systems such as S3 is a common part of the architecture design today. However, we can still use ingestion frameworks such as Sqoop, NiFi, Kafka, Flume, and so on by setting up infrastructure over the cloud. But cloud providers have their own managed tools for ingestion purposes. The following are a few tools that the cloud providers offer as part of their service offering:
  - **AWS Snowball**: You can use AWS Snowball to securely and efficiently transfer/ingest bulk data from on-premises storage platforms or Hadoop clusters to AWS S3 buckets. After we can create a job in the AWS management console, a Snowball appliance will be automatically created. After a Snowball is created, connect it to your local network, install the Snowball client on an on-premise data source, and then use the Snowball client to select and transfer the file directories to the Snowball device, which will eventually copy the data to S3.
  - **Cloud Pub/Sub**: Cloud Pub/Sub gives the flexibility and reliability of enterprise message-oriented middleware to the cloud. Cloud Pub/Sub is a scalable, durable event ingestion and delivery system. It decouples senders and receivers by providing many-to-many asynchronous messaging. Cloud Pub/Sub is a low-latency, durable messaging system that helps anyone quickly integrate systems hosted on the Google Cloud Platform.

- **Amazon Kinesis Firehouse**: Amazon Kinesis Firehouse is a fully-managed service by AWS for delivering real-time streaming data directly to AWS S3 storage. It automatically scales to match the volume and throughput of streaming data, and requires no ongoing administration to closely watch for failure or scalability. We can also configure Firehouse to transform streaming data before sending it to Amazon S3. Its transformation capabilities include compression, data batching, encryption, Lambda functions, and so on.

- **Amazon Kinesis**: Amazon Kinesis is somewhat similar to Apache Kafka as it is easy to collect, process, and analyze real-time streaming data. Amazon Kinesis offers key capabilities to process streaming the data at any scale, along with the adaptability to choose the tools that suits the best requirements of your application. Like Kafka, it allows the producer and consumer to work independently, meaning that both are very loosely coupled.

- **Processing**: There are many distributed data processing tools that have been in big data ecosystems, but a few of them are widely used by communities such as Apache Spark, Hive, Apache Flink, MapReduce, and so on. Since these are just processing engines, applications written using these tools need to be submitted to the resource manager for the execution of programs, which means we should have a processing engine and resource manager communication open and integrated. There will be some scenarios where two engines need to be integrated for different purposes, such as Spark, which can be integrated with Apache Hive for some reporting or analytics reasons.

  The integrated platform such as Cloudera Hortonworks comes with a well-tested integrated set of tools. Cloud service providers have their own integrated services, such as EMR, HDInsight, and so on. These services can be used based on the on-demand service.

- **Storage and analytics**: The cloud service providers have their own distributed data storage File Systems, for example, Amazon Web Services has S3, Google Cloud Services has Google Cloud Storage, Azure has the Azure Data Lake storage system, and so on. Apart from distributed file storage systems, cloud service providers also provide some distributed processing databases, such as Amazon Redshift, Big Query, Azure SQL, and so on.

  The cloud storage services are very reliable and robust in terms of cost, speed, and failure. The data can be replicated across regions to make storage system highly available with little extra cost. The database such as Redshift helps in processing terabytes of data in a few minutes, which helps in getting interactive reporting over large datasets in a cost-effective manner.

- **Machine learning**: The adoption of machine learning is speeding up across companies and there are lot of business and revenue benefits coming out of it. Cloud service providers have done significant advanced improvements in this area by providing easy to use libraries and APIs that can be used to build scalable machine learning models quickly.

Network

Today or tomorrow your organization or customers are likely to migrate their software and data infrastructure to the cloud. Given the shortage of engineers who most likely are experts on cloud infrastructure, you may also have to understand the cloud network infrastructure. In this section, we will cover different concepts of cloud networks and understand how an on-premise infrastructure is different from that available on cloud platforms. It doesn't matter which cloud provider you go with, such as AWS, Azure, GCP, and so on. The concept of the network remains same across each cloud provider.

Regions and availability zone

Regions are nothing but some geographical location in the world where the network and compute resources are available. Regions are governed by specific laws applicable to that region. For example, a region that is name based on anywhere in China would have to follow China's country policies with respect to cloud usage. Each resources may or may not be available in the specific region but in most cases cloud providers try to make each resource available in every region to generate more revenue.

Each region consists of one or more availability zones, which are physically isolated from each other. Each zone has its own set of resources, power, networking, and so on to reduce the possibility of region failure. A single zone consists of multiple physical data centers that are connected with each other over redundant private network links. The two zones in the region do not share a data center between them; each zone will have separate a data center and one zone is connected to the other via a private network link.

There are isolations of regional and zonal resources, which means regional resources can be used anywhere within a region and zonal resources can only be used within a zone. For example, a storage disk from one instance can be attached to another within the same zone, but it cannot be attached across zones. Resources such as VPC, images, and snapshots are global resources, and we can use these resources across different zones in the same region.

Companies normally build applications considering high availability and fault tolerance and therefore it is important to distribute resources across multiple zones and regions. Each zone is independent to each other, which means it has its own physical infrastructure, networking, and isolated control planes, which guarantee that failure events only affect that zone and not others. This is why companies distribute application across zones to guarantee the high availability of applications, even if one zone fails. Similarly we should also consider that although the distribution of applications across regions aims to avoid any issue during regional failure, sometimes due to region-specific policies, we can not distribute applications outside of the region. For example, recently the Reserve Bank of India strictly exposed policies that forced financial institution to keep data within India.

VPC and subnet

A **Virtual Private Cloud** (**VPC**) allows a user to create a virtually private and isolated network in the cloud. A VPC-enabled secure transfer of data between a private enterprise and a public cloud network means the data of one company on same public cloud is isolated from other companies' data on the same public cloud. A VPC has a CIDR block assigned to it which represents a subnet mask for VPC networks. An example of a CIDR block range is 10.20.0.0/16, we can create 2 power 16 IP addresses in the VPC. These CIDR blocks are then used to create subnets.

A virtual private cloud is shared pool of resources allocated from public cloud resources for private access to organization. It provides an isolation of cloud resources between the different organizations so that one organization can privately use any resources created under the VPC allocated to them. This is because the network is private to the organization and therefor it is referred to as a virtual private network.

A VPC is global resource, which means it can be used across different regions and zones. A VPC can contain resources from different regions and zones. Typically resources within a VPC can access each other but this can also be restricted by setting a valid firewall or security rules. A VPC network can be connected to different VPC networks within organizations by using VPC network peering, which allows resource of one VPC to access resources of other VPC. For example, we may have scenarios where a data analytics team may want to read data on daily basis from the RDBMS or any other database created in a different VPC. In such cases, we can use a VPC peering between these two VPCs to restrict database access to only these two VPCs.

A VPC network consists of one or more useful IP range partitions known as a subnet. Each subnet is associated with a specific region and has a subnet mask associated with it, which indicates the maximum number of resources that can be created using the subnet. A VPC network does not have any IP address ranges associated with it.
A VPC must have minimum of one subnet before we can actually use it for creating any resources. By default when we create any resources, the cloud provider automatically tries to add a new subnet to it. It's always good practice to create a subnet and then assign it to resources for use. We can create more than one subnet per region. There are basically two types of subnets, namely:

- **Private subnet**: Any instance or resource created using a private subnet would not be accessible via the internet; it can only be accessible within any subnet under the VPC. In many cases, organizations don't want to expose direct access to some sensitive resources to the internet, instead they want them to be accessible via some other internal instances. For example, creating any transaction database under a private subnet is common practice where we want to restrict database access to any application within the VPC.

- **Public subnet**: Any instance or resources created under the public subnet is accessible via the internet, which means anyone in the world can access the instance if they have valid authentication to access the resources running inside the instance. For example, you may want to have a bastion server associated with public subnet and assign specific users with credentials to log into the bastion server from anywhere, and then have internal security firewall rules to allow access to other resources in the private subnet from the bastion server.
  The other example could be website UI application that can be assigned to a public subnet so that its backend application can run in a private subnet so that users can only interact using a user interface and user interface can interact with the backend to get the required information.

Security groups/firewall rules

Security groups or firewall rules act as a virtual firewall that controls the traffic to or from any instances. Any instance created under a subnet will have a security group attached to it. VPCs and subnets have network ACLs to restrict the traffic to or from the VPC or subnets. It is always a good practice to create a custom security group and assign it to instances. Remember: if we do not create any security group while creating the instance, then the default security group is assigned to it. We can add rules to security groups that allow traffic to or from the instance associated with the security group. We can modify the rules for a security group as and when required, and the new rules will be automatically applied to all instances associated with the security group. Basically, there are two types of rules associated with groups or firewall, which are as follows:

- **Inbound rule**: The inbound rule defines the inbound traffic rules for the instances, which means it defines who can access which ports of the instances. If you define a rule that says port 8080 should be accessible for the block range 10.20.10.0/24, then any instance within the IP range defined in block can access the instance. Instead of putting a block range, we can also specify a security group name.
- **Outbound rule**: The outbound rule defines the outbound traffic rules for the instance, which means it defines what instance you can access. You can restrict your instance to access certain services such as the internet by defining respective outbound rules.

Network ACLs are associated with the VPC and subnet, which restricts access to the VPC and subnet. Network ACLs do have inbound and outbound rules with the same purpose we discussed previously.

Practical example using AWS

We have talked about basic network concepts in this section, lets now cover basic practical guides to actually see how to create these resources. Before jumping into the practical example, we recommend you create a valid AWS account.

Creating a VPC: The creation of a VPC is the first step in any project deployment over the cloud. Open a create VPC wizard in AWS, which will open a page that looks like the following, and fill in the information in the respective blocks. The following diagram shows the VPC Creation Wizard in AWS:

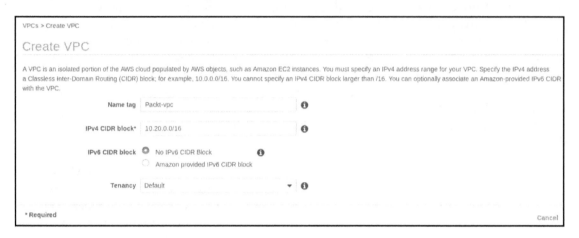

This screenshot can be explained as follows:

- **Name tag**: Unique name assigned to the VPC for reference.
- **IPv4 CIDR block**: Represents the subnet mask for the VPC that can be used by subnets to define their network range. The subnet network range never exceeds the VPC network range. It will always be less than or equal to the VPC network range.

After the VPC is created, we can see the detail of the VPC an the following screenshot. If you observe carefully, AWS has associated a few default components and configurations to the VPC, such as network ACL, route table, DHCP options set, and so on:

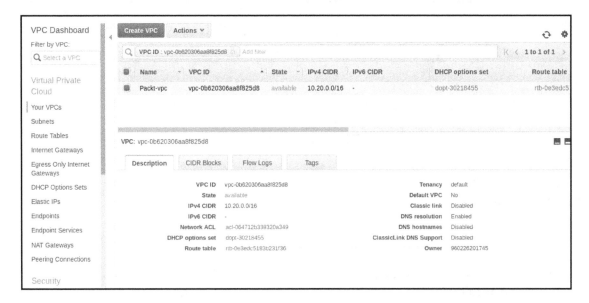

AWS assigned a unique VPC-ID to each VPC and it also assigns a **Network ACL** with default inbound and outbound rules.

Creating Subnet: Once the VPC is created, the next step is to create a subnet under the VPC that can be used at the point of creating instances. Go to the subnet creation wizard and fill in the required information. You can refer the following details:

- **Name Tag**: Defines a name tag to identify the subnet
- **VPC**: VPC-ID to which this subnet will belong. We have selected a VPC-ID created previously
- Remember the IPv4 CIDR block range must be within the range of the VPC CIDR

- **Availability Zone**: Optional, represents the choice of zone where the subnet will be created and assigned:

Similar to the VPC, the subnet also gets a default Network ACl, route table and other information as follows:

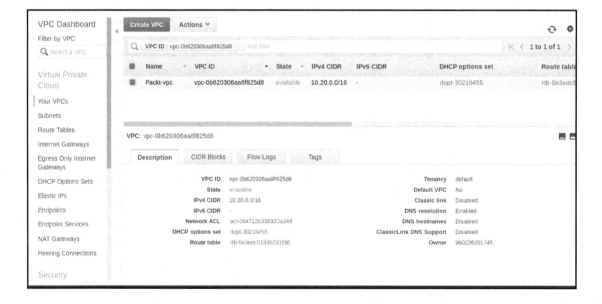

Security groups: We discussed previously that, even if we do not specify security groups when creating an instance, there is one auto-created for each instance. It is good practice to create your own security group and then assign it to instances or the EMR cluster. Go to the **Create Security Group Wizard** and fill in the information:

- **Security group name**: Unique name to identify the security group
- **VPC**: Select VPC from drop-down list in which this security group can be available as default
- **Inbound Rule**: Add an inbound traffic rule that will allow access to instances from the configured network in the rule
- **Outbound Rule**: Add an outbound rule; by default instance is open to communicate with any instance in the world
  We will see the **Security Group Creation Wizard** in the following image:

Creating EC2 instance or EMR cluster: The basic setup required for an EC2 instance or EMR cluster is done. Remember even if we don't create a basic setup for the EC2 instance or EMR cluster, there is always a default setup attached to it. But in real production or any deployment in an organization, its always good practice to create a custom setup that will be easy to maintain and manage.

Let's look into creating an EC2 instance. Go to **create instance wizard** and it will ask you to select an AMI image, which indicates which operating system we want to select, for instance:

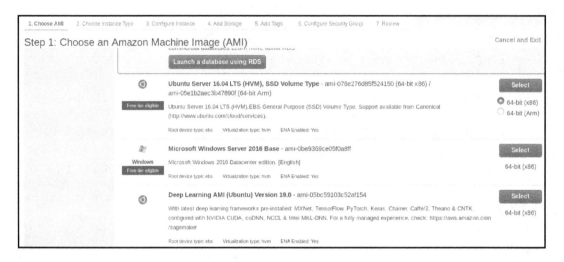

The next step is to configure an EC2 instance type and select the VPC and subnet we created previously. There are multiple choices for the type of compute engine we want to select. We recommend that you select the compute type based on your requirement. Some may need computer optimized, some may need CPU optimized, and so on. Here is our example:

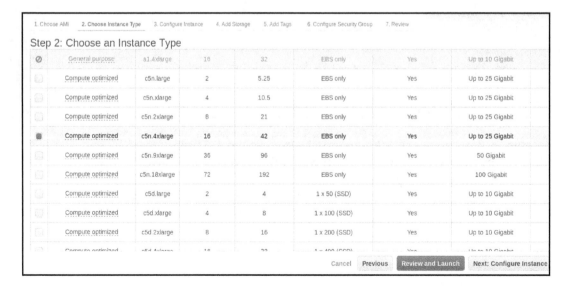

We have selected Packt-VPC. After this, subnet is created. The instance will be assigned a public IP based on what type of subnet we have. Since we have a public subnet, the public IP will also be assigned to it as shown in the following screenshot:

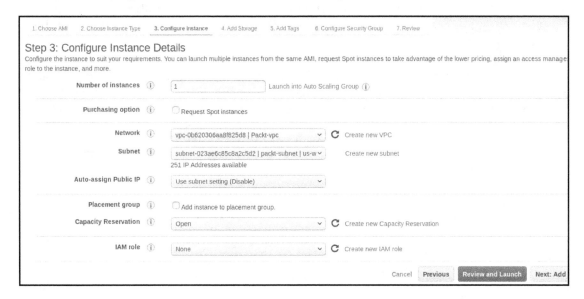

Add storage to the EC2 instance if it already exists, otherwise one will be added to the instance as follows:

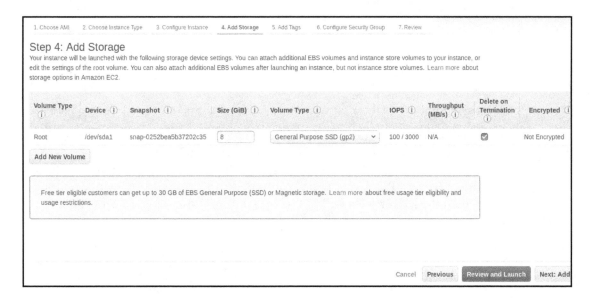

The last step is to add a security group to the EC2 instance and then launch the instance.

EMR Cluster: Similar to the EC2 instance, we can also create an EMR instance using the VPC and subnet we created previously. The EMR cluster can have multiple tools, such as MapReduce, Spark, Sqoop, Hive, and so on. Let's look into how we create and launch the EMR cluster using the same.

The first step is to launch the EMR create cluster wizard and choose advance settings. Step 1 is to select a list of software we want as a part of our EMR cluster; we can select AWS Glue as Hive metadata store, which has lot of other benefits when working with wide range of systems, for example:

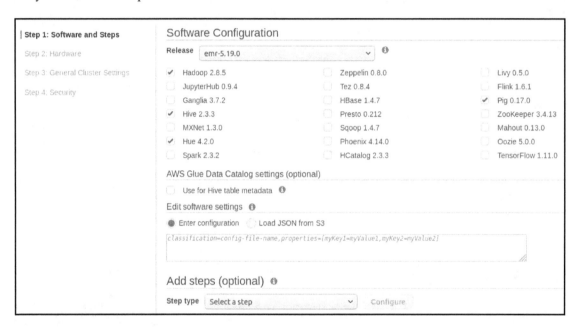

Once the selection of software is done, we can move to the hardware config, where we have the option to select where the VPC and subnet cluster nodes will be created. This is important, as there will be some other tools such as Redshift, Aurora DB, and so on whose access will be limited to the VPC, and if you do not select the required VPC while creating the EMR cluster, then the EMR nodes will not have access to those tools. Select the cluster nodes for creation as follows:

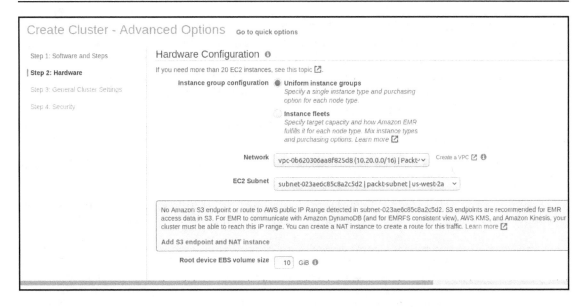

We can now launch the cluster and use it as required. We can always restrict the access to any instance that's created under the VPC by changing the security group or adding the new inbound rules to the existing security group that's attached to the instance. The best practice is to keep all prod instance only accessible to instances within the subnet or VPC. If any instance outside the VPC requires access, it's better to create a VPC peering between them.

Managing resources

Resource management is a continuous process for either on-premise infrastructures or infrastructure on the cloud. The instance you deploy, the cluster you spin up, and the storage you use all have to be continuously monitored and managed by the infrastructure team. Sometimes it may happen that you need to attach a volume to the already running instance, you may need to add an extra node to your distributed processing databases, or you may need to add instances to handle large traffic coming to the load balancer. The other resource management work includes configuration management, such as changing firewall rules, adding new users to access the resources, adding new rules to access other resources from the current resource, and so on.

Initially due to a lack of good GUI interfaces and available tools for monitoring and managing resources, it was managed using custom scripts or commands. Today almost all cloud providers have well augmented graphical user interfaces and tools that help in managing and monitoring cloud resources. Each cloud provider has their own managed Hadoop cluster, such as Amazon's EMR cluster, Azure's HDinsight cluster, and so on. Each of the cloud providers also provides easy-to-use interfaces to manage these clusters and make it easy to add users, add nodes, remove nodes, and other cluster configuration through the GUI interface. In this section, we will take an example of the Amazon AWS cloud and we will see how this cloud provider has some rich features in terms of managing resources.

The resource group page on AWS contains all the resource groups and how many resources are being used under those resource group, as shown in the following screenshot:

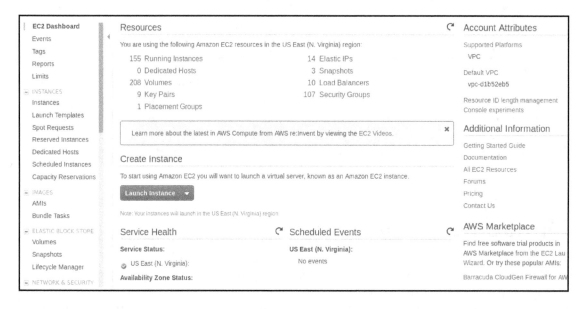

The preceding screenshot indicates that these AWS account in some regions have **155** instances running, have **107** security groups used, have **3** manual snapshots of some database, **208** volume attached to instances, **10** Load balancers running, and so on.

Now, suppose we have to manage any EC2 instance running in the region. We will go under an instance running by clicking on it and the EC2 resource manage page will look as follows:

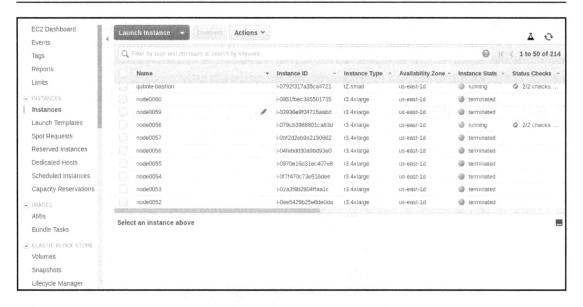

The instance page gives a list of all instances created in the region and their current state. It also shows other details, such as instance type, availability zone in which the instance is created, public DNS, security group, and so on. The following screenshot shows the instance in detail:

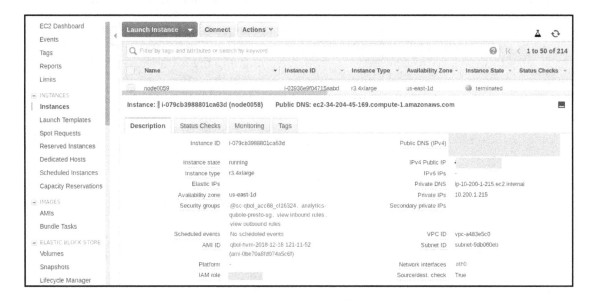

Once we select any instance, the details appear at the bottom of the instances window and tells us about some other details, such as in which instance the VPC and subnet were created, the network interface, IAM role attached to the instance, public, private DNS, and so on. The following screenshot shows the **Instance Settings**:

The configuration of instance can be managed by selecting and right-clicking the instance. There are multiple setting options available to manage the EC2 resources, such as changing the state of the instance from running to stop or terminating the instance, adding tags to instances, attaching an IAM role, adding it to a scaling group, and so on. The following screenshot shows the instance network resource management:

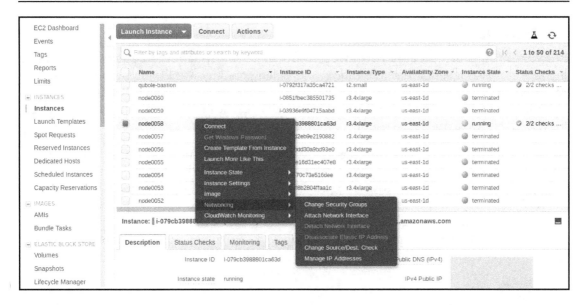

There are other settings, such as adding new security groups to instances, changing the inbound/ingress rule to allow access to instances by some specific instance or firewall group. All the screenshots in this section are just for your reference and give you an idea about how cloud service providers makes it easy to manage any resources provided by them through a simple and easy-to-use interface. The following screenshot shows the **Instance State** management:

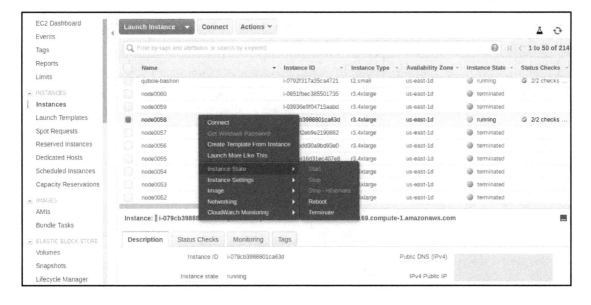

Cloud-watch

Resource management is easy when we have robust resource monitoring in place. Resource monitoring gives a better idea about how and when you may want to modify/manage resource based on metrics alert. Taking an example, you may want to add or attach a new volume to an instance wherein one storage capacity reaches 80%, or you may want to plan for cluster node expansion based on the number of failed node reported.

Amazon CloudWatch enables developers, system architects, and administrators to real-time monitor and scan their AWS applications in the cloud. CloudWatch will be automatically configured to provide metrics on request counts, latency, and CPU usage of the AWS resources, however, users can send their own logs and custom metrics to CloudWatch for monitoring. CloudWatch provides a rich set of data and reports, which helps users keep track of application performance, resource use, operational issues, constraints, and so on.

Data pipelines

Data pipelines represent the flow of data from extraction to business reporting, which involves intermediate steps such as cleansing, transformation, and loading gold data to the reporting layer. The data pipelines may be either real-time, near mealtime, or batch. The storage system may be either distributed storage, like HDFS, S3 or distributed high throughput messaging queue, such as Kafka and Kinesis.

In this section, we will talk about how we can use cloud providers' tools all together to build data pipelines for customers. If you have already gone through the preceding section about the logical architecture in Hadoop, this section will be easy to understand. We have been continuously mentioning that every cloud provider available today has some equivalent tools available with respect to open source tools. Each cloud provider claims some rich set of features and have a benchmark test available to support their claim, but remember these benchmark test are specific to their tools only; changing your test scenario may help win other tools with same dataset.

In the first section, we have covered different tools used for each steps of data pipeline. Let us look at some of the new cloud provider services that help in creating quick data pipelines using the tools discussed previously.

Amazon Data Pipeline

AWS Data Pipeline is a web service and can be used to automate the movement and transformation of data from source to destination. The Data Pipeline can be used to define workflows that indicate task flow from source to destination. The intermediate tasks are dependent on completion of its previous task. It allows us to configure and manage this workflow as a pipeline. AWS Data Pipeline manages and handles the details of scheduling and ensures that the data dependencies are met for the applications to focus on processing the data.

Data Pipeline provides an implementation of a task runner called AWS Data Pipeline Task Runner. AWS Data Pipeline has some of the default task runners for performing common tasks, such as executing database queries and running the processing pipelines using the EMR cluster. It also enables you to create custom task runners to manage the data processing pipeline.

AWS Data Pipeline basically implements two functionalities:

- **Schedule and run tasks**: Amazon EC2 instances are created to perform the defined work activities. We have to upload created pipeline definition to the pipeline, and then activate the pipeline. The user can always edit the running pipeline configuration and activate the pipeline again for its effect to take place. Once the job is finished, we can delete the pipeline.
- **Task runner**: It polls for tasks and then performs the required tasks. For example, task runner could copy log files to Amazon S3 and launch Amazon EMR clusters. The resource created by pipeline definition triggers task runner execution.

Airflow

Airflow is an advance distributed framework to author, schedule, and monitor workflows using Python programs. The workflow can also be referred as data pipeline, which consist of a series of tasks represented as a **Directed acyclic graph** (**DAG**).

The airflow executes your tasks on an array of workers while following the specified dependencies. It provides a rich set of UI interface that allows the user to track the flow and do some configuration as needed.

Airflow provides us with a few default languages and templates to define sequences of tasks. These tasks can be any number of things a computer can do, for example, executing a script on server, performing or querying the database, sending an email on task completion, business reports, or anything else, and waiting for a file to appear on a server, and so on. The user can define the sequence and execution time of tasks and it will manage when these sequences should run, what order to run the tasks in each sequence, what to do if a task fails, and so on. It also manages the number of resources necessary to run these tasks and scheduling tasks when computing resources are made available.

Airflow components

An Airflow cluster has a number of daemons that work together: a webserver, a scheduler, and one or several workers. We will explain each of them as follows:

- **Webserver**: A web server renders the UI for Airflow using which one can view the DAGs, its status, re-run, create variables, and connections. The Airflow web UI uses a Web server as its back end to provide classic and easy-to-use view for users to manage pipelines. The airflow web server accepts the REST HTTP requests and allows the user to interact with it. It provides the ability to act on the DAG status, such as pause, unpause, and trigger. In distributed mode, the workers are configured and installed on different nodes and they are configured to read the task information from the RabbitMQ brokers.

- **Scheduler**: The Airflow scheduler monitors DAGs. It also triggers the task instances whose dependencies or criteria have been met. It monitors and keeps them synchronized with a folder for all DAG objects, and periodically inspects tasks to check if they can be triggered.

- **Worker**: Airflow workers are daemons that actually execute the logic of tasks. They manage one to many CeleryD processes to execute the desired tasks of a particular DAG.

Sample data pipeline DAG example

```
import logging
from airflow import DAG
from datetime import datetime, timedelta
from airflow.operators.dummy_operator import DummyOperator
from airflow.operators.python_operator import PythonOperator,
BranchPythonOperator
from airflow.operators.hive_operator import HiveOperator
from airflow.operators.email_operator import EmailOperator
from airflow.operators.sensors import HdfsSensor
```

```
from your_task_file_path import tasks
from your_hql_file_path import hql

logger = logging.getLogger(__name__)

DAG_ID = 'my-test-dag'

default_args = {
    'owner': 'Mehmet Vergili',
    'start_date': datetime(2017, 11, 20),
    'depends_on_past': False,
    'email': 'packt.publishing@gmail.com',
    'email_on_failure': 'packt.publishing@gmail.com',
    'email_on_retry': 'packt.publishing@gmail.com',
    'retries': 3,
    'retry_delay': timedelta(minutes=5)}

dag = DAG(dag_id=DAG_ID,
          default_args=default_args,
          schedule_interval=timedelta(days=1))

hdfs_data_sensor = HdfsSensor(
    task_id='hdfs_data_sensor',
    filepath='/data/mydata/{{ ds }}/file.csv',
    poke_interval=10,
    timeout=5,
    dag=dag
)

hive_dag = HiveOperator(
    task_id='hive_dag',
    hql="DROP DATABASE IF EXISTS {db} CASCADE; CREATE DATABASE
{db};".format(db='my_hive_db'),
    provide_context=True,
    dag=dag
)
hive_dag.set_upstream(hdfs_data_sensor)

hdfs_to_hive_table_dag = HiveOperator(
    task_id='hdfs_to_hive_table_dag',
    hql=hql.HQL_HDFS_TO_HIVE_TRANSFER.format(table_name='mydata',
                                             tmp_table_name='mydata_tmp',
                                             hdfs_path='/data/mydata/{{ ds
}}'),
    schema='my_hive_db',
    provide_context=True,
    dag=dag
)
```

```
hdfs_to_hive_table_dag.set_upstream(hive_dag)

count_data_rows = BranchPythonOperator(
    task_id='count_data_rows',
    python_callable=tasks.count_data_rows,
    templates_dict={'schema': 'my_hive_db'},
    provide_context=True,
    dag=dag
)
count_data_rows.set_upstream(hdfs_to_hive_table_dag)

stop_flow = DummyOperator(
    task_id='stop_flow',
    dag=dag
)

create_source_id = PythonOperator(
    task_id='create_source_id',
    python_callable=tasks.create_source_id,
    templates_dict={'source': 'mydata'},
    provide_context=True,
    dag=dag
)
create_source_id.set_upstream(hdfs_data_sensor)

clean_data_task = HiveOperator(
    task_id='clean_data_task',
    hql=hql.HQL_clean_data_task.format(source_id="{{
task_instance.xcom_pull(task_ids='create_source_id') }}",
                                    clean_mydata='clean_mydata',
mydata='mydata'),
    schema='my_hive_db',
    provide_context=True,
    dag=dag
)
clean_data_task.set_upstream(create_source_id)
count_data_rows.set_downstream([stop_flow, clean_data_task])

move_data_mysql = PythonOperator(
    task_id='move_data_mysql',
    python_callable=tasks.move_data_mssql,
    templates_dict={'schema': 'my_hive_db'},
    provide_context=True,
    dag=dag
)
move_data_mysql.set_upstream(clean_data_task)

send_email = EmailOperator(
```

```
        task_id='send_email',
        to='packt.publishing@gmail.com',
        subject='ingestion complete',
        html_content="Date: {{ ds }}",
        dag=dag)

    send_email.set_upstream(move_data_mysql)
```

High availability (HA)

High availability (HA) is a primary focus for all the framework or application available today. The application can be deployed either on-premise or over the cloud. There are many cloud service providers available today, such as Amazon AWS, Microsoft Azure, Google Cloud Platform, IBM Cloud, and so on. Achieving high availability using on-premise deployment has limited capability, for example even if we have multi node clusters available on-premise that have both HDFS storage and a processing engine up and running, it does not guarantee the required high level of availability in case any disaster happens. It requires also strict monitoring of the on-premise cluster in order to avoid any major loss and guaranteeing high availability.

In other words, cloud services provide more robust and reliable high availability features and there are multiple scenarios for considering what level of high availability we want to achieve it. Let us look into few conceptual scenarios.

Server failure

Applications run on instances in the cloud and each instance belongs to a specific cloud resource, such as region, zone, VPC, subnet, and so on. There are many possibilities why the instance running on your application may fail or crash including memory issue, network issues, or region outage. Nobody wants to have a situation where applications are not reachable due to instance failure.

Server instance high availability

Deploying the restful micro services are the most commonly used use case across industry where each service running on any instance is responsible for handling specific tasks. For example, if we consider any e-commerce company, they may have multiple micro services running the support for the e-commerce platform, such as one service may only deal with user and order detail, one service may provide the payment service, while another micro service may provide product functions, and so on. All these services work together to achieve the overall functionality. Since each service plays an important role, they should be highly available to serve millions of requests at a time, so it is important to plan for high availability and scalability in advance. The following diagram is example of using **Load Balancer** to provide High Availability for services running under instances:

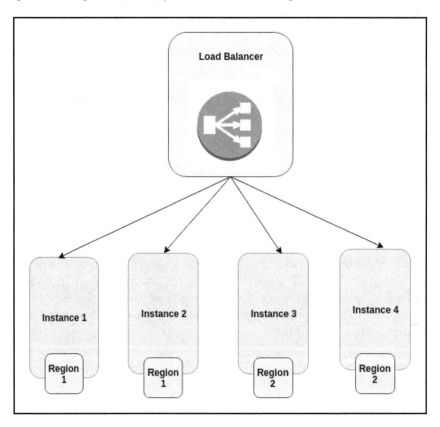

There are multiple use cases in big data that sometime require building a restful service in order to consume or produce responses from other applications. The preceding architecture can be taken into consideration if there is any such need. If you closely look at the instance boxes, they are available in different regions and thus provide High Availability, even if one region goes down.

Region and zone failure

Failure cannot be predicated and it is always better to take care of all the failure scenarios when designing an architecture. The cloud service provider has a physical infrastructure in specific regions, and each region may have multiple availability zones. It is very rare but possible that one or more zone might be unavailable or an entire region might become unavailable due to any unavoidable problems. We need to make sure while deploying our applications to the cloud that our applications are tolerant to zone and region failure, which means that if these are instances under the load balancer, then there has to be multiple instances, and they should be available. The following diagram shows the high availability (region and zone failure):

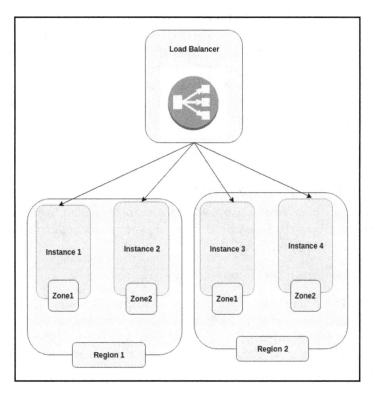

Cloud storage high availability

Companies using cloud services for their infrastructure also use the cloud storage from the same service provider to store their data. Data is a valuable asset and companies cannot be at risk of loosing data for any reason. There are multiple places where data can be stored, such as a transactional database system, messaging queue, distributed storage, and so on. We will cover the Hadoop-specific storage, such as AWS S3, in this section.

Even though most of the cloud service providers guarantee that data stored on the cloud storage systems are 99.99% available all the time, there are many scenarios where these claims will fail, and the possibility of a 0.01% chance of failure is still there, which means even in data loss and outages the protection gaps can still exist.

Nearly all cloud service providers use redundant hardware and offers the customers a service level agreement for their storage system. Cloud storage typically has redundancy in place, but that alone cannot be sufficient to protect against an outage. There are situations, such as local component failures, WAN outages, and cloud provider outages, that can lead to data becoming inaccessible.

It is always better to evaluate the cloud service provider regarding their storage protection and availability policies. A few cloud service providers do not have an easy way to provide multi-region cloud storage by default. You also need to evaluate if cloud providers are providing custom replication features or if their storage policies and features are in line with our requirement. A few cloud providers also have different tiers of storage levels and each tier has different pricing, features, and policies. If you choose a more advance tier for storage, you may get an advance feature but with additional pricing than a storage system at a lower tier.

Amazon S3 outage case history

Companies or users who have been using AWS for more than couple of years are aware of Amazon's significant outage in February 2017, when they managed to *break the internet* because of a major outage of AWS S3.

The key reasons behind the most famous outage are as follows:

- The AWS S3 storage service in the **North Virginia (us-east-1)** region was unattainable for several hours. Even though other regions were not impacted, the service outage affected the entire region, spanning all the Availability Zones, and the large customers that had their infrastructure setup in a given region had to suffer on business revenue.

- The root cause of the problem was majorly because of human error, where AWS internal were performing routine maintenance work and apparently an S3 outage occurred.
- Many companies use S3 to store there website build, application, data, and other important server configuration, which resulted in downtime of their infrastructure and revenue loss.
- The non-Amazon services that were affected by the outage included various Apple services, Slack, Docker, Yahoo mail, and other high-profile websites and services.

The following is the full detail that Amazon published on their website after the outage fix. This contents is available at `https://AWS.amazon.com/message/41926/`.

Some cloud providers, such as GCP, provide an option for multi-region storage, which means that even if one region goes down, it will not affect the availability of storage. Amazon AWS S3 does not provide the ability to define multi-region storage at the time of bucket creation, which means we need to define a strategy to have multi-region backup storage for bucket so that even if region containing a bucket goes down, data can be served from similar a bucket in another region.

Summary

In this chapter, we have studied the logical view of Hadoop in the cloud and how the logical architecture for Hadoop would look over the cloud. We also learned about managing resources, which is a continuous process for either on-premise infrastructure or infrastructure on the cloud. We got introduced to the data pipelines and how we can use cloud providers' tools all together to build a data pipeline for customers. This chapter also focuses on High Availability, which is a primary focus for all the frameworks and applications available today. The application can be deployed either on-premise or over the cloud.

In the next chapter, we will study Hadoop Cluster Profiling.

12
Hadoop Cluster Profiling

A Hadoop cluster is a complex system to manage. As a cluster administrator, one of your prime responsibilities is to manage the performance of your Hadoop cluster. The first step toward managing Hadoop performance is to find out the optimal combination of Hadoop configuration to suit your different job workloads. This is a daunting and challenging task. This can be attributed to the distributed nature of Hadoop. There are many Hadoop configurations that an administrator needs to configure to ensure performant Hadoop operations. The nature of these configurations also varies. Some of themhave a broader impact on Hadoop cluster performance and some of them have a minor impact on it.

To achieve optimal Hadoop cluster performance, you have to systematically understand how different components of the Hadoop ecosystem react to different configuration parameters and how they eventually impact your Hadoop job performance. You can always categorize these parameters into I/O, JVM, memory and other such categories. Perhaps I/O is the most impactful category in performance tuning of big data applications. The first step toward Hadoop performance tuning is to understand thoroughly how your job workloads respond to different configurations. Based on this understanding, you will come up with the best cluster configurations catering performance requirements of all your workloads. In this chapter, we will understand how Hadoop cluster performance can be optimized by benchmarking and profiling your Hadoop cluster. We will also talk about the different tools that you can use to benchmark and profile your Hadoop cluster.

Introduction to benchmarking and profiling

The Hadoop cluster are used by the organizations in different ways. One of the primary ways is to build data lakes on top of the Hadoop cluster. A data lake is built on top of different types of data sources. Each of these data sources varies in nature, such as the type of data or frequency of data. Every type of data processing for those sources in data lakes varies. Some are real-time processing and some are batch-time processing. Your Hadoop cluster on top of which the data lake is built has to take care of such different types of workloads. These workloads are memory intensive, and some are memory as well as CPU intensive. As an organization, it becomes imperative that you benchmark and profile your cluster for these different types of workloads. Another reason for benchmarking and profiling your cluster is that your cluster nodes may have different hardware configurations. For varying workloads, it is important that organizations ensure how these nodes behave under load from different data sources.

You should be benchmarking and following important components in Hadoop:

- **HDFS I/O**: This is important because when you run MapReduce jobs and Hive jobs, lots of data gets written to disk.
- **NameNode**: NameNode is the heart of the Hadoop cluster. If NameNode goes down then your entire cluster will go down. It is always necessary to benchmark NameNode for operations such as reading, writing, deleting, and renaming files. NameNode also performs a lot of file metadata operations while interacting with the DataNode. So NameNode memory consumption is also important.
- **YARN scheduler**: YARN is the job scheduling management tools for Hadoop. There are different types of queues available in YARN. The three schedulers, FIFO, capacity, and fair, have different types of features and they offer different kinds of algorithms. These algorithms take scheduling decisions based on multiple factors, such as YARN user settings, the available capacity in the cluster at the time of running the job, minimum capacity assurances, and so on. So it is important that you identify the correct scheduling algorithms for your cluster. Benchmarking and profiling YARN schedulers for your typical workloads always helpful.
- **MapReduce**: MapReduce is fundamental to the Hadoop cluster. When you run Pig jobs, the Hadoop cluster runs MapReduce jobs. The MapReduce engine is fundamental to any Hadoop cluster. So it is absolutely important to benchmark and profile the Hadoop cluster.

- **Hive**: This is again an important component used in an organizations' data lake jobs. Benchmarking and profiling this is essential, especially with SQL support on big data. Running SQL queries on big data may end up using all the cluster's resources as developers are writing simple joins, but those joins are converted once to Tez executions. DAG may end up performing lots of I/Os, utilizing all the cluster cores, or end up consuming a lot of memory, causing out of memory issues.
- **PIG**: Pig scripts get converted to MapReduce jobs when running on the Hadoop cluster. Pig is written in Pig latin, which gets converted to Java code by the Pig compiler. This Java code is then executed as a MapReduce program in the cluster. However, it is always beneficial to test if the conversion is causing some performance drop or not. Moreover, different types of operations, such as aggregation, sorts, or joins generate different types of Java code. It is important to understand how that generated Java code would work in your cluster.

The following diagram shows how you should divide and plan your Hadoop cluster benchmarking and profiling:

Benchmarking Hadoop Cluster		
HDFS	TestDFSIO	
Namenode	NNBench	NNThroughputBenchmark
	Synthetic Load Generator (SLG)	
YARN	YARN Scheduler Load Simulator (SLS)	
HIVE	TPC-DS	TPC-H
MIX-WORKLOADS	GRIDMIX	RUMEN

The preceding diagram also indicates the tools that you can use to benchmark different components. We will cover these tools in detail in the next sections.

HDFS

HDFS plays a major role in the performance of batch or micro jobs, using HDFS to read and write the data. If there is any bottleneck on the application during writing or reading the file from HDFS, then it will lead to overall performance issues.

DFSIO

DFSIO are the tests that are used to measure read and write performance of MapReduce jobs. They are file-based operations that read and write tasks in parallel. The reduce tasks collect all performance parameters and statistics. You can always pass different parameters to test the throughput, the total number of bytes processed, average I/O, and much more. The important key is that you match these outputs with the number of cores, disks, and memory in your Hadoop cluster. Understand your current cluster limitations, try to mitigate those limitations to the extent possible, and then modify your jobs scheduling or coordination to get the maximum out of your cluster resources. The following is the command to run DFSIO:

```
hadoop jar <HADOOP_CLIENT_INSTALLATION_PATH>/hadoop-mapreduce-client-
jobclient-<HADOOP_VERSION>-tests.jar TestDFSIO <OPTIONS>

OPTIONS can be:
-read[-random | -backward | -skip [-skipSize <FILE_SIZE_TO_SKIP>]]
-write |-append | -truncate | -clean
-nrFiles <NO_OF_FILES>
-fileSize <SIZE_OF_FILE>
-compression codecClassName
-resFile <LOCATION_OF_RESULTING_FILE_NAME>
-storagePolicy <HDFS_FEDERATION_STORAGE_POLICY_NAME>
-erasureCodePolicy <ERASURE_ENCODING_POLICY_NAME>
```

After data generation, each file is processed by map tasks. The reducer collects the following statistics:

- Tasks completed
- Bytes written or read
- Total time of execution
- The rate at which I/O happened
- The square of I/O rate

The final report has the following parameters:

- Type of test (read/write)
- Date and time of when the test is finished
- Number of files
- Number of bytes processed
- Throughput in MB (total number of bytes/sum of file processing times)
- Average I/O rate per file
- Standard I/O rate deviation

NameNode

NameNode is mater daemon in the HDFS and every client request for read and write goes through NameNode. If NameNode performance decreases, then it will eventually lead to the application performance decreases because NameNode will respond slowly to any request made to it. Let's look into how we do profiling for NameNode performance.

NNBench

NameNode is the heart of the Hadoop cluster. Any file operations in HDFS first goes through the NameNode. NameNode, apart from managing file operations, keeps track of all file locations on DataNodes. So it is important that you test NameNode performance against chosen hardware configurations. NNBench is one such tool that can help you in evaluating that. Based on the NNBench output, you can decide on the optimal configuration of NameNode as well. The following is the command to run NNBench (Ref: *Hadoop 3 Apache Document*):

```
hadoop jar <HADOOP_CLIENT_INSTALLATION_PATH>/hadoop-mapreduce-client-
jobclient-<HADOOP_VERSION>-tests.jar nnbench <OPTIONS>

OPTIONS can be:
-operation [create_write|open_read|rename|delete]
-maps <NO_OF_MAPPERS>
-reduces <NO_OF_REDUCERS>
-startTime <EPOCH_TIME_IN_FUTURE>
-blockSize <HDFS_BLOCK_SIZE_IN_BYTES>
-bytesPerChecksum <BYTES_PER_CHECKSUM_PER_FILE>
-numberOfFiles <NUMBER_OF_FILES>
-replicationFactorPerFile <REPLICATION_FACTOR>
-baseDir <HDFS_BASE_PATH_FOR_FILES>
-readFileAfterOpen <TRUE_OR_FALSE>
```

A few points to note about NNBench are as follows:

1. NNBench runs multiple operations on NameNode via DataNodes. It is especially used for a `stress-test` on the NameNode when the number of files is small.
2. For read, rename, and delete operations, you have to first create files using NNBench.
3. The `-readFileAfterOpen` option should be utilized as it reports the average time to read the file.

NNThroughputBenchmark

This test is more specific toward running multiple client threads on NameNode and capturing its throughput. This test focus is to capture NameNodes throughput purely by minimizing overheads. For example, the client that performs operations on NameNode runs on a single node but uses multiple threads to simulate multiple operations. This is to avoid the communication overhead that is caused by multiple **Remote Procedural Calls (RPC)** and serialization-deserialization. This benchmark test first starts with generating the input for each thread. This is again done at the start to avoid overheads that may affect the throughput statistics. It runs tests against specific NameNode operations with a specified number of threads to collect stats about the number of operations performed by NameNode in a second. This test also outputs the average execution time of specific operations. The following is the command to run this test (Ref: *Apache Hadoop 3 Document*):

```
hadoop org.apache.hadoop.hdfs.server.namenode.NNThroughputBenchmark
[genericOptions] [commandOptions]

  For genericOptions:
    Refer Link
https://hadoop.apache.org/docs/r3.0.0/hadoop-project-dist/hadoop-common/Com
mandsManual.html#Generic_Options

  For commandOptions:
  -op
[all|create|mkdirs|open|delete|fileStatus|rename|blockReport|replication|cl
ean]
  -logLevel [ALL|DEBUG|ERROR(Default)|FATAL|INFO|OFF|TRACE|TRACE_INT|WARN]
  -UGCacheRefreshCount <INTEGER_VALUE>
  -keepResults [TRUE|FALSE]
```

The following table explains each of the commandOptions parameters:

op	It specifies the operations that you want to perform on NameNode. It is a mandatory field and has to be provided first. Please note that the [all] option is available on different types of operations on NameNode.
loglevel	You can put any logging level that is available with the Apache Log4J library. The default is error. Refer the following link for all available log levels: https://logging.apache.org/log4j/1.2/apidocs/org/apache/log4j/Level.html.
UGCacheRefreshCount	This specifies the number of times to refresh the user to the = group mappings cache maintained in NameNode. This is by default, set to 0. That means it is never called.

keepResults	This ensures that clean is not called on the created namespace after execution is completed. By default clean is called.

The `op` parameter has several other options. They vary for each different types of operation. The following table covers this list:

all	This will have options for all other operations since it runs on every available option
create	[-threads] [-files] [-filesPerDir] [-close]
mkdirs	[-threads] [-dirs] [-dirsPerDir]
open	[-threads] [-files] [-filesPerDir] [-useExisting]
delete	[-threads] [-files] [-filesPerDir] [-useExisting]
fileStatus	[-threads] [-files] [-filesPerDir] [-useExisting]
rename	[-threads] [-files [-filesPerDir] [-useExisting]
blockReport	[-datanodes] [-reports] [-blocksPerReport] [-blocksPerFile]
replication	[-datanodes] [-nodesToDecommission] [-nodeReplicationLimit] [-totalBlocks] [-replication]

Finally, at the following table contains the different options available with the `op` parameter:

threads	Number of total threads to run the respective operation
files	Number of total files for the respective operation
dirs	Number of total directories for the respective operation
filesPerDir	Number of files per directory
close	Close the files after creation
dirsPerDir	Number of directories per directory
useExisting	If specified, do not recreate the name-space, use existing data
datanodes	Total number of simulated datanodes
reports	Total number of block reports to send
blocksPerReport	Number of blocks per report
blocksPerFile	Number of blocks per file
nodesToDecommission	Total number of simulated data-nodes to decommission
nodeReplicationLimit	The maximum number of outgoing replication streams for a data-node
totalBlocks	Number of total blocks to operate
replication	Replication factor. Will be adjusted to the number of datanodes if it is larger than that

With Hadoop 3, code changes have been made to `NNThroughputBenchmark.java`. This is mostly it is due to the erasure encoding feature of HDFS and is internal. It does not have any impact on how you use `NNThroughputBenchmark`. Refer to the following Jira link: `https://issues.apache.org/jira/browse/HDFS-10996`

Synthetic load generator (SLG)

Synthetic load generator (**SLG**) helps us evaluate NameNode performance. It gives you options to generate a different kind of read and write workload for NameNode. It divides the read and write operation based on the probability provided to it by the user. These probabilities help you get closer to the type of workload your cluster has. If you have a read-intensive workload, then you can increase read probabilities. This is similar for write-heavy clusters.

SLG also lets you control the way read and write requests can be made to NameNode. Like delays, read/write requests can be performed on the number of working threads simultaneously making the requests. The following diagram represents how synthetic load can be used and how it runs its tests against the NameNode:

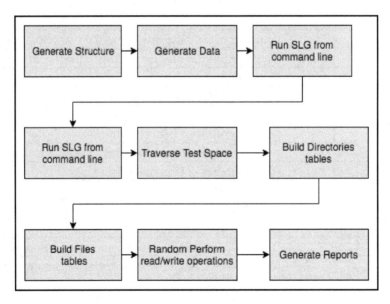

This diagram represents how SLG works. For running SLG you have to first generate the test data. It has two parts. First, you have to generate the structure of directories and sub-directories by issuing the following command (Ref: *Apache Hadoop 3 documentation*):

```
yarn jar <HADOOP_MAPREDUCE_CLIENT_INSTALLATION_PATH>/hadoop-mapreduce-
client-jobclient-<hadoop-version>.jar NNstructureGenerator [options]


Options can be:
/*The Default value is 5 that represents Maximum depth of the directory
tree.*/
-maxDepth <MAX_DEPTH_HIERARCHY_COUNT>
/* The Default value is 1 that represents Minimum number of sub directories
per directories */
-minWidth <MIN_SUBDIRECTORIES_COUNT>
/* The Default value is 5 that representsMaximum number of sub directories
per directories. */
-maxWidth <MAX_SUBDIRECTORIES_COUNT>
/*The Default value is 10 that represents The total number of files in the
test space*/
-numOfFiles <NO_OF_FILES_TO_GENERATE>
/* Average size of blocks; default is 1. */
-avgFileSize <FILESIZE_IN_TERMS_OF_NO_OF_BLOCKS>
/*Output directory; default is the current directory.*/
-outDir <OUTPUT_REPORT_DIRECTORY_LOCATION>
/*Random number generator seed; default is the current time.*/
-seed <JAVA_RANDOM_LONG_TYPE_SEED>
```

Second, you have to generate data for the generated directory structure using the following command (Ref: *Apache Hadoop 3 Document*):

```
yarn jar <HADOOP_MAPREDUCE_CLIENT_INSTALLATION_PATH> hadoop-mapreduce-
client-jobclient-<hadoop-version>.jar NNdataGenerator [options]


Options can be:
/*Input directory name where directory/file structures are stored; default
is the current directory.*/
-inDir <INPUT_DIRECTORY_LOCATION>
/*The name of the root directory which the new namespace is going to be
placed under; default is "/testLoadSpace".*/
-root test space root
```

Now, you have to run the following command to run the final diagnosis (Ref: *Apache Hadoop 3 documentation*):

```
yarn jar <HADOOP_MAPREDUCE_CLIENT_INSTALLATION_PATH> hadoop-mapreduce-
client-jobclient-<hadoop-version>.jar NNloadGenerator [options]

Options can be:
/* The probability of the read operation; default is 0.3333.*/
-readProbability <READ_PROBABILITY>
/* The probability of the write operations; default is 0.3333.*/
-writeProbability <WRITE_PROBABILITY>
/* The root of the test space; default is /testLoadSpace. */
-root test space root
/*The maximum delay between two consecutive operations in a thread; default
is 0 indicating no delay.*/
-numOfThreads <NUMBER_OF_THREADS>
/*The number of seconds that the program will run; A value of zero
indicates that the program runs forever. The default value is 0.*/
-elapsedTime <TIME_FOR_PROGRAM_TO_RUN>
/* The time that all worker threads start to run. By default it is 10
seconds after the main program starts running.This creates a barrier if
more than one load generator is running.*/
-startTime <TIME_TO_START_THREADS>
/*The random generator seed for repeating requests to NameNode when running
with a single thread; default is the current time.*/
-seed <JAVA_RANDOM_LONG_TYPE_SEED>
```

With Hadoop 3, one major bug related to file close time of SLG has been fixed. This fix has also been applied to previous versions of Hadoop. Please refer to the following link:
https://issues.apache.org/jira/browse/HADOOP-14902.

YARN

YARN is a new generation resource manager and plays the role of scheduling and executing the application over the Hadoop cluster. In this section, we will look at how we can run benchmarks against a YARN cluster.

Scheduler Load Simulator (SLS)

Hadoop provides three different kinds of scheduling algorithms in the form of queues. They are called FIFO, Capacity and Fair schedulers. Each of these schedulers takes different factors like available capacity, fairness among different running jobs, and guaranteed resource availability. Now, an important point to decide is what type of queue is suitable for your workload in the production environment. This test helps you decide that. One thing to note here is that the simulator works on prediction. It does not run jobs on the entire cluster. It is always time-consuming and expensive to run it on a very large cluster. Moreover, very few organizations run on a very large cluster. This test predicts how well the queues fit into your workloads. The following diagram briefly explains the workings of the YARN scheduler load simulator:

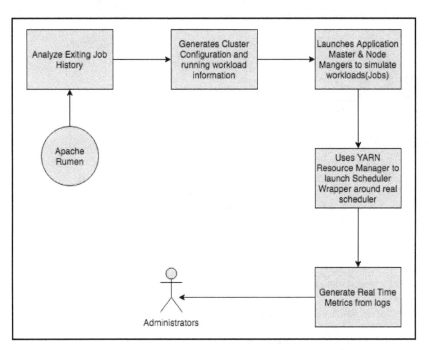

As depicted in this diagram, this test first generates a cluster and application configuration using Apache Rumen. Then it launches Nodemanagers and ApplicationMasters in thread pools to utilize the existing YARN resource manager, and forms a wrapper around a scheduler used. The wrapper generates different matrices based on scheduler behavior and logs. Finally, these outputs can be analyzed by the administrators.

This section covered YARN SLS in brief. If you need to deep dive into YARN SLS, we suggest you go through the following link. It covers this test in detail, along with its architecture and usage.

```
https://hadoop.apache.org/docs/r3.0.0/hadoop-sls/
SchedulerLoadSimulator.html
```

Hive

Hive is a widely used data warehouse tool on top of Hadoop and plays an important role in running daily batch jobs and business reporting queries by using an execution engine such as MapReduce, Apache Tez, Apache Spark, and so on. It is important to do a benchmark test for it.

TPC-DS

One of the important benchmarking paradigms for Hive is TPC-DS. This benchmarking standard is created especially for big data systems that cater for multiple business needs and different kinds of queries, such as data mining, ad hoc, transaction-oriented, and reporting. You can use the Hortonworks hive-testbench open source package to run TPC-DS benchmark. The following are the steps to execute with HIVE 13:

- Clone the lastest GitHub repository Git clone from `https://github.com/hortonworks/hive-testbench.git`
- Build TPC-DS, as follows:

  ```
  cd hive-testbench
  ./tpcds-build.sh
  ```

- Generate tables and load data, as follows:

  ```
  ./tpcds-setup.sh [SCALE_FACTOR] [DIRECTORY]

      /* SCALE_FACTOR represents how much data how much data you want to
  generate. A
      factor of 1
      represents roughly 1GB. DIRECTORY represents temporary HDFS
  directory where
      tables data would be
      stored.*/
  ```

- Run sample TPC-DS queries, as follows:

```
cd sample-queries-tpcds
hive -i testbench.settings
/* After login to HIVE Console */
use tpcds_bin_partitioned_orc_<SCALE_FACTOR>;
source query55.sql
```

TPC-H

TPC Benchmark (TPC-H) consists of business relevant ad hoc queries and data modifications at the same time. They try to model real-world scenarios of querying and modification simultaneously. Basically, this type of test benchmark is a support system that helps businesses take decisions in the right manner. It takes care of large volumes and very complex queries that give answers to critical and important business questions. You can use the Hortonworks hive-testbench open source package to run TPC-H benchmark. The following are the steps to execute that with HIVE 13:

- Clone the latest Git repository git clone from the link: https://github.com/hortonworks/hive-testbench.git
- Build TPC-H, as follows:

```
cd hive-testbench
./tpch-build.sh
```

- Generate tables and load data, as follows:

```
./tpch-setup.sh [SCALE_FACTOR] [DIRECTORY]
```

```
    /* SCALE_FACTOR represents how much data how much data you want to
generate. A factor of 1
    represents roughly 1GB. DIRECTORY represents temporary HDFS directory
where tables data would be
    stored. */
```

- Run sample TPC-H queries, as follows:

```
cd sample-queries-tpch
hive -i testbench.settings
/* After login to HIVE Console */
use tpch_bin_partitioned_orc_<SCALE_FACTOR>;
source tpch_query1.sql
```

Mix-workloads

This section covers the benchmarking strategy for mixed loads on clusters such as MapReduce history job profiling and other production job profiling.

Rumen

Apache Rumen is the tool that parses your MapReduce job history logs. It outputs meaningful and easily readable text. The output from this job is used in other benchmarking tools like YARN Scheduler Load Simulator or Gridmix. It has the following two parts:

1. **Tracebuilder**: Converts Hadoop job history logs to an easily parsable format, JSON. The following is the command to run Tracebuilder (Ref: *Hadoop3 Documentation*):

   ```
   hadoop rumentrace [options] <jobtrace-output> <topology-output>
   <inputs>

       <jobtrace-output> - Location of the Json output file
       <topology-output> - Cluster layout file
       <inputs> - Jobhistory logs location

       Options are
       -demuxer  Used to read the jobhistory files. The default
   isDefaultInputDemuxer.
       -recursive Recursively traverse input paths for job history logs.
   ```

2. **Folder**: This part is used to scale the trace runtime. You can increase and decrease the trace runtime to see how you cluster behaves while upscaling and downscaling. The following command is used to run folder (Ref: *Hadoop3 Documentation*):

   ```
   hadoop rumenfolder [options] <TRACEBUILDER_OUTPUT_JSON>
   <FOLDER_OUTPUT_LOCATION>

       Options can be:
       -input-cycle Defines the basic unit of time for the folding
   operation. There is no default value for
       input-cycle. Input cycle must be provided.

       -output-duration This parameter defines the final runtime of the
   trace. Default value if 1 hour.
   ```

-concentration Set the concentration of the resulting trace. Default value is 1.

-debug Run the Folder in debug mode. By default it is set to false.

-seed Initial seed to the Random Number Generator. By default, a Random Number Generator is used to
    generate a seed and the seed value is reported back to the user for future use

-temp-directory Temporary directory for the Folder. By default the output folder's parent directory
    is used as the scratch space.

-skew-buffer-length Enables Folder to tolerate skewed jobs. The default buffer length is 0.

-allow-missorting Enables Folder to tolerate out-of-order jobs. By default mis-sorting is not
    allowed.

Gridmix

Gridmix basically models the resource profiles of each production job to specify the exact resource requirements of the job and how much resource should be allocated to those jobs. It helps in identifying bottlenecks and guides the developers as well. Gridmix uses a job trace of the cluster that is generated by Rumen. It also needs input data and that should be in a binary format. It cannot use any other format. Please remember that you have to run Rumen before running Gridmix. The following are the commands to run Gridmix (Ref: *Apache Hadoop 3 documentation*):

```
java org.apache.hadoop.mapred.gridmix.Gridmix [JAVA_OPTS] [-generate
<SIZE>] [-users <USERS>] <IOPATH> <RUMEN_TRACE_PATH>

/*
[JAVA_OPTS] - Configuration parameters like -
Dgridmix.client.submit.threads=10 -Dgridmix.output.directory=foo

<SIZE> - Size of input data and distirbuted cache file. 1G would result in
1*2^30
        bytes.
<USERS> - path to users file (Ref below link for more details:
        http://hadoop.apache.org/docs/current/hadoop-
            gridmix/GridMix.html#usersqueues)
<IOPATH> - Working directory of Gridmix can be local or HDFS
```

```
<RUMEN_TRACE_PATH> - Location of Traces generated by Rumen. It can be
compressed   by one of the compresseion codec supported by Hadoop.

Gridmix expects certain jars to be present in CLASSPATH while running the
job. You have to pass those jars -libjars options. It definitely needs
hadoop-rumen-<VERSION>.jar to be present in CLASSPATH.
```

This section is just an overview of Gridmix. It is actually a very powerful tool and helps you analyze the cluster and jobs running on the cluster in detail. It gives you a lot of options to simulate the production workload. We did not cover all those options. However, we strongly suggest that you refer to the following link to understand how Gridmix can be used in your Hadoop environment.
`http://hadoop.apache.org/docs/current/hadoop-gridmix/GridMix.html`.

Summary

This chapter covers different types of benchmarking tools that can be used in your Hadoop environment. At the end of the chapter, you should have a clear understanding of the different open source benchmarking tools available for different Hadoop components, such as HDFS, Hive, and YARN. You should also refer to the links given in the chapter for a more detailed understanding of each of the respective benchmarking tests.

In the next chapter, we will study some details of Hadoop security concepts that are being used across the world. In next chapter, we will also learn about authentication and authorization in Hadoop.

Section 4: Securing Hadoop

4

This section covers the overall security aspect of Hadoop, including authorization and authentication, securing data at rest, and securing data in motion. This section also covers monitoring Hadoop ecosystem components.

This section consists of the following chapters:

- Chapter 13, *Who Can Do What in Hadoop*
- Chapter 14, *Network and Data Security*
- Chapter 15, *Monitoring Hadoop*

Who Can Do What in Hadoop

13

This chapter introduces you to security in the Hadoop ecosystem. When you are adopting Hadoop in your enterprise, then security becomes very important. You do not want people with unauthorized access to be able to reach the data stored in the HDFS File System. Security not only concerns a single aspect; you have to think about multiple aspects while securing your Hadoop enterprise application. Let's look at these aspects and understand what roles these play in securing Hadoop-based enterprise applications.

In this chapter, we will cover the following topics:

- Different aspects of Hadoop security pillars
- Security systems
- Kerberos authentication
- User authorization

Hadoop security pillars

Before designing security for your Hadoop cluster, you should be very clear about the different aspects of security that have to be incorporated. This section talks about the different pillars of security that are required to make your Hadoop cluster secure and threat-proof. We will discuss each of those pillars in brief in this section. Later, they will be elaborately discussed in different sections of this chapter.

The following diagram gives you a glimpse of the Hadoop security pillars:

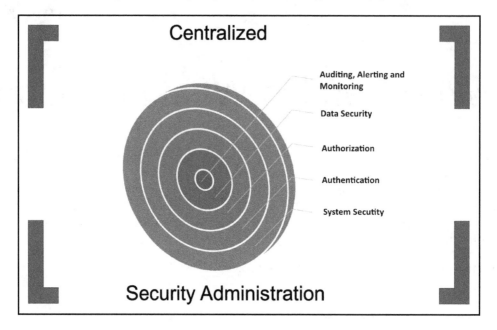

Before discussing the rings in the preceding diagram, we should understand one important aspect of securing the Hadoop cluster, and that is **Security Administration**. As a Hadoop security administrator, you have to perform the following activities at a high level:

- Get or develop a means of centralized Hadoop security enablement in terms of automated scripts or security tools.
- Get or develop a means of a centralized Hadoop monitoring and alerting system. This system should comply with your enterprise-grade security rules and deeply integrate it with enterprise alerting and monitoring systems of choice.
- Provision and plan for different types of users and roles (groups). All users and roles should be uniformly synced and integrated with the **Active Directory** (**AD**) users and groups. The AD should be integrated at the OS level on each Hadoop node as well.

Now, let's look into the different security pillars in brief. We will explain them in the following points:

- The first outer ring in the preceding security diagram talks about the system security. System security mostly covers network security and OS level security. Here, we cover network segmentation and attacks against brute-force security breaches.

- The second outer ring covers the most fundamental part of any security system, that is, authentication. It establishes the identity of end users and Hadoop services being used in the cluster.
- The third outer ring is about authorizing who can do what in your Hadoop cluster. For example, who can use Hive services in your cluster or who can run Storm jobs in your cluster. There are multiple ways this can be achieved in the Hadoop cluster and we will look at those in the following sections.
- The fourth outer ring represents data security. Data security can be divided into two parts:
    - One is about securing data that is at rest, which means securing data stored on the hard drives.
    - The second one is about data in motion, which means securing data as and when it is transmitted over the network. No security system is of use if it cannot detect and notify security breaches.
- The most inner circle is about how to detect, audit, and monitor any malicious attempts that are made on your cluster, or any breaches that may have occurred. All security systems should have the auditing, alerting, and monitoring systems in place.

Before we move on to the next section, please keep in mind that you cannot have a fully secure Hadoop cluster if you miss any of the security pillars. These security pillars are very important and they support each other for a comprehensive and complete secure system.

System security

System security is mostly related to the **Operating System** (**OS**) security and remote **Secure Shell** (**SSH**) access to nodes. OS security consists of regular checking and resolution of OS security vulnerability by applying patches or workarounds. As an administrator, you need to be aware of OS vulnerabilities and new malware that's released by hackers. You should also be aware of the different security patches and workarounds for those vulnerabilities.

The following link has details of the latest OS vulnerabilities and malware:

https://www.cvedetails.com/

A Hadoop cluster consists of a variety of nodes with different profiles. Some are master nodes consisting of NameNodes and journal nodes. Some are worker nodes consisting of HDFS DataNodes and HBase region servers. Especially in the case of remote SSH access, your firewall rules may also vary as per profile types of nodes. However, the following table is specific to SSH access and what kind of roles should have SSH access to which node profile. Please note that it may not contain a comprehensive list of all node types.

The following table represents the different variety of nodes that you have to keep in mind while securing a Hadoop ecosystem:

Profile type	Nodes names (examples only and may vary from cluster to cluster)	SSH access type
Master nodes	• HDFS primary and secondary NameNode • ZooKeeper failover controller • MapReduce JobTracker • YARN Resourcemanager and JobHistoryServer • Hive Metastore and HiveServer2 • HBase master • Oozie server • ZooKeeper servers	Administrators only
Worker nodes	• DataNodes • HBase region servers	Administrators only
Management nodes	• Ambari server • Git servers • Database servers	Administrators only
Management nodes	• Edge node	Developers and end users only

The preceding table is just for a representational perspective to give readers ideas about how to plan SSH access for different node profile types.

Kerberos authentication

There are various challenges involved in Big Data like storing, processing, and analysis, and managing and securing large data assets. When enterprises started implementing Hadoop, securing Hadoop from an enterprise context became challenging due to the distributed nature of the ecosystem and a wide range of applications that are placed on top of Hadoop. One of the key security considerations in securing Hadoop is authentication.

Kerberos is chosen by the Hadoop team as the component for implementing authentication in Hadoop. Kerberos is a secured network authentication protocol that brings in major authentication for client-server applications without transferring the password through the network. Kerberos implements time-sensitive tickets that are created using symmetric key cryptography, which was chosen over the most widely used SSL-based authentication.

Kerberos advantages

There are different advantages of Kerberos, which are as follows:

- **Better performance**: Kerberos uses symmetric key operations. Symmetric key operations are always faster in operations than SSL authentication, which is based on public-private keys.
- **Easy integration with enterprise identity server**: Hadoop is a store of many services like HDFS, Hive, YARN, and MapReduce. These services are used by the user accounts, which are managed by identity servers like AD. Kerberos installations can be easily made local to the Hadoop cluster while still ensuring end user authentication with remote AD servers. All services would still be authenticated with local Kerberos ensuring a lesser load on the AD servers.
- **Simpler user management**: Creating/deleting/updating users in Kerberos is very simple. All you need to do is create/delete or update the user from the Kerberos KDC or AD. However, if you are going for SSL-based authentication, deleting a user means the generation of a new certificate revocation list and the propagation to all servers.

- **No passwords over the network**: Kerberos is a secured network authentication protocol that brings in major authentication for client-server applications without transferring the password through the network. Kerberos implements time-sensitive tickets that are created using symmetric key cryptography.
- **Scalable**: Passwords or secret keys are only known to the KDC and the principal. This makes the system scalable for authenticating a large number of entities, as the entities only need to know their own secret keys and set that secret key in KDC.

Kerberos authentication flows

Kerberos authentication flows need to be looked at from different perspectives. There is a need to understand how services are authenticated, how clients are authenticated, and how communication happens between authenticated clients and authenticated services. We also need to understand in detail how the symmetric key cryptography works in Kerberos authentication and how passwords are not communicated over the network. Lastly, there is a need to understand how Kerberos authentication works with Web UIs. The following diagram (https://access.redhat.com/) represents how Kerberos authentication flows works at a high level:

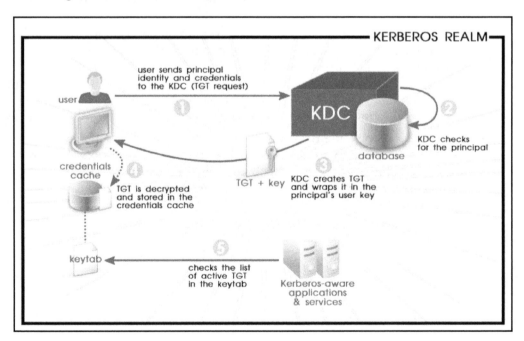

Service authentication

Services authenticate themselves with Kerberos during startup. During startup, Hadoop services will authenticate with KDC directly using the service principal and the keytab configured in `core-site.xml` or similar configuration files. The principle asserts that it is the right service that can be proved by the right key held in the keytab. After successful authentication, KDC issues the required ticket, which will be put into the subject's private credentials set. The service can then serve the client requests.

User authentication

It is essential that the end user should authenticate to Kerberos KDC when the Hadoop service is accessed via a client tool or another mechanism, using his/her own user principals. First, the user should log in to a client machine that can talk to the Hadoop cluster, then execute the `kinit` command with the principal and password. kinit does the work to authenticate the user to KDC, gets the result Kerberos TGT ticket, and puts it into the ticket cache in the filesystem.

Communication between the authenticated client and the authenticated Hadoop service

After both the server side and client side are authenticated to Kerberos successfully, the server waits for the client requests, and the client is ready to issue a request as well. On issuing a service command, the client stack picks up the client TGT ticket from the credential cache that's created after successful login using kinit. Using the TGT, it then requests a service ticket from KDC, targeting the right service/server that the user or the client software is accessing. After getting the service ticket, it shows the resultant service ticket to the server, which decrypts and thus authenticates it, with its own ticket issued by KDC upon service startup.

Symmetric key-based communication in Hadoop

The following diagram indicates a typical Kerberos authentication flow based on symmetric keys. The flow depicts how time-sensitive sessions are created and how communication messages are encrypted with three different types of keys, namely client, KDC, and HDFS. All steps are depicted with sequential numbers. The important point to note is that KDC is aware of all three types of keys and the server authority is established based on the ability to decrypt the messages with keys known to them.

For example, if the HDFS server is able to decrypt an ST issued by a client using its own key, Kf, then it ensures that this ST is valid and issued by KDC. Another important point to note here is that keys or passwords are not transferred over the network. Encryption/decryption of messages happens with keys stored at server locations. The following diagram shows the Kerberos Symmetric key communication:

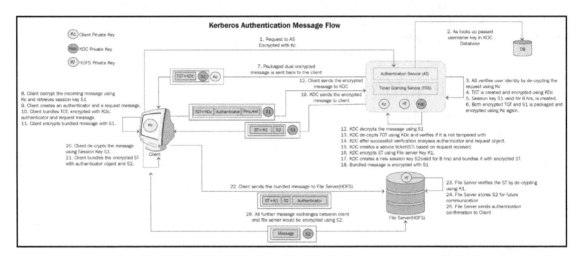

User authorization

Once the identity of the end user is established via Kerberos authentication, the next step in Hadoop security is to ensure what actions or services those established identities can perform. Authorization deals with that. In the following sections, we will look into how authorization rules can be established for different users across different services and how data is stored in HDFS. We will look into two different types of tools that facilitate centralized security policy management for authorization. Let's look into these in brief.

Ranger

The following diagram represents the architecture of the **Ranger** tool, which lets you centrally manage security policies for different Hadoop services:

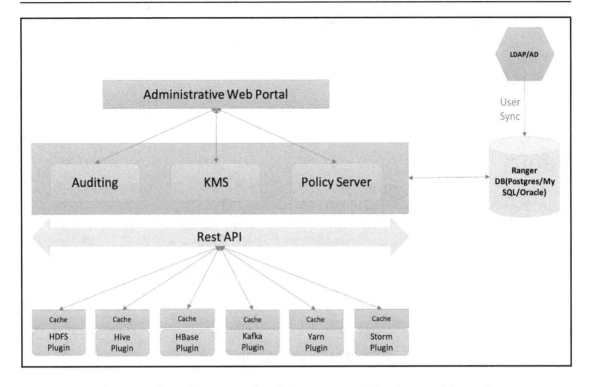

As shown in the preceding diagram, all policies are centrally managed through an administrative web portal. The portal has three distinct parts, namely auditing, KMS, and the policy server. The policy server has several different functionalities. The following are the prime functions of the web portal:

- The repository manager, to add or modify Hadoop services like HDFS or Hive repositories, as shown in the preceding diagram
- The policy manager, to add or modify repository policies for groups or users
- The users/groups section, to manage users and groups' permissions
- The audit section, to monitor user activity at the resource level, and audit log search based on certain filters

Policies are stored locally in the cache that's managed by different service plugins, as shown in the preceding diagram. Policies are synced on a regular basis from the policy server using REST APIs. The other component is KMS, which is used to store keys that are used in HDFS data encryption. We will look into KMS in more detail in the next chapter. The third component lets you capture every user activity with its authorization result of access, denied, or granted. Audit data can be captured in SOLR servers (for searching) or HDFS (for detailed reports) or in DB as well.

This section only covers Ranger at a very introductory level. If you want to read about Ranger in detail, please visit the following links:

```
https://cwiki.apache.org/confluence/pages/viewpage.action?
pageId=57901344.
https://hortonworks.com/apache/ranger/.
```

Sentry

As we mentioned previously, Ranger is a resource (Hadoop services) and user-based authorization control tool. On the contrary, Sentry is an authorization tool that's focused on role-based access control. We will look into that in a moment. But first, let's understand what some of the technical components of the Sentry architecture are. Well, Sentry has some common architecture patterns with Ranger. We have Sentry plugins, which are the same as Ranger plugins, sitting with Hadoop services. However, the internal architecture of the Sentry plugin is somewhat different from the Ranger plugin. The following diagram represents the high-level architecture of a Sentry plugin:

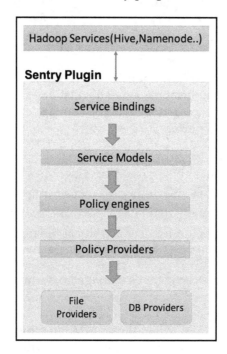

As shown in the preceding diagram, the **Sentry Plugin** has bindings for every Hadoop service. Each of those bindings are mapped to the models like SQL or Search. For example, Hive service bindings are mapped to SQL models, Solr service bindings are mapped to Search models, or HBase service bindings are mapped to BigTable models. Sentry plugins using these models use policy engines to make decisions about authorization. The policy engine uses authorization data stored in the policy providers. Providers can be file-based or DB-based. Users are different identities that are supposed to use the Hadoop services. They are supposed to perform actions on data stored in HDFS using Hadoop services. Users belong to a group. A group can be defined as a set of users that perform the same actions and require the same set of privileges. Roles are a collection of privileges that you want to grant to a group of users. Lastly, privileges are defined as a combination of data objects and actions that can be performed on those data objects. Table is the data object and create/update/drop is the action. As a general practice, you should define privileges logically and map them to roles as per your organization structure. Finally, map those to users and groups defined in your enterprise LDAP/AD. The following diagram represents how the policy engine enforces policies for a particular user:

List of security features that have been worked upon in Hadoop 3.0

The following is the a of the JIRAs that have been solved or worked upon with the Hadoop 3.0 release:

AliyunOSS: update oss-sdk version to 3.0.0 `MajorResolvedFixed`:

Issue Type	Issue key	Issue ID	Parent ID	Summary
Bug	HADOOP-15866	13192984		Renamed `HADOOP_SECURITY_GROUP_SHELL_COMMAND_TIMEOUT` keys break compatibility
Task	HADOOP-15816	13189089		Upgrade Apache ZooKeeper version due to security concerns
Bug	HADOOP-15861	13192122		Move `DelegationTokenIssuer` to the right path
Bug	HADOOP-15523	13164833		Shell command timeout given is in seconds whereas it is taken as millisec while scheduling
Improvement	HADOOP-15609	13172372		Retry KMS calls when `SSLHandshakeException` occurs
Improvement	HADOOP-15804	13188359		Upgrade to commons-compress 1.18
Bug	HADOOP-15698	13181280		KMS log4j is not initialized properly at startup
Bug	HADOOP-15864	13192767		Job submitter/executor fail when SBN domain name can not resolved

Subtask	HADOOP-15607	13172317	12989378	AliyunOSS: fix duplicated `partNumber` issue in `AliyunOSSBlockOutputStream`
Bug	HADOOP-15614	13172717		`TestGroupsCaching.testExceptionOnBackgroundRefreshHandled` Reliably fails
Improvement	HADOOP-15612	13172576		Improve exception when `tfile` fails to load `LzoCodec`
Improvement	HADOOP-15598	13171339		`DataChecksum` calculate checksum is contented on hashtable synchronization
Bug	HADOOP-15571	13169010		Multiple `FileContexts` created with the same configuration object should be allowed to have different `umask`
Improvement	HADOOP-15554	13167452		Improve JIT performance for Configuration parsing
Subtask	HADOOP-15533	13165709	13125961	Make WASB `listStatus` messages consistent
Test	HADOOP-15532	13165626		`TestBasicDiskValidator` fails with `NoSuchFileException`
Bug	HADOOP-15548	13167176		Randomize local directories
Subtask	HADOOP-15529	13165448	13160080	`ContainerLaunch#testInvalidEnvVariableSubstitutionType` is not supported in Windows
Bug	HADOOP-15610	13172471		Hadoop Docker Image Pip Install Fails
Subtask	HADOOP-15458	13158705	13160080	`TestLocalFileSystem#testFSOutputStreamBuilder` fails on Windows
Bug	HADOOP-15637	13175019		`LocalFs#listLocatedStatus` does not filter out hidden `.crc` files
Improvement	HADOOP-15499	13162512		Performance severe drop when running `RawErasureCoderBenchmark` with `NativeRSRawErasureCoder`
Subtask	HADOOP-15506	13163293	13125961	Upgrade Azure Storage SDK version to 7.0.0 and update corresponding code blocks
Bug	HADOOP-15217	13137278		`FsUrlConnection` does not handle paths with spaces
Improvement	HADOOP-15252	13140188		Checkstyle version is not compatible with IDEA's checkstyle plugin
Bug	HADOOP-15638	13175291		KMS Accept Queue Size default changed from 500 to 128 in Hadoop 3.x
Subtask	HADOOP-15731	13183700	13160080	`TestDistributedShell` fails on Windows
Bug	HADOOP-15755	13185076		`StringUtils#createStartupShutdownMessage` throws NPE when args is `null`
Bug	HADOOP-15684	13179708		`triggerActiveLogRoll` stuck on dead name node, when `ConnectTimeoutException` happens.
Bug	HADOOP-15772	13185604		Remove the `'Path ... should be specified as a URI'` warnings on startup
Bug	HADOOP-15736	13183931		Trash: Negative Value For Deletion Interval Leads To Abnormal Behaviour.
Bug	HADOOP-15696	13181222		KMS performance regression due to too many open file descriptors after Jetty migration
Improvement	HADOOP-15726	13183478		Create utility to limit frequency of log statements
Bug	HADOOP-14314	13064501		The `OpenSolaris` taxonomy link is dead in `InterfaceClassification.md`
Bug	HADOOP-15674	13179075		Test failure `TestSSLHttpServer.testExcludedCiphers` with `TLS_ECDHE_RSA_WITH_AES_128_CBC_SHA256` cipher suite
Bug	HADOOP-10219	12688260		`ipc.Client.setupIOstreams()` needs to check for `ClientCache.stopClient` requested shutdowns
Subtask	HADOOP-15748	13184562	13173308	S3 listing inconsistency can raise NPE in globber
Bug	HADOOP-15835	13190458		Reuse Object Mapper in `KMSJSONWriter`
Bug	HADOOP-15817	13189267		Reuse Object Mapper in `KMSJSONReader`
Bug	HADOOP-15850	13191397		`CopyCommitter#concatFileChunks` should check that the blocks per chunk is not 0
Bug	HADOOP-14445	13073925		Use `DelegationTokenIssuer` to create KMS delegation tokens that can authenticate to all KMS instances
Bug	HADOOP-15822	13189805		`zstd` compressor can fail with a small output buffer
Task	HADOOP-15815	13189087		Upgrade Eclipse Jetty version to 9.3.24
Bug	HADOOP-15859	13192011		`ZStandardDecompressor.c` mistakes a class for an instance
Task	HADOOP-15882	13194079		Upgrade maven-shade-plugin from 2.4.3 to 3.2.0
Subtask	HADOOP-15837	13190483	13173306	`DynamoDB` table Update can fail S3A FS init

Bug	HADOOP-15679	13179254		`ShutdownHookManager` shutdown time needs to be configurable and extended
Bug	HADOOP-15820	13189502		`ZStandardDecompressor` native code sets an integer field as a long
Bug	HADOOP-15900	13196160		Update JSch versions in `LICENSE.txt`
Bug	HADOOP-15899	13196153		Update AWS Java SDK versions in `NOTICE.txt`
Subtask	HADOOP-15759	13185417	12989378	
Subtask	HADOOP-15671	13178804	12989378	`AliyunOSS`: Support Assume Roles in AliyunOSS
Subtask	HADOOP-15868	13193163	12989378	`AliyunOSS`: update document for properties of multiple part download, multiple part upload and directory copy

Summary

In this chapter, we have covered the Hadoop security pillars, and it should now be very clear about the different aspects of security that have to be incorporated along with system security and Kerberos authentication. We studied the different advantages of Kerberos, along with how Kerberos authentication flows. This chapter also talked about user authorization, which includes two different tools, namely Ranger and Sentry. Lastly, we were also introduced to the list of JIRAs that have been solved or worked upon with the Hadoop 3.0 release.

In the next chapter, we will study network and data security, which includes aspects like Hadoop networks, perimeter security, data encryption, data masking, row, and column level security.

14
Network and Data Security

In the previous chapter, we briefly looked into all the different aspects of Hadoop security. We elaborated on the authentication and authorization aspects of Hadoop security. This chapter is dedicated to looking at other aspects, such as Hadoop networks, perimeter security, data encryption, data masking, and row and column-level security. We'll start by looking into network security.

In this chapter we will cover the following topics:

- Securing Hadoop networks
- Encryption
- Masking
- Row-level security

Securing Hadoop networks

There are multiple steps in securing Hadoop networks. The first step in designing the Hadoop cluster is to set up the network. In the next subsections, we will talk about different types of networks, network firewall usage and different tools available in the market to secure the network.

Segregating different types of networks

Segregating or segmenting your enterprise network is one of the most basic aspects of securing your Hadoop network. In general, segmentation is one of the practices followed by enterprises. However, when you are setting up a Hadoop cluster you need to ensure that certain aspects are in your network design.

You should think about the following aspects one by one:

- What kind of traffic would there be? Are we getting any traffic from the internet or will it all be internal network traffic?
- Do we have inbound or outbound traffic over internet or intranet? What services would have inbound or outbound traffic, or both?
- Does your Hadoop cluster have integrations with external systems that are exposed over the internet?
- Do you have external users outside the enterprise network accessing the Hadoop network?

These are some of the aspects that you should keep in mind while designing a Hadoop network. However, this list is brief and for enterprise network design you should think it through and cover the aspects more deeply in practice. The following diagram shows an example of the Hadoop network segmentation:

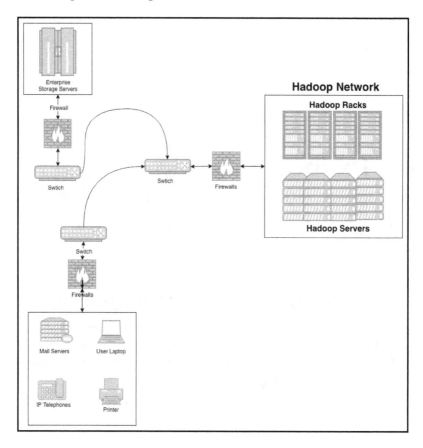

As shown in the previous diagram, the key is that you should isolate the Hadoop cluster and services from the rest of the enterprise network both logically and physically. Physical separation means the Hadoop network should be sectioned off with physical devices such as routers, switches, and firewalls (hardware). That means all nodes (master, worker, or edge nodes) are connected to these separated or isolated switches or routers.

Logical separation means putting all cluster nodes under a separate subnet with IP ranges based on the nodes in the cluster. Ideally, for any Hadoop cluster, it is a good idea to have both physical and logical network segmentation present. The most common approach in achieving physical and logical segregation is by using **virtual local area networks (VLANs)**. VLANs enable sharing physical switches between multiple switches. Each VLAN can be configured on one switching port or, in the case of one port availability, you can use packet tagging for routing inbound or data packets to their respective VLAN destination. Segmentation has the following advantages:

- It lets you define firewall policies at one entry point where the segmentation is started.
- It helps you restrict entries from the internet or from any other enterprise network easily.
- It is easier to maintain. For example, if you add one node in the subnet range defined for a VLAN, security policies would be applied automatically without having to apply them specifically.

Next, let's see how we can protect these network segments using firewalls.

Network firewalls

Network firewalls are actually a wall that monitors and prevents any access to a segregated Hadoop network. Firewalls are the first entry points to the Hadoop cluster and ensure that unauthorized access can be made to the Hadoop cluster. For Hadoop, firewalls have to be used with segmented network and authentication.

Firewalls can be hardware- or software-based. They can be used as network packet filters where they examine each inbound and outbound packets based on user-defined rules. They can apply security mechanisms based on networking protocols such as TCP or UDP. They can act as proxy servers to protect the true identity of Hadoop servers and can be used for whitelisting IPs. They are also used in intrusion prevention and intrusion detection systems.

The following diagram represents how walls are created by network firewalls:

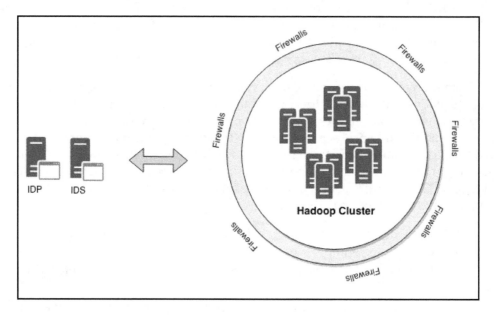

Tools for securing Hadoop services' network perimeter

One of the common tools for securing Hadoop services' network perimeter is Apache Knox. There are different functionalities of Knox gateway, which are set out in the following list:

- It works as an authentication layer for REST services, Hadoop web UI, and other services. It can be used as an SSO layer for using multiple services and has support for LDAP/AD integration, Kerberos, and OAuth.
- It works as a proxy layer for Hadoop HTTP services such as YARN UI and Oozie UI.
- It can also work as network traffic authorization.
- It can be used as network traffic auditing and monitoring and can be integrated with alerting tools.
- It also has its own SDK, which can be integrated with your application that uses Hadoop services to provide proxy and authentication services.

The following diagram represents the overall functioning of the Knox gateway's logic:

> This section is just a brief introduction to Knox services and not for detailed explanation. If you want to understand the details about Knox Gateway, please refer to the following link: `https://knox.apache.org/`.

In the next section we will learn about the encryption types.

Encryption

There are two types of encryptions in Hadoop. One is for encrypting data that is transferred over the network. That is called data in transit encryption. Another is for encrypting data that is stored on disks, which is called data at rest encryption. We will look at both of these types of encryption techniques in the following sections.

Data in transit encryption

To understand in transit encryption of any Hadoop cluster, you need to understand how different components are communicating with each other. By *how*, we mean what kind of network protocol they are using. Enabling encryption over the network depends upon what kind of communication protocol is being used for communication.

We can think of Hadoop cluster components using three different types of protocols, namely **RPC**, **TCP/IP**, and **HTTP**. **RPC** is used for network communication of **MapReduce** programming, **JobTracker** communication, **TaskTracker** communication, and **NameNode** communication. The **TCP/IP** protocol is used for communication involving HDFS CLI clients. Finally, **HTTP** communication protocols are used during MapReduce data shuffles and web UIs that interact with different Hadoop components.

The following diagram represents the logical view of data in transit encryption in Hadoop:

Hadoop Data In Transit Security		
Transit Protocols		
RPC	**TCP/IP**	**HTTP**
Mapreduce		Mapreduce Shuffles
JobTracker	HDFS CLIENTS	
TaskTracker		Web Interfaces
NameNode		

There are different provisions or configuration settings provided in Hadoop to encrypt communication using these protocols. **RPC** communication in Hadoop uses the **simple authentication security layer** (**SASL**). Apart from supporting authentication, it also provides support for message integrity and encryption support. **TCP/IP** communication protocol is mainly used for communication between DataNodes. Now, **TCP/IP** does not have encryption built in or directly supported by default. To address this deficiency, the existing data transfer protocol is wrapped with a SASL handshake. SASL supports encryption. That is how **TCP/IP** protocol encryption is supported in Hadoop. Hadoop uses **HTTP** for its **Web Interfaces**, for the **Mapreduce Shuffles** phase and for fsimage operations between the NameNode and the secondary NameNode. HTTPS is used for encrypting **HTTP** communications. HTTPS is a proven and widely adopted standard for HTTP encryption. Java and browsers support HTTPS, and many libraries and tools in most operating systems have built-in support for HTTPS.

Data at rest encryption

Transparent data encryption (**TDE**) is about keeping HDFS data on disk encrypted. This HDFS data on disk is also called data at rest. This type of encryption is security key based. Keys are generally stored in a key management server either internal to Hadoop or as an external key storage.

As the name suggests, TDE is about encrypting data on the disk in a way that is transparent to the user accessing the data. As long as the user has access to the relevant security key, the Hadoop system would automatically encrypt data upon writing and decrypt data upon reading. For the user, it is as good as reading and writing non-encrypted data. All underlying encryption would be automatically managed by the Hadoop system. You just have to configure the directory that needs to be encrypted. This is also called the encryption or security zone. As long as any file is written to that encrypted zone, it will be encrypted by the system.

The goal of TDE is to prevent anyone who is inappropriately trying to access data from doing so. It guards against the threat, for example, of someone finding a disk in a dumpster or stealing one, or someone poking around HDFS who is not a user of the application or use case. The following diagram represents how data at rest encryption works in Hadoop:

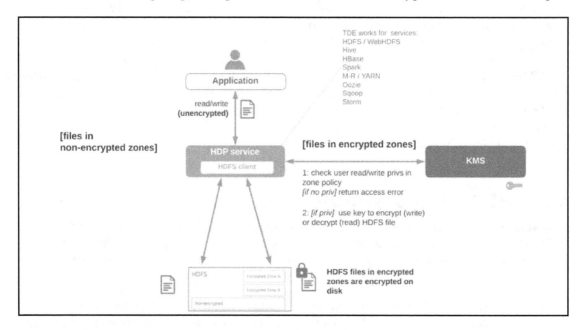

Whenever a user or application tries to read or write data in an encrypted zone, the underlying HDFS client tries to access the encryption key from the configured KMS. In that process, first the access privileges are checked and if access privileges are established, files are encrypted and decrypted by Hadoop.

Masking

Masking is the technique of showing masked data to users who do not have access to some data. This can be seen as hiding personal data, be it financial or health-related information, from those who are not authorized to see it. Masking methods can be different. The following diagram represents one of the **Data Masking** techniques where you hide **Employee Salary** with simple **XXXX** substitution:

Data Masking		
ID	**Employee Name**	**Employee Salary**
1	John	10,000
2	Tim	20,000

ID	**Employee Name**	**Employee Salary**
1	John	XXXXX
2	Tim	XXXXX

Another common masking method is substituting the masked column with random replacement. In this table, **Employee Salary** is replaced by random salary numbers. The following diagram shows the **Data Masking By Random Substitution**:

Data Masking By Random Substitution		
ID	**Employee Name**	**Employee Salary**
1	John	10,000
2	Tim	20,000

ID	**Employee Name**	**Employee Salary**
1	John	5000
2	Tim	1000

The following diagram shows one of the other common masking techniques using encryption:

Data Masking By Encryption		
ID	Employee Name	Employee Salary
1	John	10,000
2	Tim	20,000
ID	Employee Name	Employee Salary
1	John	AB2H345EDNE98TYUO
2	Tim	SDF2096FT32UO7I9OP

Filtering

Filtering is the technique of filtering information from users who do not have access to it. It is different from masking in the way that it filters out the complete column or complete row instead of showing random values or a masked value. There are two types of filtering, as they are described in the following sections.

Row-level filtering

As shown in the following diagram, **Row-Level Filtering** refers to hiding certain rows from users who do not have access to them:

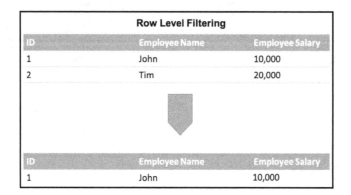

Row Level Filtering		
ID	Employee Name	Employee Salary
1	John	10,000
2	Tim	20,000
ID	Employee Name	Employee Salary
1	John	10,000

Column-level filtering

As shown in the following diagram, column-level filtering refers to hiding entire columns from users who do not have access to them:

Data Masking By Random Substitution

ID	Employee Name	Employee Salary
1	John	10,000
2	Tim	20,000

ID	Employee Name
1	John
2	Tim

Summary

In this chapter, we have learned some of the important aspects of network and data security in the Hadoop ecosystem. We have seen some important concepts of masking and filtering with respect to data security. One thing we have to understand here is that there are different tools and frameworks available to achieve the different security methods in Hadoop. However, you should evaluate these carefully with respect to the security features you want to achieve.

In the next chapter, we will focus on how we do monitoring in Hadoop and what the monitoring systems for security are. We will also look into monitoring in the world of growing data.

15
Monitoring Hadoop

In the previous chapter, we focused on the different aspects of Hadoop security. So far, we have walked you through the different components in Hadoop, some advanced concepts of the Hadoop ecosystem, and a few of the best design practices that have to be taken into consideration while designing and implementing Hadoop applications. Above all, it is also important to monitor and alert any application system to avoid unnecessary losses or system failure by taking appropriate actions. In this chapter, we will cover the following topics:

- General monitoring
- Security monitoring

General monitoring

The of applications goes through various stages, such as the development environment, load test environment, stage environment, and then, finally, it goes to the production environment. Most of the application architecture has more than one component, such as the UI server, backend server, and database server. All components interacts with each other to fulfill the overall application objectives in any enterprise, no matter how big or small, so it is very important to monitor the health of the services. These server are intended to run 24/7 and if any of the servers go down it may lead to the failure of the business objective and may cause huge losses to the company. It is very important to have the proper mechanisms in place to continuously observe the health, failure, network issues, database performance, application performance, and so on, of the applications. Monitoring is the process of capturing important application matrices that can help us obtain a server report. These reports can be used by the alerting system to send necessary alerts if any alerting rule matches the condition.

The monitoring tool may want to send an alert when 60–70% of the disk space is full, an instance is not able to send the health heartbeat for two to three minutes, CPU utilization is reaching 90%, or for many other reasons. There are already some open source tools available that can help us to do general monitoring over Hadoop. The primary objective of monitoring and alerting is to make sure the applications and the infrastructure where the application is running are healthy; if there is any indication of failure, it must alert users to take the appropriate action. Let's discuss a few important metrics and how to collect them.

HDFS metrics

Even though most of the applications are moving to cloud-based distributed storage similar to HDFS such as S3, Azure storage, and GCP storage, still there are companies who prefer to have their own HDFS storage on-premises or over the cloud. In this section, we will focus on two major HDFS component metrics: NameNode and DataNode. We have already covered the detail of all the Hadoop components in the initial chapters. Let's start looking into NameNode and DataNode metrics in detail.

NameNode metrics

NameNode is the master HDFS daemon that is responsible for managing HDFS metadata and acts as a single point of failure, which means the failure of NameNode without any backup or High Availability configuration will results in all the entire being lost. Since the NameNode is the master daemon, the HDFS does not work without it. It is also very important to give priority to NameNode metrics over DataNode. The following are a list of NameNode metrics:

- `CapacityRemaining`: This metric represents the total available capacity remaining across the entire HDFS cluster. The capacity threshold should be set to monitor the HDFS cluster based on how frequently data landed to the HDFS; the basic rule is that you should immediately get an alert if the value exceeds 75%. You can then add new volume or a new data node to the Hadoop cluster.
- `UnderReplicatedBlocks`: This metric represents the number of blocks that do not match in the configured replication factor. We can configure different replications for different directories or files. If the number of metrics is very large, we must immediately take remedial action. The sudden spike may be sure to be due to a failure of one or more DataNodes.

- `MissingBlocks`: It is said that missing blocks are more dangerous than corrupt or under-replicated blocks. Upon receiving the corrupt block signal from the client, NameNode begins copying the block from other replicas to some DataNodes and upon completion removes the corrupt block; but missing blocks cannot be recovered using this method because there are no replicas present in the block. This may be due to the DataNode having those blocks that are taken for maintenance, but it is not the case that immediate action should be taken to avoid any measure of data loss.

- `VolumeFailuresTotal`: The DataNode has a number of disk volumes attached to it. Unlike older versions of Hadoop, where failure of a volume leads to the shutdown of the DataNode entirely, in newer versions, the DataNode can be configured to tolerate a number of disk failure at a time. It helps the DataNode not to shutdown immediately if one or two instance have failed.

- `NumDeadDataNodes`: The DataNode sends a continuous heartbeat to the NameNode to indicate it is alive and all the alive nodes are represented by metrics named `NumLiveDataNodes`. If the DataNode does not send a heartbeat for a defined time of period, then it is added to the list of dead DataNodes list. We must carefully watch these metrics to avoid major problems later.

- **JMX metrics**: The garbage collection is a standard process in any JVM-based process and if there are more HDFS operations, the number of times garbage collection calls may also increase, which may lead to low-performing clusters. CMS is the recommended garbage collector for the HDFS and we may allocate sufficient JVM memory for the process.

DataNode metrics

DataNodes are slave nodes in the Hadoop cluster and we have already covered their internal makeup in the previous chapters. Since the DataNode sends heartbeats to the NameNode, it also sends various metrics to the NameNode; therefore, we can also get most metrics about the DataNode from the NameNode. Let's look into a few important DataNode metrics:

- **Remaining**: This metric represents the amount of free space remaining on the DataNode. Remember, even if a single DataNode runs out of disk space, it may lead to failure across the entire cluster. We must always set a threshold percentage for monitoring and alerting, so if the disk space reaches the specified limit, we can immediately take action to avoid any failure.

- `NumFailedVolumes`: We mentioned in the NameNode metrics section that one DataNode is attached to multiple disk volumes. By default, the configuration is set in such a way that if any attached disk fails, it will cause an entire DataNode to fail. But in the production system, it must be set to a defined tolerance of a few disks. We should remember that for every DataNode failure, it will result in a few under-replicated blocks in the cluster and thus the NameNode will start copying those blocks to other DataNodes; thus, we should always set this limit to a calculated number to avoid performance bottleneck.

YARN metrics

YARN is a Resource Manager that was introduced in Hadoop version 2. In previous chapters, we have already covered the details of the architecture and the internals of its components. The Resource Manager and Node Manager are two major components of a YARN cluster and we are going to look into a few useful metrics of a YARN cluster:

- `unhealthyNodes`: Unhealthy nodes are those nodes whose disk utilization exceeds the configured limit number. Node Managers in a YARN cluster are responsible for executing application in memory and each Node Manager is assigned a defined number of disks and memory. If a node is marked as unhealthy by YARN, then it will not be used for any processing and another node in the cluster has to step into the breach, which may lead to performance degradation. It's always a good idea to add or clear disk space after a monitoring alert.
- `lostNode`: Like NameNode and DataNode, the Node Manager also sends a heartbeat to the Resource Manager at regular intervals and, if the Resource Manager does not receive a heartbeat for a configured period of time, which is 10 minutes by default, it marks the Node Manager as lost or dead. If the count of `lostNode` is one or more than one for a long period of time, we must immediately take the appropriate steps to find out the root cause and take action.
- `allocatedMB/totalMB`: As the name indicates, these metrics represent the total amount of memory available in MB and how much is allocated to resources in MB. These metrics play an important role in deciding whether to add a new Node Manager when `allocatedMB` regularly comes close to `totalMB`.
- `containersFailed`: This represents the Node Manager metric that indicates the total number of failed containers on a given Node Manager. If there are more failed containers on any given Node Manager, most likely the issue could be related to a hardware failure, such as a disk space issue.

ZooKeeper metrics

Production Hadoop and YARN clusters are always configured with High Availability in mind. ZooKeeper plays an important role in a High Availability deployment. ZooKeeper continuously monitors the master daemon and triggers the replacement of the master daemon if it fails. Both YARN and HDFS High Availability are managed via ZooKeeper. Let's look into a few important metrics of Zookeeper:

- `zk_num_alive_connections`: This metric represents the number of clients connected to ZooKeeper. The number generally does not change dynamically and remains static. If the number drops, it is recommended that you check the dropped client check logs to detect the reason and fix it, as it is most likely a connection or network issue.
- `zk_followers`: This metric indicates the number of ZooKeeper followers currently available, which must be equal to the total number of ZK nodes minus one. If this number is less than that, then we must check the failed nodes and get them up as soon as possible to avoid any significant issue later.
- `zk_avg_latency`: This metric represents the average time ZooKeeper takes to respond to any client requests. ZooKeeper only responds back to a client when it successfully writes the transaction to its log.

Apache Ambari

It is always possible to build your own monitoring and alerting tool for Hadoop, but we feel there are already open source tools available to serve your purpose and it is a good idea to reuse them until and unless there are very critical custom requirements for your application. Let's focus on a few tools that are available.

Apache Ambari is an open source project that eases the management and monitoring of Hadoop clusters. It is widely used across multiple organizations as it supports the installation, management, and monitoring of softwares such as HDFS, MapReduce, HBase, Hive, YARN, Kafka, and so on.

Its monitoring GUI user interface looks like the following:

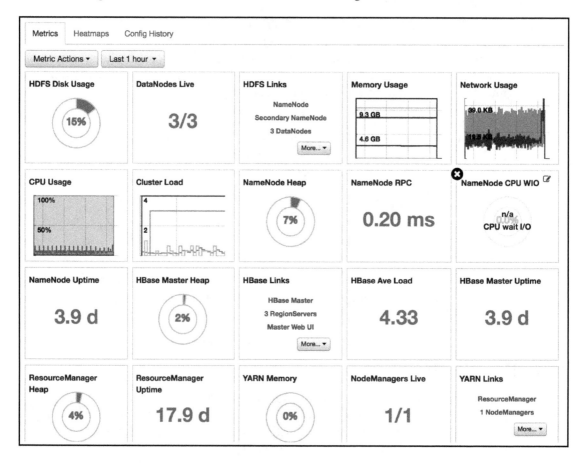

There is also continuous ongoing development on integrating more tools into Apache Ambari's. All the metrics we discussed previously are already integrated into Apache Ambari monitoring GUI.

Security monitoring

Production-level Hadoop ecosystems are implemented with sufficient authentication, authorization, and data security in place. We have already covered various ways to implement security in Hadoop in previous chapters. But, as discussed, while implementation is one thing, monitoring and alerting are another. What if someone log into your system using some other mechanism or someone tries to enter your system by some other route? What if a user performs operations they are not allowed to?

Security information and event management

Security information and event management (**SIEM**) is an audit that logs entries and from the security system and converts them into an actionable item. This actionable information can be used to detect any potential threat, take action, and add a new investigation into the compliance process. Depending on how the SIEM system is designed, this entire process can be either in batch or real time, based on how critical the security threat is. The following diagram shows the SIEM architecture:

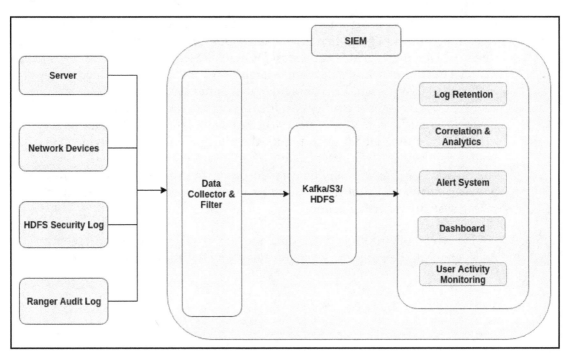

How does SIEM work?

SIEM has defined a process whereby any proprietary tools that have SIEM in place may have a standard set of steps and a design architecture in place. In this section, we will talk about how SIEM works and some common steps involved in the process are:

- **Collection layer**: The first step in any monitoring and alerting system is to get data that we can analyze and say if it has any information to trigger a threat alert. The basic practice is to deploy applications to perform any filtering and forward logs to any specific storage system. Data sources for SIEM could be a firewall, IDS/IPS system, web filters, domain controllers, log collector systems, and so on. SIEMs can also be integrated to cloud services to obtain log data for cloud-deployed infrastructure. Events can be filtered at the data-collection level so that only required logs get stored.

- **Storage layer**: The collector is responsible for collecting and filtering events based on defined rules and then storing valid events to a target storage system. Today, we have distributed and high-throughput storage systems available such as HDFS, S3, Kafka, and so on. The collector can push the data to these target storage systems.

- **Correlation and security analytics**: The primary and core step in SIEM is to have rules and policies in place to define what events are categorized into security threats. Given the available capability for machine learning, we can always have a model to automatically detect and categorize events into lower, medium, and higher threat events and then pass them to another layer to take the respective actions. Correlation is the process of identifying the relationship between different events to conclude that a particular event falls into a threat category. For example, imagine that a user continuously fails in their attempts to log in to a system from some IP addresses, using different user and credential combinations, but that finally the user succeeds. In this case, there is correlation between events that indicates it might be a threat and it can be sent to an action-taking system for further action.

 In correlation, multiple data points are analyzed into meaningful security events, and delivered to an action system by notifications or dashboards.

- **Action and compliance layer**: This layer plays a very critical role in SIEM as it takes appropriate actions and sends alerts to the security team to let them know about the security incident. The action system can be designed to have the capability to block any further processing of requests for correlated events and to send an alert to the security team to look into the incident on a priority basis. These incidents can then be used to define a compliance document that can be used to avoid similar incident reporting.

Intrusion detection system

An **intrusion detection system** (**IDS**) monitors network traffic for any suspicious activity and immediately sends alerts when any such malicious or suspicious activity is detected. Anomaly detection and reporting are the main function of an IDS but it is capable of taking the relevant actions when any malicious activity is detected, such as blocking traffic sent from suspicious IP addresses. The IDS system can be categorized into two types:

- **Active IDS:** An active IDS is nothing but the integration of an IDS with IPS and is therefore referred to as an intrusion detection and prevention system. It will not only generate alerts and log entries, but can also be configured to take actions such as blocking IP addresses and shutting down access to restricted resources.
- **Passive IDS**: Passive IDS systems are standalone intrusion detection systems that are designed to detect malicious activity and generate alert or log entries. They do not take any action upon receiving any incident.

Depending upon where in the network the IDS system is deployed, it is categorized into types:

- **Network intrusion detection system** (**NIDS**): NIDS is deployed at strategic points within the network and monitors all the traffic from all the devices. Upon receiving any suspicious event, it can then generate an alert and log entry for the incident. Since it is deployed over a network, it does not have the capability to detect any threat within the network.
- **Host intrusion detection systems** (**HIDS**): An HIDS is deployed on all devices in the network. It has direct access to both the internet and the enterprise internal network. Since the HIDS is available on each host under the network, it has the capability to detect any malicious network traffic within the network or from the host itself.

There are also other types of enterprise-level IDS system, such as the signature IDS and anomaly IDS system designed for specific use cases:

- **Anomaly-based intrusion detection system:** In this detection system, the intrusion detection system tries to detect abnormalities in the network. When any such alteration occurs in the network, the incident gets detected by the system. This type of IDS may generate many false alerts.
- **Signature-based intrusion detection system:** In this approach, there are already predefined sets of patterns that are used to match with traffic events. If any traffic packet matches the defined pattern, then the IDS triggers an alert on that network.

Intrusion prevention system

An **intrusion prevention system** (**IPS**) audits network traffic events to detect and prevent susceptibility deeds. The applications or services that attackers use to interrupt and gain control of a machine or application are the primary source for vulnerability exploits. If an attacker successfully exploits the machine or application, he/she can perform unwanted and malicious activity that can result in the complete shutdown of an application or the loss of a huge amount of revenue.

The IPS is often placed directly behind the firewall and provides a layer of security analysis that prevents dangerous content. The IDS scans traffic and reports back on threats and we get an active IDPS system after integrating the IDS with the IPS, which actively analyzes and take automated actions on all traffic flows that enter the network. The IPS's action could be anything that could prevent an event getting into the network, such as the following:

- Sending an alert alarm to the administrator
- Dropping the malicious network traffic packets
- Blocking traffic from the source IP addresses

Network performance should not be affected much when the IPS is in place. IPSs have the ability to detect and take appropriate action in real time to avoid any security threat later.

Summary

In this chapter, we covered how we monitor the Hadoop ecosystem. We started by covering general security parameters such as a few metrics that can be helpful in identifying system bottlenecks. We also looked at the basic rules for configuring monitoring and alerting systems are. In the security monitoring section, we talked about the SIEM system and how this system works. There are many tools on the market that have SIEM implementation and can be used as plug and play modules. Later in the chapter, we covered intrusion detection systems and intrusion prevention systems.

Other Books You May Enjoy

If you enjoyed this book, you may be interested in these other books by Packt:

Big Data Analytics with Hadoop 3
Sridhar Alla

ISBN: 978-1-78862-884-6

- Explore the new features of Hadoop 3 along with HDFS, YARN, and MapReduce
- Get well-versed with the analytical capabilities of Hadoop ecosystem using practical examples
- Integrate Hadoop with R and Python for more efficient big data processing
- Learn to use Hadoop with Apache Spark and Apache Flink for real-time data analytics
- Set up a Hadoop cluster on AWS cloud
- Perform big data analytics on AWS using Elastic Map Reduce

Apache Spark 2.x Machine Learning Cookbook
Siamak Amirghodsi et al.

ISBN: 978-1-78355-160-6

- Get to know how Scala and Spark go hand-in-hand for developers when developing ML systems with Spark
- Build a recommendation engine that scales with Spark
- Find out how to build unsupervised clustering systems to classify data in Spark
- Build machine learning systems with the Decision Tree and Ensemble models in Spark
- Deal with the curse of high-dimensionality in big data using Spark
- Implement Text analytics for Search Engines in Spark
- Streaming Machine Learning System implementation using Spark

Leave a review - let other readers know what you think

Please share your thoughts on this book with others by leaving a review on the site that you bought it from. If you purchased the book from Amazon, please leave us an honest review on this book's Amazon page. This is vital so that other potential readers can see and use your unbiased opinion to make purchasing decisions, we can understand what our customers think about our products, and our authors can see your feedback on the title that they have worked with Packt to create. It will only take a few minutes of your time, but is valuable to other potential customers, our authors, and Packt. Thank you!

Index

W

warm data 61
Word Count, summarization patterns
  about 129
  combiner 131
  mapper 130
  reducer 130
write once read many principle 24
write-forward logging (WAL) 374

Y

YARN cluster
  benchmarking 462
  benchmarking, with Scheduler Load Simulator
    (SLS) 463
YARN command reference
  about 112
  administration commands 114, 116
  user command 112
YARN container
  running, as docker container 105
YARN job scheduling 83
YARN metrics
  allocatedMB/totalMB 500

  containersFailed 500
  lostNode 500
  unhealthyNodes 500
YARN scheduler 454
YARN Timeline server
  about 98, 99
  configuring 99, 101
YARN
  about 118
  Docker containers 103
  MapReduce, executing 122, 124
Yet Another Resource Negotiator (YARN)
  about 76
  architecture 76, 77, 79

Z

ZKFailoverController (ZKFC) 29
ZooKeeper 289
Zookeeper failover controllers 29
ZooKeeper metrics
  zk_avg_latency 501
  zk_followers 501
  zk_num_alive_connections 501
Zookeeper Quorum 29

CPSIA information can be obtained
at www.ICGtesting.com
Printed in the USA
LVHW101706180719
624478LV00011B/94/P